Water Resource Economics

Water Resource Economics

The Analysis of Scarcity, Policies, and Projects

Ronald C. Griffin

The MIT Press
Cambridge, Massachusetts
London, England

MIT Press books may be purchased at special quantity discounts for business or sales promotional use. For information, please e-mail ⟨special_sales@mitpress.mit.edu⟩ or write to Special Sales Department, The MIT Press, 55 Hayward Street, Cambridge, MA 02142.

This book was set in Times New Roman on 3B2 by Asco Typesetters, Hong Kong. Printed and bound in the United States of America.

Library of Congress Cataloging-in-Publication Data

Griffin, Ronald C.
Water resource economics : the analysis of scarcity, policies, and projects / Ronald C. Griffin.
  p.   cm.
Includes bibliographical references and index.
ISBN 978-0-262-07267-0 (hc : alk. paper)
1. Water resources development—Economic aspects. 2. Water resources development—Government policy. 3. Water-supply—Economic aspects. 4. Water-supply—Government policy. I. Title.
HD1691.G745   2006   333.91′15—dc22   2005051097

10 9 8 7 6 5 4 3 2

Dedicated to wondrous Trish

Contents

Preface

Who is this for? What should they know?

Because of the powerful insights that economics brings to water management, books like this should reach beyond an audience of economists. Therein lies a challenge. Due to other pressing demands, few water managers or planners have invested in economics. Because they come mainly from the engineering and science disciplines, most water professionals have limited exposure to economic fundamentals. For these people, it's rarely practical to study microeconomics and natural resource economics before getting schooled in water resource economics. Few have that kind of time or patience. For these reasons, this text is designed for economists, engineers, and natural scientists.

Economist readers possess conceptual knowledge that is readily adapted to water resources, especially if they have studied natural resource economics. The comparative advantage for audiences from the engineering and natural science disciplines is their strong math skills. With the aid of mathematics, important economic principles can be accessed quite quickly. It turns out that the initial wisdom emerging from economics is quite practical, yielding positive feedback regarding the merits of knowing "some" water resource economics. You don't have to go all the way to the end to enjoy benefits. Such affirmations inspire continued study too. Fortunately, many dedicated individuals consider themselves to be publicly assigned stewards of water resources, making it easier for them to welcome new tools. Of course, there will always be old-school defenders who didn't have to learn any economics and can't imagine why anyone should. Oh well.

The intended level of reader includes graduate students of many disciplines, water planning professionals with baccalaureates, and upper-level undergraduates possessing solid math backgrounds. The needed mathematics pertain to optimization (setting derivatives equal to zero) and integral calculus (finding areas under curves). In addition, the presentation will not be shy about using vector notation, although our use of linear algebra will be confined to simple vector products. A lot of the economics contained in this book is not mathematically oriented, but at times the insights enabled by mathematics are indispensable.

It is helpful to have prior familiarity with microeconomics or natural resource economics, but all the needed economics is developed in the text. Hopefully, by developing all the required tools in a self-contained book, a point of access to this important topic will be fruitfully realized. In this way, self-study becomes practical too. Special diligence by noneconomist readers will be needed, for the path is a steady and rigorous climb. Do not skip things. Do not move forward until you have a good grasp of the present topic. Missed ideas and concepts will become detrimental later on, as no economic tools are developed here unless they are useful in water planning or management. Chapters 2–4 are pivotal in this regard. For those readers desiring only a foundational exposure to water resource economics, chapters 1–4 and 6–8 should serve nicely.

One of the book's goals is to assemble and apply the minimal set of economic theory needed to understand and operationalize water resource economics. To bind empiricism (number crunching) and theory more tightly, all graphic portrayals of economic theory and most calculations will be performed using Mathematica, an analytic mathematics software package. Consequently, this material is less abstract than what is usually encountered in economics. The programming code for these graphics and routines is not included with the text, but the programs are freely available for anyone who wants to "follow along," and it is hoped that this code can serve as a model for readers' future work in water resource economics. Perhaps readers will contribute additional material of this type too. The makers of Mathematica (⟨http://www.wri.com⟩) distribute a free application known as MathReader that enables users of any computer platform to read the programming code and output of Mathematica programs. The accompanying programs of this book, including programs for reproducing many of the figures, are accessible through the author's Web site, ⟨http://waterecon.tamu.edu⟩. Most of this code is sufficiently transparent to guide programming in other languages. Although these tools are useful learning and "doing" aids, their retrieval is completely optional.

Many of the water topics discussed here, if not all of them, are also addressable using the doctrines of other disciplines (sociology, geography, political science, law, etc.). In most instances, a good policy design will draw insight from many places. We will embark on a purer course—adhering strictly to economic directives in developing management advice. This approach does not dilute or muddy the messages of economics—which would occur if one pursued some manner of blending, as performed in typical water management books. We will be true to the economics source material so as to let it stand on its own two feet and be clearly visible—for its successes, possibly its faults, and certainly for its differences. As a result, it will be interesting to contrast economic ideals about water to your usual thinking as you proceed through this text.

To keep the topic manageable, we will focus on the scarcity of water *quantity*. Yes, water quality is a serious topic too, and economics has a lot to say about it. There are even important social problems in which issues of water quantity and quality interface. It suits an introductory text, however, that the scope be workably delimited.

A final orientation deserving of explanation is the geopolitical focus. We will emphasize U.S. situations and applications whenever it is important to select an institutional or physical context. The fundamental water resource economics presented in this book is devoid of U.S. definition, but water resource economics is an inherently policy-oriented field of inquiry. That is, the ultimate contributions of water resource economics have to do with improving management policies. To speak about improving policy it is often useful to have a starting place. Wherever necessary in this text, U.S. policy constitutes the primary background.

Acknowledgments

Sincere appreciation is extended to several water specialists who commented on earlier drafts of this book. These reviewers are John Boland, Greg Characklis, Chuck Howe, Ray Huffaker, Jay Lund, Frank Ward, and Bob Young. Their efforts resulted in many improvements, yet they bear no responsibility for remaining shortcomings. In addition, I relied on Texas A&M colleagues for assistance with isolated topics. These friends include Lonnie Jones, David Leatham, John Penson, and Rich Woodward. Students in graduate courses at Texas A&M University and the University of North Carolina at Chapel Hill contributed to readability and accuracy in important ways. My administrative assistant, Michele Zinn, provided crucial support for which I am grateful.

Water Unit Conversions

For Volumes, Flow Rates, and Values (to 7 Significant Digits)

Volumes	acre-foot	1,000 gal	100 f^3	1,000 m^3
1 acre-foot =	1	325.8514	435.6000	1.233482
1,000 gal =	0.003068883	1	1.336806	0.003785412
100 f^3 =	0.002295684	0.7480519	1	0.002831685
1,000 m^3 =	0.8107132	264.1721	353.1467	1

Flows	af/yr	gpm	f^3/s	m^3/s
1 af/yr =	1	0.6195365	0.001380333	0.00003908668
1 gpm =	1.614110	1	0.002228009	0.00006309020
1 f^3/s =	724.4628	448.8312	1	0.02831685
1 m^3/s =	25584.16	15850.32	35.31467	1

1 million gallons per day (mgd) = 1120.910 af/yr

Values	$/af	$/1,000 gal	$/100 f^3	$/1,000 m^3
$1/af =	1	0.003068883	0.002295684	0.8107132
$1/1,000 gal =	325.8514	1	0.7480519	264.1721
$1/100 f^3 =	435.6000	1.336806	1	353.1467
$1/1,000 m^3 =	1.233482	0.003785412	0.002831685	1

Abbreviations

af = acre-feet
(1 acre = 0.4046856 hectares [10,000 m^2])
af/yr = acre-feet per year
f^3 = cubic feet
f^3/s = cubic feet per second

m^3 = cubic meters (1 m^3 = 1,000 liters)

m^3/s = cubic meters per second
gal = gallons (U.S. liquid)
gpm = gallons per minute

Water Resource Economics

1 Introduction

Why might any of this matter?

By long-standing definition, "economics is 'the study of the allocation of scarce resources'" (Russell and Wilkinson 1979, 1). So it is not astonishing that economics is being applied with rising frequency in water management. One of economics' prime advantages is that it is accustomed to addressing trade-offs among the disparate factors, such as food, lawns, pipe, fish, and electricity, that are constantly encountered during decision making about water. Indeed, economics is actually about such trade-offs.

It is a mistake to confuse economics with accounting, as the uninitiated are prone to do. Although accounting principles are useful for managing the ledgers of water utilities and projects, economics transcends accounting in most decision-making respects while occasionally making use of accounting-based information.

Economics is action oriented, seeking to guide decision making on multiple levels. Water resource economics is strongly prescriptive. It is not content to merely describe water problems from an economic vantage. This is not to say that economics is 100 percent effective in these pursuits, or that it can accomplish them without assistance from the technical and social sciences. So one of the goals of this book is to distinguish the legitimate power of economics in water management. As we demystify the methods of water resource economics, the reader will encounter topics where work remains to be done or economic guidance is weaker than desired.

1.1 An Array of Decision Types

Water-related decision making occurs at various levels, in both governmental and nongovernmental arenas. Properly applied, economics can be of assistance for most of these decisions. For some decisions, the information offered by economics is paramount in framing the selection. In others, it can be helpful without being pivotal.

In some of the most momentous choices faced in water planning, decision makers are trying to refine a property right system or a legal doctrine for guiding the future use of water. These are normally national or state/provincial decisions. Although preexisting legal doctrines tend to be well rooted, ever-mounting scarcity fueled by rising demand has a way of revealing inadequacies in existing rules. So the laws always seem to need incremental improvement and occasionally a complete rewrite. Economics can help us understand the consequences of alternative rules so that better choices can be made.

In other cases, different parties may be voicing conflicting claims to a limited water resource. Regardless of whether the contest is waged in court, in the legislature, or before an agency, its resolution requires a partitioning of the available resources. A key capability of economics is being able to speak to optimal allocation among competing parties. Sometimes this partitioning is indirectly governed by setting a water price and letting water users consume what they wish, as long as they pay their bills. Pricing is an intimately economic undertaking, so the guidance of economics is quite strong here.

Some water-related decision making concerns infrastructure development. Here, we're interested in what kind of infrastructure to undertake. Given limited public funds, which projects should be built, how should they be sized, and who should pay for them? The economic tool called cost-benefit analysis was constructed for the very purpose of analyzing such things. While this tool has been primarily applied to nationally sponsored projects, it is also highly applicable to state and local projects as well as unconventional project proposals. (As a simple example, should the water utility acquire and freely distribute water-conserving showerheads?)

Collectively, these matters of allocation, policy analysis, and project analysis, as well as others, call for an understanding of the behavioral consequences of people and businesses, the determinants of value, and the manners in which alternative decisions shape our future.

1.2   Amid the Noise

A distinguishing feature of water resource decision making is the high degree of public involvement. Whether it is true or not, people think of water resources as public property. They feel entitled to water. They have an opinion about it. Because they drink it and know that life isn't possible without it, they can get emotional about water. They use it in religious ceremonies. Any modification of their access to water generates reactions that can be disproportionate to the modification. Every change proposed in water management has the potential to become a lightning rod for attracting public opinion.

Under these conditions, decision making can be onerous, both in terms of time and costs. Status quo positions can be hard to change. (Why else would there still be communities in the western United States that do not meter water deliveries to residential customers?) Elected officials have lost their seats when they pursue water policy changes before their constituents are ready for it (Martin et al. 1984). To better anticipate and manage public sentiment, it has become standard practice in water management to have public hearings so that "stakeholders" can voice their opinions. Such hearings may guard against postdecision revolt by providing a forum for the public and their leaders to exchange information and opinions.

This high degree of public involvement exposes water managers to forces that can be whimsical and unsettling. Unfortunately, the attitudes of the public can be inaccurate as well as fervent. Water managers can get stuck in their ways too. If we are to make progress under these difficult conditions, it would be helpful to inject clear information about the actual *human* consequences of alternative choices. Translating hydrologic paths into humanly experienced outcomes has clear relevance for this kind of decision making. Economically derived insights can often be of assistance in these situations.

In the water arena, there are plenty of myths and lore to be dispelled, and economics can contribute mightily here. When water consumers contend that the sky will fall if new water supplies are not obtained, it is useful to investigate how much the losses will really be. When someone argues that a proposed change in water rates is too burdensome for large water consumers, it's appropriate to understand how costly these things are, all things considered. If a region's leaders are weighing possible participation in a large water project, public sentiments regarding what should be done will be a mixed bag of emotive appeals for varied and conflicting objectives. Economic procedures offer a means of separating these disparate matters and individually considering each. All such information made available for planning processes can be very helpful.

1.3 Supply Enhancement and Demand Management

Although dichotomies often gloss over noteworthy middle ground, the distinction between *supply enhancement* and *demand management* is a useful one. Whenever water demand exceeds water supply, there are two general methods for addressing the problem.[1] We may either carry out alternatives designed to enhance water supply or

---

1. The prevailing economic wisdom is that the quantity of water demanded cannot exceed the quantity of water supplied unless the price is wrong. It is unfortunately true in many water resource situations that the water price is indeed wrong in that it does not equilibrate demand and supply. Often, the water price omits important values and places us into a position of "excess demand," the economic term for demand > supply.

pursue approaches meant to control (manage) demand. The first harnesses another water source in some way, and the second invokes ways to operate within the limits of current supplies. Of course, we can jointly undertake both types of measures, and this is normally best. Examples within each category are listed below:

Supply Enhancement Strategies	Demand Management Strategies
1. Build/enlarge dams	1. Establish water-conserving plumbing codes requiring certain fixture types (such as low-flow toilets and showerheads)
2. Drill/improve wells	
3. Build interbasin water transfer facilities	2. Establish drought contingency plans
4. Repair leaky infrastructure	3. Ration water or constrain water use (e.g., alternate-day watering schedules)
5. Build desalinization plants	
6. Reprogram reservoir operations (e.g., more storage with less flood protection)	4. Buy/lease/sell water rights
	5. Raise water rates
	6. Educate water users about conservation options

Supply enhancement has dominated water resource planning in the modern era, but this dominance has been suspended in most of the United States. Traditional forms of supply enhancement have run much of their course, because fresh water supplies are physically limited. New dams and wells generally deprive water from some existing or future use category, even if it is estuary inflows, which have become increasingly valuable due to the great amount of human diversions of water from its natural courses. Moreover, these forms of supply enhancement are much more expensive than they have been in the past. This is not to say that we are through developing water supplies—just that we are unlikely to rely on this approach as we have in the past, and future water developments will tend to be less conventional (e.g., desalinization plants). Some experts will argue that supply enhancement options remain strong, but such assertions may exploit the middle ground of this dichotomy or misclassify demand management approaches.[2]

As the role for supply enhancement has ebbed, the opportunities of demand management have simultaneously increased. While individual demand management options lack the scale of supply enhancement facilities, and they are certainly not viewed as the monuments to human achievement that our dams have become, demand management strategies are powerful tools for balancing demand and supply.

2. As a middle-ground example, is leak repair really a supply enhancement given that leaked water is already part of the supply? Some experts call water marketing a supply enhancement because they are visualizing water transfers as a way of increasing supply for particular user groups. On the other end of such transfers, however, someone is reducing their use, so that there is no net increase in usable supply. So whether a strategy constitutes supply enhancement or demand management may ultimately depend on the accounting stance from which it is viewed.

The rise in the usefulness of economic methods for water planning is partly linked to the rising role of demand management. Competing demands are not strangers in the world of economics, and markets and pricing are inherent concepts to economics. But economics also provides methods for assessing the merits of supply enhancement, and even to compare demand management and supply enhancement options. As a consequence, next-generation water managers can profit from adding economic acumen to their toolkits. Even those water managers who will not practice economic analysis, at least not formally, will benefit from developing their economic intuition. Moreover, noneconomists are likely to find themselves collaborating with economic specialists because of the substantial power that economics brings to water planning. When this occurs, possessing a common language will have obvious rewards.

1.4 Future Forces

While the pivotal water issues lying ahead bear a strong resemblance to those we have been facing in recent decades, some differences promise to emerge. It is useful to keep these in mind as we develop our thinking on foreseeable responses and the types of economic analysis that will be useful.

• A key item is continued population growth and the rising water demand (economically defined) it brings. This continual increase in demand will result in increased water scarcity over time. Some water demands will grow faster than others. The consequences will be a public desire for the reapportionment of available supply, continued interest in new water developments, and the further evolution of water policy. Populations will not rise forever, and the U.S. population will peak within this century, but the force of continued growth will remain strong over the next few decades.

• Economic advance and development will cause added water demand too. When members of a constant population become more affluent due to economic development, their collective water demand rises.

• Environmentally oriented demands for water have risen rapidly in recent decades and may continue to do so. To a large extent, these demands ask that water stay in place, either instream or inground, and that it stay relatively uncontaminated.

• Water supply is not rising; in fact, it is shrinking due to pollution and ground water depletion. The fallout will magnify the consequences of rising water demand. Scarcity will certainly increase.

• A warming global climate promises to raise water demand. Induced shifts in the location of people and agricultural production may have far-reaching implications for the spatial distribution of water demand relative to its current locations (U.S. Global Climate Change Research Program 2000). Because a higher energy climate is projected to cause more evaporation and precipitation, with more precipitation occurring in large storm events, the demands for reservoir storage and flood control are expected to rise. Spring melting of high-altitude snowpack will be quicker, thereby adding to these demands.

• The best dam sites are occupied. Lesser-quality ones are available, but construction costs are high as is the regulatory burden stemming from ecosystem protection. While additional water development can play a role in managing growing scarcity, development must be shaped differently than it has been in the past. The options of the new era are different.

• Our amassed assets in water infrastructure are depreciating. Most of our large-scale water developments were constructed since 1930. They were not intended to last forever (U.S. Environmental Protection Agency Office of Water 2002). In addition to normal forms of infrastructural aging, sedimentation has progressively claimed reservoir storage capacity. Replacing underground conveyances in urban areas is a huge expense, as older cities in the eastern United States have already discovered. Postponing infrastructure maintenance is a common tactic to avoid unpopular rate increases, but there is an eventual cost to be faced (National Research Council 2002b, 42).

• Public health concerns pertaining to the quality and security of drinking water continues to boost the costs of water and wastewater treatment operations. Unlike the other forces observed here, this one has the capability to lower the quantity of water demanded for certain uses, providing that higher costs are reflected in higher water rates. Rising costs also diminish the net benefits people receive from the water they consume.

• Energy prices will be rising because of the rising scarcity of depletable fossil fuels. Renewable energy options will be induced as prices rise. The demand for hydropower will rise. We should be mindful that water is a heavy commodity relative to its value. The implications for water planning are several. Pumping, conveying, and pressurizing water will become more expensive. Infrastructure construction and replacement are energy intensive, inferring that water supply enhancement strategies will become more costly.

Collectively, these forces will propel social water issues into more serious matters than those we currently experience. This does not mean that water problems will be grave in every region or even in every year. Water scarcity will, however, become a more common condition—it will occur with greater frequency and intensity in regions already familiar with it, and it will emerge in regions where it is foreign. Rising scarcity will increasingly pressure the capacity of our institutions and wisdom.

1.5 Economics, Environment, and Equity

Water is employed for such a great variety of things. We use it in our homes, businesses, and industries. We transport goods on it. We apply it to our crops and serve it to our livestock. We swim in it, fish in it, and recreate on it. We take pleasure in seeing and listening to it flow by. We directly generate power with it and cool our fossil fuel plants with it. We dump our wastes into it, relying on natural forces to transport and assimilate what we discard. Commercial fisheries, even offshore ones, depend on fresh water availability. Water is a vital substance for the maintenance of the environment, and the environment is similarly vital for supporting humankind. Although our knowledge remains incomplete about the extent of humankind's dependence on the environment and water's role in it, we have come to know that much is at stake.

Given the multitude of water demands expressed by people, how should we proceed? Which water demands are we to elevate in planning for the future and which are we to slight? For example, are environmental water demands as important as water directly used by people in production or consumption activities? The stance of economics with respect to such questions is simple: If someone cares about it, it counts. More formally, economics is ***anthropocentric*** or human centered (Tietenberg 2003, 20). Hence, environmental demands for water have equal standing with other demands because they stem from humanly derived wants. On the other hand, only humanly sponsored water demands count in economics.

Box 1.1
The Diamond-Water Paradox

One of the earliest problems to be posed among economists was the so-called diamond-water paradox. Diamonds have been long regarded as an especially valuable commodity, even though their most acknowledged use has been "decorative." Water, fundamental to life on the other hand, has long been exchanged for fairly low prices. Water prices seem especially low relative to the prices of luxury commodities such as diamonds. How can it be that an essential resource like water commands a much lower price per unit weight or volume than diamonds?

The answer to this paradox emerges when we learn that the price of a commodity is determined not by its most important applications but by its most *marginal* uses. The most marginal use is the one that would be rationally eliminated if the supply of the commodity were decreased by one unit. The marginal use of household water is liable to be for an activity like lawn irrigation or sidewalk washing. Hence, the value of water is not normally associated with its essential uses. If scarcity ever advances to a point where the marginal water uses are essential uses, we may witness a reversal of diamond and water prices.

In the late 1700s A. R. J. Turbot, a French economist, came close to pointing out the solution to the paradox (Rothbard n.d.), but he stopped a trifle short of fathering accurate "marginalist" economic principles, perhaps due to a short life focused on public administration (Schumpeter 1954). Final explanation of the paradox is attributed to Alfred Marshall, who developed our most fundamental marginalist principles in the late 1800s (Schmidt 1992). The application of these principles to water will be of the utmost concern in the forthcoming chapter.

If an endangered species requires a certain water flow to guarantee its survival, this is an economic demand for water only to the extent that people assign value to the species' continued existence. In economics, nonhuman species do not, in and of themselves, have standing. That is, economics is not *ecocentric*, but this does not imply that environmental values do not count. Because people derive sustenance and products from the environment, all resources contributing to human welfare have economic value. But that is not all. Because people are caring and exhibit demands for nonhuman welfare, environmental water demands have standing beyond water's "productive" ability. How these demands are compared to direct human water demands in economic methodology will be a subject introduced within the next chapter.

Much of the focus of water resource economics is to identify *efficient* choices. In other words, given the demands, supplies, and scarcities at hand, and given the great number of alternative choices that can be made, what action(s) should be selected to advance our goal(s)? These goals are carefully developed in the next two chapters. While the goals of economic efficiency are not fundamentally concerned with egalitarian objectives such as equality, fairness, intergenerational equity, or sustainability, such objectives are well illuminated by economic investigation. The inherent fuzziness that accompanies these alternative expressions of *equity* can be clarified by purposeful economic study. Hence, even though the main pursuits of water resource economics direct modest attention to equity, it is certainly possible—and often desirable—to examine how alternative choices will affect different people and groups. Because decision makers commonly care about the social distribution of the gains and losses of a new decision, it is worthwhile to prepare this information for general consideration.

1.6   Organization and Conventions

Although this book is constructed to be completely accessible and digestible by non-economists, it does not sidestep the frontier issues and methods of water resource economics. The overriding goal is to build a practical platform for performing economic analysis, both theoretically and empirically. In the forthcoming chapters, we will progressively

· develop the basic economic theory of resource allocation and customize it for water's peculiarities (chapter 2);

· expand the basic theory to encompass time-defined matters (chapter 3);

· inspect water law as well as the role of economics for critiquing laws and rules (chapter 4);

· establish how economics is employed to investigate proposed policy changes (chapter 5);

- establish how economics is employed to investigate proposed projects (chapter 6);
- analyze the role of water marketing in solving water scarcity problems (chapter 7);
- examine water pricing and the design of efficient water prices (chapter 8);
- develop various methods for empirically specifying water demand functions (chapter 9);
- study how water supply functions can be estimated, and scrutinize the choice between private and public ownership of water supply systems (chapter 10);
- overview methods and studies that combine demand and supply functions into models for specific water settings (chapter 11);
- reassemble, in abridged form, the major contributions available from economics (chapter 12).

Progressing through these topics, both theory and numerical examples will be utilized. As observed in the preface, a feature of this book is the linkage between the theory, graphic portrayals, and empiricism provided here. Complementing this text are the associated Mathematica programs (available at ⟨http://waterecon.tamu .edu⟩) that parallel each chapter containing numerical calculations or graphics.

Wherever possible, end-of-chapter questions are offered as direct applications of the material in each chapter. Many of these questions require no calculations. The exercises that do necessitate computations can ordinarily be accomplished by hand or using a spreadsheet program. Few exercises require unique programming (such as in Fortran or C), or the application of numerical or symbolic programs (such as Mathematica, Matlab, or MathCAD). While the concepts and messages of this book are digestible without performing any of the exercises, future practitioners may wish to undertake these problems as a means of honing insight and skills.

As a matter of standardization, all words appearing in boldface italics in this text are important terms that are redefined in the glossary at the rear of the book.

1.7 Exercises

1. Think of two methods or policies of dealing with water scarcity (not directly listed in this chapter), and then classify them as supply enhancing or demand managing.

2. Download the program MathReader from ⟨http://www.wri.com⟩ and use it to review a program downloadable from ⟨http://waterecon.tamu.edu⟩.

3. Characterize the following sentence as either ecocentric or anthropocentric, and justify your position: "Endangered species have a right to continued existence within the earth's environment, and no water project expected to extinguish a species should ever be constructed."

Ecocentric → The endangered species has no contract for water.

2 Optimal Allocation and Development

What are we trying to accomplish?

The main objective of this central chapter is to firmly establish the economic goals we seek to promote in water resource planning. A second objective is to establish the basic economic nomenclature and concepts used to perform static (time-insensitive) economic analysis. For the most part, this information arises from the branches of economics called welfare economics and microeconomics, with some needed tweaking to accommodate the peculiarities of water. Because of the tweaking as well as our cautious attention to goals, veterans of economics should not overlook this material. Noneconomists will find this information to be an essential foundation for any real understanding of water resource economics.

2.1 Establishing Goals

The anthropocentric orientation of water resource economics narrows the available objectives for guiding decision making, but the alternatives are still many. A specific objective is needed for economic analysis. A useful objective would ideally have sufficient scope and power to guide a broad range of water-related decisions.

The water issues faced by society are numerous and varied. For example, when apportioning limited water supplies, how are we to weigh water used for irrigation (and its resulting food production) against alternative uses such as household hygiene or instream flow for ecosystem habitat maintenance? How are we to select between expanding a particular water use or expanding a water-conserving practice when the first consumes water resources and the second consumes other resources? How much of a depletable ground water resource should we pump for immediate use and how much should we leave in the ground for use by people who have yet to be born? These issues embed trade-offs between different people, between substantially different uses of water, between water resources and other resources, and between current people and future people.

Since these matters are of human origin and involve society at large, how does the public want them resolved? Unfortunately, proponents of particular water uses are self-interested so they naturally argue, as well as lobby and vote, on behalf of their interests vis-à-vis other interests, and they will even submit skewed information to elevate their own causes. Public debate about water generates varied perspectives and emotive appeals, as noted in the prior chapter. In the face of all this noise, how can water resource professionals assemble helpful information, and how can we employ it to make socially advantageous decisions about the use of water?

Economists dismiss the idea that there might be an accurate ranking of alternative water uses.[1] It cannot be said, for example, that the residential use of water is always more desirable (or more valuable) than irrigation, or vice versa. Protagonists in public debates about water may sponsor the idea that water is universally more desirable in one sector than another, but economic evidence does not support such thinking. (Whenever a water resource issue is cast as black or white, you might suspect that the correct assessment is a shade of gray—the challenge is to identify it.)

In the course of comparing one use of water against another, or in comparing water use against a sacrifice in other resources, we need both a common metric and an objective that utilizes the metric. The selection of a metric is not of great consequence; it could be many things. Its job is merely to reduce everything to common units, so that apples and apples are being considered rather than apples and oranges. In economics, it has been convenient to select dollars as the metric. Any currency would do just as well. The convenience of currency stems from its familiarity because people are accustomed to employing money in exchanges and making psychological trade-offs assisted by this common denominator.[2]

The selection of an objective is much more difficult because the objective must often embed relative weights for different people or different groups of people. Having such weights are clearly important, because a great many public decisions about water (or any resource or issue) involve trade-offs about advancing the welfare of one person or group as compared to others. How this gets done depends on the relative weights.

Economists have devised two alternative, guiding social objectives, and they address the weighting issue in rather different ways. Both concern *allocative efficiency* because the primary issue is how to allocate limited resources. The first we shall

1. It is noteworthy that the official water codes of many U.S. states expressly identify such hierarchies as a supposed means of resolving legal disputes involving water. The existence of such lists implies that not everyone understands the economic findings on this matter. This is one of many issues where simple economics offers a strong basis for correcting a policy error.

2. Deciding whether to spend one hundred dollars on a camera is not so much a choice between having a camera or a hundred dollars; it is a choice between a camera or the other things that one hundred dollars commands.

uniquely term *neutral economic efficiency* because it sidesteps the weighting issue entirely by emphasizing a spectrum of "good" decisions. Economists commonly call this concept Pareto optimality.[3] The second we shall call *aggregate economic efficiency*, and it performs the weighting task by treating the values experienced by different people as commensurate and then maximizing total value summed over all water users. This second definition permeates the customary conduct of water resource economics so completely that we will drop the "aggregate" adjective in much of this volume. Yet it can be important for practitioners to recognize, and sometimes to report, the occasional shortcomings of the aggregate efficiency goal. Also, some water issues are better illuminated by the neutral vision of efficiency, as we shall see later in this text.

Distinguishing neutral and aggregate economic efficiency is best concluded after we have fully developed the goals and desires of individual water users. Not surprisingly, people have *private* objectives that count in the pursuit of *social* objectives, for society is an aggregation of individuals. To establish a solid footing, we shall start by investigating the costs of water supply, and then examine the demands for water expressed by people and businesses. These matters can then be combined to inform us about how water can be efficiently allocated across its various demand groups.

Part I: The Fundamental Economic Theory

We begin by developing the important principles of microeconomics, so that the knowledgeable practitioner (you) can perform needed analyses and properly interpret analyses performed by others.[4] There are two building blocks to emphasize: the character of water supply by its providers, and the character of demand by water users.

2.2 The Costs of Water Supply

Although it is practical for some water users to supply their own water, the typical scenario is one where a single organization supplies finished, processed, or *retail water* to all individuals in a given area. Usually, the organization is designated as a water utility or water district. It may be privately or publicly owned. It may be

---

3. Surprisingly, many economists have a dismal grasp of the distinction between neutral and aggregate efficiency, perhaps because Pareto optimality sometimes seems to capture both types (Griffin 1995). To promote better respect for the separate ideals, the neutral/aggregate terminology is introduced here. Definitionally, Pareto optimality is achieved when the only available options for improving any person's welfare will necessarily harm one or more other people.

4. Microeconomics refers to that branch of economics concerned "with individual consumers, producers, etc., and ... with the allocation of resources among these economic agents" (Russell and Wilkinson 1979, 2).

operated as a for-profit venture or a nonprofit organization. The supplier's customers may be composed of irrigators, commercial establishments, households, or publicly owned facilities. The supplier may specialize by serving only one user group or it may supply multiple user types. Competition in the local provision of retail water is normally not viable due to the great expense of replicating water delivery infrastructure. Because pipelines and canals are expensive to build and maintain, it is not economically sensible to encourage competition in any given locale. Bottled water is the exception here, but that is a small proportion of overall water use.

The task of the utility or district is to handle raw, unprocessed, or **natural water** from either a surface watercourse—such as a river, stream, or lake—or an underground aquifer, and then transform the natural water into the retail water that is received by clients. Some suppliers buy partially processed water from another supplier. Some suppliers employ natural water from both surface and ground water sources. The transformation tasks may be few or many, depending on the differences that exist between the natural water source(s) and the desired properties of retail water. Even the act of storing water in a reservoir represents a transformation, meaning that the water is no longer 100 percent natural.

For organizations supplying only irrigation water, the differences may relate solely to the location of water. In this case, the supplier need only pump and convey water to farm gates. Such suppliers have pumping plants to construct and maintain, and they have conveyance facilities such as canals and pipelines to establish and maintain. Clearly, they also make expenditures on pumping energy, and they must perform administrative services for planning, management, accounting, billing, and customer relations.

In more urban settings, suppliers must do more than pump and convey when they transform water. Depending on natural water quality, various sorts of water treatment may be undertaken to remove, modify, or deactivate contaminants. Such treatment(s) can be performed mechanically, chemically, or biologically, but all methods will entail additional costs for the supplier. To enhance the usability of water, clients may prefer to receive consistently pressurized water, thus motivating the supplier to incur expenses for additional pumps, energy, and aboveground storage tanks (i.e., water towers). Consumers also have preferences regarding the *reliability* of their water supply. That is, they have desires relating to the riskiness of supply shortfalls that might occur as a consequence of system failures or climatic aberrations. To obtain some measure of insurance against such problems, the supplier may incur further costs for keeping equipment and facilities in top condition or installing additional system capacity that can be available during shortfall events. These expenses also raise the costs of water supply. As compared to suppliers of only irrigation water, urban administrative costs are enlarged by the added complexities of tending to treatment, pressurization, reliability, and a greater multitude of customers.

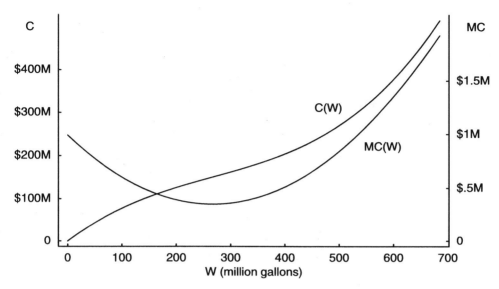

Figure 2.1
Total and marginal costs of water supply

As a first approximation to investigating water supply costs, we may envision that these costs are driven by the amount of retail water that is delivered. As a generic expression of this idea, it can be said that the total cost of operating a particular supply organization is a well-defined function of the amount of delivered water, W. This idea is captured by the function C(W) in which total cost is a function of W. The function C will vary from place to place and from year to year depending on the exact circumstances, but that only means that the function must be properly specified for each situation. Figure 2.1 contains a common vision of such a total cost function. Total costs are read on the left-hand vertical axis. Embodied in this particular curve are several features that may not fit every situation:

• As a point of standardization consistent with usual practice, C(W) incorporates no costs for natural water. If we did want to include these costs, C(W) would be rotated upward by an appropriate amount.

• Embedded in and implicit to the total cost function is the notion that every level of W is being achieved using the most cost-effective techniques available. This is fundamental for all total cost functions.

• The cost of supplying zero units of water is zero dollars. This infers that all costs are portrayed as *variable costs* in figure 2.1. That is, the supplier has full control over potential expenditures in that there are no precommitted obligations. This is not an appropriate depiction for circumstances in which the water supplier is already established and has costs to cover even in the absence of water deliveries. Such preestablished costs are termed *fixed costs* in economics. They result from irreversible commitments such as long-term contracts and debt incurred for construction investments.

• As the amount of delivered water increases, total costs strictly increase. This is fundamental.

• As deliveries rise from a zero level, costs rise somewhat more rapidly than they do for intermediate levels of water delivery. This is most readily witnessed by inspecting the curve representing *marginal costs*, MC(W). Marginal costs are read on the right-hand vertical axis. Definitionally, marginal cost is the derivative of total cost with respect to W; it specifies the slope of the total cost function. Marginal costs are falling across the range of low water deliveries (0–267 million gallons), presumably because additional deliveries allow the supplier to employ more fully its capital items (such as pumping plants, pipelines, and treatment facilities) and because some administrative functions do not increase proportionately with water deliveries.

• At some point, total costs start to rise more rapidly as the supplier begins to encounter capacity limitations requiring more expensive approaches, administrative complexities that challenge managerial talent, and/or resource limitations pertaining to the availability of natural water. This point is signaled by the inflection point of the total cost curve or, equivalently, the bottoming out of the marginal cost function. From this point onward, total costs increase at an increasing rate.

Later, when water supply and demand elements are pulled together, it will become clear that marginal cost is a key concept. The marginal cost function is the same thing as the *supply function* in idealistic economic situations. For us, however, two worries remain. The value of natural water has been omitted, conforming with the usual accounting procedures of utilities and districts. If this value is included or if it is zero, the marginal cost function can be said to be the supply function. Still, most water suppliers do not engage in marginal cost pricing—a fact to be revisited later—so the supply function cannot be safely equated to marginal costs just yet.

It bears emphasis that total and marginal costs are portrayed as functionally dependent on W, not on the many outlays made by the water supplier for inputs such as energy, trucks, pipe, and workers. In our basic theory, this representation works well because increasing amounts of delivered water involve increasing amounts of costly inputs. Economic theory is well attached to the idea that total costs are fully dependent on the amount of the commodity produced, or W in this case. In water supply circumstances, however, there can be major costs that are largely unrelated to water deliveries. An important example is the urban distributional networks that connect all residences to a central water supply. This distribution system is costly regardless of how much water is passing through it. When these costs begin to matter more, as they will later in this text, we shall have to expand our vision a bit.

The bottom line is this: the cost function C(W) portrays cost-effective action on the part of the supplier. For any given amount of supplied water, C(W) tells us the lowest total costs of supplying that water. Therefore, whenever efficiency in water resource management is insisted on, one of the things being requested is that suppliers operate on their total cost function (and not above it). Efficiency requires cost-effectiveness—all levels of water supply must be provided at minimum cost, but that is not all.

What exactly does this mean?

2.3 Efficiency for a Single Water-Using Agent

Having established the simple efficiency precepts lying on the supply side of water planning, we can look at the decision-making calculus of a single agent using water. The term *agent* is purposely broad so that the analysis may apply to a person deciding how deep to fill the bathtub, an irrigator deciding how much water to pump to fields, a corporation deciding how much coolant to circulate at a thermal plant, or any number of similar decisions undertaken by a single entity, be it a person, household, farm, or business. Entrepreneurial agents such as farmers or companies are normally treated in economics as striving for profit-maximizing decisions. Efficient decisions for these agents are ones that maximize profit. Other agents such as individuals, families, and households are thought of as employing their limited budgets to maximize the satisfaction or **utility** they derive from all consumption activities, including water consumption.

Both profit maximization by firms and utility maximization by people generate value-sensitive water **demand functions** that analysts can use to measure the total benefits of water consumption. Such measurements turn out to be crucial to the practice of water resource economics.

Efficiency for a Single Firm

A firm producing some quantity, y, of an output (rice, electricity, roadway, hamburgers, etc.) per period will normally have the technological capability to employ alternative quantities of water, w, and other inputs $(x_1, x_2, \ldots, x_n)$ per period to produce y. The amount of w used per unit of y is usually not fixed by available technology. Instead, there are various degrees of substitutability among the inputs. For example, less w can be used to produce the same amount of y if more of some other input(s) is (are) used.

While the principles of physics, chemistry, and biology place absolute limits on the degree of substitutability among inputs, and may even establish the minimum amount of water required, these limits are rarely, if ever, germane. The reason phys-ical boundaries are not relevant is that the relative value of water does not lead us to test these limits in real-world business operations. Water is not so valuable that it is ever sensible to maximize the amount of y per unit of w. By the same token, there is not a fixed water requirement for each unit of y production in an economic world.[5]

Existing technology for y production by a firm can be specified by a **production function**, f, indicating how much y can be produced from alternative combinations of water and other inputs:

$$y = f(w, x_1, x_2, \ldots, x_n). \tag{2.1}$$

To envision it, consider the typical cross section provided in the upper panel of figure 2.2 in which the x_is have been fixed at arbitrary levels. If we change the other input levels, the curve of figure 2.2 will likely shift, but its shape tends to be preserved. The derivative of output with respect to water is displayed in the lower panel. Similar graphs apply for all other inputs as well. Typical features displayed are as follows:

1. Positive marginal product, defined as a positive first derivative ($y' = \partial f / \partial w$), occurs up to the point $\bar{w}$, beyond which additional water usage will reduce production.

2. Increasing returns to scale, defined as a positive second derivative ($\partial^2 f / \partial w^2$), occurs up to the point $\vec{w}$, and decreasing returns to scale ($\partial^2 f / \partial w^2 < 0$) exists beyond $\vec{w}$.

Both of these features turn out to be important for profit maximization. From the first feature, water usage above $\bar{w}$ cannot be profit maximizing because it would lower output while raising water costs. From the second feature, water usage below $\vec{w}$ cannot be profit maximizing under most situations because the usual second-order conditions for maximization may not be obeyed. Expressing the latter point more intuitively, if profit is positive for water use levels below $\vec{w}$, then even greater profit can be achieved by increasing w.

While we will set aside this point because it alters none of our water-focused results, some of the x_is may be fixed by prior decisions. This may be particularly true for fixed assets such as land, structures, and equipment. For the remaining deci-sions, the profit-maximizing firm wishes to optimize w and x levels with respect to resultant profit. Such decision making also infers that y will be produced at minimum cost, so cost minimization is fully implied by profit maximization—cost minimiza-

---

5. Although analysts may sometimes model an enterprise's water use *as if* it had a water requirement, such abstractions overlook management options as they simplify modeling. When the results of such models are interpreted, it is a good idea to be mindful of all assumptions, for some "results" are more thoroughly driven by assumptions rather than the facts.

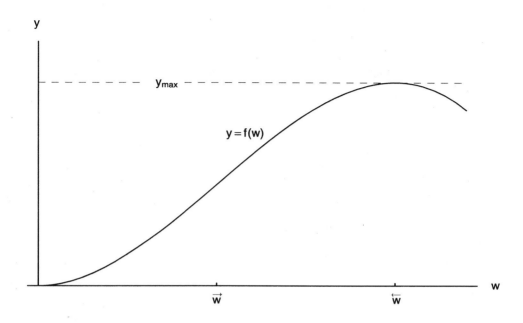

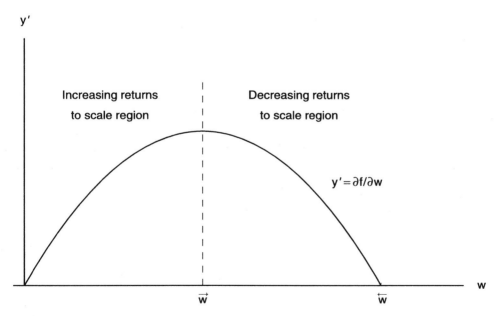

Figure 2.2
Production and marginal product functions

tion need not be separately pursued. (On the other hand, cost minimization does not imply profit maximization, thus indicating the superiority of the latter objective.)[6]

Formulation and solution of the profit-maximization problem is enabled by adding some simple economic details. Let us assume that the y producer can sell output at p_y dollars per unit, and that the firm is sufficiently small not to exert any price-influencing market power over price (it's not a monopoly or close to being one). Similarly, assume that any of the x_i inputs can be purchased by the firm at a constant price of p_i dollars per unit. A comparable assumption about the price of water available to the firm can be made, but many firms supply their own water or face a rate structure that contains more than a single water price. Instead, we will initially presume that the cost of water to the firm is given functionally by $c(w)$ where it is also true that $dc/dw > 0$ (more water costs more). This cost function pertains only to the firm's costs, so it is quite distinct from the total cost of water for the entire supply system discussed earlier. Of course, if the firm does face a single price, p, of water, then $c(w) = p \cdot w$.

Combining these elements, the firm must

$$\text{maximize } p_y \cdot f(w, x_1, x_2, \ldots, x_n) - c(w) - \sum_{i=1}^{n} p_i \cdot x_i, \qquad (2.2)$$

which if one prefers, can be readily rewritten using vector notation as

$$\text{maximize } p_y \cdot f(w, \mathbf{x}) - c(w) - \mathbf{p} \cdot \mathbf{x}. \qquad (2.3)$$

Each of the x_is, as well as w, constitute a decision variable to be optimized. A first-order condition can be obtained for each decision via the usual calculus procedure.[7] Focusing on the water decision and assuming it is optimal to employ a nonzero amount of water, we take the first derivative of the above profit equation and set it equal to zero. The result,

---

6. For a water engineering perspective on the inadequacies of emphasizing cost minimization exclusively, see Walski (2001).

7. To assure that the level of w satisfying this condition provides a profit maximum and not a profit minimum, there is also a second-order condition that may need to be verified. In most circumstances, however, this is not necessary. The applicable second-order condition is

$$p_y \cdot \frac{\partial^2 f}{\partial w^2} - \frac{d^2 c}{dw^2} < 0.$$

If the firm's cost function incorporates a single price of water, then the latter term on the left side of the inequality is zero, and the second-order condition is guaranteed if the production function exhibits decreasing returns to scale at optimal x. If the second derivative of the cost function is negative, though, as might occur in the presence of a decreasing-block rate structure, decreasing returns to scale in production will not be sufficient to guarantee the second-order condition.

$$p_y \cdot \frac{\partial f}{\partial w} = \frac{dc}{dw}, \tag{2.4}$$

implicitly indicates the profit-maximizing amount of water to use. If the $\partial f / \partial w$ term contains any of the x_i terms, as it commonly will, then equations (2.4) and (2.5),

$$p_y \cdot \frac{\partial f}{\partial x_i} = p_i \quad \text{for each } i = 1, 2, \ldots, n, \tag{2.5}$$

will need to be solved as a simultaneous system in order to get an explicit solution for profit-maximizing w.

Hence, from the firm's perspective the *efficient* amount of water to use is given by these combined first-order conditions, (2.4) and (2.5). When the function f is known, a useful algebraic approach is to eliminate all x_i from (2.4) by employing each x_i's known market price and the simultaneous solution to (2.5) to determine every x_i, with the possibility that each is functionally dependent on w. Substituting these results into (2.4) yields a revised (2.4) containing only p_y, w, and dc/dw.

The efficient level of water use indicated by (2.4)–(2.5) is dependent on the output price, the marginal productivity of water in terms of y production, and the marginal cost of water. To illustrate the role of each determinant, the two panels of figure 2.3 provide the graphic analog of equation (2.4). The upper graph portrays a typical production function and the consequent marginal product function, $\partial f / \partial w$, once levels of all other inputs have been selected and substituted into f. Notice that the vertical axis of the upper panel is in units of y. In the lower panel, units have been converted to \$ by first multiplying the marginal product function by the fixed price of y. The resultant *value of marginal product* (VMP) function (the left side of [2.4]) is graphed in the lower panel along with the *marginal cost* (MC) function (the right side of [2.4]). The efficient choice for this firm is w^*.

Notice how w^* might change in response to changes in its determining factors. A technological change or a change in the usage of other inputs could shift the VMP curve upward, thereby raising w^*. Likewise, a rise in p_y would increase w^*. Finally, if the marginal cost of water decreased (shifted down), w^* would be increased.

The first-order condition (2.4) can also be manipulated to obtain the firm's demand for water—an important concept in water resource economics. In the case of a single firm, the water demand function tells how the firm's desired employment of water changes in response to the value of water. Substituting the value of water, p, for marginal water costs in (2.4) produces

$$p_y \cdot \frac{\partial f}{\partial w} = p, \tag{2.6}$$

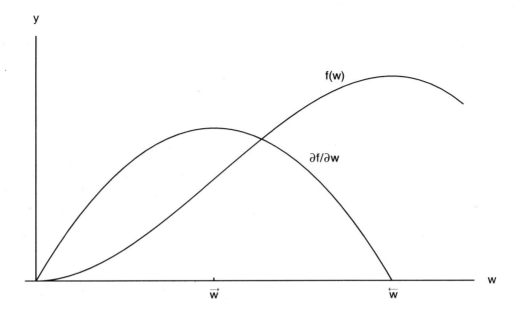

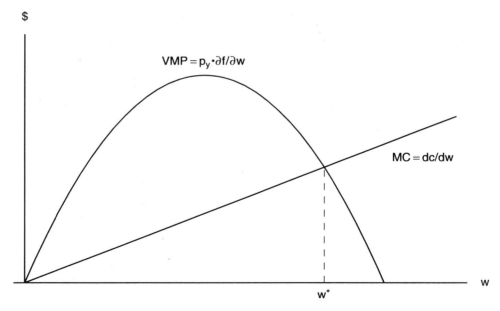

Figure 2.3
Optimal water employment

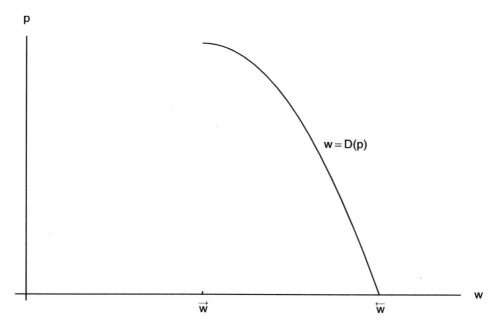

Figure 2.4
Water demand for a producer

which is a functional relationship among p_y, w, and p. Substituting the existing price of y (or as another example, y's projected future price) eliminates one variable, leaving us with an equation in two variables that can normally be inverted/solved for w. This solution is the firm's demand for water,

$$w = D(p), \tag{2.7}$$

which is depicted in figure 2.4 using economists' odd tradition of placing the price variable on the vertical axis. In the case of profit-maximizing firms, the downward slope of the demand function is a consequence of the declining marginal productivity of water (i.e., decreasing returns to scale) across the relevant range of w. Because it is not optimal for the firm to select water usage outside the $(\vec{x}, \overleftarrow{x})$ interval, the demand curve does not exist outside this range.

Efficiency for a Single Consumer

Analyzing efficient choices for consumers is more problematic than for firms because consumers are not trying to advance something as tangible as profits. After much scrutiny, which continues to this day, the science of economics has settled on a framework in which consumers are modeled as rational utility maximizers. "Utility"

Box 2.1
Extracting Water Demand from a Production Function

Suppose that all other inputs are preestablished at specific levels, and the amount of an output y is functionally determined by water use according to $y = a + bw - cw^2$, where a, b, and c are positive numbers. (The minus sign before c is needed to establish decreasing returns to scale.) The corresponding water demand function is resolved by differentiating profit with respect to w, setting it equal to zero (because we want to choose a level of w maximizing profit), and then algebraically processing the result until it is in proper form.

$$\text{profit} = p_y \cdot (a + bw - cw^2) - p \cdot w$$

$$\frac{d(\text{profit})}{dw} = p_y \cdot (b - 2cw) - p = 0$$

$$-p_y 2cw = p - bp_y$$

$$w = \frac{bp_y - p}{2cp_y}$$

A multi-input production function is more difficult to deal with because there is more algebra to do after setting derivatives equal to zero for each input. For the production function $y = ax^b w^c$, where $b + c < 1$, the best path is to write the profit function, set both derivatives equal to zero, rearrange the two-term equations so that one term is on each side, and divide one of the resulting equations by the other one. Solve for x and substitute the result back into one of the original first-order equations. The result is messy, but it can be solved for w, yielding the demand equation

$$w = (ab^b c^{1-b} p^{b-1} p_x^{-b} p_y)^{1/(1-b-c)}.$$

This result qualifies as a demand equation because there are only fixed parameters (a, b, and c) and prices (p_x, p_y, and p) on the right-hand side. The other decision variables (x and y) are absent, as they must be.

---

connotes the sometimes nebulous "satisfaction" consumers derive from consuming a good. Consumers face an array of goods they can purchase in different amounts, and they have a limited income with which to make these purchases. Different consumers have different incomes and different preferences about the goods they may buy. Water is one of these goods.

While commonplace rhetoric outside of economics often speaks of consumers' "need" for water, need has little to do with relevant ranges of a consumer's demand for water. Yes, consumers use water for high-value applications such as for drinking, cooking, and hygiene. These applications compose the "high end" of a person's demand for water. A portion of these applications can be regarded as needs in a survival sense, but others involve choice and substitution possibilities. Substitutions are especially apparent for hygienic applications of water, where for example, water-saving models of customary appliances are readily available (such as washing machines, showerheads, and toilets). Household leaks are often a large, and sometimes the largest, "use" of indoor water use (DeOreo, Heaney, and Mayer 1996;

Heaney et al. 1998; Dziegielewski 2000), in spite of their easy correction. More important, households apply water to many "low-end" uses such as car and sidewalk/patio washing, lawns, and pools. Such uses cannot be portrayed as needs, and it is misleading to lump such uses together with true water needs. With average water use exceeding a hundred gallons per capita per day across U.S. homes (van der Leeden, Troise, and Todd 1991, 335), it is apparent that low-end water uses must compose a sizable portion of overall water use. In arid regions of the United States where water resource management tends to be more significant, the proportion of low-end water uses can be much higher. When we combine this fact with a recognition that some of the high-end uses of water are also discretionary (or leaky), we discover that water *needs* is not accurate vocabulary for a water resource professional. Water *demand* is what we need to know, and as in the case of businesses, water demand by the individual consumer or household is not a single level of water use. It is a value-dependent function. As the value (scarcity) of water increases, people demand less. Most crucially, changing policies and new projects do not impinge on high-end water uses anyway, so they are generally irrelevant for policy and project evaluation. What we might legitimately call needs are outside the range of evaluation.

This is not merely a semantic matter. The word need is a powerful expression, and it conveys a sense of urgency that is useful to groups who "want" a particular decision outcome and wish to obtain approval for it.[8] One such group may be ourselves. As water management specialists, we are easily tempted to aggrandize our subject so as to attract public attention and social energy. But we are also ethically obligated to portray our efforts with as much accuracy as we can muster. For this reason, as well as a scientific desire for precision and good judgment, it is a good planning practice to focus on the specification of water demand, economically defined.

The vital consumer theory is that a consumer's preferences about all goods can be condensed into a ***utility function*** that is dependent on the amount of every good consumed: $U(w, x_1, x_2, \ldots, x_n)$. In our water-focused theory, it is noteworthy that many of the important x goods will be water substitutes in some fashion while other x_is will involve water as a complementary good (e.g., pool size or lawn area). Although no consumer is explicitly aware of their utility function, if a person's preferences satisfy rather modest requirements (Varian 1992, 97), that person's choices and behavior can be modeled as if the individual were acting to maximize utility. Fortunately, application of this theoretical construct does not require that we actually determine each individual's utility function, as we shall soon see.

---

8. It is smart to be wary of claims based on alleged water needs. According to Miller and Underwood, there is a "three-point water creed" that has typified traditional water-using interests: "(1) get it first; (2) get someone else to pay; and (3) if you have to pay, shift as much of the burden as possible away from water users" (1983, 638). A well-employed argument by these interests is that this water is *needed*. Genuine analysis rejects such contentions in favor of more balanced thought.

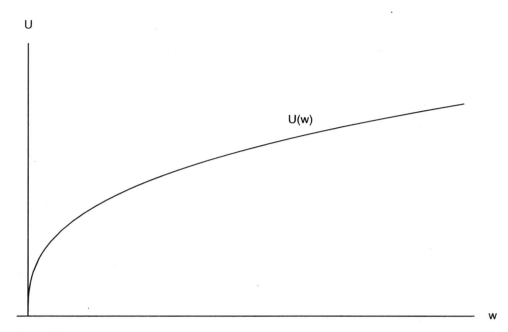

Figure 2.5
Utility of water

A utility-water cross section of a typical utility function is provided in figure 2.5. The general features important to demand formulation and its application are as follows:

1. More water is preferred to less ($\partial U/\partial w > 0$) throughout the relevant range of w.

2. Diminishing **marginal utility** (defined as a negative second derivative, $\partial^2 U/\partial w^2$) occurs throughout the relevant range of w.

3. Any order-preserving transformation of a person's utility function—such as multiplying the entire function by three, adding a thousand to it, or taking its logarithm—is also a legitimate utility function representing the same preference pattern.

Visiting the first feature, if water consumption were to become large enough, the consumer would find additional quantities to be useless ($\partial U/\partial w = 0$), and even larger quantities might begin to lower utility ($\partial U/\partial w < 0$). Such levels of water consumption would obviously be uneconomic, and they will not be observed under realistic conditions because the consumer will not choose them. The second feature is a consequence of consumer rationality in consumption. The first units of any acquired good, including water, will be applied in their most preferred applications. In the case of water, this means the high-end uses will be served first. Subsequent units will generate progressively lower satisfaction. The last feature implies that the vertical axis of figure 2.5 has only *ordinal* or relative significance. Utility cannot be interpreted as a *cardinal* measure, and it cannot be used as the basis for conducting "interpersonal" (across different people) comparisons.[9]

A consumer maximizing their utility subject to an income constraint (I is income) can then be modeled as facing the following formal problem:

$$\text{maximize } U(w, x_1, x_2, \ldots, x_n) \quad \text{subject to } c(w) + \sum_{i=1}^{n} p_i x_i = I, \tag{2.8}$$

or using vector notation,

$$\text{maximize } U(w, \mathbf{x}) \quad \text{subject to } c(w) + \mathbf{p} \cdot \mathbf{x} = I. \tag{2.9}$$

The above problem incorporates a cost function for water rather than a single price, because it is common for water rate structures to include more than a single water price. Formal solution and investigation of this problem's solution is assisted by the Lagrangian method of optimization in the presence of constraints.[10] The resulting system of first-order conditions will, as in the case of the single, profit-maximizing firm, require simultaneous solution to obtain the consumer's $n + 1$ demand functions. In general, the consumer's demands for water and each of the n other commodities will depend on the marginal cost of water, the prices of other goods, and income. Our notation can sometimes be simplified by referring to water's marginal cost as water price, p, so that resultant water demand by the consumer can be written as

$$w = D(p, p_1, p_2, \ldots, p_N, I). \tag{2.10}$$

The second feature above implies that $\partial D / \partial p < 0$ (demand is downward sloping), and it is also apparent that $\partial D / \partial I > 0$ (increases in income increase demand).

---

9. For example, if we are trying to decide whether to allocate a unit of water to person A or person B, we cannot base the decision on which person will experience more utility from the water. Because of the third feature, the "util" measurement is not unique, so it doesn't convey the power necessary to make such decisions.

10. See the appendix to this chapter if you are unfamiliar with this approach and feel that you can make good use of it. An example generating a water demand function from a utility function is also offered in the appendix. The Lagrangian method is very useful, and we will refer to it twice more in this chapter. In both cases we use the Lagrangian method to obtain first-order equations for a constrained optimization problem. Later chapters will also refer to this method, and there is a useful Mathematica routine that performs it (first used in chapter 3).

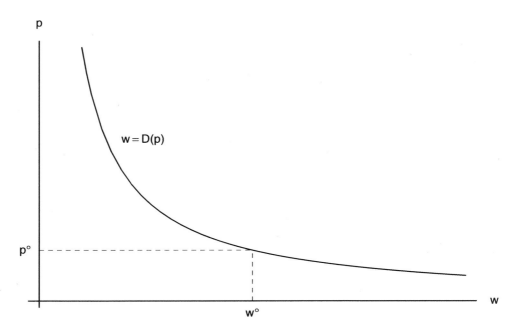

Figure 2.6
Water demand for a consumer

Whether $\partial D/\partial p_i$ is positive or negative for the various commodity prices will depend on whether those goods are substitutes or complements to water.

If known nonwater commodity prices and consumer income are substituted into the above demand function, then the resulting function can be plotted as in figure 2.6. All points lying on the demand curve are personally efficient for the consumer in the sense that they are the consumer's optimal water choices for each possible water price. If the prevailing marginal cost of a unit of water is p°, then the only personally efficient consumption level is w°.

In contemplating and using demand curves such as the one portrayed in figure 2.6, analysts must exercise care in their use of the economics term *demand*. Economists have agreed on the following terminology to standardize communications. A *change in demand* is a shift in the demand curve, such as would occur if income increased or the individual installed a water-saving appliance. A *change in quantity demanded* constitutes a movement along the demand curve due to a change in water value or price.

Given the nature of water demand for both business and household agents—especially the fact that *demand is a function rather than a number*—the shortcomings of terms like *water needs* or *water requirements* is becoming increasingly evident.

2.4 Aggregation and Acquisition of Marginal Net Benefit Functions

The prior sections generated basic information about efficient actions from the perspective of the two main types of water users: firms and people. In both cases, it can be said that agents' efficiency is captured well by the simple expression "their marginal benefits equal their marginal costs." The marginal benefit side of this equation is differently defined and differently obtained for firms and people, but it applies nonetheless. In both instances, the concept of water demand emerges because efficient water choices depend on water value. What, then, is water value? This question is why economics has an important role in water resource management.

Water value is a consequence of water scarcity. Water scarcity can only be measured by comparing the desires (demands) for water to its availability. As a first step in assessing scarcity, the various demands for water must be aggregated into a total demand. This is a trickier matter for water than it is for most commodities, for three reasons:

Differential Processing Different types of water demand often involve differing degrees of water processing and therefore differing supply costs. For example, irrigators value mainly the delivery of untreated water to their land; households value delivery, pressurization, and purification; industries value delivery, possibly pressurization, and various degrees of water treatment depending on the products being manufactured.

Reuse Depending on the circumstances, water can be used to satisfy one demand and then reused to satisfy another. Reuse may be a natural consequence of a user's return flow reentering a watercourse and being used downstream by another user. Or reuse may be humanly assisted, such as when facilities are constructed to collect, treat, and deliver used water to yet other users.

Nonrivalness (and Jointness) Some demands for water can be simultaneously satisfied by the same units of water because the two demands are *nonrival* or can be jointly served. An example is reservoir releases that yield both hydropower and water for households. Facilities such as this can jointly supply multiple uses. Another example is the demand for instream water, which may simultaneously satisfy many peoples' demand for biodiversity along a watercourse. Biodiversity demands for water and some other water demands (like recreation) can be nonrival in that the same units of water may be simultaneously beneficial to more than one agent.

The implication of differential processing is that disparities in supply costs must be considered prior to any attempts to aggregate (add) individual demands to obtain total water demand. It is only proper to combine the demands of firms or people who are receiving similarly processed retail water. Whenever reuse is a relevant

matter for planning, the methodology of combining demands must include information about the water flows of the situation. Hence, economics must be married with
basic hydrology to study any water planning issue for which natural return flow or
purposeful reuse is a possibility. Nonrivalness does not affect the matter of whether
demands can be added; it influences how they are added.

Assuming multiple firms or households (or some of both) are to receive similarly
processed retail water, reuse is not a concern, and water consumption is rival, then
the aggregation of demands is a simple matter. If agent 1's water demand is given
by $w^1 = D^1(p)$, agent 2's water demand is given by $w^2 = D^2(p)$, and agent 3's water
demand is given by $w^3 = D^3(p)$, then their total demand, $D(p)$, is readily obtained
as

$$D(p) = D^1(p) + D^2(p) + D^3(p). \tag{2.11}$$

This addition is graphically shown in figure 2.7. Although water demand is not often
truly linear in price, three linear demand functions are added in figure 2.7 to clarify
what economists call *horizontal* addition. Demand curves must be horizontally combined when the good in question is rivally consumed. A good is rivally consumed
when the units consumed by one agent are no longer available for consumption by

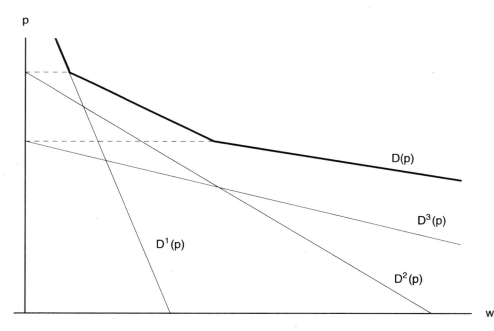

Figure 2.7
Adding rival water demands

other agents. For example, agents 1–3 might be three households within the same community or three irrigators within the same water district. The bold "kinked" line of figure 2.7 is total demand.

A Detour into Demand Estimation

In actual application, analysts might acquire demand function information through a variety of methods. These methods are the subject of chapter 9. It is fruitful, however, to introduce the simplest method, *point expansion*, to appreciate how easily demand functions can sometimes be obtained, at least approximately. This approach will be used often in the forthcoming chapters. Understanding it is aided by the concept of *elasticity*.

Whereas most sciences rely on the notion of "slope" or "rate of change" to characterize system responsiveness to changing conditions, economists tend to speak and think in terms of a dimensionless measure called elasticity. Thus, demand functions are said to have a price elasticity, an income elasticity, and elasticities for any other independent variable serving as an argument of the demand function. Similarly, supply functions also have multiple elasticities. The price elasticity of supply functions is especially important, just as the price elasticity of demand is of special significance.

The price elasticity of demand, ε, is defined as the percentage change in quantity demanded that will occur for a percentage change in price:

$$\varepsilon = \frac{\frac{\Delta w}{w}}{\frac{\Delta p}{p}} = \frac{\Delta w}{\Delta p} \cdot \frac{p}{w}. \tag{2.12}$$

Because w demanded falls as p rises, ε is negative. In the limit, as the percentage change in price becomes small so that we can speak of price elasticity at a specific point on the demand function,[11] we may write

$$\varepsilon = \frac{dw}{dp} \cdot \frac{p}{w}. \tag{2.13}$$

Some economists spend a lot of time collecting real-world data and statistically estimating demand functions. When they do, they normally report their elasticity findings. Nowhere is this more true than for urban water demand where hundreds of studies have been conducted (Dalhuisen et al. 2003). Hence, estimates of ε are

---

11. The elasticity formula given by equation (2.12) is formally called an "arc elasticity" because it is computed over an interval, Δp, of the demand function whereas the elasticity given by (2.13) is an instantaneous elasticity measured at a point on the demand function.

commonly available to water resource analysts, even if estimates from other study regions must be used. Water demand functions are generally found to be price *inelastic*, meaning that $-1 < \varepsilon < 0$. This does not mean that quantity demanded does not respond to price; it means that a 1 percent change in price induces a less than 1 percent change in quantity demanded. (Sometimes, noneconomists have taken the inelasticity of water demand to mean that price does not affect demand, but this is a false interpretation, usually employed to denigrate demand management strategies.) When the price elasticity is less than -1 (e.g., -1.4), demand is said to be *elastic*. Thus, if one demand function has a "larger" price elasticity than another, it means that its elasticity is larger in absolute value.

The point expansion method of demand estimation takes an externally obtained estimate of demand elasticity and a known point on the demand function to estimate the function. A known point can be easily obtained. For example, we might observe that households in Little Town are paying \$3 per thousand gallons of tap water, and the average household is choosing to consume 7,000 gallons during December at this price. If there are 5,000 households, then the ordered pair (35 million gallons, \$3) is a point on the city's December demand curve for tap water. Completing this procedure requires that we be willing to assume that the demand function exhibits either constant slope or constant price elasticity throughout its range.

Suppose the price elasticity of demand is thought to be -0.5. If we assume linear demand, then the "known" elasticity estimate and the known point can be substituted into equation (2.13) to obtain the slope of the demand curve. Then, substitution of the slope and point into $w = \text{slope} \cdot p + b$ allows b to be determined, thereby completing the job:

$$w = -5833.3 \cdot p + 52500,\qquad \text{\textit{→ Not sure how they get this?}} \tag{2.14}$$

where units for w are thousands of gallons and p is a dollar per thousand gallons. This is a demand function.

Alternatively, if we assume constant elasticity demand, then (2.13) is first rearranged into a manageable differential equation, which is then solved via integration. The solution procedure given below determines the only demand form with the property of constant price elasticity throughout its domain. Although it is not important to understand the solution procedure, some readers like to be acquainted with these things. Only the resultant relationship, (2.18), is crucial.

$$\frac{dw}{w} = \varepsilon \frac{dp}{p} \tag{2.15}$$

$$\int \frac{dw}{w} = \int \varepsilon \frac{dp}{p} \tag{2.16}$$

$$\ln w = \varepsilon \cdot \ln p + \ln k \tag{2.17}$$

(where ln k is an arbitrary constant)

Hence,

$$w = kp^{\varepsilon}. \tag{2.18}$$

Substituting the point and an elasticity into the latter expression determines k. For example, if demand elasticity is -0.5 and the example point given previously is used, the resulting constant elasticity December demand function is

$$w = 60622p^{-0.5}, \tag{2.19}$$

where w again indicates thousands of gallons. This function and the linear alternative are plotted in figure 2.8. Observe that they only have one point in common. (What point is this?)

Note that the point expansion method enabled us to obtain demand without maximizing consumer utility and without maximizing business profit. Theoretical modeling of consumer and business behavior offers us insights into the properties of the

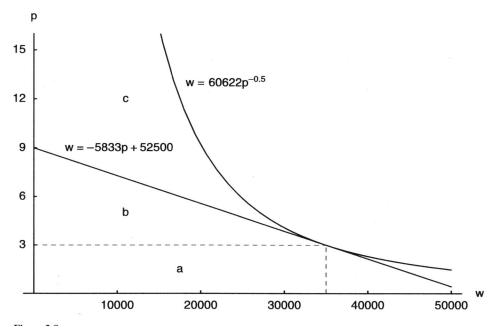

Figure 2.8
Two water demand functions

water demand function, like its negative slope, but it is not always necessary to simulate the theory in order to estimate demand.

Marginal Benefits and Changes in the Total Benefits

The demand curves of figure 2.8 can also be called *marginal benefit* or willingness-to-pay curves. The two terms, demand and marginal benefit, can often be used interchangeably, but care should be exercised here. Sometimes the word demand is thought to suggest the presence of a true marketplace, which is often false in the case of water because of the absence of either competition for retail water or private property rights to natural water. In such situations, marginal benefit can be a preferred term. Demand might also be suggestive of a function having a quantity, such as w, standing alone on the left side of the equation. Marginal benefit and willingness-to-pay terminology can suggest an inverted form having marginal benefits or price on the left side. Regardless of what we call them, both the "w = ⋯" and "p = ⋯" forms embed identical information—and highly useful information too.

Because the adjective marginal means "derivative of" in the common parlance of economic theory, the presence of the word marginal immediately indicates what information can be recovered by mathematically integrating. Integrating under a marginal benefit curve yields total benefits. Thus, referring again to figure 2.8, integrating under either of the two demand curves from w = 0 to w = 35,000 provides estimates of the total benefits received by consumers of city-provided water. Operationally, we must first invert the demand function (solve for p) before integrating. Appropriate integrals for the linear and constant elasticity forms are:

$$\text{area a} + \text{b} = \int_0^{35000} (-.00017143w + 9.)\, dw \tag{2.20}$$

and

$$\text{area a} + \text{b} + \text{c} = \int_0^{35000} 3.675 \times 10^9 w^{-2}\, dw. \tag{2.21}$$

Hence, there are two different estimates of total benefits depending on which demand function is used. This is not to imply that each demand function is equally correct. Each is an estimate of actual demand, and one may be a better estimate than the other.

There's an important lesson in the difference between these two measures of total benefits. Area a + b is $210,000 whereas area a + b + c is infinite. The first measure is likely an underestimate, and the second is an overestimate, but the crucial matter is that both measures make use of the estimated demand curve far away from the point of expansion, (35000, 3).[12] The actual point of expansion is a reliable one for the demand curve. As we move into p and w ranges distant from the point of expansion, the estimated demand curve becomes more unreliable and any applications of it are more unreliable as well.

Fortunately for the point expansion method of demand estimation, as well as other methods, total benefits is rarely a necessary value. Most useful applications of demand functions do not involve large deviations from baseline conditions. For example, proposed water resource projects often enlarge available water quantities, and planners may wish to estimate the change in total benefits attributable to a project. In other circumstances, potential infrastructure failures or water supply shortfalls will lower available water deliveries, and planners may wish to know the potential value of losses so they can decide how much defensive expenditures might be justifiable. As an example of the latter, a decrease in available water to 28 million gallons would generate the following measures of loss for the two demand functions:

$$\int_{28000}^{35000} (-.00017143w + 9.)\,dw = 25200 \tag{2.22}$$

and

$$\int_{28000}^{35000} 3.675 \times 10^9 w^{-2}\,dw = 26250. \tag{2.23}$$

Therefore, such a loss in water supply would result in a community loss of $25,200 using the linear relationship and $26,250 according to the constant elasticity function. In many planning and modeling scenarios, this type of information is useful. It should be acknowledged, however, that these are estimated *gross* losses in consumer benefits. They are not *net* losses to the community, due to the fact that the utility will save money by not having to pump or treat the undelivered seven million gallons. That can make a big difference. To more completely assess the true effects, we need to develop one more element. It's called marginal net benefit.

Marginal Net Benefits and Changes in Net Benefits

We have been able to use an aggregated demand function for Little Town's water customers because all the clients are receiving similarly processed retail water from

---

12. The linear demand curve imposes a "choke price" (the p-axis intercept), which is a price where tap water demand goes to zero. In this case, the choke price is nine dollars per thousand gallons. It is improbable that the quantity demanded at this price would be zero. The constant elasticity demand function imposes the opposite scenario that there will be nonzero demand regardless of how great the price becomes. Keeping in mind that this demand curve pertains to tap water and that people can get drinking water from other sources, there is likely to be a choke price at some level.

the same facilities. When water resource issues crosscut different sectors (agriculture, industry, or residences), regions, or infrastructure, as is commonplace, aggregation requires that we account for water supply cost differences. A basic way of accomplishing this is to rely on marginal net benefit (MNB) functions. By definition, marginal net benefits equal marginal benefits (demand) minus marginal costs (supply, almost):

$$MNB = MB - MC. \tag{2.24}$$

Both terms on the right-hand side pertain to a water-using group or locale. MB represents inverted, aggregated demand for the system, such as was estimated in the prior section. Except for the omitted value of natural water, MC is systemwide marginal costs of delivered water, as illustrated earlier in figure 2.1. So the MNB curve is obtained by vertically subtracting the MC curve from the MB curve. To put it another way, instead of setting demand equal to supply, demand minus supply is the focus of inquiry.

From consumers' perspectives in the example we are building on, marginal cost is $3 per thousand gallons. But this might only be MC for the community when the quantity demanded (and supplied) is precisely 35 million gallons. Suppose that the total costs of operating Little Town's water utility are functionally dependent on delivered water according to

$$C = 50000 + 1.95w + 0.000015w^2.$$

Using the constant elasticity MB relationship, the correct elements for obtaining the MNB are illustrated in figure 2.9. The equation for the result is

$$MNB = -1.95 + 3.675 \times 10^9 w^{-2} - 0.00003w. \tag{2.25}$$

The reader may wish to obtain the alternative MNB function pertaining to linear demand.

MNB functions have interesting and useful interpretations in water resource economics. Together with the simple method of point expansion, it can form a basis for the extensive analysis of water issues and solutions (as an example, see Jenkins, Lund, and Howitt 2003). Consequently, it is a key concept in the forthcoming chapters. If a group of agents is taking water from a watercourse and the subtracted MC function is derived from a cost function that includes all operations performed in the withdrawal, processing, and delivery of this water, then the *MNB of retail water is the agent's MB of natural water in the watercourse*. This is crucial information. To say it another way, the MNB of retail water is the MB of natural water before it is removed from the watercourse. Whereas different agents' demands for retail water present apples-to-oranges issues, such as with the residential demand for tap water

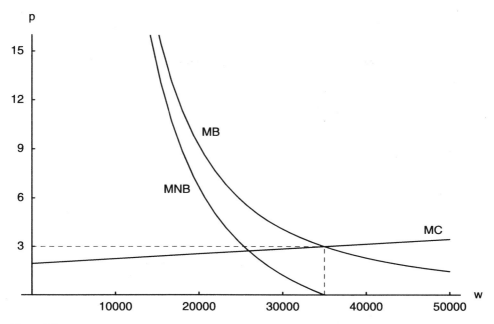

Figure 2.9
Constructing a marginal net benefit function

and the irrigation demand for water at the farm gate, MNB functions present no such difficulties if the agents are using water from the same watercourse. Possible applications of MNB functions include the following:

· MNB curves can be added to get the summed marginal benefits of natural water.

· Optimal allocation of limited water supplies across differing sectors or differing jurisdictions can be identified.

· Integrals beneath MNB curves measure the benefits of raising a group's natural water use. This is helpful in analyzing the benefits of a proposed water project or a water market transaction.

Obtained and applied correctly, these are powerful achievements, and they can guide important decisions.

2.5 (Aggregate) Economic Efficiency

Using the building blocks assembled thus far, we can proceed to investigate the optimal allocation of water from *society's* perspective. Public policy and public projects

Box 2.2
Which Sector Values Water More Highly?

> A common misstep in water resource discussions is to casually say that urban users value water more highly than irrigators. This claim might be true in some sense, but one must be clear about what is being discussed—retail or natural water. What's true for one type of water (retail) is irrelevant, and such statements are commonly false for the other type (natural) at the margin.
>
> If local irrigators are paying $25 per acre-foot of water applied to their crops and getting all they want, then the marginal value of *farm-gate water* is $25 per acre-foot. If local households are paying $3 per thousand gallons at the tap and getting as much as they want, then we may similarly conclude that the marginal value of *tap water* is $3 per thousand gallons. It is wrong, however, to convert this $3 into an acre-foot amount ($978) and then observe that $978 > $25. Tap water is far more processed than farm water, so these two goods are like apples to oranges. Their differences amount to differences between the nonwater resources employed in processing. This tells us nothing about relative water values.
>
> To infer their implied natural water values correctly, and thereby enable an accurate comparison, one should subtract all the embedded processing costs from the retail water prices. Often, the correct procedure will identify a zero natural water value for both sectors because there are no price-embedded costs associated with natural water, especially in water-rich regions, but often in arid regions too. That natural water is unvalued is a distressing finding, but it is an honest one, and it clearly underscores one of the major policy flaws in water resource management. This matter will be of further concern in the forthcoming chapters.

should be selected to advance social objectives, so we need to isolate those objectives if we are to frame good policy and build desirable infrastructure. Because society is an aggregation of individuals, aggregation is a good place to start.

A primary vision of social economic efficiency in water use is that of aggregate economic efficiency: maximize the total value of water (before processing) across all users, or equivalently, maximize the total net benefits (after processing) across all users. In this vision, the weight assigned to each user group is contained within its own MNB functions. All valued applications of water count in this objective, including instream uses for recreation, ecosystem maintenance, and so on. In the remainder of this section we will inspect graphic portrayals of this criterion followed by a more formal optimization framework.

Suppose there are only two user groups making use of a watercourse containing W units of water. Suppose further that their uses of water are completely rival (what water one group takes provides no benefits to the other), and recycling is uneconomic at current scarcity levels. Figure 2.10 contains two MNB curves, and they have been horizontally added to obtain an aggregate MNB curve. The intersection of summed MNB with $w = W = 50000$ indicates the social value of natural water, p^*. Moreover, the intersection of $p = p^*$ with MNB_1 and MNB_2 indicates the optimal division of available water between the two user groups. Extension of this graphic device to three or more water-using groups is obvious, though not as pretty.

A second graphic device for illustrating aggregate economic efficiency makes use of a three-axis graph in which the fixed length of the horizontal axis indicates the

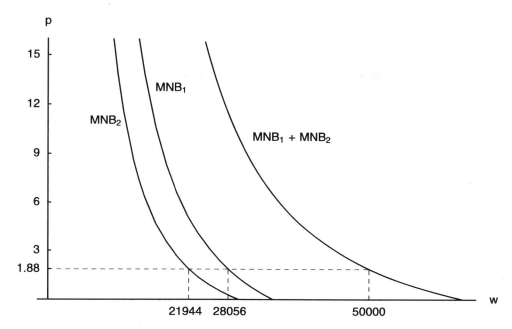

Figure 2.10
Efficient allocation for two agents

available amount of water, W. In figure 2.11, MNB_1 is placed normally. Water use by group 1 is measured from the left-side vertical axis. Group 2's water use is measured from the right-side vertical axis, so it is necessary to flip the MNB_2 curve of figure 2.10 and place it relative to the right-side axis of figure 2.11. In this framework, left to right movements along the water axis indicate increasing w_1 and decreasing w_2 while maintaining $w_1 + w_2 = W$. In this graphic model, aggregate economic efficiency is determined by the intersection of MNB_1 and MNB_2. Clearly, this device is only a practical representation for two user groups.

The validity of these graphic approaches stems from the fact that the areas beneath MNB curves are the net benefits of water use. When total net benefits of water use are maximized across user groups, equal MNBs emerges as a first-order condition. Let's demonstrate. Assuming J rival user groups on a watercourse with no return flow or reuse, the maximization of total value results in the following problem:

$$\underset{w_1, w_2, \ldots, w_J}{\text{maximize}} \sum_{j=1}^{J} (B_j(w_j) - C_j(w_j)) \quad \text{subject to} \sum_{j=1}^{J} w_j = W. \tag{2.26}$$

$B_j(w_j)$ is the only new notation in this problem, but it's not really new. It's the gross benefits received by user group j when it consumes w_j units of water. This is the area

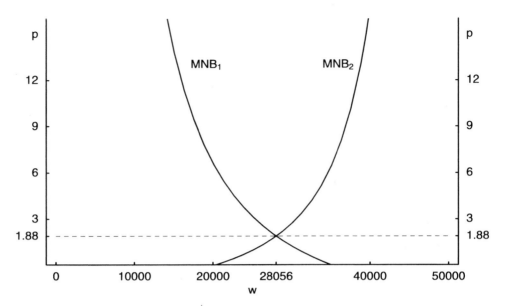

Figure 2.11
Two-agent efficiency with three axes

under the group's demand curve, as we've already noted. Because net benefits (NB) are defined as the excess of benefits over costs, it is possible to rewrite the above problem as

$$\underset{w_1, w_2, \ldots, w_J}{\text{maximize}} \sum_{j=1}^{J} NB_j(w_j) \quad \text{subject to} \quad \sum_{j=1}^{J} w_j = W. \tag{2.27}$$

As long as it is optimal for each group to receive some water, the Lagrangian optimization procedure (see appendix) results in J first-order conditions:

$$\frac{dB}{dw_j} - \frac{dC}{dw_j} = \lambda \quad \text{for all } j = 1, 2, \ldots, J. \tag{2.28}$$

Here, λ is the introduced Lagrange multiplier, and it captures an important parameter: the marginal value of natural water ($p^* = 1.88$ in the prior two figures). These J equations can be rewritten in a few useful ways:

$$MB_j - MC_j = \lambda \quad \text{for all } j = 1, 2, \ldots, J, \tag{2.29}$$

$$MNB_j = \lambda \quad \text{for all } j = 1, 2, \ldots, J, \tag{2.30}$$

or

$$MNB_j = MNB_k \quad \text{for all } j, k = 1, 2, \ldots, J. \tag{2.31}$$

Solving for aggregate economic efficiency in water allocation does not require that we build and solve an elaborate optimization problem. We do, however, need to know the MB and MC functions so that the system of J first-order conditions given by (2.31) can be solved simultaneously.

Engineer readers may observe that we have been developing a *lumped parameter* model. The emphasis is entirely on a single water factor: the amount of available water. No spatial detail regarding the physical location of water availability or use is being modeled. Water quality is not being tracked. There is a single dimension of interest. Whereas greater detail is achievable using *distributed parameter* models in which more dimensions and features are acknowledged, the most significant insights of water resource economics can be captured with simple models. The extension to distributed parameter settings (e.g., nodes along a river, two-dimensional finite-difference model of an aquifer) is entirely practical.

2.6 The Universal Advisory Term: Opportunity Costs

A useful economic distinction is captured by the term ***opportunity costs***. Each time an agent makes a choice and pursues it, other choices become forfeit and are sacrificed. The opportunity cost of an action is the value of the next best selection that could have been undertaken. Opportunity costs can be different than financial (or accounting) costs. Or they can be the same. Whenever financial costs do not overlap entirely with opportunity costs, the latter has more decision-making significance.

For example, an irrigated farm with gravity-delivered, yet limited water might be able to grow several crops profitably. Regardless of how the farm employs its limited water, there are no financial costs associated with the water, because there are no pumping costs and the water is "free" to the farmer. Under these conditions, the producer can profitably apply a great deal of water to a low-value crop because the water is costless. If this water could have been applied to a more valuable crop, however, the farmer would experience an opportunity cost, if not a financial cost, for the water. The knowledgeable farmer will recognize the personal opportunity cost of using water in a low-value application even though the water is free. Paying attention to opportunity costs will motivate the farmer to avoid low-value uses of water.

Like the farmer, society should also be attentive to the opportunity costs or else resources will be misallocated. Indeed, efficient water use is fundamentally about the recognition of water's opportunity cost. (The λ term on the right side of (2.29) and (2.30) is the opportunity cost of natural water.) Nevertheless, it is one thing to say that water use has a social opportunity cost, and another thing to get everyone to recognize it and behave accordingly. The burden here is on public policy. If policies do not signal water's opportunity costs to all agents, then agents cannot be expected to observe them. For example, while the farmer with limited "free" water can easily see the opportunity cost of not irrigating the most profitable crop mix, how can we get the farmer to behave efficiently when there are off-farm opportunity costs? That's a key inquiry for water resource policymakers. Its importance will begin to occupy us more intensely during chapter 4's focus on institutional options.

Part II: Further Adjustments for the Idiosyncrasies of Water

2.7   Economic Efficiency in the Presence of Return Flows

In performing their jobs, water resource practitioners encounter many unique circumstances, which is part of the interest and vibrancy of water issues. Every hydrologic condition seems to be different from the previously examined one, so it's difficult to design a standard model that applies well to all scenarios. Earlier in this chapter it was observed that demand aggregation for water is trickier than for ordinary goods due to differential processing, reuse, and nonrivalness. Thus far, differential processing is the only one of these challenges that we have addressed. In this section and the next, the peculiarities of reuse and nonrivalness are tackled.

The issue of water *reuse* is a varied one. As a consequence of our planet's water cycle, only a small fraction of our water is actually created or destroyed by natural or human forces. Water may change its form (liquid, solid, or vapor), location (in three dimensions), or character (such as its temperature or purity), but the mass of water remains little changed. Through their "use" of water, humans interfere with the underlying natural forces, but the water is still present after it is used. As a result of their water use, humans often diminish, at least transitionally, the usability of specific units of water due to changes in form, location, or character. Once out of human control, these units are again subjected to natural forces that may or may not ameliorate the humanly imposed changes. The end result is that water is not usually destroyed in use, and it may become available for reuse.

When reuse of water can be physically and economically contemplated within both a given study region and a given planning horizon (e.g., within the growing season or the next twenty years, depending on the goals of the study), there may be grounds for incorporating such reuse within models, including the efficiency model developed above. The manner in which reuse is modeled depends on the hydrologic and economic circumstances.

A commonplace situation in which reuse should be modeled is the case of a flowing watercourse with multiple water diverters (cities, irrigation districts, and factories) lying along its length. Each user group withdraws water for its use, but the subsequent return flow from these groups reenters the watercourse and becomes available for reuse by entities downstream. If there are only two water-using groups, economic efficiency can be graphically portrayed. (The adjective aggregate is henceforth implied when the term economic efficiency is used.) Suppose that group 1 is located upstream of group 2. Thus, group 1's return flow can be subsequently reused by group 2, but group 2's return flow is irrelevant. Although there may be a time lag between group 1's use and its return flow, we will set this issue aside because dynamic (time-defined) issues are postponed until the next chapter.

Suppose that group 1's return flow is a function of its diversions from the watercourse and is given by $R(w_1)$. A little thought suggests that $0 < dR/dw_1 < 1$ is to be expected. (Do you agree?) Economic efficiency is then specified by the solution to the following problem: *↳ Yes, you can't change more than 100% of what's supplied*

$$\underset{w_1, w_2}{\text{maximize}} \ NB_1(w_1) + NB_2(w_2) \quad \text{subject to } w_1 + w_2 = W + R(w_1). \quad (2.32)$$

The constraint in this problem implicitly allows group 1 to make use of its own return flow, which is not realistic, so it may be necessary to add the constraint $w_1 < W$ to the problem as well. Here, the latter constraint is suppressed because it's unlikely to be disobeyed.[13] Processing the two first-order conditions from problem (2.32) gives us

$$\frac{MNB_1}{1 - dR/dw_1} = MNB_2. \quad (2.33)$$

This result can be graphically depicted by recognizing that the denominator of the left-hand side constitutes a rotation of the MNB_1 curve. The rotation and its implications are presented in figure 2.12. In addition to the rotation, MNB_2 is shifted to account for group 1's return flow availability. Overall, the marginal value of water has fallen as compared to figure 2.11 because water is less scarce. The availability of reusable water means that efficient MNBs are no longer equal (equation [2.33]).

The above example is merely suggestive of the changes introduced when the possibility of water reuse matters (Johnson, Gisser, and Werner 1981). Important hydrologic conditions will have to be accommodated within the modeling or optimization work. Distributed parameter modeling may be needed. For these reasons, economically astute simulations of optimal water use are normally conducted numerically, using detailed computer programs. Thus, the theory assembled in this chapter is ordinarily a precursor to the computer modeling of water resource issues. If the

---

13. The willingness to pay by group 2 for initial units of water would have to be quite low for this to happen.

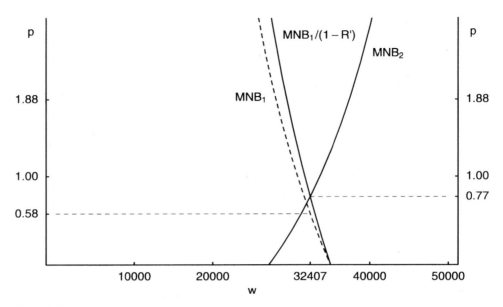

Figure 2.12
Efficiency with return flow

modeler does not possess an accurate vision of water resource economics, however, the modeling may be inappropriate and it may support poor decision making.

2.8   Economic Efficiency with Nonrivalness

If miraculously, 100 percent of group 1's water withdrawals became return flow in the prior model, then both groups could use all the available water. Total net benefits would then be the sum of net benefits at W for both groups. That's basically what occurs for nonrival uses of water (although nonrivalness is a more general concept). Nonrival users are not in competition for water, at least not with each other. The same units of water can serve all nonrival users, so each unit of water has a value given by the sum of users' values.

The operational importance of nonrivalness is that nonrival demands must be summed vertically rather than horizontally. Presuming linear demands for clarity, vertical summation of two demands is portrayed in figure 2.13, and is contrasted with summation in the case of normal rival goods. The upper panel represents summed demand for the nonrival case. Keep in mind that the manner in which water is consumed determines whether it is employed rivally or nonrivally. So for any specific circumstance, only one of the summation methods will be applicable.

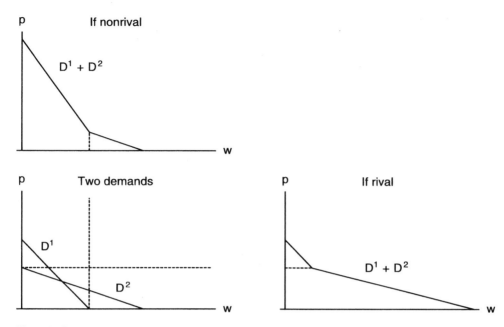

Figure 2.13
Rival versus nonrival demand addition

   What kinds of demands are then nonrival? A good example is water applied for the purpose of enhancing biodiversity. Suppose that an endangered species of slug or serpent exists only in a particular river segment. For various reasons, a person might have some demand for the continued existence of this species apart from eating or taking it. Examples include the following:

· Knowledge of the continued existence of this species may be pleasurable.

· The individual may enjoy witnessing the unique appearance or behavior of this creature in person or on television.

· The person may believe the presence of this creature is an indicator of ecosystem health and the general power of the environment to reliably support humankind.

Regardless of the reasons, if there are people who value the preservation of this species, then there are marginal benefits associated with the units of water allocated to its survival.[14] Adding these marginal benefits across all people valuing the creature must be performed vertically.

---

14. Even though other people, perhaps even the analyst, may feel that the preferences of biodiversity-loving people are misplaced, the analyst faces a large burden if one decides to dismiss such values.

Box 2.3
The Origins of Rivals

Did you know that the term rival "evolved from the Latin *rivalis*, meaning 'one living on the opposite bank of a stream from another'" (Maass and Anderson 1978, 2)?

There are other types of nonrival uses of water. Some recreational uses of water tend to be nonrival (until congestion sets in). Inevitably, nonrival uses of water will also be rival with competing uses of water, so attention to nonrivalness is part of the scarcity problem. Attention to nonrival uses of water seems to be increasing in much of the developed world. In these places, population and development pressures have lowered the availability of environmental resources, thereby raising their value. Environmental goods tend to be what economists call "luxury goods"—goods for which demand grows rapidly in response to income. Hence, as an economy develops and its people prosper, they demand proportionately more of these things. Poor people tend to exhibit little demand for environmental quality.

2.9 Neutral Economic Efficiency

This chapter has progressively developed an efficiency criterion that can be succinctly condensed to "maximize net benefits." In some instances, maximizing society's net benefits is a problematic goal. In this section we consider these problems and introduce a substitute objective for instances where the problems may be worrisome.

Whereas maximizing net benefits is compelling for the decisions of individual agents, extending it to social decision making constitutes a moral leap of faith. In order to render maximize net benefits operational for social decisions, it is necessary to add the benefits and costs experienced by different people. But in most cases, a water-related decision will aid some people while harming others. How are the different people to be weighed? Expressed so as to underscore the importance of the matter, does a $100 benefit to one person offset a $100 loss to another? (If so, a public policy that benefits one faction $1,000,001 while costing another faction $1,000,000 is a good policy.) What if one is a poor person and the other is rich? Does it matter if the loser is the poor person or the rich one?

In the procedures implemented above, net benefit optimization for a watershed was accomplished using a net benefit curve that was the sum of the net benefit curves for individual agents. If all individuals are alike and have identical demands, then summing their net benefits seems quite sensible. There is no "fairness" issue to con-

Box 2.4
Adding Rival versus Nonrival Demands

Suppose that each of the H households in a community has two important demands for water. Each demands water for home and public park use. Suppose that home uses are purely rival whereas the fountains and greenery of city parks are purely nonrival. Furthermore, for convenience of expedient analysis, demands are identical across households.

Suppose every household experiences the following marginal benefits of home and park water use, respectively,

$$mb_{hm} = \left(\frac{a}{w_{hm}}\right)^{1/c} \quad \text{and} \quad mb_{pk} = \left(\frac{b}{w_{pk}}\right)^{1/d}, \tag{2.34}$$

where a, b, c, and d are known positive constants. Reorganizing these functions algebraically, we recognize that they are constant elasticity functions similar to equation (2.18), so they can be empirically established via the point expansion method:

$$w_{hm} = \frac{a}{mb_{hm}^c} \quad \text{and} \quad w_{pk} = \frac{b}{mb_{pk}^d}. \tag{2.35}$$

For all H households, total home water demand is

$$W_{hm} = \frac{aH}{MB_{hm}^c}, \tag{2.36}$$

where uppercase W and MB are employed to clearly indicate community demand, distinguishing it from household demand. Using similar notation, total park marginal benefits are

$$MB_{pk} = H \cdot \left(\frac{b}{W_{pk}}\right)^{1/d}, \tag{2.37}$$

which is invertible to

$$W_{pk} = \frac{bH^d}{MB_{pk}^d}. \tag{2.38}$$

Computational Observation Notice most crucially that summed rival demand, (2.36), is obtained starting with the "w =" form of (2.35), whereas summed nonrival demand, (2.38), is obtained commencing with the "mb =" form of (2.34). Although the results are specific to the constant-elasticity demand form, compare (2.36) and (2.38) to see how the rival/nonrival distinction causes the number of households to enter the total demands differently.

If the community incurs the same costs for supplying park water as it does for home water, then the total community demand for all water is

$$W_{total} = W_{hm} + W_{pk} = \frac{aH}{MB^c} + \frac{bH^d}{MB^d}. \tag{2.39}$$

Observe that the latter addition treats park and home water demands as mutually rival. For this reason, W_{pk} and W_{hm} are directly (horizontally) added (instead of adding MB_{pk} and MB_{hm}).

Being able to add demands correctly is an important element of model building. Whereas certain assumptions in this model are overly simplistic, especially identical demands across all households and only two demand types, such assumptions can be readily avoided. Complemented by additional details, such models can be useful devices. Once quantitatively specified, they can indicate how much water should be dedicated to different uses. The impact of variable water supply or population growth can be inspected. Potential policies and projects can be assessed. And it is possible to use such models to retrieve information about how water should be priced. After a sufficient quantitative foundation has been established, chapter 11 will pull together the empirical pieces to demonstrate these prospects more clearly.

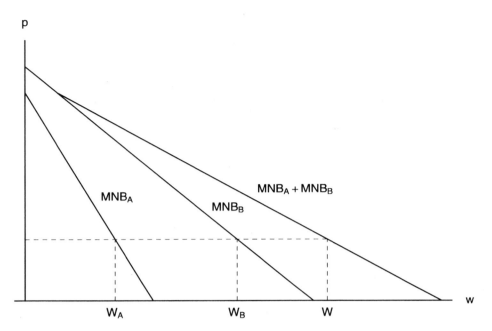

Figure 2.14
Aggregate economic efficiency

tend with. In more realistic settings, however, the agents will be different, and their net benefits will be different. To gain insight, suppose that there are two people with different demands, as in figure 2.14, and for simplicity neither has any costs of withdrawing and processing the water. Hence, MNB = MB for each person. If the total available water is W, then aggregate economic efficiency requires that person A receive w_A units of water and that person B gets w_B. The reason B gets more is that B values the same units of water more highly than does person A. That is, person B's demand is greater. But does B value water more highly than A because that individual has a greater preference for water or a greater income? While it seems compelling for optimal allocations to respond to relative preferences for water, weighting people by their relative incomes is more tenuous, ethically speaking.

By the same token, A and B may represent sectors of a regional economy, in which case w_A may indicate the optimal amount of water for agricultural users and w_B may be the optimal amount for industrial water users. Are industrial users to receive more water because their marginal productivity of water is higher ($\partial f/\partial w$ in equation [2.4]) or the price of their product is higher (the p_y term of [2.4])? Again, the marginal product part of this is fairly sensible, but what about weighting by output prices?

Therefore, we see that part of the weighting decision employs relative incomes or relative output prices experienced by the agents (people and companies) involved. For this reason, the criterion is "nonneutral"—weighting is not equal, nor does it provide a neutral weighting of agents. Expressed another way, the "willingness to pay" captured by agents' demand functions is predicated on their "ability to pay." Is that what we want to do? In most instances, the answer is yes. These incomes and prices are not arbitrarily generated in a market system. Higher incomes are the consequence of developing and maintaining socially valued assets, such as stocks, land, and skills. Higher prices are the result of greater social preferences for such commodities. Societal values for these things mean that income/price differences are motivating signals for encouraging the production and maintenance of the most desirable things possible. Higher income is the market's reward for performing more social service. Higher price is the market's reward for producing more desirable goods.

Thus, the heightened buying power afforded by greater incomes and prices is the carrot that induces agents to assume risks, make costly investments (such as attending college), develop technologies, undertake difficult tasks, and so forth. For such an incentive system to function, it is crucial for demands to be income and price weighted. These arguments suggest that the maximize net benefits criterion has merit as a social objective in normal circumstances.

In the same vein, whereas marginal costs have been equal and zero for both agents in the discussion aided by figure 2.14, the same conclusions hold when marginal costs are positive and different for agents. When a person, firm, or sector is disadvantaged by higher marginal costs than the marginal costs faced by others, the disadvantage arises from real resource costs. Efficiency-based analysis should incorporate cost advantages and disadvantages. Retail water costs can be higher because distances are greater (more pipe), elevation is higher (more energy), water quality requirements are greater or natural quality is poor (more treatment), the demand for water supply reliability is larger (more capacity), and so on. The heightened costs are relevant to the maximization of social net benefits, so it is a good thing that attention to these costs results in less water being employed in more costly applications.

There are, however, social situations in which the promotion of aggregate/nonneutral economic efficiency does not sufficiently describe the choices and decisions under study. Because total net benefits collapses all consequences into a single economic metric, distributional details become masked, and some of these details may be important for decision making. In less developed countries, for example, water projects have often been employed as a means to improve the welfare of disadvantaged people. It is customarily the case that these people have a low demand for water because of their impoverished condition. If their demand information is employed to assess project desirability, the measured benefits will be low and they will also be a poor measure of project objectives.

Even in developed countries, there are often concerns about who gains and who loses due to a proposed public action. For these reasons, it is sometimes useful to apply a more expansive objective than that provided by aggregate economic efficiency.

Neutral economic efficiency, referred to in economics as Pareto optimality or Pareto efficiency, declines to assign relative weights to different agents or agent classes (Griffin 1995). As a consequence, rather than finding a single efficient allocation of resources as aggregate efficiency does, neutral efficiency emphasizes a range of allocations that are efficient.[15]

Formally, neutral economic efficiency is determined by maximizing the net benefits received by one agent subject to available water and subject to an arbitrary level of required net benefits being received by other agents:

$$\underset{w_1, w_2, \ldots, w_J}{\text{maximize}} \ NB_i(w_i) \quad \text{subject to} \ \sum_{j=1}^{J} w_j = W \text{ and } NB_j(w_j) \geq k_j \text{ for all } j \neq i. \qquad (2.40)$$

The choice of agent i is inconsequential to the outcome; it can be any of the J agents. By varying the required net benefits received by other agents (the k_j terms), we can generate a range of neutrally efficient choices. The entire range is then regarded as equally efficient. The range of neutrally efficient choices normally includes an infinite number of options. Not too surprisingly, one of these choices (possibly more than one) will also be efficient in the aggregate/nonneutral way.

To illustrate this simply, whereas the content of figure 2.14 showed an allocation of w_A to A and w_B to B to be aggregately efficient, there are many (infinitely many) other ways to apportion W. These ways are depicted by the line segment in figure 2.15. Each point on it represents an alternative allocation. At the extreme, one agent (or sector) could receive all the water and the other none, as indicated by the end points of this line segment. The outcomes of these infinite allocations can be substituted into each agent's net benefit function to determine the gains each receives from the allocation. Plotting these generates a *Pareto frontier* of all the neutrally efficient possibilities, as in figure 2.16.[16] Also depicted on this frontier is the single allocation that is aggregately efficient.

15. Pareto optimality (neutral efficiency) is occasionally confused with the concept of "Pareto improvement," which is gauged relative to a known starting position. If a policy or project exists that would make some people better off (in terms of their utility) while making none worse off relative to their starting positions, that action would constitute a Pareto improvement. Pareto optimality, on the other hand, is not assessed relative to a fixed starting position. Pareto improvements are an exceptionally rare find in the real world. New water projects or policies are bound to cause a loss for some group regardless of how well-intentioned its designers may be.

16. The usual textbook depiction of a Pareto frontier is more abstract than the one plotted in figure 2.16. The frontier plotted in figure 2.16 corresponds precisely to the quantitative information shown in figures 2.14 and 2.15.

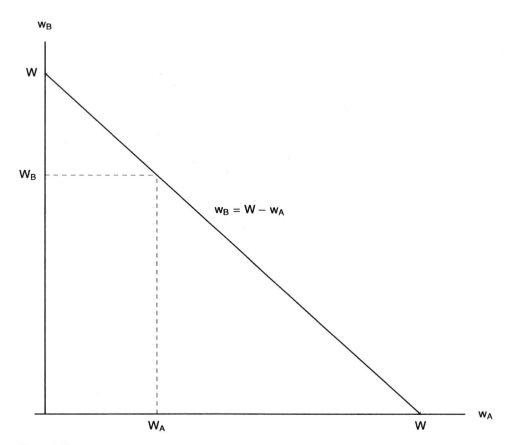

Figure 2.15
Neutrally efficient water allocations

It is clear that the two efficiency objectives take different approaches to agent weighting. This is the root of other differences between the two criteria (listed in figure 2.17). Aggregate efficiency weights by income and commodity prices. Neutral efficiency does not weight at all and therefore indicates an array of efficient selections instead of one. Because there are good reasons for income/price weighting in a well-functioning market economy, aggregate efficiency is sensible and has the advantage of resolving a single efficient allocation. But circumstances can arise in which the implicit weights embodied in aggregate efficiency are disagreeable, or are possibly so. In such cases, neutral efficiency can be an illuminating social objective for examining particular water resource issues.

As a revealing example of how these two different objectives work in practice, suppose that our investigation of a water reallocation or a new policy or project reveals

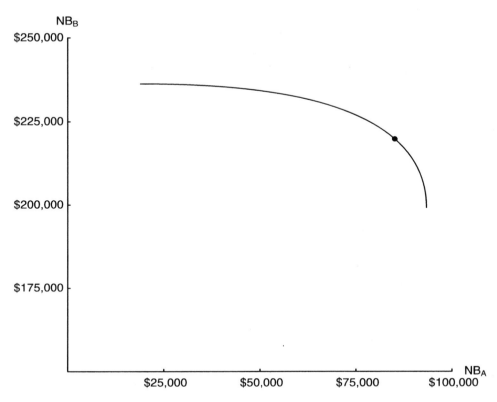

Figure 2.16
Neutrally efficient outcomes

the following information: group A is harmed (has costs) in the amount of $600,000, and group B benefits in the amount of $1 million. These impacts may be the result of water reallocations, taxes, or other reapportioned resources (as with project construction). According to aggregate efficiency, the net benefit of this action is a positive $400,000, and the change is therefore desirable (efficient) because the net social rewards are positive. According to neutral efficiency, A loses $600,000 and B gains $1 million, and it is appropriate to report both consequences (for A and B) without addition. Furthermore, the neutral efficiency perspective is that it is equally efficient to have an economy with the project or not.[17] Only in cases where everyone either loses or wins is there a single, neutrally efficient choice. Aggregate efficiency, on

17. Yet an odd nuance in this situation is that while the economy is neutrally efficient with or without the proposed project, it is not a neutrally efficient move (a Pareto improvement) to pursue the project, because someone will lose. See note 15 above.

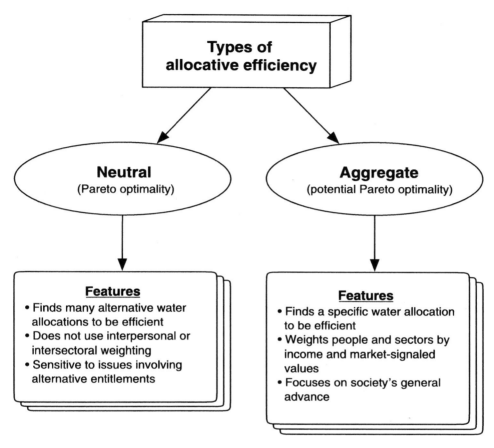

Figure 2.17
Alternative efficiency objectives

the other hand, usually finds a single efficient decision. Although both of these criteria will find application in the forthcoming chapters, aggregate efficiency will be predominant.

2.10   Is Water Conservation an Additional Goal?

Many public policy sentiments favor water conservation, so a relevant question is whether the pursuit of economic efficiency will contribute to water conservation. The answer to this question depends on what we mean when we say "water conservation." There are many available perspectives. Indeed, part of the allure of water conservation may be that it can be molded into a concept that is attractive to anyone. It is professionally disappointing to employ loose jargon because it is difficult to operationalize, so what might water conservation mean when it is tightly defined?

According to Mann, "there are at least four definitions of conservation" (1982, 12–13): (1) the full use and development of water, (2) preservation from use, (3) technical efficiency in water use, and (4) economic efficiency in water use. Definition 1 is consistent with U.S. policy during the latter 1800s and the majority of the 1900s. During this period, the term conservation often expressed a desire to fully harness available water resources for the purpose of economic development, primarily through irrigation, hydropower, and navigation. Definition 2 is consistent with the intentions of preservationists who wish that more water remained in its natural state, either instream or inground. Definition 3 expresses a desire to obtain the most physical output per unit of water, such as trying to transport water to end users with minimum leakage and evaporation, or trying to encourage the adoption of low-flow showerheads, low gallons-per-flush toilets, or advanced irrigation technologies. Definition 4 is, well, it is what this chapter is all about.

Not surprisingly, the economic perspective is less than enthusiastic about definitions 1–3. Definition 1 fails to find value in in situ ("in place") uses such as ecosystem sustenance, recreation, and freshwater inflows for coastal environments and offshore fisheries. U.S. application of this definition until the 1970s led to an overcommitment of water resources to water diversions. On the other hand, definition 2 is too ecocentric to do a good job of managing water resources in most circumstances. While the overallocations of an earlier era make a preservationist reaction understandable, we must take care that the pendulum does not swing back too far. Good water stewardship should acknowledge all the demands of a growing population. That is, good stewardship should be anthropocentric and holistic.

Economic disappointment with definition 3 arises from its intrinsic "water theory of value." Other resources have value too, so it is not a good idea to squeeze as much as is technologically possible out of every unit of water. Such pursuits undervalue other resources. For example, canal water lost in conveyance due to leaks and evaporation is costly to prevent in the sense that other resources must be expended to "conserve" this lost water. From the technical efficiency standpoint, it is water conserving to undertake the expenditures to prevent all so-called wasted water. From the economic perspective, this water is not wasted; indeed, it is optimally used *unless* the costs of preventing it (the value of other resources) are less than the value of the water saved.

Do these arguments mean that proper water conservation is nothing more than economic efficiency in water use? Perhaps. Defining conservation in this way is sensible in that it leads to good decision making.[18] But we will leave the matter for the reader to consider further. There are other conceivable perspectives that may matter in some circumstances. Some analysts believe that the term *water conservation* should contribute something not already embedded in economic efficiency. For example, Baumann, Boland, and Sims (1984) have argued that a water-conserving practice is an alternative that saves water *and* is economically efficient as well. If, however, an economic efficiency criterion is not part of the equation, then economics-savvy professionals understand that water conservation is not necessarily a desirable thing.

2.11 Summary

The densely relayed material of this chapter includes several essential economic topics. Modeling of individual and social goals has been the primary pursuit here. The concept of marginal costs can describe either the added total costs a water supplier encounters when deliveries of retail water are increased or the added costs an individual agent must pay when consuming an additional unit of water. Individual agents are modeled as profit or utility maximizers depending on whether they are businesses or not. Both profit and utility maximization are demonstrated to result in a price-sensitive water demand, yielding the important finding that an agent's water demand is not a single amount of water. Water demand is a function. It is also called the marginal benefit function when mathematically solved for price or value. Although there are many ways to empirically acquire water demand functions (to be considered in a later chapter), the point expansion method was introduced to solidify the manners in which demand information can be subsequently utilized.

For agents using similarly processed retail water from the same water source(s), demand aggregation across agents is demonstrated. The methodology of aggregation depends on whether water is used rivally (as is most common) or nonrivally. Nonrival uses of water are distinguished by the fact that each agent's water use does not diminish the amount of water available to others, such as might occur for aesthetic uses of water.

A crucial tool for optimizing water allocation, marginal net benefits, subtracts marginal costs from demand (marginal benefit) functions. The power of knowing marginal net benefits is that we can use these functions, which are different for different agent groups, to examine optimal water use across different parties. Marginal net benefit functions encompass demand differences as well as cost-of-service differences

18. "Conservation is incorporated into the economic efficiency concept but economists generally do not view decreasing consumption in itself as a meaningful goal" (Beecher, Mann, and Landers 1991, 65).

across agents, so these functions have the advantage of being combinable for agents using differently processed water, like irrigators and households.

From society's perspective, economic efficiency in water allocation among competing parties is shown to be of two varieties. Henceforth, the unqualified term efficiency shall mean aggregate economic efficiency. This version of economic efficiency occurs when water is apportioned (allocated) among agents in such a way that net benefits, summed over all users, is maximized. Aggregate efficiency dominates the practice of water resource economics—and with good reason. Because this version of efficiency is only concerned about summed net benefits, it is indifferent regarding the way in which water benefits are bestowed on alternative people, businesses, or groups. Whenever such distributional detail is important to decision making, it can be useful to employ a broader vision of economic efficiency, neutral economic efficiency (more formally termed Pareto optimality).

Neutral economic efficiency underscores a range of allocations that are efficient depending on which agents or groups are to be favored. The distinguishing characteristic of all neutrally efficient allocations is that the only way to improve one agent's welfare is to decrease another's. Neutral economic efficiency serves as the foundation of a sort of policy analysis in which decision makers want to know more than summed net benefits across all users—that is, when they want to know how these net benefits are distributed.

Across all of these topics, we have illustrated concepts with graphic models. In several instances, mathematical examples have been constructed to further amplify the application possibilities. One of the more fruitful approaches for locking in these principles is to apply them—beginning with the exercise questions that follow.

2.12 Exercises

1. Build a spreadsheet in which you sample from the production function $y = 3x^2 - 0.2x^3$ from $x = 0$ to $x = 12$ in increments of $\Delta x = 0.5$ or smaller. Place the following information in the parenthetically numbered columns of your spreadsheet: (1) x, (2) y, (3) Δx, (4) Δy, and (5) $\Delta y/\Delta x$. Place the production function formula in each entry of column 2. Use formulas elsewhere when you can. The entries in column 3 will all be the same. The entries in column 4 will be obtained as $y_{row} - y_{row-1}$ computed using column 2 information. The results contained in column 5 are your estimates of marginal product, and these estimates get progressively more accurate as Δx becomes smaller. Plot columns 2 and 5 against column 1 to reproduce the upper panel of figure 2.2. If you also want to assume a specific fixed price for y (anything will do), you can create a sixth column containing price $\cdot \Delta y/\Delta x$. Graphing this new column against column 1 produces a demand function.

2. Suppose that irrigated corn can be produced using water and nitrogen fertilizer according to the following statistically estimated production function (using data from field experiments):

$$corn = -10586 + 688.36W + 36.421N - 10.039W^2 - 0.0772N^2 + 0.4133WN,$$

where corn and nitrogen units are pounds per acre, and water units are acre-inches (Hexem and Heady 1978, 78–81; many similar functions are described in their book). Using a spreadsheet or other program and the following assumptions, generate each panel of figures 2.2 and 2.3. Assumptions: $N = 240$, $0 \leq W \leq 50$, corn price $= 4$ cents/lb., and marginal cost of water $= \$5$/acre-inch. What's the profit-maximizing amount of water to apply? (Don't be too surprised if your functions have a different shape than those in the text. Shape is dictated by functional form, and Hexem and Heady use a quadratic form for this production function.)

3. Given only the definitional information for average and marginal costs ($AC = C/w$ and $MC = dC/dw$), prove that the average cost curve is intersected by the marginal cost curve at the minimum of average costs. (Hint: given the definition of average costs, minimize it.)

4. Make up an original (w, p) demand point (choose numbers). Select a believable value for demand elasticity. Apply the point expansion method to precisely identify a demand function corresponding to your assumptions. Clearly state the resulting demand function. Suppose that marginal costs are given by $MC = w/10$. Determine the applicable MNB function.

5. How should we interpret a situation in which aggregate MNB of figure 2.10 does not intersect $w = W$ or, equivalently, the curves of figure 2.11 do not intersect at a positive price?

6. Two distinct agents have the following marginal net benefit functions for retail water:

$$MNB_1 = 300 - 5w_1 \quad \text{and} \quad MNB_2 = 200 - 2w_2.$$

Seventy-six units of water are available for allocation between these agents.

a. What is the aggregately efficient allocation of water? What are the consequent marginal net benefits and net benefits for 1 and 2?

b. Quantitatively describe the neutrally efficient allocation of water with an equation relating w_1 and w_2. As a consequence of this efficient range of allocations, quantitatively describe the relation between MNB_1 and MNB_2. Now describe this efficiency relation between MNB_1 and MNB_2 parametrically, writing both as a function of a single variable, w_1.

c. For arbitrary water allocations w_1 and w_2, compute the relationships $NB_1(w_1)$ and $NB_2(w_2)$. Assuming neutral efficiency, rewrite $NB_2(w_2)$ as a function of w_1. Given this parametric specification for relating NB_1 and NB_2 under neutral efficiency, determine if the aggregately efficient allocation is also neutrally efficient.

Appendix 2.A: Constrained Optimization Using the Lagrangian Method

Instances of unconstrained optimization can be managed by setting one or more derivatives equal to zero and algebraically processing the resulting first-order condition(s). It is also advisable to check second-order conditions to verify what type of optima one has found: a maxima or a minima.

In the case of constrained optimization, where the objective function is optimized subject to one or more constraints, one might be able to proceed in *two ways*. If the constraints are equalities, it might be possible to solve each one for a specific variable and then substitute this relation into the objective function, effectively imposing the constraint directly and eliminating a variable from the problem. If this can be successfully performed for every constraint, then the constrained optimization problem can be converted into an unconstrained problem to which ordinary calculus can be applied.

If it is not algebraically practical to solve each constraint for a single variable or if one of the constraints is an inequality that may be nonbinding, then the proper procedure is to attach each constraint to the objective function using an introduced *Lagrange multiplier*. This is a common approach in economics because theoretical constraints often cannot be solved for a single variable and the resulting knowledge of the Lagrange multiplier's value can be useful. In economics, simple nonnegativity constraints (quantities and prices must be nonnegative) are often suppressed in that they do not formally appear in the optimization problem, but attention is restricted to positive solutions.

Consider the following generic problem involving an objective "value" function, V, to be maximized with respect to a vector of decisions, $\mathbf{x}$. (Changes appropriate for minimization problems shall be listed later.) For whatever external reasons, the various elements of $\mathbf{x}$ are related to one another or are constrained in some fashion, or at least some of them are. The single relation or constraint is either an inequality or an equality of the general form $h(\mathbf{x}) \leq a$, where "a" is a constant number.

The generic problem is then

$$\text{Max } V(\mathbf{x}) \quad \text{subject to } h(\mathbf{x}) \leq a. \tag{2.41}$$

In the Lagrangian method we first rewrite the constraint, paying careful attention to the direction of the inequality sign:

$$a - h(\mathbf{x}) \geq 0,$$

and then we construct the following Lagrangian:

$$L(\mathbf{x}, \lambda) = V(\mathbf{x}) + \lambda \cdot (a - h(\mathbf{x})). \tag{2.42}$$

2.A.1 Necessary Conditions

The so-called Kuhn-Tucker (necessary, first-order) conditions for problem (2.41) are the four following inequalities and equalities:

$$\frac{\partial V}{\partial x_i} - \lambda \cdot \frac{\partial h}{\partial x_i} \leq 0 \quad \text{for all i,} \tag{2.43}$$

$$\left(\frac{\partial V}{\partial x_i} - \lambda \cdot \frac{\partial h}{\partial x_i} \right) \cdot x_i = 0 \quad \text{for all i,} \tag{2.44}$$

$$a - h(\mathbf{x}) \geq 0, \tag{2.45}$$

and

$$(a - h(\mathbf{x})) \cdot \lambda = 0. \tag{2.46}$$

While these four conditions are the most accurate requirements for a maxima, in economic settings it can often be presumed that inequality constraints will be binding and that the solution will be "interior" ($x_i > 0$ for all i). In such cases, (2.43)–(2.46) reduce to much simpler equalities:

$$\frac{\partial V}{\partial x_i} - \lambda \cdot \frac{\partial h}{\partial x_i} = 0 \quad \text{for all i,} \tag{2.47}$$

$$a - h(\mathbf{x}) = 0. \tag{2.48}$$

If $\mathbf{x}$ possesses I elements, then (2.47) and (2.48) constitute a system of $I + 1$ equations with $I + 1$ unknowns (the x_i and λ). Algebraic solution of this system completes the Lagrangian procedure.

2.A.2 Interpretation of Lagrange Multipliers

The Lagrange multiplier is a "shadow price" associated with the constraint it premultiplies. If the constraint could be "relaxed" a little, the value of λ tells us how much we will gain in V. In some situations, this type of information is very useful. While it is not especially useful in this instance because utility has only ordinal significance, solving for λ in the boxed example tells us how much utility the consumer

Box 2.A.1
Getting Demand from Utility Maximization

A consumer has preferences between the total value of all other goods one consumes, x, and water, w, that are given by the utility function $U = x^{30}w$. The consumer has \$40,000 of income to spend. What is the consumer's demand for water?

Because of the simple way x is defined, its price is 1. (You can get another unit of the good if you pay \$1.) Because we are seeking a water demand function, the price of water must be treated as variable. Let p be the price of water. The objective function is $x^{30}w$ with decision variables x and w. The consumer's budget constraint is $1 \cdot x + p \cdot w \leq 40000$ or $40000 - x - p \cdot w \geq 0$. The appropriate Lagrangian is

$$L(x, w, \lambda) = x^{30}w + \lambda \cdot (40000 - x - p \cdot w).$$

Necessary equations (2.47) and (2.48) are

$$30x^{29}w + \lambda \cdot (-1) = 0,$$

$$x^{30} + \lambda \cdot (-p) = 0, \quad \text{and}$$

$$40000 - x - p \cdot w = 0.$$

The first two equations can be combined to obtain optimal x in terms of w, yielding $x = 30pw$, which can be substituted into the third necessary equation. Solving for w yields the water demand function

$$w = \frac{40000}{31p},$$

which has the expected negative slope.

would gain if one had another dollar of income. The result will be functionally dependent on water price.

2.A.3 Sufficient Conditions

To guarantee that (2.43)–(2.46) or (2.47)–(2.48) yield a maxima rather than a minima, it is important to verify sufficient conditions. We will first observe the technical sufficient conditions and then note the simple conditions that are required when V is a function of a single variable.

There are three sufficient conditions that must be simultaneously satisfied (Chiang 1984, 738–740, 347):

1. $V(\mathbf{x})$ must be a *concave* function. This is equivalent to $D^2[V(\mathbf{x})]$, the matrix of second derivatives, being *negative definite*.

2. $h(\mathbf{x})$ must be a *convex* function. Hence, $D^2[h(\mathbf{x})]$ must also be *positive definite*.

3. There must exist a feasible selection of $\mathbf{x}$ such that any inequality constraint holds with a strict inequality.

Recall that linear functions are both concave and convex.

2.A.4 Minimization and Multiple Constraints

If the problem given by (2.41) is one of minimization, then everything stated previously is accurate as long as we reverse the inequalities in (2.41), (2.43), and (2.45), and change the sufficient conditions 1 and 2 to require concavity and convexity, respectively.

In cases where there is more than one constraint to be obeyed, each should be appended to the objective function to form the Lagrangian function, and each constraint should have a distinct Lagrange multiplier.

3 Efficiency in a Dynamic World

What happens when time matters?

Our work in the prior chapter concerned tools to allocate limited water among competing current users. Both social efficiency criteria of chapter 2 emphasize this crucial matter. We also examined optimizing decisions for firms wishing to maximize profit and consumers wishing to maximize satisfaction (utility). All of these matters, while important, are quite *static*—there is no time element to contemplate or any scheduling to do. When time becomes an important matter in decision making about water, as is often the case, we need *dynamic* tools.

Dynamics are important for water resource decision making in two primary ways.

In the first, a single agent is faced with a current decision that has implications for the agent's future prospects. The agent must resolve a trade-off between current and future net benefits. Water conservation investments are noteworthy examples.[1] If the agent undertakes a conservation investment, there is an up-front cost to be paid (net benefits in the current period are negative for the decision), but in future years the expected water savings will lower water costs (positive net benefits). To make a decision, the agent must possess some vision of what the current and future net benefits are, and the agent must assign relative weights to these net benefits. If the agent is typical, it takes more than one dollar's worth of future net benefits to offset one dollar's worth of net costs today. The same relative weights must be known to resolve reversed situations in which an agent can receive up-front net benefits in return for negative future net benefits.[2]

---

1. Examples are numerous. Households can install low-flow showerheads or low gallons-per-flush toilets. Manufacturers can convert to a water-recycling system specific to their production processes. Golf courses can change their grass species. Depending on crop type, irrigators can change their water application technology from furrow irrigation to low-pressure sprinkler irrigation or drip irrigation.

2. For example, an irrigator can reduce current water applications and save irrigation costs if one accepts the future productivity losses of not clearing accumulated salts from the root zone (which will reduce future crop yields).

The second manner in which time is relevant is an extension of the first. Society, which is an aggregation of agents, must also make trade-offs between temporally defined net benefits—present versus future. For instance, a public agency might be considering how much ground water to pump this year. Agency managers may know that pumping now will decrease the amount that can be pumped in the future. Other important examples include public works projects such as reservoirs and water conveyance facilities. Like present versus future decisions for a single agent, social decisions typically involve differential weighting of current and future net benefits. The present is weighted more heavily. For reasons to be discussed in this chapter, public decision making can involve different weights than those encountered for the private decision making of individual agents.

At first glance, these matters are not fully dynamic. While they certainly involve time-defined schedules of benefits and costs, it is not apparent that they involve movement or rates-of-change in some interesting phenomena. Yet a whether-or-not decision to adopt a particular water management strategy is really just a simplified version of a broader question: When is the optimal time to adopt a water management strategy, and how should it be scaled? Population growth and changing water demands interact with various supply-side influences to bring about continually changing water scarcity. Within these changing circumstances, new or modified tools (projects and policies) can be utilized, and these tools should be efficiently scheduled. This is a very dynamic setting. To work in this environment, we must have a mechanism for comparing values experienced in differing time periods.

To understand how future net benefits can be compared to present net benefits, one must grasp the concept of *time preference rate*. Also called the *discount rate* or the *time value of money*, rates of time preference are derived from human preferences. The first half of this chapter focuses on determining these rates. The second half is about putting them to work in dynamic analysis such as applies to ground water depletion and project assessment. (If you have no interest in the behavioral origins of discounting or the standards for selecting appropriate discount rates, then you should advance several pages to section 3.5.)

3.1 Rates of Time Preference

Suppose someone you trust without reservation offers you the following choice: with no obligation, they will give you either $100 today (tax free) or $100 one year from today (also tax free). You get to choose which one. The only stipulation is that you must spend the money when you get it. You cannot save or invest it. A typical individual faced with such a choice will choose to take the money today because their **private rate of time preference** is such that now is more important than tomorrow.

Now what if the choice is between $100 today and $150 in one year? Remember that you trust this individual completely. Even if that person is dead a year from now, their estate will automatically send you $150 if that's the selection you make. Many people facing these options will choose to take the $150 one year from now, although some may wish to take the $100 now.

We can continue these experiments until we narrow in on a number x such that you are roughly indifferent between $100 today and $100 + $x in one year. For future offers less than $100 + $x, you prefer the $100 today. For future offers greater than $100 + $x, you prefer the future money. Different people will have different x amounts for many reasons. You might expect to be in better financial circumstances a year from now, so a dollar today may yield more utility than a dollar in one year. Tomorrow you may be dead, or the social order may collapse and render dollars worthless. We humans find that today is more tangible than tomorrow. We are more desirous of goods today. Different people weigh these sorts of things differently within their personal preference structures. Whatever x is for you, it is your annual rate of time preference expressed as a percentage; your annual rate of time preference is x percent. This is a key parameter for personal dynamic analysis. It allows you to turn the apples-to-oranges matter of net-benefits-now versus net-benefits-later into an apples-to-apples comparison.

Suppose your rate of time preference is 15 percent and you expect it to stay at 15 percent over the next five years. Assume that you have the opportunity to install a water-saving showerhead for $20. Based on the provided data, you reasonably anticipate that this showerhead will save you $5 in water and energy costs every year for the next five years with the first $5 benefit occurring one year from now. After five years, you expect the unit to fail in the sense that it no longer will yield any water or energy savings. Assuming no other effects, should you install this product? Knowing your rate of time preference, you can successfully weight and add your annual net benefits to reach a decision. The components of this calculation are collected in table 3.1, where it is shown that this is not a worthwhile purchase for you.

3.2 The Underlying Theory

It is insight building to examine time preference a bit more deeply now. Figure 3.1 contains a representative two-period model of an ordinary individual's trade-off between year 1 and year 2 wealth. Other periods are ignored as a simplification. The *indifference curve* I_1 in figure 3.1 captures all combinations of this year's money ($\$_1$) and next year's money ($\$_2$) that yield the same total welfare for this person. Said another way, this person is indifferent among all the points on this curve. Consulting our personal preferences to verify this notion, each of us can generally agree that we can "break even" on small decreases in the money we enjoy in year 1 if we receive an

Table 3.1
Economics of showerhead replacement

Year	Net benefits	Net benefits $\dfrac{}{1.15^{\text{year}}}$
0	$-\$20$	$-\$20.00$
1	$+\$5$	$+\$4.35$
2	$+\$5$	$+\$3.78$
3	$+\$5$	$+\$3.29$
4	$+\$5$	$+\$2.86$
5	$+\$5$	$+\$2.49$
	Total:	$-\$3.24$

acceptable increase in next year's money. For this reason, the indifference curve has a negative slope. Other indifference curves (indeed, infinitely many) can be drawn for this same person, because there is a distinct indifference curve for each level of this individual's two-period welfare. An additional indifference curve (I_2) is also drawn in figure 3.1. Because the additional curve involves higher-value levels than the bold curve, it results in more total welfare. Other things being equal, this person wishes to be on the highest indifference curve possible (most distant from the graph's origin), but is limited by income, knowledge, and a host of other economically relevant constraints.

Suppose that given all the underlying opportunities, this person chooses point A in figure 3.1 because they can achieve no higher total welfare. This choice is, among other things, an expression of this person's desires for using money this year versus next year. There's a trade-off to be made, and it's a psychological one involving one's specific preferences. By definition, this individual's private rate of time preference, d, is the negative of the slope of the tangent line (the dashed line) to the indifference curve, measured at point A, minus 1. That is, $d = -\text{slope} - 1$. This representation of the rate of time preference is useful because it indicates how the rate depends on choice. Movements to indifference points rightward and below A lower this person's implied rate of time preference. Leftward and higher movements raise this person's rate of time preference. Figure 3.1 demonstrates that a person's rate of time preference is not a fixed parameter. It is a consequence of a person's options and preferences. As these options and preferences change, a person may make different decisions and reveal a different private rate of time preference.

3.3   Time Values of Money

Financial markets can have a dramatic impact on a person's rate of time preference. The existence of financial markets means that different people have a mechanism for creating win-win opportunities out of their differing rates of time preference. This is

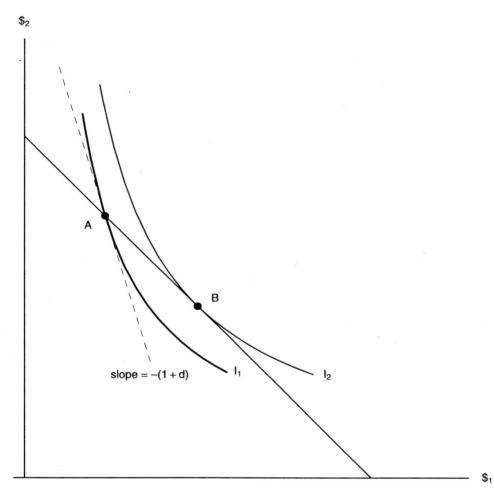

Figure 3.1
Interperiod preferences and the discount rate

accomplished by exchanging access to present and future wealth—what we call borrowing and lending. Suppose the person represented in figure 3.1 can borrow or lend money at an interest rate less than their rate of time preference. This person can then convert point A into any ($_1$, $_2$) combination on the solid line passing through A.[3] The consequences are twofold, with the second being more momentous:

1. This person will borrow money in order to achieve a higher total welfare at point B. (If the market rate had been greater than the rate of time preference, this person would improve their total welfare by lending.)

2. This individual's new private rate of time preference will be the same as the market rate of interest.

Consequence 2 should not be interpreted as meaning that market rates of interest determine private rates of time preference. It's the other way around.

A market interest rate is essentially a price—a price of leasing money—that equilibrates the amount of wealth supplied by lenders with the amount demanded by borrowers. In the absence of such financial markets, some people have relatively low personal rates of time preference, possibly because their higher-than-normal wealth makes them eager to transfer some of their wealth to the future. Others have relatively high rates of time preference, meaning that they have a greater desire to transfer future wealth to the present, if only they could. Financial markets allow these people to conduct swaps. Financial markets therefore blend people's rates of time preferences into an agreed-on intermediate value and alter their rates of time preference in the direction of this intermediate value (point 2 above). Such a value can be observed in the marketplace, and it can be called a time value of money. This term and the term discount rate are fully interchangeable with the phrase rate of time preference.

Although some writers (like engineering economists) expeditiously define the time value of money as the rate of return enabled by a capital (investment) good, that's too mechanistic and circular. Time value is behaviorally rooted in people's preferences. We should always keep in mind that positive rates of return—the time value of money—cannot exist without the positive rates of time preference psychologically held by people.[4]

---

3. If the interest rate is i, then the slope of the solid line through A is $-(1+i)$. This slope is computable by solving the following intertemporal budget constraint for $_2$: $_1 + \$_2/(1+i) = \$_{1A} + \$_{2A}/(1+i)$, where ($_{1A}, \$_{2A}$) is the coordinates of point A. The right-hand side of this equation is a constant, so it only influences the intercept of the budget line.

4. If all people's preferences embedded a zero rate of time preference instead of the positive rates normally seen, then the added savings people would undertake would drive the rate of return to capital downward. In this case, people's equal regard ($d = 0$) for present and future consumption would increase the availability of investment funds, as compared to $d > 0$, and lower the return on investments to zero.

What of businesses? Businesses have to make water decisions too. What rate of time preference might they apply for their dynamic decisions?

Businesses also have private rates of time preference that are extensions of their owners' preferences. People own, invest in, or loan their wealth to businesses because they expect to earn a rate of return sufficient to compensate them for their private rate of time preference. The expected reward must exceed the provider's private rate of time preference. Hence, business rates of time preference are associated with the psychologically rooted time preferences of the business's owners (or stockholders) and its creditors or debtors.

Because many bargains are being struck among many different types of borrowers and lenders in the marketplace, there isn't one private time value of money. There are many. If financial markets were perfectly informed and frictionless, the interaction of many agents would conclude in a single rate of time preference shared by all agents (Mishan 1976, 202). Unfortunately, perfect information is infinitely costly and friction is inevitable, so there will always be multiple rates of time preference and multiple time values of money. Even with the moderation and advantages provided by financial markets, different agents will have different rates of time preference that they employ for resolving their personal and corporate dynamic decisions.

For businesses involved in dynamic water decision making, it is technically correct to apply whatever time value of money is in force. For the majority of firms, money's time value is bounded by the cost of borrowed funds. This is most apparent for water development and conservation projects under consideration by firms. If projects require borrowed funds (or keep the firm from retiring its existing debt) and the firm can borrow funds at an interest rate of y percent, then y percent is the firm's time value of money for such projects. If the firm can borrow only a limited amount of money at y percent and will have to forgo investment opportunities yielding z percent $(z > y)$, then the true "opportunity cost" of firm funds is z percent. In the latter case, the effective time value of money is the opportunity cost, z percent. Even if the firm does not have to borrow funds to undertake the project, it can loan its cash or make other investments. In such cases, the opportunity cost of the alternative returns is, again, the business's time value of money.

3.4 What Is the Social Time Value of Money?

Private rates of time preference (that is, private time values of money and private discount rates) are fine for resolving private trade-offs and making private decisions, but what might the *social rate of time preference* be for making public policy and public project decisions? Examples of such decisions include how a city establishes water rates when it is making use of depletable ground water and whether a water district should improve leaky conveyances to lessen its future water deficits. These are crucial issues that are profoundly impacted by the selected rate of time preference. Given that there are many people composing society and its subsets (such as a city or a water district), how might we condense many different private rates of time preference into something representing social preferences? There are two juxtaposed answers to this question, and there is a lot of gray area between them. Water management is significantly affected by the ethical choices embedded in the path we choose (Rosenblum and Stanley-Jones 2001).

The Opportunity Cost of Capital Argument

On the one hand, social decisions are being conducted in an economic environment where financial markets have condensed and disclosed the range of private time values of money. Individual behavior has been shaped, to a large extent, by these markets, which are mechanisms for interpersonal interaction. Because of these markets, people have more uniform rates of time preference. Interest rates indicate these discount rates. This is the basis for a strong argument in favor of using a representative private value for the social time value of money.

The argument can be made even stronger for public projects (Randall 1981, 210–212). Because funds for public projects are obtained from people, often via taxation, the opportunity cost of the timely use of these funds is given by private rates of time preference. Remembering figure 3.1, people have gone to some lengths to balance present versus future expenditures according to their private discount rates. If they are to be denied funds because of taxes, we may be remiss in not acknowledging the opportunity costs represented by these people's discount rates. Even for dynamic matters not involving up-front construction and investment, a desire for consistency and grounding social decisions in the real world requests that social decision making reflect all costs incurred by people. Proponents of this view contend that the social discount rate for all public decisions should be the opportunity cost of capital.

Depending on the scope or, more formally, the *accounting stance* of the public entity engaged in dynamic decision making, the opportunity cost of capital might be easily determined.[5] For a local authority such as a district or a city, the social discount rate may be the same as the authority's borrowing cost—the rate the authority must pay on bonds. Or if it has limited borrowing capability, the opportunity cost of capital may be higher than the bond rate. That is, it may be the returns available from the next most gainful project.

---

5. The concept of accounting stance—the breadth of all costs and benefits considered by the decision-making authority—will be more fully utilized in chapter 5. It is a simple idea. Benefits or costs experienced outside the authority's jurisdiction and clientele are not relevant to the authority's decision, but all the interior benefits and costs count.

For a federal (or state) authority, however, it should be recognized that taxation policy causes the opportunity cost of capital to be higher than rates directly revealed by financial markets. The actual returns to investment are divided between the investor and the government. If a market rate of return is i percent and people have to pay a tax rate of t percent on all their investment income, then the true *social* returns to private investment must be $i/(1 - t)$ percent. That is, if a public project or policy is going to divert dollars from the private sector, these dollars have a time value of i percent to people, and they were generating tax revenues of t percent. This means, importantly, that the social opportunity cost of capital is higher than the market-revealed rates. Similar to public project costs that sacrifice time values and taxable returns to capital, public actions contributing dollars to the private sector have the reverse effect. Depending on the different taxes involved—especially personal and corporate income taxes—the computation of the social opportunity cost of capital can become quite elaborate (see chapter 13 of Zerbe and Dively 1994). Including the average state and federal personal and corporate taxes, we may find that the social opportunity cost of capital is more than twice the market-revealed rate.[6] Such calculations constitute a substantial modification to the social discount rate and can have deep impacts on dynamic analysis.

The Future Is Underweighted Argument

On the other hand, opposition to the market-oriented perspective comes from those concerned about the ethical treatment of future people (Rosenblum and Stanley-Jones 2001). Due to the compounding involved in discounting, use of a market-chosen discount rate can assign extraordinarily little weight to future people. For example, suppose the discount rate is 10 percent and we are thinking about *not* using an acre-foot of ground water this year because it's only worth a hundred dollars now, but will be worth one million dollars one century from now due to rising scarcity, even without any inflation in the economy. (Having such refined information is admittedly far-fetched, but it allows us to concentrate on the discounting issue.) Given that $1.1^{100} = 13{,}781$, such ground water conservation would appear to be a bad idea because \$1 million $\div$ 13,781 = \$72 < \$100.

Faced with the denial of the conservation proposal, some may argue that it is unfair to treat present people as almost fourteen thousand times more important than people living one hundred years from now. Proponents of the market-oriented view counter that this statement has misframed the matter. Their view is that if we set aside a hundred dollars now (in exchange for present consumption of the water) at

---

6. For personal income derived from corporate sources, it is reasonable to contemplate a 28 percent personal federal income tax rate, a 4 percent personal state income tax rate, a 35 percent corporate federal income tax rate, and a 5 percent corporate state income tax rate: $1/(0.72 \cdot 0.96 \cdot 0.65 \cdot 0.95) = 2.34$.

10 percent, this money would be worth more than one million dollars in a hundred years and future people would prefer that. Opponents say, "Fine, invest the hundred dollars now, dedicate it to be used in a hundred years, and let it grow until then." Market-oriented proponents claim that's unnecessary—present people are engaged in all sorts of investments furthering the welfare of future people, and in any case, the opportunity cost of such investment is well measured in the marketplace—it's 10 percent.

Over the decades during which such sparring has occurred, various arguments have been forwarded for why the social discount rate should be selected as *something less* than private discount rates and the opportunity cost of capital. Some of these thoughts are enlightening to consider:

· Over fifty years ago, A. C. Pigou "observed that individuals have faulty 'telescopic' vision concerning the future, and are inclined not to make sufficient provision for it" (Sassone and Schaffer 1978, 105). Such a claim suggests that market-obtained discount rates are too high.

· Providing for future generations is a nonrival good, as viewed from the perspective of the current generation. We get satisfaction from knowing that future generations will be well-off, and these feelings are nonrival. As individuals, we can do little to advance the welfare of future generations, so we don't really try except for our own immediate descendants. Although the concept of public goods is not fully discussed until the next chapter, there is a public good problem here. It leads us to suspect that individual actions in support of future people are inefficiently low. Using collective action, we can be more successful. One way to accomplish this is to employ a low rate of social discount in assessing all public endeavors (Prest and Turvey 1965, 696–697).

· Market-obtained time values of money are resolved in an economic system where current people own all property and future people own nothing. If we envision our society in a way that includes future generations (an ethical question), might it make sense to implicitly grant them some property entitlements so they could pursue "life and happiness"? If, hypothetically, they did have such entitlements and could participate in current financial markets, wouldn't a significant result be a lowering of the rates of time preference as revealed by markets? (Since future people care about future goods, their involvement in current financial markets would lower the market rates of time preference.) In other words, what's so great about market-obtained discount rates if future generations have no role in their determination?

· When the real-life decision making of people is experimentally studied, their discounting is found to be more "hyperbolic" than "exponential" (Angeletos et al. 2001). Simply put, the exponentially based discounting relied on in this text (and virtually everywhere else too) fails to account for the higher discount rates that people apply to "sooner" decisions. For example, most people would now think it optimal to commit a certain percentage, say S percent, of their income ten years from now to retirement savings, but when year ten arrives, they will set aside less than S percent. One consequence of hyperbolic discounting is that people make inefficiently low provisions for the future, and this is a failure that government can partially remedy by using a discount rate that is about 2 percent lower than private discount rates (Cropper and Laibson 1999).

Arguments such as these advocate that we soften the idea of rigidly using private time values of money for all social decision making, though these ideas are still not resolute. If the market rates of discount are too high, we still need to know by how much.

How Can the Opposing Arguments Be Balanced?

A useful, partial resolution of these matters is to distinguish between those decisions involving only the next forty years and those involving more than forty years (Portney and Weyant 1999, 7). Within the next forty years, special ethical considerations pertaining to future generations are negligible, so private rates of discount can be adopted as social rates of discount.

For dynamic decisions going beyond forty years, market-oriented rates are less satisfactory. Here, the analyst may be obliged to devote effort to the selection. Familiarity with the material contained in this chapter will then be a useful starting place.

In certain cases, analysis can proceed with an ordained social discount rate. For example, a social discount rate is decreed for federally funded water projects undertaken in the United States. The federally decreed rate changes from year to year according to a specified procedure (to be discussed in chapter 6) and applies only to water projects. In cases where such directives are unavailable, the analyst or analysis team may be uncomfortable about accepting responsibility for choosing a social discount rate. It may be useful in such cases to obtain counsel from the ultimate decision-making authority. Alternatively, one may perform the needed analysis using alternative discount rates as a means of exploring the "sensitivity" of final results to this subjectively selected parameter.

3.5   Not Risk, Not Inflation

So for less than forty-year dynamic decisions, what have markets revealed about the discount rate? In the numerous financial markets, lenders provide their monies for various prices known by a variety of instrument-specific terms (interest rates, stock dividends, coupon rates); borrowers agree to pay these prices for the temporary use of the money; and financial intermediaries (banks, brokerages) help link borrowers and lenders for a fee. Some examples of these instruments include credit cards, savings accounts, mortgage loans, stocks, corporate bonds, and government bonds. Observable rates of return vary greatly across these examples, not only due to differing rates of time preference, but also because each involves different levels of risk for the lender, and lenders must be compensated for their exposure to risk as well as the use of their money.

Credit card borrowers sometimes pay high rates of interest because their credit worthiness is not well-known and many cardholders default. Such risk is *not* relevant to the determination of rates of time preference. Compensation for bearing risk is a separate matter. So if we want market observations on the rate of time preference, we should find financial instruments devoid of any risk. Government bonds, particularly U.S. bonds, are highly regarded here because the chances of the U.S. government defaulting on its payment obligations are judged to be very low. In particular, U.S. Treasury bonds are instruments auctioned periodically by the U.S. Department of the Treasury for the purpose of financing the federal debt. These bonds are commonly traded in the marketplace, and such trades are closely watched because they clearly disclose the implied rate of return.[7] Hence, data on bond interest rates are readily available.

Like risk, inflation is distinct from rates of time preference. **Inflation** means a *general* reduction in the buying power of money. If we define a representative "basket of goods" purchased by the average person during each month and find that the total cost of this basket of goods has increased 2 percent during the past year, then the apparent inflation rate is 2 percent. Alternatively, if this basket of goods costs 50 percent more than it did ten years ago, then the average inflation rate has been 4.14 percent. (Solve $1.5 = (1 + x)^{10}$ for x.) Because rising scarcity of *particular* goods is *not* evidence of inflation, it is improper to say that inflation has occurred because the price of gasoline has risen or water rates have increased.

National agencies such as the U.S. Bureau of Labor are concerned about the measurement of inflation because of the changing real value of money and its impact on real wages. (If your personal income has doubled, but all prices and fees in the economy have doubled too, then your buying power has not increased, has it?) The most popular measure of inflation is the Consumer Price Index or the CPI, and a historical record of the CPI is readily available via the Internet (⟨http://www.bls.gov⟩).

Unfortunately for our purposes in ascertaining the time value of money, market-observed discount rates include an allowance for inflation. Lenders are not willing

---

7. Although the U.S. Treasury issues each bond at a fixed rate of interest, market interest rates can change over time. Bonds trade at higher prices as market interest rates decline. Because bonds are an investment alternative to stocks, their returns are well tracked and reported. For example, see ⟨http://money.cnn.com/markets/bondcenter⟩.

to lend at their rates of time preference if they believe inflation will occur. If my rate of time preference is 10 percent and I expect the inflation rate to be 1.5 percent, then I will engage in riskless lending at rates greater than 11.65 percent, and I will borrow at rates less than 11.65 percent ($1.1 \cdot 1.015 = 1.1165$).

Economists have adopted a pair of adjectives to clearly demarcate whether prices or discount rates include inflation allowances. ***Real prices*** include no inflationary component and are stated relative to prices in a particular reference period. ***Nominal prices*** incorporate inflation. Market-observed prices and rates are always nominal. Most forward-looking water resource economics is performed using projected real prices and a real discount rate. It is equally acceptable, however, to employ projected nominal prices and a nominal discount rate. As long as the analyst consistently employs real values or nominal values without mixing them, the results will be equivalent.

3.6   Market Revelations of the Discount Rate

So what does available market evidence tell us about the real discount rate? The first thing market data tell us is that the discount rate is an elusive parameter. Figure 3.2 contains graphs of two primary U.S. Treasury rates: the three-month Treasury bill

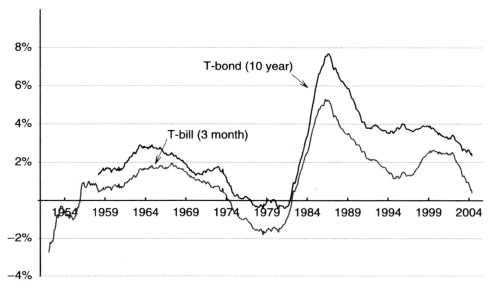

Figure 3.2
Market time preferences (running averages)

(T-bill) and the ten-year Treasury bond (T-bond). These rates reflect monthly data that have been adjusted to remove inflation.[8] To remove some of the fluctuations in month-to-month changes and obtain a steadier picture, the data represented in figure 3.2 have also been smoothed by graphing an average of the preceding sixty months.

Not only does the market-indicated, real discount rate move up and down in figure 3.2 but it has been negative at times—indicating that investors have not anticipated inflation accurately. For example, investors underforecast inflation during the late 1970s and the early 1980s, and they would have been better off holding their wealth as cash instead of in Treasuries.

Over the last thirty years, the T-bill rate has averaged 1.5 percent, and the T-bond rate has averaged 3.1 percent. For the most recent twenty years, those averages are 1.9 and 3.8 percent, respectively. The ten-year T-bond rates generally exceed those of the three-month T-bill because longer-term bonds lock up money longer, thus adding risk exposure that real rates of return will change in the marketplace. Although they are concealed by the sixty-month averaging used in figure 3.2, there have been brief periods during which T-bill rates exceeded T-bond rates.

Based on this information, one might comfortably conclude that private rates of time preference generally lie between 2 and 4 percent in real terms. If we wish to apply such a discount rate to a federal-level decision where a particular discount rate has not been mandated, then 5 to 9 percent is the social opportunity cost of capital reflecting lost tax revenue.[9]

3.7   Discounting: A Summary

The discount rate is the single most important parameter in dynamic decision making. Small changes in this parameter can dramatically alter certain decisions, so its resolution is worthy of our close attention. A recent overview, resulting from a discounting workshop assembling some of our most respected economists, noted "the unease even the best minds in the profession feel about discounting, due to the technical complexity of the issues and to their ethical ramifications" (Portney and Weyant 1999, 5). Discount rate selection can be a tough issue, but it does no good to sidestep it, so we have confronted it directly here. Let's restate the most important findings and their logical extensions.

---

8. Monthly T-bill, T-bond, and CPI data can be obtained from the Web pages maintained by the Federal Reserve Bank of St. Louis (⟨http://www.stls.frb.org⟩). Inflation for month t, f_t is calculated as $(CPI_t/CPI_{t-1})^{12} - 1$. The real rate of discount is then calculated from the nominal bill/bond rate (i_t) using $((1 + f_t)/(1 + i_t)) - 1$ (Halvorsen and Ruby 1981, 44).

9. This new range employs the 2.34 factor indicated by note 6 above.

For shorter planning horizons, perhaps forty years or less, one sees the following:

• For private agents as well as many cities and districts, the discount rate will be well captured by the entity's cost of borrowed funds. If the entity is not able to borrow enough funds to undertake all its economically beneficial opportunities, however, the applicable discount rate is actually higher than the cost of borrowing, and the correct discount rate is the returns available on the best project that cannot be undertaken.

• For federal water undertakings subject to a mandated discount rate, the prespecified social discount rate must be employed. This approach may also be required in other jurisdictions such as states.

• For federal and state projects and policies not subject to a mandated discount rate, there is a strong argument in favor of the social opportunity cost of capital. For federal activities, using a real discount rate in the 5 to 9 percent range seems advisable. For state activities, similar calculations based on applicable state tax rates are advised.

For long, multigenerational planning horizons where market-derived rates may underweight the importance public planners wish to attach to future people, one finds the following:

• To assign greater weight to the future, a less-than-market rate of discount can be purposefully selected and applied.

• Instead of aggregating net benefits over all time using discounting, estimated net benefits can be tabulated by time period (perhaps by decades or longer) and reported to decision makers without further aggregation. The decision-making body can then apply its own weights, either implicitly or explicitly, to make the present versus future trade-off necessary to reach a decision.

In most of these bulleted cases, there is an inescapable feature present in dynamic decision making: the discount rate matters, yet it is imprecisely known. In such situations, it is often advisable to perform all analysis using alternative values for the uncertain parameter. This approach, formally called *sensitivity analysis*, provides the analyst (and the analyst's audience) with information about how sensitive the decision recommendation is to the questionable parameter. While sensitivity analysis can be employed for other imperfectly known parameters, it is especially useful in the case of the discount rate.

3.8 Dynamic Improvement and Dynamic Efficiency

Having established guidelines for discount rate selection, it can be presumed (finally) that we now know how to weight temporally separated net benefits:

• NBs occurring during the same period will be weighted equally as is done in static, aggregate efficiency.

• NBs occurring during different periods will be weighted according to the discount rate and the number of separating periods using compounding. Accordingly, a decision has the property of **dynamic efficiency** if it maximizes net present value. A decision constitutes a **dynamic improvement** if it increases net present value above baseline levels. **Net present value** is the sum, over the chosen planning horizon, of all net benefits accruing to an action and discounted to current value terms:

$$\text{NPV} = \sum_{t=0}^{T} \frac{NB_t}{(1+d)^t},$$
(3.1)

where

t is the time period index (generally year by year),
T is the planning horizon (how far out we are looking),
NB_t are net benefits in period t, and
d is the discount rate.

Among other things, this formula replicates the computation performed in table 3.1 for the water-conserving showerhead.[10] There we found the proposed showerhead investment did not offer a dynamic improvement because its NPV was less than zero. Such calculations are methodologically simple and proceed as follows: a change is proposed, a schedule of NBs is obtained for the change, NPV is calculated using (3.1), and the change is found to be a dynamic improvement only if NPV > 0.

To analyze dynamic efficiency, NPV must be functionally dependent on a decision variable to be optimized. In our most common situation, NPV is functionally dependent on a set of continuous decision variables, one for each period. If each decision variable is denoted x_t and the vector $\mathbf{x}$ refers to the set of decisions, $\{x_0, x_1, \ldots, x_{T-1}\}$, then the dynamically efficient $\mathbf{x}$ is the vector solving the following problem:

$$\underset{\mathbf{x}}{\text{maximize}} \ \text{NPV}(\mathbf{x}) = \underset{\mathbf{x}}{\text{maximize}} \sum_{t=0}^{T-1} \frac{NB_t(x_t)}{(1+d)^t}.$$
(3.2)

10. If NB_t is constant for all t, then equation (3.1) can be employed to generate empirically useful relations. For example, economic theory holds that the market value of a permanent water right is the net present value of the annual gains that this water right supports. So knowing a repeating annual value and (3.1) gives a benchmark market value. The importance of such calculations has made it useful to have simplifying formulas. For this reason, the most practical formulas are given in appendix 3.A at the end of this chapter.

This sort of problem is commonly seen in water resource economics, though the problem setting can also be more complex, such as when there are multiple decisions for each period instead of just one. Noncomplex examples include the amount of ground water to pump each period, the amount of water to release from a reservoir, and the amount of water to apply each week to a growing crop. Generally, in addition to the objective function captured by (3.2), there will also be physical constraints causing net benefits in later periods to be related to decisions made earlier. This is the essence of dynamic issues—decisions made today affect results achieved today *and* those results to be achieved later.

Even though the structure of (3.2) is to calculate an optimizing value for every element of **x**, it is often the case that we are only going to implement decisions required for the current period. When it comes time to implement the next period's decision, we can solve the problem again using updated information. Each time we do so, however, we are considering the impact of the immediate decision(s) on future net benefits.

3.9 Other Metrics

The economist's focus on NPV as the guiding light for dynamic decision making is a little different from that encountered in engineering economics and business economics, where the internal rate of return is commonly emphasized. Some other governmental organizations have an affinity for the benefit-cost ratio instead of NPV. Federal analysts who assess water supply projects in the United States are focused on the calculation of annualized benefits and annualized costs. How do these differing measures relate, and in what cases might one be preferred to the other?

The *internal rate of return* (IRR) is that discount rate causing the NPV of a proposal to be zero:

$$\text{IRR} = d \quad \text{such that } 0 = \sum_{t=0}^{T} \frac{\text{NB}_t}{(1+d)^t}. \tag{3.3}$$

This calculation can be performed without first choosing the applicable discount rate—a temporary advantage—but a proposed policy or project can only be judged a dynamic improvement if IRR is greater than a chosen threshold rate. Hence, an applicable personal, corporate, or social threshold discount rate is needed to apply this criterion, even though none is needed to do the calculation.

Applied to the showerhead proposal summarized in table 3.1, equation (3.3) reduces to

$$0 = -20 + \frac{5}{1+\text{IRR}} + \frac{5}{(1+\text{IRR})^2} + \frac{5}{(1+\text{IRR})^3} + \frac{5}{(1+\text{IRR})^4} + \frac{5}{(1+\text{IRR})^5}, \tag{3.4}$$

or, multiplying both sides by $(1 + IRR)^5$,

$$0 = -20(1 + IRR)^5 + 5(1 + IRR)^4 + 5(1 + IRR)^3 + 5(1 + IRR)^2 + 5(1 + IRR) + 5. \tag{3.5}$$

Notice that (3.5) is a polynomial of degree five ($= T$, the planning horizon) and can therefore have five possible answers for IRR. In general, the roots of the IRR polynomial will all be equal because the schedule of net benefits changes sign only once.[11] In this case, IRR $= 7.93$ percent, which is less than the required return of 15 percent.

The **benefit-cost ratio** (BCR) of a proposal is calculated as the present value of benefits divided by the present value of costs:

$$BCR = \frac{\sum_{t=0}^{T} \frac{B_t}{(1+d)^t}}{\sum_{t=0}^{T} \frac{C_t}{(1+d)^t}}. \tag{3.6}$$

If a proposal is a dynamic improvement, then BCR > 1. The showerhead proposal provides a BCR of 0.84, which is not acceptable.

A fourth measure, **annualized net benefits** (ANB), is obtained by subtracting *annualized costs* (AC) from *annualized benefits* (AB). Definitionally, annualized costs and benefits are those amounts that, if occurring each and every year without variation, would produce the same present values as the proposal. AC and AB can be determined by solving the following two polynomials:

$$\sum_{t=0}^{T} \frac{AC}{(1+d)^t} = \sum_{t=0}^{T} \frac{C_t}{(1+d)^t} \quad \text{and} \quad \sum_{t=0}^{T} \frac{AB}{(1+d)^t} = \sum_{t=0}^{T} \frac{B_t}{(1+d)^t}. \tag{3.7}$$

Hence, the mathematical act of annualizing effectively levels uneven streams of costs and benefits into two recurring amounts. In the same way, annualized *net* benefits is the recurring amount of net benefits yielding the same NPV as the proposal:

$$\text{Solve for ANB:} \quad \sum_{t=0}^{T} \frac{ANB}{(1+d)^t} = NPV = \sum_{t=0}^{T} \frac{NB_t}{(1+d)^t}. \tag{3.8}$$

The decision criterion here is that ANB should be positive if the proposal is to be accepted. Applied to the "showerhead water conservation project," for which we

---

11. The T roots of the IRR formula will normally be real valued (not complex numbers) and identical because NBs either are negative initially and become positive later or vice versa. When the temporal schedule of NBs exhibits multiple sign changes (e.g., from negative to positive and back to negative again), multiple IRR solutions to (3.3) are possible (Zerbe and Dively 1994, 201n).

have already computed a net present value of $-\$3.24$, we must determine the value of ANB for which

$$\sum_{t=0}^{5} \frac{ANB}{(1.15)^t} = -3.24. \tag{3.9}$$

Processed algebraically, (3.9) can be transformed as follows:

$$ANB \cdot \sum_{t=0}^{5} \frac{1}{(1.15)^t} = -3.24; \tag{3.10}$$

$$ANB \cdot 4.35 = -3.24; \tag{3.11}$$

$$ANB = -0.74. \tag{3.12}$$

Because the obtained value is negative, this is not a worthwhile project.

3.10 NPV versus the Others

Sometimes, it is incorrectly presumed that the purpose of cost-benefit analysis is to calculate a BCR, but NPV, IRR, or ANB can be an end result of cost-benefit analysis. Economists generally prefer NPV over IRR because NPV does not require polynomial root computation, and there are situations in which IRR yields errant advice when comparing alternative projects (Brealey and Myers 2003, chapter 5; Sassone and Schaffer 1978, 17–18) or assessing projects with negative net benefits in the future (Halvorsen and Ruby 1981, 49).

When determining whether a water proposal is a dynamic improvement, the BCR has one noteworthy advantage as compared to NPV and one primary disadvantage. In some situations, decision makers are faced with multiple projects that can be undertaken, but available funds are limited. If there are several alternatives having positive NPV yet all cannot be feasibly undertaken, then it would be nice to prioritize them so that the returns to available funds can be maximized. The BCR performs this task more directly because it explicitly tells us the benefits per unit of costs.[12] A possible disadvantage of the BCR metric is that it can occasionally be manipulated depending on the interpretation of benefits and costs (Lund 1992). For example, a public project objective may be to protect and enhance biodiversity (or environmental quality), and this objective may lead to proposals to replace the water that

12. Even here, the BCR is not a perfect tool unless it is only possible to select a single project due to the constraint. If the budget limitation makes it possible to select multiple projects, then some "trial and error" should be combined with the BCR measure (Au 1988).

formerly was habitat streamflow. (Prior water development has lessened streamflows in most regions.) Do such proposals entail a reduction in environmental costs or an increase in environmental benefits? That is, is the value of added biodiversity or environmental quality to be registered in the numerator or the denominator of the BCR formula? The answer matters for a BCR calculation, although it makes no difference in NPV.[13]

ANB is functionally equivalent to NPV. It has no strong advantages or disadvantages relative to NPV. In some decision-making forums involving noneconomists, ANB or its two components might be easier for people to understand, thereby yielding a possible advantage. A minor matter for proposal analysis is that ANB requires an additional computation that is not required for NPV, but that is ordinarily a small concern.

All of these decision criteria use the same information so they are, to a large extent, a transformation of units—like metric versus English measurement systems. Proposals are dynamic improvements if $NPV > 0$, $IRR > d$, $BCR > 1$, or $ANB > 0$. Other criteria are possible as well, but any that do not consider the time value of money, like the well-known "payback period" method, do not reliably support decision making (Sassone and Schaffer 1978, chapter 2).[14]

Thus far, the comparison of metrics has been confined to applications assessing dynamic improvement. A notable advantage of the NPV criterion is the direct manner in which it can be used for dynamic efficiency analysis. Maximizing IRR is not as practical because of the nonlinear way in which IRR depends on net benefits. IRR is, after all, the root of a high-degree polynomial in real-world settings. So maximizing IRR presents some technical challenges. Similarly, the fractional nature of the benefit-cost *ratio* introduces an unnecessary complication for the calculus of finding the most efficient decision(s) possible. The additional computation involved in obtaining ANB also limits the measure's practicality for optimization. Because of NPV's ease of use for matters of both dynamic improvement and dynamic efficiency, it is a fundamental tool of water resource economics.

3.11   Is Dynamic Efficiency/Improvement Neutral or Aggregate?

The additive nature of NPV suggests that it and related metrics are analogous to *aggregate* economic efficiency. This suggestion is true. Dynamic efficiency is an ag-

---

13. Consistently applied protocols such as reserving the denominator for all project implementation actions and the numerator for all project results might effectively eliminate this problem, yet such protocols are unnecessary precautions for NPV calculations.

14. Observe that the earlier showerhead example yields a payback period of four years. There are at least two problems: the value of the "payback dollars" is actually less than the value of the initial investment (because of time preference) and knowing the payback period does not tell us anything definitive about what we should do.

gregate approach to combining time-separated economic impacts. Whereas static economic efficiency of the aggregate variety weighs impacts by prices and incomes, and subsequently adds them (chapter 2), dynamic efficiency performs identically to static efficiency within a single time period, but it weighs using discounting when net benefits occur in different periods. This weighting significantly affects the results that are obtained, and it is for this reason that economists have ardently debated the choice of discount rate.

Given that neutral economic efficiency sidesteps aggregation over agents and thereby emphasizes a range of efficient outcomes instead of just one, it is interesting to ask whether there is a dynamic companion to neutral economic efficiency. Such a criterion has not been popularized as yet in economic methodology. Presumably, a neutral version of dynamic efficiency would operate without any discounting and would report economic impacts without aggregation. Its independence from discounting would render it best applied to long planning horizon issues involving multigenerational matters. Instead of making a policy or project recommendation on the basis of NPV, the analyst would estimate how the decision would impact net benefits in different time periods, and report those estimates without addition or discounting. Such an option could be attractive for policies or projects having long-term implications. As noted previously, intergenerational issues can raise doubts about the ethical application of discounting. When this occurs, it may be best to report impacts as a temporally indexed tabulation or description.

3.12 Dynamic Efficiency: A Two-Period Graphic Exposition

Whereas the computation of NPV is straightforward when examining whether we have a dynamic improvement, the analysis of dynamic efficiency is more complex. That's not entirely surprising because in dynamic efficiency we are looking for the ultimate dynamic improvement. To better appreciate the situation, it is worthwhile to apply a reinforcing device—the two-period model. This model uses the same three-axis system employed for figure 2.11 in the previous chapter. Because this tool limits us to two periods, and real-world issues involve many future periods, the primary purpose is to build understanding. It is also a useful device for penetrating the complexities of dynamic analysis when talking to clients and decision-making groups.

Suppose there is a planning task of allocating a limited supply of water among users in two consecutive periods. Because the water source is depletable, whatever water is used in period 0 will not be available in period 1. Suppose we have already done the analysis needed to determine MNB in each period.[15] In other words,

---

15. Recall from chapter 2 that MNB = MB − MC, where MB is inverted water demand and MC is the marginal cost of supplying water to customers.

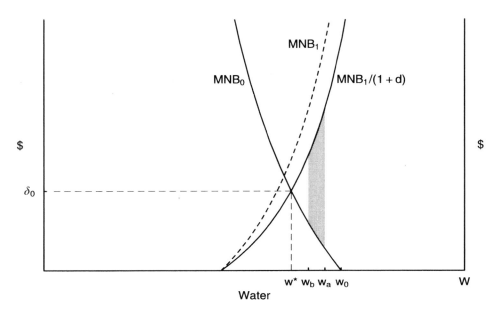

Figure 3.3
Dynamic efficiency and dynamic improvement

MNB_0 and MNB_1 are known. A simple extension of figure 2.11 is to place both curves on the graph, orienting the second one with respect to the right-hand origin as in figure 3.3. The length of the bottom axis is the amount of available water. To account for discounting, MNB_1 is rotated by dividing it by $1 + d$. The resulting curve is the present value of MNB_1.

The dynamically efficient allocation of water between the two periods is given by the intersection of MNB_0 and $MNB_1/(1 + d)$. In the figure this occurs at w*, which tells us how to allocate available water between the two periods. Knowing that allocation, we would then use the static methods of chapter 2 to determine how each period's water should be partitioned among the various users active in each period. Notice three crucial findings illustrated by this illuminating device:

· Increases in the discount rate will pivot discounted MNB_1 clockwise, resulting in less water for the second period. This observation indicates the strong role that the discount rate selection plays in dynamic efficiency.

· If we start with an intertemporal allocation other than w*, such as w_a, and propose a "policy" to move the water allocation closer to w*, such as w_b, that policy will be found to be a dynamic improvement. (You can use the information given here and in chapter 2 to verify that the NPV of this policy is positive and is equal to the shaded area of figure 3.3.)

· If period 0 users are charged δ_0 for every unit of natural water they consume (in addition to marginal processing costs), they will be motivated to use the optimal amount of water without further coercion.[16] In the absence of such a charge, however, they will underconserve water by consuming at w_0. All of these findings are important properties of dynamic efficiency in water allocation.

3.13 Dynamic Efficiency: The Basic Calculus

The graphic depiction of figure 3.3 is a two-period illustration of the many-period results attainable via the Lagrangian method of optimization. Adding a water constraint to equation (3.2) to obtain a clearly dynamic problem having the same spirit as figure 3.3, we obtain

$$\underset{w_0, w_1, \ldots, w_{T-1}}{\text{maximize}} \sum_{t=0}^{T-1} \frac{NB_t(w_t)}{(1+d)^t} \quad \text{subject to} \sum_{t=0}^{T-1} w_t = W. \tag{3.13}$$

Maximization using the Lagrangian procedure immediately yields

$$\frac{MNB_t}{(1+d)^t} = \delta_0 \quad \text{for all } t = 0, 1, \ldots, T-1, \tag{3.14}$$

where δ_0 is the introduced Lagrange multiplier. Knowing δ_0 can be useful, so economists have given it a formal name, **_marginal user cost_** (MUC). It is the period 0 value of scarce water in figure 3.3 and tells us, essentially, how to price depletion as noted in the last bulleted item above.

The T equations represented in (3.14) can be algebraically rewritten as

$$MNB_0 = \frac{MNB_1}{1+d} = \frac{MNB_2}{(1+d)^2} = \frac{MNB_3}{(1+d)^3} = \cdots = \frac{MNB_{T-1}}{(1+d)^{T-1}} = \delta_0. \tag{3.15}$$

Written this way, the $MNB_0 = MNB_1/(1+d)$ element forming the basis of figure 3.3 is clearly evident, and it is also seen how this dynamic efficiency requirement can be extended when we must care for many periods instead of just two. When faced with a water issue in which some parameter requires dynamic optimization, the specific first-order conditions will depend on the dynamic relationship(s), and they may appear different than those of (3.14) or (3.15), but something similar in structure will likely emerge.

---

16. This proposed charge is in addition to the marginal cost charge already implicit to the construction of MNB_0. The appropriate price of water to consumers is then $\delta_0 + MC$. This and other important pricing implications of water resource economics will be more fully developed in chapter 8.

Another useful observation concerns the change in δ_0 over time. If problem (3.13) is rewritten as soon as period 0 has expired (and it is time to decide w_1), analogous results for (3.14) and (3.15) are obtained. Comparing these with the prior results, it is seen how the value of depletable water grows over time:

$$\delta_1 = (1 + d)\delta_0, \tag{3.16}$$

which is generalizable to

$$\delta_{t+1} = (1 + d)\delta_t \quad \text{or} \quad \delta_{t+n} = (1 + d)^n \delta_t. \tag{3.17}$$

Hence, for a dynamically efficient allocation the value of the water resource must grow over time at the rate of discount. This is quite useful for our work. Equation (3.17) is known as Hotelling's rule in recognition of its originator (Hotelling 1931). Because these results stem from the growing *real* value of depletable water, it is incorrect to refer to it as *inflation*. If there is also inflation present, it must be added to d.

3.14   A Fundamental Example: Drawing from a Reservoir

Let's construct an illustrative dynamic setting that one can modify and improve to study realistic circumstances. (For example, if pumping costs are added to the model, optimal ground water depletion can be investigated.) Assume that there is a "reservoir" serving a city, and the planning task is to schedule reservoir releases over the next forty years. Hence, the problem has forty decision variables, but we are really interested in determining them so the first one can be implemented: "Planning for the future allows us to make good decisions today." Let the city be Little Town of the prior chapter, initially serving five thousand households. Whereas the demand and cost parameters given previously for Little Town pertained to December water use, let us pretend that these are annual water use parameters. As a new wrinkle, the number of households is growing at g percent per year due to population growth.

To make the setting more interesting, the amount of water initially contained in the reservoir plus water inflows over the forty years are inadequate to allow static efficiency to occur every year. (Recall that this occurs at a water level where MNB = 0 each year.) Suppose that 160 million gallons are in the reservoir initially, and inflows are 27 million gallons every year.

Years are indexed 0 to 39. Using the constant elasticity demand form and a demand elasticity of -0.5, thousands of gallons demanded in period t is given by

$$w_t = (1 + g)^t 60622p^{-0.5}, \tag{3.18}$$

as demonstrated previously within equation (2.19) (except for the nonzero growth factor, g). To obtain total benefits in period t, (3.18) must be solved for p (which is the same as marginal benefits) and integrated across the range of consumed water from 0 to w_t. Integration is a problem for this demand form because it is infinitely valued at $w = 0$. This problem can be sidestepped if we begin the integration range above 0, but below the relevant scheduling range. Beginning at one million gallons will work. *Truncated* total benefits in year t, as a function of water consumption, are as follows:[17]

$$B_t(w_t) = \int_{1000}^{w_t} MB_t \, dw_t = 3.675 \times 10^9 (1+g)^{2t} \left(\frac{1}{1000} - \frac{1}{w_t} \right). \tag{3.19}$$

Total costs are also the same as before:

$$C_t(w_t) = 50000 + 1.95w_t + 0.000015w_t^2. \tag{3.20}$$

This is all the information needed to fully specify NPV as a function of the water consumption schedule once both growth and discount rates are selected. Let's use a growth rate of 1 percent and a discount rate of 6 percent. Although it is too lengthy to write out here, forty substitutions of (3.19) and (3.20) into the equation below completely specifies the objective function as a function of the forty decision variables.

$$NPV(\mathbf{w}) = \sum_{t=0}^{39} \frac{B_t(w_t) - C_t(w_t)}{1.06^t}. \tag{3.21}$$

All that remains is to formalize the hydrology into mathematical constraints and solve the optimization problem. The manner in which the constraints are written influences the optimization method, and higher-level optimization techniques are normally employed for dynamic problems such as this. (See appendix 3.B of this chapter for an overview and literature resources.) The constraint set is most accurately written as follows:

$$\left. \begin{array}{l} w_t \leq R_t \quad \text{for all} \quad t = 0, 1, \ldots, 39, \\ R_0 = 160000 + 27000, \quad \text{and} \\ R_t = R_{t-1} + 27000 - w_{t-1} \quad \text{for all} \quad t = 1, 2, \ldots, 39, \end{array} \right\} \tag{3.22}$$

where R_t indicates the amount of water contained in the reservoir at the beginning of year t. Equations (3.22) include the constraints that in each period, we cannot use

17. These are not really the total benefits because the integral commences at one million gallons instead of zero. Doing things this way does not alter the optimization results because the calculus of optimization responds to slopes, and this truncation does not modify the slope of the TB function.

more water than is in the reservoir; during the first year, available water is equal to the initial amount in the reservoir plus the annual inflow; and reservoir water quantity in each year is equal to the reservoir quantity one year ago plus annual inflow and minus the amount withdrawn last year.

In settings like this, where there is ample storage and inflows are known, it may be possible to collapse the annual constraints into a single cumulative constraint obtained by combining the several elements of the constraint set above. The resulting constraint is:

$$\sum_{t=0}^{39} w_t \leq 160000 + 40 \cdot 27000. \tag{3.23}$$

We can proceed by maximizing objective function (3.21) subject to (3.23) because the simple nature of this constraint allows for the use of the Lagrangian method of optimization. Still, care must be exercised, and the resulting schedule of reservoir storage should be checked to verify that the optimizing solution never results in a negative reservoir level. That is, each part of (3.22) must be obeyed.

This problem is too complicated to solve by hand, so one would normally resort to one of several available computer packages. Here, the problem is formulated as a Mathematica program and solved using a numerical, Lagrangian-based algorithm. The important aspects of the solution are then summarized using Mathematica to create figure 3.4. In the figure, water units are also thousands of gallons.

The solution is the series of starred points labeled as w_t^*. For context, the dotted line placed at thirty-one million gallons is an equal apportionment of available water across all periods. For additional context, the series s_t is the amount of statically efficient water that would be consumed if the reservoir had enough water in it and no planning for the future were performed. That is, s_t will occur if the net benefits are maximized in each period. Because the number of households in the city is growing and causing water demand growth, the s_t series is rising over time. R_t^* is the amount of water annually available in the reservoir as the optimizing plan, w_t^*, is followed.

Notice that the amount of water used in early periods is higher than in later periods even though the demand in later periods is certainly higher. This is an artifact of discounting. The larger the discount rate, the more pronounced this will become. On the other hand, notice that forward planning causes all periods to use less water than they would if they followed a static efficiency objective. The sacrifice made in period 0, $s_0 - w_0^*$, is not large, but it is positive. As an additional note, the shadow price variable for this problem, recognizable as δ_0 in figure 3.3 and equation (3.14), turns out to be 0.79 for this problem. Hence, charging people in period 0 an extra seventy-nine cents per thousand gallons (above their marginal costs as given by the derivative of (3.20) with respect to w_0) will induce them to behave optimally. This type of policy

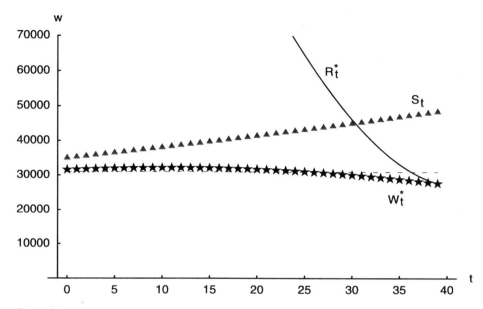

Figure 3.4
Optimal water use scheduling

is sufficiently important to justify more refined inspection, which we will undertake in chapter 8.

3.15 Extendable in Many Possible Directions

The prior exercise provides some useful insights into dynamic efficiency and the impact of discounting. The most significant of these revelations are that:

• Planning for the future with a dynamic efficiency objective causes less water to be used in early periods as compared to a simple efficiency goal. The extent of the difference depends on the discount rate as well as future marginal net benefits.

• Dynamically efficient levels of water use can be achieved with an appropriate revision of water price.

Many interesting enhancements of the "drawing from a reservoir" setting are possible. For this reason, it constitutes a basic model usable as a jumping off point for more complex inquiries. For example,

• withdrawals of water from the reservoir may involve pumping costs, such as when the reservoir is an underground water body;

• releases from the reservoir may generate additional benefits, such as occur with hydroelectricity;

• time steps need not be years—they can be months, days, or decades;

• demand or supply parameters may involve seasonality such as would occur with a monthly time step and summer demand peaks;

• water sitting in a reservoir may incur losses, such as evaporation and seepage; or

• stored water may generate recreational benefits dependent on the amount of water in the reservoir.

Thus, the notion of NPV maximization subject to constraints can be modified to investigate many issues involving water resource dynamics. In general, these problems will necessitate higher-level optimization techniques, but the prior example does reveal much about the typical character of solutions to these problems.

3.16   How Fast Should Ground Water Be Depleted?

Underground water bodies (aquifers) may receive periodic or continuous recharge from other parts of the hydrologic cycle. If an aquifer's natural and pumped discharge exceeds its recharge, then depletion and eventual loss of the aquifer's service are social concerns. Of course, some aquifers receive negligible recharge, so pumping is more problematic in these cases. Recharge can be augmented by *artificial recharge*, defined as purposeful operations conveying surface water into underground storage, but most of humanity's ground water activities involve one-way withdrawal. *Mining* is said to occur when the rate of pumping exceeds the rate of aquifer recharge. The usual public sentiment is that ground water mining is an undesirable thing.

Although economic findings are critical of it, perhaps the oldest concept advising us about ground water pumping is *safe yield*, first defined in 1915 (Domenico 1972, 43). The engineering-oriented water management literature now contains several perspectives on safe yield. All of these emphasize pumpage limitations so that bad hydrologic consequences will be avoided in the future (Young 1970). According to various safe yield concepts, annual pumping should be low enough *not* to either lower an aquifer's water table, use up the aquifer anytime during the next Z years, induce aquifer contamination by neighboring "bad" water, and/or interfere with the legal rights (surface or ground) of other water users. Some of these requirements are stricter than others, but the unifying message of all safe yield definitions is "use without impairment."

A newer concept is that of *sustainability*, a term that has achieved buzzword status in recent years. In common usage, sustainable ground water pumping is redundant with safe yield. Both focus on the repeatability with which an aquifer can be utilized;

as long as current users do not harm the productivity of a ground water resource "too much," this resource can continue to serve users in future years, perhaps even in future generations. It is easy to salute the moral code involved here. If our collective footprint on ground water resources is not too great, use can be perpetuated for a long time, perhaps indefinitely.

One of the difficulties with these visions of safe yield and sustainability is that they do not explain current use patterns. Ground water is being mined throughout the world. Can wrongful decision making be that widespread? As a second difficulty, it is hypocritical to rail against ground water mining while accepting the mining of other resources, not just fossil fuels, but resources that, like water, might be renewable and recyclable. Is ground water so unique that it warrants immunity from depletion? After all, the hydrologic cycle guarantees that water will be available in other forms once ground water is depleted. A third problem is the variety of safe yield concepts and their consequent imprecision. It is confusing to have multiple safe/sustainable yield definitions unless a preferred one can be identified. One hasn't.

As a fourth and most unsatisfying problem, physical criteria such as safe yield and aquifer sustainability lack human reference (Toman 1994). Instead of thinking about the repeatability of ground water use, why not emphasize what we really care about—the repeatability of human welfare? In the resource and environmental economics literature, inquiries about sustainability understand that depletable natural resources are always in decline due to their exploitation by humankind. Yet each generation seems to be successively better off than the one preceding it.[18] Historically, the depletion of resources has been overcome in some way(s). A primary way is that some economic activities create physical capital (machines, equipment, buildings, and infrastructure) and human capital (knowledge, technology, and experience) that have, up to recent times anyway, offset the sacrifice in natural capital (resources such as water, petroleum, and timber). From this perspective, it might even be claimed that there is an opportunity cost for *not consuming* resources such as ground water bodies at the "proper" depletion rate. If human advance through capital formation depends on the expenditure of natural capital such as water, then it is conceivable that safe yield ideals are actually counterproductive. That is, if the development of advanced physical and human capital is stalled in order for future people to have more natural capital, will they be any better off? There would be a stronger basis for a preservationist argument if we were addressing something truly unique (like

18. It is not good to be too confident about this point, for there is no guarantee of ever-rising welfare even when economically measured output (e.g., gross domestic product) is rising on a per capita basis. Economics does not regard output measures such as gross domestic product as adequate measures of our well being because output measures omit too much. There is even evidence that the U.S. may have turned the corner a generation ago, and per capita welfare may be in decline now (⟨http://www.redefiningprogress .org/projects/gpi/⟩).

an individual species, an irreplaceable resource, or a special natural monument), but here we are merely considering ground water for which surface water is an excellent substitute.

Answering questions about the trade-off between natural and advanced capital is always tough to do, but treating the issue accurately is helpful. Perhaps safe yield guidance is too conservative because it does not engage the larger question of human welfare. As an alternative, NPV maximization offers a point of human reference instead of physical reference. Economists have long championed dynamic efficiency, and some hydrologists have come to regard it as a crucial tool for analyzing ground water depletion (Domenico, Anderson, and Case 1968; Domenico 1972, sec. 3.2). Dynamic efficiency tells us that mining is desirable as long as each pumped gallon provides benefits in excess of its costs. Most important, the costs considered here must include MUCs. Because MUC is the future value of the scarce resource, discounted to present terms, concern for the future is explicit. If water from all sources is locally scarce, then MUC is high and the social incentive to conserve will be strong. Empirically, this kind of analysis strongly resembles the prior drawing from a reservoir example. Only pumping costs might have been omitted in that example. The results illustrated by the water use trajectory over time in figure 3.4 are typical for recommended ground water use trajectories as well. In the face of constant or even slowly rising water demand, optimal ground water pumping declines over time, as will the water table. For literature examples, see Burt (1964, 1967), Provencher (1993), and/or Krulce, Roumasset, and Wilson (1997, includes Mathematica code).

Economically oriented investigations lack interest in whether or not ground water mining should occur. The real issue lies in determining the optimal rate of pumping, and as an extension, whether or not society is achieving it at each moment in time. Rarely will the optimal pumping rate be constant over time, as suggested by physically based advice such as safe yield. This is not to say that physical constraints are not binding. It is just that realistically, "all ground water developments initially mine water, and finally do not" (Balleau 1988, 280).

Economics indicates that the most challenging policy issue for ground water depletion is to design public strategies, including property assignments and pricing rules, that encourage efficient behavior by individual agents. We shall examine these important topics more deeply in the coming chapter. For now, it suffices to understand that the drawing from a reservoir example is sufficiently extendable to encompass matters of ground water depletion.

3.17 Summary

The notion of discount rate is crucial for doing any dynamic analysis pertaining to water resources. The social discount rate that might be employed for assessing public policies or public projects arises, fundamentally, from the private rates of time preference psychologically held by individual agents, but it is difficult to be more precise. Clearly, agents making private dynamic decisions are to use their private discount rate in resolving their preferred choices. Yet the identification of a single social discount rate to be applied in social decision making is more complex because of the immense importance of this parameter and its ethical basis. As a consequence of the ethical foundations of discounting, there are divergent positions on its precise value, all of which are admissible to some extent. This is certainly an area in which economic advice is not as resolute as we would like. When a social discount rate is needed, perhaps the best advice is to reconsult the midchapter summary section for this matter.

The two most prevalent versions of dynamic analysis are dynamic improvement and dynamic efficiency. A dynamic improvement is a decision that will increase dynamic efficiency. A dynamically efficient decision is a decision maximizing dynamic efficiency. The primary tool for assessing both versions is NPV. To evaluate dynamic improvement, NPV is evaluated to see if it is positive for the proposed decision. To evaluate dynamic efficiency, NPV is maximized with respect to a specific parameter (e.g., how much water to use). Analytic tools similar to NPV—such as IRR, BCR, or ANB—can sometimes be employed in lieu of NPV for analyses of dynamic improvement, but they are not as tractable for evaluating dynamic efficiency.

As a criterion for assessing the optimality of water use over time, dynamic efficiency is a primary tool. It can be readily operationalized, and empirical optimization models can be used to investigate the scheduling of water use over time. Optimal ground water depletion is an important issue for which such studies can be conducted.

3.18 Exercises

1. The local utility charges Sand City households $2.50 per thousand gallons of metered water. Analysts figure this rate omits 50¢ in natural water value, but city leaders are opposed to an efficient rate increase. As a band-aid, the city utility is contemplating a new rebate program for people who install permanent conservation fixtures in their homes. The purpose of the program is to promote conservation investments that would not occur otherwise. As a first step, subsidizing low gallon-per-flush (gpf) toilets is going to be tried. How big of a rebate per toilet is justifiable under the following assumptions?

· Each replaced toilet is expected to save thirty gallons per day.

· Whereas a toilet possesses a longer average life than fifteen years, analysts expect all residential toilets to be low gpf in fifteen years, even without this program, because rising rates will eventually encourage everyone to make the conversion.

· There are no social costs for disposing of old toilets.

· Except for their water use, low gpf toilets have no other advantages or disadvantages.

· Sand City's discount rate is 5 percent.

2. Redraw figure 3.3 omitting w_b, w_a, and the shaded area. Suppose that a new water conservation technology is discovered, but it cannot be established quickly enough for use in period 0. Suppose that this technology will be widely applied in period 1, however, and this fact is known in period 0. What, if anything, happens to dynamically efficient water use in period 0, dynamically efficient water use in period 1, marginal user cost, and retail water price? Show all of these results, making appropriate modifications to your figure by shifting the proper curve(s). (Other scenarios can be quickly examined using figure 3.3 as a basic tool. They include modified population projections or irrigated crop prices, modified water processing costs due to changing energy or labor costs, and changes to the discount rate.)

3. Suppose the average market-implied return on U.S. Treasury bonds has been 4.9 percent during the past year while the rate of inflation was 1.4 percent. What real and nominal social discount rates are indicated by these data?

4. A revolving loan fund has just been established by the state. Its purpose is to provide money for the conservation projects undertaken by irrigation districts. The state can borrow more cheaply than districts, so passing along this borrowing ability might lessen water use. Districts repayments will include the same interest paid by the state, and all repayments will be returned to the fund for additional projects. Loan applicants are expected to submit a properly computed BCR for their intended project. The state is currently issuing bonds at 3.5 percent (real) to initiate the revolving fund, and program managers are wondering what discount rate to tell districts to use in their computation of BCR. If managers wanted to use the opportunity cost of capital, what is its numerical value? Use the parameters given in note 6 while recognizing that this is a state policy instead of a national one.

5. How are the return flow results of chapter 2 (figure 2.12 and equation [2.33]) modified if return flow does not become available for reuse until the next period?

6. Make up a three-period "project" for periods 0–2 by selecting dollar amounts for project-caused costs and benefits in all three periods (six numbers). Make sure net benefits have a differing sign in the first and last periods. Use these values and a reasonable social discount rate to compute NPV, IRR, BCR, and ANB.

7. A group of people are exclusive users of an enclosed stock of stored water. Precipitation and other water supplies are absent in the desert where these people live. The group wishes to exploit their water for three periods, after which they will relocate. Their retail water demand is $w = 20 - p$ in every period. The total costs of convert-

ing natural water to retail water is $C = 24 + 0.5w^2$ in every period. There are no conveyance or transformation losses of any kind. Because they possess twenty-two units of stored water, it is required that $w_0 + w_1 + w_2 \leq 22$. Use this information together with equation (3.15) to determine the optimal schedule of water use, and marginal user costs during the first period. The applicable social discount rate is 50 percent.

Appendix 3.A: Amortization

It is useful to have shortcuts relating a capital asset's value to a smoothed one-period value. If V is asset value and v is the asset's repeating, single-period use value, then it is definitionally true that

$$V_t^T = \sum_{\tau=t}^{T} \frac{v}{(1+d)^\tau}$$

$$= v \cdot \sum_{\tau=t}^{T} \frac{1}{(1+d)^\tau} \tag{3.24}$$

where t is the time index, T is the planning horizon, and d is the discount rate. Knowing any three of the four variables (V, v, T, d) in this equation permits the fourth to be computed. As a geometric series, the $\sum_{t=0}^{T} \ldots$ term can be reduced to a more readily computable expression that greatly simplifies certain types of analysis. For an infinite planning horizon,

$$\sum_{t=0}^{\infty} \frac{1}{(1+d)^t} = \frac{1}{1 - \frac{1}{1+d}} = \frac{1+d}{d}, \tag{3.25}$$

so for infinite T, (3.24) becomes

$$V_0^\infty = v \cdot \sum_{t=0}^{\infty} \frac{1}{(1+d)^t} = v \cdot \frac{1+d}{d}. \tag{3.26}$$

Using the same procedure when the summation commences at $t = 1$ instead of $t = 0$:

$$V_1^\infty = v \cdot \sum_{t=1}^{\infty} \frac{1}{(1+d)^t} = v \cdot \frac{1}{d}. \tag{3.27}$$

To obtain a similar shortcut for finite planning horizons, we can still exploit the known sum of a geometric series by taking a difference between two series sums.

One begins at t = 0 and the other begins at t = T + 1. We have to apply the mechanics behind (3.25) twice and do some algebraic simplifications:

$$\sum_{t=0}^{T} \frac{1}{(1+d)^t} = \sum_{t=0}^{\infty} \frac{1}{(1+d)^t} - \sum_{t=T+1}^{\infty} \frac{1}{(1+d)^t} \tag{3.28}$$

$$= \frac{1+d}{d} - \frac{\dfrac{1}{(1+d)^{T+1}}}{1 - \dfrac{1}{1+d}} \tag{3.29}$$

$$= \frac{1+d}{d} - \frac{\dfrac{1}{(1+d)^{T}}}{d} \tag{3.30}$$

$$= \frac{(1+d) - (1+d)^{-T}}{d}. \tag{3.31}$$

More algebra is possible, but the last result is easy to apply in practice. Using it, we have

$$V_0^T = v \cdot \sum_{t=0}^{T} \frac{1}{(1+d)^t} = v \cdot \frac{(1+d) - (1+d)^{-T}}{d}. \tag{3.32}$$

Equations (3.26), (3.27), and (3.32) are often useful in the conduct of water resource economics, and they will be called on later in this text.

Appendix 3.B: Advanced Methods of Dynamic Optimization

The challenge of dynamic optimization is the addition of a dimension. Not only do we want to determine the optimal levels of various decision variables; we also want to determine their levels for each point in time across some time interval. Methods such as Lagrangian optimization or linear programming can sometimes be adapted to handle the new complexity, but other methods offer greater power and range. Advanced methods of optimization applicable to dynamic circumstances include dynamic programming, optimal control, and calculus of variations. Each possesses advantages in particular settings, although the latter method's advantages are slight. In situations where more than one of these techniques is applicable, they can be expected to produce the same results.

Dynamic programming is well suited for discretized, numerical solution (by computer) where objectives and constraints are not continuously represented but are "sampled" at chosen points. This is analogous to the conduct of linear programming where multiple, fixed "activities" are available, and one wishes to determine an optimal selection of activities. The activities themselves are finite in number and are established by the investigator. Dynamic programming is capable of solving discrete-time, continuous-decision problems of water resource significance, and it is finding increased application for such problem classes. Dynamic programming is also a good choice for situations involving uncertainty.

The comparative advantage of *optimal control* usually lies in the investigation of circumstances where time is continuous (not just $t = 1, 2, \ldots$) and attention is not restricted to preselected activity levels. Thus, optimal control is prevalent in theoretical inquiries. The additional detail and demands of continuous settings imposes analytic costs, however, so many applied problems favor dynamic programming as the preferred methodology. *Calculus of variations* is also applicable for continuous scenarios, but optimal control has sufficient generality to handle these too. Moreover, calculus of variations has less scope in that it cannot handle every problem solvable via optimal control.

Because dynamic programming and optimal control can be applied to dynamic efficiency problems such as the drawing from a reservoir example, as well as its extensions and theoretical generalizations, and because these methods can capture constraint sets more satisfactorily than the Lagrangian method, they are useful tools for professional water resource economists. They can be difficult to master, though. Economists' favorite textbook resources for learning about these methods include Chiang (1992), Intriligator (1971), Kamien and Schwartz (1991), Kennedy (1988), Leonard and Van Long (1992), and Stokey and Lucas (1989). For additional study incorporating natural resource depletion, consult Conrad and Clark (1987), Dasgupta and Heal (1979), Howe (1979), and Krautkraemer (1998).

4 Social Institutions

How might our rules help us achieve our goals?

The stage is well set to now consider the institutions that guide water use. Water management institutions are seriously intertwined with all aspects of water planning, including project analysis. Indeed, it is difficult to craft any good public decisions for water until one understands the many institutional features and options that are present.

Although the approach of this chapter may look like a departure from the content and methods of the prior two chapters, the only true departure is the reduced employment of mathematics to illuminate our subject. We are still interested in pursuing the alternative visions of efficiency isolated previously. Here, the primary objective is to search for institutions that enhance efficiency.

Economics offers exceptional insights when the water management task is to select, modify, or interpret institutions, as is often the situation. The term "institutions" has a different meaning than "organizations" in economic parlance: "Institutions are the humanly devised constraints that structure political, economic and social interaction. They consist of both informal constraints (sanctions, taboos, customs, traditions, and codes of conduct), and formal rules (constitutions, laws, property rights)" (North 1991, 97; North earned a Nobel Memorial Prize in 1993 for his contributions to institutional economics). Thus, **institutions** are the *informal and formal rules* forming the "system of mutual coercion" by which humans relate to one another (Samuels 1972, 64). Thought of another way, "institutions are sets of ordered relationships among people which define their rights, exposure to the rights of others, privileges, and responsibilities" (Schmid 1972, 893). Institutions are the instruments we employ to avoid chaos, standardize our interactions, and promote human welfare. The economy is an important part of this system. As "humanly devised" methods for people to interact with one another, the notions of *markets* and *prices* are important institutions, both in general application and for water management. Every *policy* that can be applied to water management problems is also an institution. Hence, institutional choice is highly relevant to us.

Everyone knows that a species' survival is a consequence of its ability to compete, and that business enterprises also endure or perish based on their capacities to outperform rivals. Just as species supplant one another over time, so do business ventures. A few percentage points in profitability between two firms can lead to expansion of one and dismantling of the other.

Less well-known is the idea that institutions (rules) hold their own struggles to see which will survive and which will be abandoned. These contests can be waged over long periods of time, so it may be difficult to observe the process. From a social perspective, each institution can hinder or help. Societies that employ hindering rules will chafe under the strain. Societies with helpful rules can flourish. As in the biological and business worlds, societies with weakening institutions are sometimes overrun (economically, culturally, or even militarily) by societies with more encouraging institutions.

The economic literature indicates that the success of countries is closely linked to their institutional choices and that bad choices are not necessarily eliminated by internal forces (Olson 1982), so it is advisable to be attentive to these choices. One reason bad institutions can persist is because agents benefiting from weak rules may have sufficient influence to block change even when change presents net benefits for society at large. The lesson here is that the same observations apply for states, cities, and water districts. Like adaptive species and opportunistic firms, all societies can improve their conditions by refining their institutions. Rules can be changed over time. It is socially productive to periodically update institutions to reset them for changing preferences, technologies, and scarcities. Institutions that served well under one set of scarcity conditions may be ill tuned to new conditions.

In the next part of this chapter, we begin developing the important economic concepts needed to understand institutional choice in general settings. Once all the needed tools are in place, we will turn to the key water-specific institutions, especially laws.

Part I: The Economics of Institutions

4.1   What If You Had to Choose?

Suppose that substance X has been around forever, but there are no institutions governing its use because it has no known applications. No one is interested in it, so no rules have ever been formulated. Then, overnight, multiple applications for X are discovered. Businesses and individuals begin to gather as much X as they can because they can use it or profit from it. Soon, there's not enough X to go around, and tension rises among its demand groups. One or more new institutions are needed if we are to achieve the orderly development of resource X. Why do we want orderly development? Among other things, we do not want people to be injured in confrontations over X; it is socially advantageous for X to be harvested as cheaply as possible and applied to its most highly valued uses (efficiency); and if it is an exhaustible resource, we want to conserve the right amount of X for the future (dynamic efficiency). Given these social desires, what institutions should we choose?

One may feel there is no need for rules to allocate limited X among people. After all, we can use the analytic methods of the prior two chapters to solve for the optimal allocation of X. Once MB and MC information for X is obtained, optimal allocations of X across uses and time can be calculated. After performing these computations, why not simply follow the advice?

The simplistic response to this suggestion is as follows: if this is to be the manner in which X is to be allocated, then we have adopted a particular institution. Institutional selection has not been sidestepped at all. The adopted rule is to determine an X allocation maximizing net benefits or net present value, and then to apply that allocation by decree. This is a form of centralized planning. Centralized planning occurs when a governmental authority possesses allocative duties.

The deeper response to this suggestion is that "optimize and decree" institutions are not resilient in the face of change. Given that MB and MC functions are always changing, it is preferable to establish institutions pertaining to a *process* of allocation. That is, particularized allocations become inefficient over time—sometimes quite quickly—so society is often better served if a continual process of efficient allocation can be identified. A crucial aspect of such a system pertains to the choice of property form. *Property* delimits who is empowered to use any given resource, and the extent of their powers and responsibilities.

Available Property Forms

In the absence of more specific information, it will be difficult to select a preferred institutional regime for managing X, but it is possible to lay out four fundamental alternatives. The initial institutional setting described for X is one of open access. An ***open access resource*** is a resource having no rules establishing conditions for its use. Anyone can use it and use as much as they like—first come, first serve describes this situation. In today's world, you will be hard-pressed to find an example of a completely open access resource. Over the millennia during which humans have harnessed enumerable resources, we have established and revised rules for nearly everything. Not all of these rules are codified (written down), but even informal customs and agreements constitute institutions. Hence, if you are contemplating a resource setting and think it may be one of open access, you are probably not looking closely enough. Visit with the resource users and you will uncover the guiding institutions.

In spite of the virtual nonexistence of open access resources, it is a useful backdrop concept against which other rules can be contrasted. Open access constitutes a polar extreme—useful for defining the endpoint of a spectrum of rule types. In the historical chain of events, as people have discovered uses for a new resource, we have abandoned open access for that resource and have typically adopted a second form of allowed use: common property. A **common property resource** is owned "in common" and managed according to the adopted social institutions of the "common" (Ciriacy-Wantrup and Bishop 1975). Such institutions may provide for an elaborate management program or leave management decisions to the group composing the common. Here, the *common* refers to the entirety of people enjoying similar rights to resource access. Well-acknowledged examples of common property resources include fisheries, pastoral lands used for grazing, the atmosphere, and many water resource settings. Depending on the circumstances, the common may be composed of anything from a few people to the world's population.

Common property resources are distinguishable from open access resources in that common property embeds conditions of use and rules for who can use the resource. Open access entails no such restraints.

For example, an oceanside town may contain a number of lobster fishermen who benefit from an evolving set of traditions governing who can catch lobster (who can be a member of the common), how many traps each may deploy, size limits, prohibited seasons, inherited fishing grounds, or daily harvest allowances. Regardless of whether these rules are set by Congress or annually renewed at a local pub, they may promote the efficient use of lobster resources and may be the most efficient available institutional structure for managing the resource.

It is too bad that the now-popular phrase "tragedy of the commons" derived from Garrett Hardin's impactful article (1968) wasn't called "tragedy of open access" instead (Turner, Pearce, and Bateman 1993, 210). *Open access* implies an absence of management rules, and it is destined to fail for anything we might call a resource. *Common property* implies no such absence of rules, although it is often true that specific common property rules are outdated and ill tuned to a resource's current scarcity level. There is great variety in the types of common property institutions that may be deployed, as the lobster fishery example begins to illustrate, and it is often possible to replace obsolete common property rules with better ones (Ostrom 1990). In any case, one cannot conclude that certain institutions are inefficient merely because they constitute common property, as the phrase tragedy of the commons insinuates.

A **state property resource** refers to situations in which a resource is expressly owned by a government. In ordinary application, an agency of a government will establish rules that agents must follow when they use the resource. In centrally planned economies, which are increasingly rare because they underperform relative to other systems, the state property form is heavily used. In this case, the government performs most decision making, specifying how things are to be used and in what quantities. In less rigid application common to many nations, state property allows the state to exclude certain types of uses and limit any use as long as the controlling agency employs accepted procedures for establishing its rules. State-approved uses may be freely undertaken, or agents may have to pay a fee. State property may coexist with other property forms, such as when part of the resource is state owned. For example, some portion of a society's land may be owned and managed by the state (parks, forests, etc.) while other portions are privately or commonly held. The same can be true of water resources, and this possibility will be examined in the second part of this chapter.

The fourth and final category of rule forms is private property. A ***private property resource*** has been partitioned among individual agents and can be transferred by an owner to someone else. In the normal chain of events, a society will only adopt private property institutions for a resource after it has been applying common or state property institutions to the resource and heightened scarcity induces a shift to private property. In most cases, the shift can be portrayed as a historically evolving process, perhaps taking hundreds of years, in which common/state property institutions are developed to manage new resources, common/state property institutions are progressively refined to deal with ever-rising scarcity, and the resource is eventually allocated (perhaps across members of a common) as well-defined and transferable private property rights. The last step in this process may never occur. Or it may be the product of various mechanisms: possibly through a series of court decisions, deliberations among common members or within a government, extended application of prior traditions or legal rules, or even by forcible appropriation of the resource by internal agents or outsiders with a tradition of private property.[1] Or we might skip the intermediate steps altogether, and immediately adopt private property for new resources. Following the transition to private property, it is still quite possible that private powers will be adjusted occasionally to sort out conflicting rights and adapt to changing technologies and social preferences.

The important feature of private property is that the possibility of trade unlocks resources from their established use and development patterns. Private property— not open access, common property, or state property—is the foundation of market activity. Trading produces prices, and prices are the signals that communicate rela-

---

1. Property rights to an ore within the earth's crust *may* be inferred from preexisting property rights to overlying land, for example. Also, appropriative actions must be sanctioned by a government before the "owners" can be said to hold a property right.

tive value. These signals induce production and consumption behavior that tend to be in tune with actual scarcity levels. For this reason, many economists view private property as the pinnacle of institutional innovation.

If private property is so advantageous, one is inclined to ask, Why mess around with common or state property at all? Why don't we assign private property rights to *all* resources? There are three general reasons why a full transition to private property may be infeasible or undesirable:

1. Establishing private property in natural water replaces group or state ownership with a set of individual and distinct owners, so there are likely to be equity issues over the fair partitioning of the resource. If the user group is large and the policy change to private property requires widespread agreement, the inertia of trying to placate everyone may be difficult to overcome. If some members of the user group believe that they will lose access (receive property rights lower than their typical use levels), they in particular and a sympathetic society in general may be unsupportive of a move to private property.

2. Private property is more expensive to support than common property. The initial division can be expensive. Thereafter, records must be maintained regarding ownership and transfers, and "boundaries" must be enforced. In some fashion, individual use must be measured to ensure compliance with each agent's held rights. Conflicting claims will arise and require resolution, often by the judicial system. While these same classes of operational costs can be encountered under other property systems, the refined nature of private property can be accompanied by greater costs. In circumstances such as these, it is not always clear if the increased benefits of private property are sufficient to justify the greater costs.

3. There are technical situations such as externalities and public goods that may not be remedied by private property. Indeed, these issues may be aggravated. Consideration of these technical problems is postponed until more rigor can be established regarding the prospective efficiency of a system of markets (as we shall soon see below).

How Should We Choose?

Returning to substance X, which is now resource X because we have discovered human uses for it, what institutional structure should we select? The primary choice is between common property, state property, and private property, but that is a simplification. There are a great many variations of common property, and they are too numerous to contemplate. Later in this chapter, as we discuss institutional alternatives pertaining only to water, some of the options will be identified as common property forms and it will be useful to understand why. Even in the case of private property, there are alternative selections. For example, should each owner be granted a fixed amount of X or a share/percentage of total X? Will the property right expire after a fixed time period? Can the owners do anything they wish with the resource, such as destroying it or letting it sit idle? Will the owner's interests in X be protected by a *property rule* requiring one's agreement prior to transfer of the property or a *liability rule* granting compensation should anyone else decide to infringe on one's property (Kaplow and Shavell 1996)? Given all the variants of common, state, and private property, how should we decide?

While any rule society might establish can be revisited and revised, it is likely that each selected institution is going to be around for a while (Howitt 2002). Institutional change is too stressful and expensive to pursue often. Hence, each new rule set is going to have some permanence. Because water users must make capital expenditures on conveyances as well as water-processing and water-using equipment, it's appropriate for institutions to have some stability so as to limit water users' uncertainty about their future access to water. Agents and organizations cannot justify socially efficient levels of infrastructural investment unless their rights to water are secure. Because institutional change is a dynamic choice then, it is rational to request dynamic efficiency in institutional selection. Given this, it is reasonable to think that each rule change should maximize NPV.

The major problem in seeking dynamic efficiency in institutional change is that it is so difficult to assess. Compared to the MB and MC of water, the benefits and costs of an institutional change are harder to estimate, although we shall devote the forthcoming chapter to it. In these difficult empirical circumstances, some added economic guidance would be helpful.

4.2   The Invisible Hand and the First Theorem of Welfare Economics

Most contemporary dialogue about reforming water law includes arguments favoring *water market* formation. Water markets are enabled when private property rights to a water resource (e.g., a river or aquifer) are assigned to agents who are then allowed to transfer any portion of their water rights to others—who can then do the same. (The term *water marketing* does not apply to cases where a water supplier sets prices for services and then consumers choose how much water to use. Nor does it apply to the marketing of infrastructural capacity.) The considerable importance of this matter requires a solid basis for understanding and critiquing it. In chapter 7, the topic of water marketing shall be addressed in detail.

What is important to understand now is the foundation and limits of the economic theory buttressing water marketing. It is a theory spanning the most momentous accomplishments of economists, and it assigns considerable social significance to the ideals of open markets, entrepreneurial spirit, and decentralization. It is also a theory that encounters hurdles when applied to peculiar resources such as water. These hurdles can be difficult to overcome, and *in the end it may require some measure of faith or vision to privatize water rights and thereby initiate water marketing*, as we shall see.

With or without markets, an economy with millions of people and perhaps millions of different goods is a complex thing to orchestrate. There is an enormous number of decisions to make. Which goods are going to be produced, in what quantities, and by which firms? Which inputs are going to be used for each good and in what quantities? Who is going to work, where are they going to work, and what is to be their duties? Who is going to receive which goods and in what quantities? Given that all these questions are dimensioned by the number of resources, goods, and people in the economy, the multitude of decisions is incredibly vast.

Although the analytics of the prior two chapters emphasize water, efficiency is a compelling request for the allocation of *all* goods and resources. How is society to accomplish this? How are we to process all of the necessary information and achieve economic efficiency in a general economy? From a calculus perspective, reflecting on our work in chapter 2 and extending it to encompass nonwater goods as well, the number of first-order conditions is hard to contemplate, but it certainly must exceed trillions. The informational burden of this task seems as incalculable as the simultaneous solution of all these first-order conditions.

Today's economic doctrine on this matter originated over two centuries ago with the invisible hand notion coined by Adam Smith: "[Each] individual . . . by directing that industry [one's work] in such a manner as its produce may be of the greatest value, he intends only his own gain, and he is in this, as in many other cases, led by an invisible hand to promote an end which was no part of his intention. Nor is it always the worse for society that it was no part of it [his intention]. By pursuing his own interest he frequently promotes that of the society more effectually than when he really intends to promote it" (1776, II: 258). This powerful idea originating with Smith can be overextended (and it often is), so close inspection is worthwhile. As formalized over the past half century, the argument is as follows. Society would be best served if a complex set of relationships representing economic efficiency were achieved simultaneously. Neutral economic efficiency, usually termed Pareto optimality by economists, as noted earlier, is the focus of this pursuit.[2] When this desired set of relationships is compared to the outcome of a market system under idealized

2. Whereas most economic appraisals of policy/project desirability use the stricter, aggregate version of efficiency, neutral economic efficiency is always the objective in the context of the current topic. The reason is the axiomatic relationship connecting neutral efficiency and the results of an idealized marketplace, which is about to be disclosed.

circumstances, a striking correspondence arises. The results of idealized markets achieve the sought-after conditions of economic efficiency. No individual firms or consumers are pursuing economic efficiency on society's behalf. Yet in the acts of maximizing their individual profits or utilities, businesses and people bring the economy to a point of neutral economic efficiency. This is the most significant finding in the entire field of economics. During the twentieth century, this discovery was mathematically formalized as a theorem, now widely known as the *First Theorem of Welfare Economics*. Nobel Prize winners Kenneth Arrow and Gerald Debreu are two prime contributors to this development.

The First Theorem, as we will abbreviate it, provides economists with a useful policy tool for addressing many of society's allocative issues. According to this tool, a good way for a society to "be all it can be" is to rely on the market system. By extension, all we need to do is to assign property rights to problematic resources and "let the market work." As a consequence, market solutions to social issues are the favorite recommendation of economists.[3]

It is crucial, however, that markets are found to attain economic efficiency only when circumstances are ripe. Expressed more formally, the First Theorem is a theorem in the true sense. It takes the logical form of "if p, then q" or "p implies q." The q part is "a system of markets will produce economically efficient (neutral) results." What, then, is the p part, and can we as a society generally rely on p to be satisfied so that q will occur?

4.3 Market Failure

The number of assumptions used by the First Theorem has declined over time due to the efforts of mathematical economists in generalizing the result. Still, assumptions remain. Some of them are benign because they can be expected to hold true in most circumstances. For example, it is required that people prefer more of any given commodity to less (Mas-Colell, Whinston, and Green 1995, 549). This is not an especially objectionable assumption. Others are more troublesome. Of course, if one or more assumptions are false in certain settings, it cannot be concluded automatically that inefficiency will result from markets. It merely means that the theorem does not apply, and we do not have its assurance that the marketplace is an unbeatable institution for organizing human activities.[4]

---

3. Examples include school vouchers, transferable development rights for open space preservation, international free trade, the Kyoto Protocol for addressing climate change, nonsocialized medicine, and bandwidth pertaining to the Internet and radio/satellite frequencies.

4. As a matter of logic, the truth of "p implies q" does not establish that "not p implies not q."

While the First Theorem is quite technical and makes use of advanced mathematics in both its proof and presentation (see, for example, Debreu 1959), the crucial assumptions can be put into words. In cases where an assumption is not met, a **market failure** is defined to exist (Bator 1958, 351; Mas-Colell, Whinston, and Green 1995, 350). Unfortunately, the main classifications of market failure are rather common occurrences in the water resource arena. This is not surprising when you think about it. If the First Theorem applied widely to water issues, all U.S. water resources would have been converted to private property by now, and water allocation would be driven by market forces—just like farmland, music CDs, and automobiles. There would be nothing especially distinctive about water, and you would not be contemplating it now.

The primary market failures of relevance in particular water management scenarios are listed below, along with their definitions. This listing does not do justice to the great importance of these matters in economic theory and policy analysis, but it does tersely convey the nature of each problem together with water-related examples.

Public Goods   A **public good** (or bad) is a good possessing two properties— *nonrivalness* and *nonexclusion* (Myles 1995). Nonrivalness was discussed in chapter 2, where it was shown that demand is aggregated differently for nonrival goods. Both nonrivalness and nonexclusion are technical properties of a good.

• A good/bad is **nonrival** if its "consumption" by one agent does not diminish the amount available to other agents.

• A good/bad is **nonexclusive** if it is prohibitively expensive to exclude someone from consuming the commodity.

Note that a public good is not defined to be a publicly owned good; *ownership is irrelevant here*. Whether or not something is a public good depends totally on the technical properties of the good, with no attention to in-place institutions such as state ownership.

While some water uses constitute public goods, it is economically incorrect to label water as a public good. Many water uses are immediately rival—one person's use of specific units of water makes those units unavailable to others—rendering those uses private goods. Return flow does not necessarily imply nonrivalness, because the return flow is not available in the same time/place. Most water uses are excludable, so they do not qualify as public goods either.

An important instance of nonrivalness occurs when water is used for biodiversity maintenance. Units of water used for instream flows result in habitat support for vegetation and animals. Some of these species may even be threatened or endangered. Seeing this habitat, or just knowing that it exists, benefits some people. Although I may benefit from "consuming" this habitat through sight or knowledge, my consumption does not detract from the amount available to you. Hence, our consumption is nonrival.

The First Theorem is founded on a presumption of rival goods, so it does not apply when some goods are nonrival. The theorem has been successfully rebuilt for situations in which some goods are nonrival (Myles 1995, 271–279), but the ideal for market prices becomes modified for each nonrival good. Instead of there being a single price faced by all agents for each commodity, nonrival goods must be priced *personally* in the revised First Theorem. That is, each person benefiting from a nonrival good must pay a price targeted to that person, and (here's the regrettable part) that price depends on the individual's personal evaluation of the worth of the good. Now, imagine a situation in which a water management worker says, "You must pay a fee for the provision of habitat on river Z and the fee is equivalent to what this habitat is worth to you. What's it worth to you? You will be receiving a bill in the mail." Not only are you and everybody else prone to underreport the good's worth, you know and everybody knows that you get to consume the good regardless of how much you pay (due to nonexclusion).

The consequence of this problem is that marginal benefits are understated by almost everyone who is asked for their valuation, *free riding* occurs, and not enough financial resources are obtained to achieve a neutrally efficient level of public good provision. Therefore, public goods are underproduced by a system of markets, even when those "markets" incorporate personalized prices and, symmetrically, public bads are overproduced.[5]

The primary policy alternative for managing public goods is to turn away from markets. Usually, the public sector makes decisions on the level of public good production and resorts to taxation as a means to cover costs. While certain aspects of production may be contracted to private enterprises, the crucial decision making is performed by a public authority.

Externalities An ***externality*** occurs when a "third" agent's utility or production function contains items (such as positively or negatively regarded commodities) that are chosen by one or more other agents without regard for the third agent's welfare (Baumol and Oates 1988, 17). As tersely and accurately stated by Myles, "An externality represents a connection between economic agents which lies outside the price system of the economy. As the level of externality generated is not controlled directly by price, the standard efficiency theorems on market equilibrium cannot be applied" (1995, 312).

---

5. A public bad is a dislikable "commodity" also possessing the properties of nonrivalness and nonexclusion. The nonrivalness character is key here. For example, many matters of pollution do not constitute public bads because they are experienced rivally. (Think about ingested pollutants.)

Pollution is the prototypical example of an externality, so matters of water quality often stand as externality situations. Because other agents do not have cause to pay attention to their influence on the third agent, they select a socially inefficient level of activity. If the item is a "good," termed a *positive externality*, consideration of the third agent's welfare would lead the other agents to produce more.[6] If the item is a "bad," termed a *detrimental* or *negative externality*, consideration of the third agent's welfare would lead the agents to produce less.

Referring to the affected agent as the third agent in this definition acknowledges the common situation in which *market* bargains struck between two agents affect third parties in an economically inefficient way. Hence, the term *third-party effects* is similar to *externalities*. Market failures of this type inevitably involve many agents of all types, and it is often the case that items affecting third agents are determined collectively by many first and second agents. For example, in a coal-producing region there may be many mines producing coal that is being sold to many electricity producers throughout the country. If mining practices result in ground water pollution affecting area households and enterprises, then there are many affected third parties.

It can be said that externalities constitute "missing markets" which also serves to indicate one form of externality resolution—assign property rights to the item in question (e.g., ground water quality) so that the other agents have reason to have "regard for the third agent's welfare." The reason will be a new price signal.

Other policy instruments (institutions) for correcting externalities include merger with the third agent (if both are firms), economic incentives such as subsidizing or taxing the interdependent item, regulating[7] the item or factors relating to its determination, and moral suasion (appealing to the social ethics of first and second agents). All such policy devices seek to *internalize* the externality by aligning first and second agent choices with socially desired choices. Characteristics of the externality in question often eliminate one or more of these policy options.

All of these policy options, including market creation via property right assignment, will be accompanied by information costs, called **transaction costs** in economics literature (Dahlman 1979). Moreover, the transaction costs of establishing

6. Presumably, a first/second agent will select a profit- or utility-maximizing level of personal consumption or production of the item. If the additional benefits accruing to a third agent could be "communicated" to other agents through some mechanism, such as would occur if the third agent compensated the other agents, they would be motivated to consider the third agent's interests and increase the activity. Absent such a device, too little of the activity will be undertaken.

7. Here, "regulation" means to compel (by rule) the appropriate agents to undertake the efficient level of activity.

and operating each policy will be unique to the selected policy. Some or even all policy options may have transaction costs that exceed the value of correcting the externality. Hence, certain policies may be advantageous relative to others, and if transaction costs are great enough, the best choice may conceivably be to have no policy for the externality at all (Griffin 1991).

This treatment of externalities has been fairly abstract thus far, so let's make it more tangible with a couple of examples. The following examples pertain to a few of the many externalities that arguably affect private property forms of water management (National Research Council 1992, 5). Others will be observed as they become relevant in forthcoming chapters.

Return flow externalities arise from the fact that water is not normally destroyed in use. After water is used by any agent (a farm, a business, or a household), some portion of the water returns to the watercourse or some other water body to become usable by third agents. Consideration of return flows in chapter 2 resulted in a generalizable optimality condition (equation [2.33]) showing how conditions for economic efficiency are altered in the presence of return flows:

$$\frac{MNB_1}{1 - dR/dw_1} = MNB_2.$$

Unfortunately, individual agents do not pursue this condition in their activities because they tend to ignore the effects of their behavior on return flow. They do not derive personal benefits or costs from their own return flow, so they are not motivated to control return flow to the benefit of agents lying downstream.

As a second example, when different water users pump from the same aquifer, each pumper may know that their withdrawals lower the water table incrementally and increase everybody else's pumping lift, especially nearby pumpers. Greater lifts imply greater costs. Such *pumping cost* or *well interference externalities* can be reciprocal in that everyone is both a first and third agent, but in the absence of corrective policy, no pumper has reason to reduce their pumping in recognition of the costs imposed on others.

Natural Monopolies A **natural monopoly** is a production setting in which economic efficiency is injured, not aided, by marketplace competition. The injury is due to prevalently declining average costs (AC) of production. (The average cost of supplied water is simply the total costs divided by the amount of water supplied.) In plainer language, the greater production is, the lower per unit costs are. Declining average costs often occur for water suppliers. As a technical consequence, the marginal costs of supplying an additional unit of the good are always lower than the average costs (figure 4.1). Two important implications then arise: per unit costs of production are

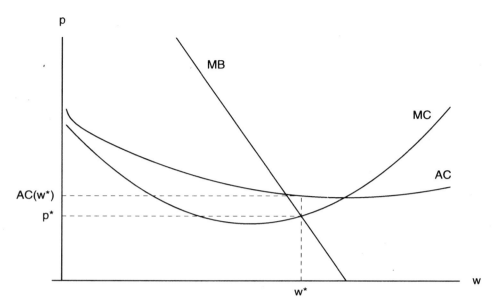

Figure 4.1
A natural monopoly scenario

lowest when a single producer supplies all consumers, and marginal-cost pricing of the good does not yield enough revenue to cover all of the producer's costs.[8] Both of these implications are to be revisited in later chapters.

Why might average costs be declining? As Kahn notes, "The principle source of this tendency is the necessity of making a large investment merely in order to be in a position to serve customers on demand." He adds that "this tendency is created or accentuated by certain common and interrelated characteristics of many public utility services: that they involve a *fixed* and essentially immovable *connection* between supplier and customer" (1988, 2: 119–120).

If there are to be competing firms, all "connection" capital (e.g., pipes) must be duplicated, so the normal social rewards of competition can be negated by the high costs of replicating service. Virtually all competition entails some duplication of capital costs. Thus, duplication is not a sufficient basis for identifying natural monopo-

---

8. Whereas marginal costs are the derivative of the total cost function with respect to water, average costs are total costs divided by the amount of water. It is a mathematical truism that the marginal cost function intersects the average cost function at the latter's minimum level (exercise 3 of chapter 2). Hence, where average costs are negatively sloped, average costs exceed marginal costs. Efficient pricing is still marginal cost pricing (as long as the marginal cost function is positively sloped where it intersects marginal benefits), so the efficient price is less than the average costs of providing water.

lies. Only when a single supplier can serve an entire market more inexpensively than multiple suppliers, such as commonly occurs for water distributors, will we have a natural monopoly.

When a single production agent supplies all consumers, an institutional mechanism for limiting the agent's market power is useful. If a single supplier is allowed to make uncontrolled decisions, its pursuit of profit will lead it to underproduce so as to influence price in an upward direction.[9] The conventional social options are twofold. Either the enterprise is operated as a not-for-profit public operation or a price-regulated firm. The choice is a classic dilemma. Public operations of this type face no competition and may not be inspired to pursue cost-minimizing activities. On the other hand, the regulated firm may attempt to overstate its costs (on which regulated price is usually based) and/or neglect reasonable quality-of-service expectations. Given that regulated rates will usually be based on publicly allowed *returns to capital*, regulated firms have a tendency to employ production strategies that are not least cost because they overinvest in capital. Further examination of this dilemma is postponed until chapter 10, where combinations of public/private responsibilities will also be considered.

Overdiscounting   When privately motivated agents make dynamic decisions regarding the property rights they control, they employ private discount rates assigning less weight to the future than indicated by social discount rates. This *overdiscounting* implies that the market system has propensities to underconserve depletable resources such as ground water and underinvest in long-term projects such as reservoirs, at least from a social point of view. (Recall that the two-period model exhibited in figure 3.3 can be usefully applied to demonstrate a reduction in first-period conservation when the discount rate rises.) Clearly, the extent of the harm caused by overdiscounting depends on the difference between private and social discount rates.

Overdiscounting can be a contentious topic for some economists as there are those who argue that the issue is nonexistent because the social discount rate cannot (according to them) be less than private discount rates. Their perspective is that all social opportunity costs are rooted in the sacrifices of today's private agents. Opposing arguments pertaining to a regard for future people were considered previously in the prior chapter.

---

9. An important assumption of the First Theorem is the absence of market power. Market power occurs when a single agent's decisions influence market price. The worst-case scenario is that of a monopoly— when a single firm supplies a particular good. Because of the agent's influence on price, the monopolist's profit-maximizing output level is less than that required for economic efficiency in the economy. Additional technical details regarding monopolistic pricing are given by note 13 in chapter 10.

4.4   Consequently, . . .

These four classifications of market failure cloud the significance of the First Theorem for recommending water policy—especially the recommendation of market-oriented institutions. But it is easy to delineate two general areas of impact—one for the distribution of retail water, and one for the optimal allocation of natural water among competing interests.

In terms of the optimal allocation and provision of retail water in any given locale, such as in a city or for a group of irrigators, the existence of a natural monopoly implies that we should choose publicly owned processing and distribution or regulating a single, profit-motivated supplier. Market competition is not a viable option for the delivery of retail water. Even though the amount of processing applied to irrigation water may be small, transporting river water to farm gates (which is a form of value-added processing) commonly involves decreasing average delivery costs because a single canal can serve multiple users. These same transportation economies apply for urban water, and there may also be economies of scale (decreasing average costs) in achieving water quality standards, water pressurization, and administration.

The second area concerns the optimal allocation of natural water. This matter concerns the allocation of water prior to its removal from the watercourse and whether society may confidently depend on private property institutions to achieve efficiency. Here, one or more issues of public goods, externalities, or overdiscounting can confound institutional choice—muddying the water, so to speak. As society attempts to refine our present institutions, which constitute instances of common property more often than not, these three market failures can present strong obstacles. Not only may the evolutionary tendency to install private property be thwarted or delayed, but (1) any common or state property regime must also wrestle with the challenges embedded in these market failures, and (2) even where private property is installed for natural water, these market failures will recommend a certain degree of "tweaking" to the new property instrument. As a consequence of (2), calls for so-called free markets in water are normally too superficial to have merit. Often, a *mixed* institutional system will be preferred, using market-oriented institutions where possible to harness private incentives, but leaning on nonmarket institutions where the prospect of market failure is worrisome.

As an example of a basic mixed system well employed in the western United States, we can (1) distribute property rights to the annual flows of rivers, (2) meter water withdrawals to assure no one exceeds their right holdings, and (3) allow trade in these rights. The resulting incentives will harness agents' self-motivated behavior, encouraging the application of water to its most valuable rival uses and in efficient amounts. To protect the livelihood of a threatened aquatic species (a public good) in this river, (4) some of the water rights can be held by the public sector, and these rights will not be exercised except to leave the water instream and sheltered from water diverters. To manage return flow externalities affecting third parties to water market transactions, (5) a publicly operated approval process for all water market exchanges can be instituted. A possible requirement is that no exchanges harmful to a third party will be authorized, thus motivating traders to design their deals differently and more expansively, so as to limit return flow externalities. All things considered, mixed systems such as this forfeit some of the net benefits that marketing provides to traders, while protecting net benefits experienced by other agents. Depending on the set of institutions employed in such a mixed system, we will achieve a differing array of outcomes in terms of which goods are produced and who gets them. These can be crucial differences.

4.5 The Nature of Property

There are features and nuances of property that are good to keep in mind, lest the water manager treat institutional choice too lightly. This is true of common, state, and private property. Above all, one should be mindful that property is both highly dimensioned and dualistic. Both are interesting elements.

To say that an agent "possesses property" in an item conveys a simple idea of ownership, but it lacks detail. Land is a good example because it is something people can relate to easily. You may "own" an acre of land, but your ownership is not absolute. There are things you are allowed to do with your land. There are other things you cannot legally do. To better reflect on this matter, legal theory speaks of property using a "bundle of sticks" metaphor. Together, all of the imaginable powers over an item constitute a bundle of sticks, with each stick representing a separate power. Your ownership of an acre of land grants you many of the sticks in its bundle, but not all. Which sticks you own will be heavily influenced by governmentally established rules for the jurisdictions in which the acre lies. You may be able to till this acre for agricultural purposes, set up a commercial enterprise on it, mine its ores, or build a home on it. You may be able to sell it to another party. You may be entitled to harvest its trees or take fish from the stream passing through it. You may be able to pave it over with asphalt. Or maybe not.

Perhaps you can build a home on the acre, but not one more than a certain height because that would block the sunlight received by other property holders. Perhaps you can pursue a commercial activity, but only if it isn't publicly regarded as a nuisance to neighbors. Perhaps the underlying ores (and ground water) are yours to use, or perhaps ownership of these resources has been separated from the land and is held by someone else or the state. Perhaps you can develop the entire acre or perhaps you are required to leave some of it as green space. The gist here is that you hold some of the sticks, and other people hold the other sticks to "your" property. Ownership is not an absolute. Sometimes people mistakenly think that ownership grants total power over a resource, but that is patently false. As shall be seen later in this chapter, property to water normally grants particular powers to the owner while withholding other powers.

The other notable nuance of property rights is their dualism. Every property right has two sides. A property right of any kind simultaneously expresses the *right* of one agent/group to behave in some manner or to expect certain behavior from others, and the *duty* of other agents/groups to be compliant with respect to the other's right (Bromley 1989, 44–45). If your property right in the acre of land assigns you the right to dig a pond and raise mosquitoes, then others have a duty to allow your digging and receive the mosquitoes that fly from your property. If mosquitoes are discovered to be a vector for a nasty disease and your neighbors dislike this exposure, then they will have to contract with you for the elimination of your mosquitoes. If social concerns for public health motivate the government to alter the distribution of this property right stick, then the right may be reversed so that you now have a duty to disrupt mosquito reproduction on your land and others will have a right to reduced peril from your mosquitoes. In this case, you may need to construct your pond in an approved, mosquito-reducing manner; contract with your neighbors in order to construct a pond; or forgo pond construction.

Unfortunately, some policy dialogue speaks of "maximizing" property rights, which is a bit odd given that a high level of right for one party must be balanced by an equally high level of duty for others. If you possess a senior water right to withdraw one hundred acre-feet of water from a river each year, then nonsenior water right holders have a duty to limit their water use until your right can be satisfied. Given the limited nature of the water resource, increases in your rights (which might be accomplished by a revision in state water law) can only be accomplished by raising the duty of others (or vice versa). For example, if rising water scarcity highlights a legal ambiguity with regard to who is legally entitled to the return flows from your hundred acre-feet of withdrawals, the government might either assign you the right to your return flow, thereby entitling you to capture and reuse it, or assign the right to others downstream, thereby handing you the duty to always return a certain amount of water. There is nothing to maximize here. The right to return flow either belongs to one party or another, or perhaps it can be divided in some way.

Dualism also pertains to common property arrangements, and common property is highly dimensioned as well. Hence, both aspects of the preceding discussion apply well to common property. There is no surprise here, for it can be said that "common property is a management regime that closely resembles *private property for a group of co-owners*" (Bromley 1991, 93).

4.6 The Assignment of Property: Who Should Get It?

It should be quite apparent that the important matters of institutional choice for water resource management involve the selection of a property form and the assignment of property. In nearly all cases, institutional choice involves the replacement or modification of a prior institution rather than the establishment of one where none stood previously (= open access). Some modifications are quite simple. Others are momentous and set in motion new forces prompting radically modified human action.

As property rights involving water are revised, there are always going to be different people and groups asking that they be assigned greater rights. Whenever new rights are created by the state, different agents will ask that the rights be assigned to them. From the point of view of efficiency—that is, the optimal allocation of water from society's perspective—does it matter who is assigned new or revised property in water?

Economic doctrine on who should be granted property rights is derived from a centerpiece contribution of Ronald Coase, another Nobel Memorial Prize holder in economics. Coase's work in "The Problem of Social Cost" (1960) has become abridged in what is now known as the *Coase Theorem*, even though the original article is devoid of mathematics and proofs. Although extendable, the focus of the Coase Theorem is the following question: When correcting an externality situation by property right creation (and subsequent transactions involving the new rights), does it matter how the rights are initially assigned? The simplistic answer provided by contemporary versions of the Coase Theorem is this: We get neutral economic efficiency regardless of how the new property rights are assigned. Different assignments, followed by market transactions, take the economy to different points on the frontier constituting neutral efficiency (recall figure 2.16), but all are efficient in the neutral sense. All are not efficient in the aggregate sense, but this is arguably a secondary concern for such matters.[10] To this extent, then, the assignment does not matter and the decision may be reasonably resolved by other social criteria, especially social ideals of fairness in the partitioning of this new right.

Exploring these assertions by example, suppose that water managers of an eastern U.S. basin are confronted with some growing pains. An all-too-common scenario is described as follows. Throughout the past, various water users along the river have coexisted amiably, for there was plenty of water for all. Because of recent population

---

10. In section 2.9, it was noted that the implicit weighting that is embedded in aggregate efficiency may be objectionable in some cases because weighting commodities by their prices and people by their incomes may conflict with some vision of "fairness." Neutral economic efficiency dodges such complaints, which is why it can only be resolved to a range of outcomes. New property rights are presumably assigned in a socially fair way, implying that the neutral efficiency of resulting transactions is acceptable.

growth, some cities have increased their withdrawals and some towns are attempting to initiate new water withdrawals because their ground water supplies are no longer "adequate." The current institutional framework treats all users, old and new, as members of a common, and it is based on a set of rules emphasizing "equitable sharing" in times of excess demand (when quantity demanded exceeds quantity supplied). The new wrinkle for managers is that excess demand is no longer an infrequent occurrence—it happens every summer as a consequence of elevated demand. The idea of equitable sharing has become hard to apply because everyone has a self-interested perspective on what is fair. Legal suits among users have become common, and the basin water authority is often named in these suits too. Everyone is talking about water being "necessary for continued economic growth," but there does not seem to be enough of it to go around.[11] The basin's institutional structure has aged beyond usefulness. Either the common property rule set should be updated or a transition into a mixed private/common system should be undertaken.

A better common property institution would be to institute water pricing that incorporates the value of natural water. This idea was introduced in chapter 2 and will be developed fully in a forthcoming chapter. A different common property upgrade would be to resolve specific water use limits for every user, so that all these limits add up to less water than is in the river each year. Of course, we would want to allot some water for instream flows too. A problem with this upgrade is that the individual limits will have to be revisited and revised in a few years. The ongoing growth in demand and new users will require it.

The previous suggestion is quite close to private property. The only additional step is to turn these limits into transferable rights. Such a step has the advantage of being able to address forthcoming new growth without intervention. New or growing users will have to obtain water from those who own it, by buying or leasing it. The newly arisen price signal will help to induce efficiency.

Let's assume that transferable rights (private property) is the chosen approach. How should the rights be initially assigned? According to the Coase Theorem, the rights can be assigned in any manner. Neutral efficiency will result as a consequence of transactions between those having rights in excess of their quantity demanded at the market price and those having rights below their quantity demanded at the market price. Because of two major factors, the postmarket (after-trade) allocation of water rights will be influenced by the initial distribution. These two matters are closely attended to by contemporary statements of the Coase Theorem.

---

11. It should be added that such "water is necessary for growth" arguments are misguided. Economic growth in output can and does occur in the face of many resource limitations. Water does not possess a uniqueness among all resources in enabling growth. Indeed, the pursuit of additional water resources can burden an economy with costs and debt in excess of the value provided, thereby serving to hinder economic development and growth.

• Being newly endowed with a valuable right provides the owner with additional wealth. Because willingness to pay (demand) for most goods is positively affected by ability to pay (income and wealth), the initial distribution of water rights has the potential to influence demands for all goods, including water. Hence, the postmarket allocation of water rights can be impacted by the way we distribute new water rights.

• Any good can be costly to buy and sell due to the information costs of exchange. Buyers and sellers must find one another; they must confirm ownership and financial backing; they must measure the quality and quantity of the good; and they must resolve legal assurances and enforce their deal. Buyers and sellers may choose to pay other people for these services. Together, these information costs (transaction costs) will prevent otherwise advantageous trades from occurring because the transaction benefits must exceed the transaction costs if a deal is to happen (Coase 1960, sec. 6). This fact imparts some measure of "inertia" to property rights, so that "post-trade allocations of rights will bear some resemblance" to the initial assignment (Griffin 1991, 607).

The second point is more noteworthy for water. As a fluid, water is not especially amenable to being "staked out" or fenced. Accurate measurement can also be a problem as meters are neither free nor 100 percent accurate and reliable. If the trading process must be publicly overseen to cope with return flow externalities, there are additional transaction costs to be dealt with. All of these burdens increase the inertia of water rights. While planners can be comforted by Coase Theorem results— saying that one of the neutrally efficient allocations will occur regardless of initial distribution—the initial distribution does matter.

As a consequence of these observations, *there truly is a role for publicly minded vision in the assignment of private property rights to water* if this is to be the chosen institutional path. If property rights are assigned primarily to one group or water use, as opposed to others, there will be a tendency for water to stay there or, at least, to stay there for a longer period of time. If initially established water rights are primarily assigned to irrigators as opposed to cities, then (1) the welfare of irrigators is enhanced, (2) population growth will encourage the continual exchange of water rights from irrigators to cities, and (3) the inertia caused by transaction costs will slow the conversion of irrigation water rights to urban water rights. A consequence of (3) is that irrigation will persevere longer if water rights are initially assigned to irrigators. *Any* initial assignment is neutrally efficient, however. Likewise, if water rights are primarily assigned to diverters (irrigators, cities) as opposed to nondiverters (recreationists, biodiversity lovers), then the same three points apply. Among other things, we end up having more water diversions under this assignment than one where nondiverters are better endowed. Any assignment is neutrally efficient, though.

The important questions are then these: Who does society wish to favor with these assignments, and what water-using activities does society envision itself emphasizing? Given our collective preferences for *both* cheap food and lush landscapes, what trade-off should we settle on? What balance is to be struck between environmentally healthy rivers and springs, on the one hand, and baskets of consumer goods, on the other? What legacies are we to leave our descendants in terms of conserved ground water and polluted water bodies?

Part II: Legal Institutions

4.7   Water Law

Having gained an economic perspective on institutional choice, it is now possible to examine the more specific social rules available for managing water. Water law is a fascinating area of study with numerous variants and nuances, so it is necessary to limit attention here to the most important matters. It is best to learn water law from specialized courses of instruction as well as the literature emphasizing this topic, so it suffices for our purposes here to highlight the major institutions and their proper economic interpretation. Indeed, it is the economic interpretation that compels this inspection now.

Water resource economics perceives water law as establishing the rules by which agents can behave regarding water. This behavior may include the exchange of water rights if the law allows it. In customary practice, the framers of water law are not entirely appreciative of the market process of reallocation. Legal designers sometimes think that an appropriate division of water can be identified and then implemented rigidly. Depending on the experience and precepts of any particular government, there can also be a discomforting tendency to "tinker" with the rules, changing them more often than is socially necessary. Two lessons offered by an economic perspective are that private exchange is a socially useful (and automatic) tactic for managing scarcity, and that water right security is desirable if we are to encourage water users to invest and conserve efficiently. Examples of these points will arise in the sections to follow.

4.8   Surface Water Law

Governments have established differing water law doctrines for managing surface water and ground water. Even though surface and ground waters are usually connected hydrologically, it is understandable, as well as unfortunate, that their institutions developed differently. Significant employment of ground water is a recent event (over the last half century) in most regions of the world, owing to the impracticality of ground water access prior to machine-driven pumps and drills. Windmills and manually operated dug wells are still used in much of the world, but the amounts withdrawn are characteristically low—too low to create problems and foster new institutions in most instances.

The use of surface water had a substantial historical jump on ground water and has even exerted a significant influence on human settlement patterns. Hence, the scarcity required for institutional development occurred first for surface water. These institutions developed as conflicts were sorted out, so the resulting array of rules can be haphazard: "In fact, water law development has often occurred in a crisis atmosphere in which resolution of a pressing but narrowly defined water resources problem was the primary objective. Thus water law generally does not consist of a comprehensive, integrated body of legal principles for managing the resource, and problems of coordination among the different bodies of law frequently arise" (Cox 1982, 107). In concert with our prior observations, the earliest institutions for surface water are forms of common property, and in relatively recent history some governments have commenced a partial transition to private property. U.S. states have substantial latitude in selecting their own water law doctrines, so it is not surprising that considerable variety has emerged.

The Riparian Doctrine: Common Property in Surface Water

In the U.S. experience, a featured system of water law is the *riparian doctrine*. This doctrine also prevails in other countries, including those of the English Commonwealth (Scott and Coustalin 1995). Historically, riparianism was mainly adopted in eastern U.S. states where low water scarcity provided tolerance for common property rule. But the less arid, nonmountain, western states have also recognized some degree of riparianism in their water law (Goldfarb 1984, 15–16). While there are notable variations, the key provisions of the riparian doctrine are that

• only riparians are legally entitled to make use of surface water;

• these water rights are not quantitatively fixed;

• each riparian's water use must be "reasonable" in relation to the water use of other riparians in the basin.

A riparian is an owner of a land parcel touched by the watercourse. Hence, the riparian doctrine establishes a common consisting of all owners of land along a watercourse. Due to specific issues that have risen over the years, courts have progressively refined the details of membership in this common. In general, riparians are constrained to use water on riparian land within the same watershed as the watercourse (should their parcel be large enough to span multiple watersheds), and if a riparian parcel is legally divided in such a way that one piece no longer borders the water, then that piece's associated water rights are forever forfeited, even if later recombined with riparian land.

Riparians must share the resource equitably; their use must be *reasonable*. "Reasonableness is a relative concept that . . . normally is determined only in the context of a specific water-use conflict" (Cox 1982, 111). Absent an agreement among competing riparians, disputes are resolved in the courtroom. The criteria used by courts in assessing reasonableness are many: "the size of the stream, its fall, the velocity of the current, seasonable rises and falls in the flow, the purpose of the use, its extent, duration and manner of application, custom of the river and the needs and uses of other riparian owners are equally all relevant factors" (Tarlock 1991, sec. 3.12[4]). The multitude of these factors makes it difficult to predict outcomes, resulting in both high transaction costs (largely for legal representation) and uncertainty about how much water a riparian may confidently expect to receive in the future. Both of these results can limit economic development because investment in land and water-using capital is sensitive to production costs and uncertainty.

Cities can be burdensome members of the riparian common due to their sizable water use, so unique rules have been fashioned for accommodating cities and their growth. "Most courts . . . have held that a city must either purchase or condemn riparian land or compensate any riparians injured by its diversions" (Tarlock 1991, sec. 3.09[2]). Because the spirit of condemnation and compensation is that cities are vested with the crucial power to take what they want, other riparians may complain about their reduced status in such a common. But at least the courts found a mechanism for moving water to rising populations.

A distinguishing feature of the riparian doctrine is that all riparians are members of the common even if they have not previously exercised their rights. Thus, new users may rightfully initiate water use. Combined with the fact that the prior users do not face quantitative limits, demand growth among all riparians can easily test the court's ability to assess and reassess reasonability. The relative nature of any reasonability criterion implies that what was reasonable under one set of demand and supply conditions can cease to be reasonable as scarcity advances. Courts must therefore apply new and ever-sharpening details to perform their tasks. Transferability might be one mechanism for escaping these problems, but transferability of riparian rights is allowed in only a few jurisdictions (Goldfarb 1984, 9), and riparian rights normally lack the quantitative precision needed for efficient market transactions. Because a riparian right does not specify the amount of water involved, the prospects for achieving efficiency through the First Theorem are remote.

Eastern Permit Systems: State Property in Surface Water

It is not surprising to find that water management problems have been progressively revealed in riparian jurisdictions. The system of common property management contained in the riparian doctrine is too loosely defined by reasonability, and conflicting rights must be balanced on an expensive, case-by-case basis. This soft approach to management is only desirable when scarcity is low and conflicts are infrequent.

As a consequence of rising dissatisfaction, many eastern U.S. states have embarked on state or regional water-planning exercises, emphasizing "inventories of existing uses, projections of future demand and the identification of problem areas" (Tarlock 1991, sec. 3.20[4]). Many riparian states have also enacted requirements that water users obtain water use permits. These permits produce planning information such as the amount and seasonality of water withdrawals. Permit requirements are also evolutionary steps in the reformation of riparianism. Previously, riparians could withdraw water without a permit. Permits may eventually heighten exclusivity and result in the quantification of riparian rights, firming up the amount of water each riparian may reasonably expect to receive. With state water planning underway, future approval of new or enhanced permits may need to find justification in state water plans (Tarlock 1991, sec. 3.20[4]). As these changes occur, ownership of riparian land will become an inadequate basis on which to receive a permit to withdraw surface water. While these possibilities are prospective and currently in progress, it is clear that many jurisdictions are transitioning beyond riparianism.

Whereas riparian institutions emphasize resolution by the judicial branch, planning and permitting reforms are being initiated by legislatures. Moreover, new administrative duties are being created and assigned to agencies. These are clear departures, and they signal a transition from common property to state property. As contrasted to riparianism, these institutions are stricter. What remains to be seen is whether these permits will evolve into transferable property rights. That is, states could feasibly treat these permits as transferable forms of private property. The new systems usually employ "term permits," which have a finite life (e.g., ten years) and must be subsequently renewed. Term permits are not as amenable to transfer as permanent rights because their short life spans limit their value. Water use of any kind is generally accompanied by nontrivial levels of infrastructure investment, so the reduced security of term permits constrains marketability and dulls users' incentive to make related investments.

The Prior Appropriations Doctrine: Private Property in Surface Water

Earlier in this chapter, we considered the generic ideal of managing society's resources by distributing those resources as private property and allowing trade. Perhaps the most widespread, active institution applying this vision is the *prior appropriations doctrine*, a legal system based on the ethical principle of "first in time, first in right." It is employed in a purer form by the Rocky Mountain states, and other western U.S. states employ its principles in some combination with riparianism. Some eastern states have contemplated it, as have some countries. Like other systems of water law, the prior appropriations doctrine is best thought of as a set of rules. A minimalist set, capturing the essence of prior appropriations, includes the following key features.

Seniority Conflict over scarce water is settled by seniority, based on whichever use(s) commenced earlier (e.g., a use originally initiated in 1889 takes precedence over a use begun in 1921).

Quantification These water rights are quantitatively expressed. For example, a right may indicate that the owner may take up to two hundred cubic feet per minute not to exceed 240 acre-feet of water per year. Traditionally, these rights emphasize "flow" quantities such as cubic feet per minute rather than volumetric quantities (Gould 1988, 8–10).

Transferability Rights may be sold independently of any land on which the water is used.

As a result of their promarket ideology, most economists speak glowingly about the prior appropriations doctrine. The most laudable feature is that transferability makes water owners think about the value of their water to others. That is, this policy signals water's opportunity costs to each water owner. It's not personally sensible to apply water to a low-value crop generating twenty dollars of income per acre-foot when someone else is offering a hundred dollars. Were it not for transferability, the twenty dollar use would continue and society would miss an opportunity. A secondary feature is that seniority provides a market mechanism for "higher-quality" water rights to have greater value. Climate fluctuations infer that water supplies vary yearly. Some water users attach greater value to more secure (less uncertain) water supplies. Municipalities are a prime example. With each water right being "tagged" with a seniority indicating its relative security during dry years, water users can trade to obtain water rights balancing the price of more secure water rights against the value this security produces for the user.

In its pure form, the prior appropriations doctrine does not constrain water use to riparian lands. Nonriparians can make use of the water resource. Indeed, this was part of the motivation for the invention of prior appropriations by western miners during the 1800s. Simple mining technologies for separating precious ores from the accompanying dirt and rock often made use of water. Operating in a loose and self-imposed legal environment, miners were free to adopt a legal system that suited their wishes. It was natural for them to extend their system of land claims to water: the first to stake out a claim and make use of the resource earned a right to continued use until the claim was abandoned. As these territories later became states, legislatures and courts found ways to write and interpret formal law so that it was respectful of these customs. In this way, prior appropriations was established formally, in some cases in lieu of riparianism and in other cases blended with riparianism (so-called dual doctrine states).

A stumbling point for the market efficiency of appropriative water rights is that these rights are historically quantified as allowed *diversions*. Yet each diversion of surface water will result in some return flow to the originating stream, thereby generating reuse opportunities and downstream benefits. If we are to respect these downstream benefits and thereby avoid the most common trading externalities—but not all of them—it is necessary to disallow transferability in excess of consumptive use (Gould 1988). Hence, consumptive use for each trader must be resolved and enforced, effectively causing a shift to consumptive use rights. The importance of this consideration, as well as other externalities, motivate added attention in a forthcoming chapter focused on water markets.

It is noteworthy that the prior appropriations doctrine is generally accompanied by provisions that are undesirable due to their inefficiency. Examples include beneficial use requirements, preferential use hierarchies, and forfeiture clauses. While these provisions may have had merit in an earlier era, they have aged beyond usefulness in regions experiencing water scarcity.

• According to beneficial use requirements, the legitimacy and extent of each water right is defined by the amount of water the right holder has put to beneficial use. Historically, this implied that the right holder had to divert water from a watercourse and apply it to an approved purpose listed in the state's water code (e.g., domestic, irrigation, or mining). The apparent intentions of this provision were to discourage hoarding and speculation, and to encourage efficiency in water use. Three complaints arise. First, beneficial use requirements have presented problems because they originally listed only offstream diversions (omitting instream uses). In recent years, some legislatures have corrected these omissions, but the whole idea of specifying any list is misdirected. Is the government sufficiently knowledgeable and evenhanded to acknowledge all conceivable and valuable uses of water? Second, given that most western streams are fully appropriated now—there are no additional water rights that can be newly assigned—the possibilities for hoarding and speculation are remote. Finally, efficiency is well policed by the market created by transferable rights, so there is no reason to employ legal proceedings to decide what is or is not an efficient water use. Except for prospective market failures, which are not addressed by beneficial use provisions anyway, the marketplace is a reliable tool for eliminating inefficiency. Even the legal community, which has helped to overextend the life of the beneficial use principle, has begun to seriously acknowledge it as an aged, failing approach. For example, Neuman (1998) nicely exposes the barrier that beneficial use poses for achieving efficient water use (without really understanding the market alternative).

• In addition to ranking water rights by seniority, most states have established a preference ordering by type of use. "The usual list is (1) domestic, (2) municipal, (3) irrigation, (4) mining and manufacturing, and (5) power generation" (Tarlock 1991, sec. 5.08[3]). In theory this listing trumps seniority, allowing a high-preference junior user to take water before a low-preference senior user does. In practice, the junior user exercising this prerogative has to compensate the senior user for the value of any sustained losses. Hence, this provision is redundant with the prospect of water marketing, which probably has lower transaction costs anyway. As an additional problem, it cannot be economically maintained that *all* type (1) uses are more valuable than *all* type (2) uses. The same is true for other neighboring preference categories. Preference rankings are therefore ill founded.

• Most state water codes have forfeiture clauses indicating that a water right is terminated after a sustained period of nonuse (normally ten years). Thus, if during a ten-year period forty acre-feet is the greatest annual use of a water right to a hundred acre-feet, the water right is reestablished at forty acre-feet. This "use it or lose it" provision encourages right holders to maintain their water rights through full and even wasteful use of their water. Such incentives are clearly unfortunate in water-scarce regions, especially given the rising scarcity of instream flows.

It should be evident that beneficial use, preference ordering, and forfeiture provisions are dispensable if we are truly interested in promoting efficiency in water use. In some ways, the negative influences of these provisions have withered, either through nonapplication or legal modifications, but they still perplex market activities because their existence degrades the security of water rights. Fortunately, it is easy to eliminate these effects: simply remove these provisions from the "duties" of water right holders.

Correlative Shares: Private Property in Surface Water

Another mechanism for managing a variable surface water supply is to employ transferable shares in the resource. This is a private property form of *correlative shares*. It is employed in many irrigation districts (Maass and Anderson 1978), in specific basins such as the Lower Rio Grande in Texas (Chang and Griffin 1992), and by some countries (Hearne 1998). In its pure form, a fixed number of shares are allocated to users, and owners of each share receive a proportion of the available water. (If there are one hundred shares and the administering authority has 1,000 cfs to allocate in the current period, then each share is entitled to receive 10 cfs.) These shares are transferable, perhaps to anyone or perhaps only to qualifying landowners or individuals. While the transfer of correlative shares may be contingent on the transfer of land, the discussion here presumes that these water rights—or "sticks"—have been legally severed from land rights so that they may be separately exchanged.

Depending on the extent of transferability, this system can be supportive of economic efficiency in water allocation. Aggregate efficiency tends to be progressively sacrificed as the pool of allowed owners is constrained. For example, irrigation districts may not allow agents outside its boundaries to purchase shares. In this case, transferability can only serve to improve efficiency inside district boundaries. Since there's normally a high degree of economic homogeneity among irrigation district members, the efficiency achievements of transferability are small here.

As contrasted to prior appropriations, correlative shares do not offer a direct mechanism for valuing more secure rights. During dry times, the prior appropriations system curtails water to the most junior right holders, while correlative shares apportions the water supply shortfall equally across all shareholders, leaving risk-averse water users with limited options for guaranteeing their supplies. If transferability of correlative shares is limited to permanent exchanges, the only recourse for risk-averse users is to accumulate enough shares to balance their quantity demanded (against the share price) during dry years. This action will leave these users with excess supplies during normal years, depressing the economic efficiency of the system because too much water is committed to risk-averse users. On the other hand, if risk-averse users can lease shares for short periods during dry spells or lease out shares when they have excess supplies, then the reduced efficiency of a correlative system can be circumvented.

Therefore, we see that economic efficiency can be advanced by properly designed correlative shares systems. For water-scarce regions, transferable correlative shares are a major improvement over riparianism. Transferable correlative shares to surface water can approach the achievements of prior appropriations, with the exception that the prior appropriations doctrine better encourages infrastructural investments that are sensitive to the security of water rights during dry periods (Ciriacy-Wantrup 1956, 302).

Other State Property Interests in Surface Water

There are crucial nonrival, as well as rival, uses of water that depend on water being left instream. Examples include fish, wildlife, and vegetation support, recreation, scenic beauty, hydropower, navigation, wastewater dumping, and channel maintenance (Shupe and MacDonnell 1993). As long as rival users of instream water are allowed to possess transferable water rights, the First Theorem provides confidence about achieving efficient results. Nonrival uses are not efficiently supported by transferable rights, however, so the public sector must develop management tools for addressing these applications. In most instances, this task will require isolating specific water units from market forces (which underappreciate nonrival water uses). While action groups such as water rafting associations, the Nature Conservancy, and Trout Unlimited can successfully employ water markets to enhance and protect streamflows, we should remain mindful that nonrivalness is an area of market failure: markets underprovide nonrival goods. Therefore, it is reasonable to believe that action groups make progress toward efficiency, but it is overly optimistic to think that their activities will go far enough.

It is evident in the prior sections that the public sector plays an important role in water rights determination and allocation. All the key rules are selected and administered by the public sector. One can say the same of resources such as land and minerals. For all such resources, initial ownership and reallocative processes are ultimately governed by the public sector. In the case of water, though, involvement by the public sector is deeper. The flowing nature of water creates a rich set of interdependencies among water users, so the public sector is more "hands on" with its administrative functions than it is for most land-based resources.

Legal scholars point out that water rights of all types are normally *usufructuary* in nature—water right holders are entitled to the *use* of water, but do not possess strong ownership interests in specific units of water, even when transferability is allowed (Goldfarb 1984, xvii). This is legal jargon for acknowledging the heightened powers of the public sector in administering water resources, as contrasted to things like land and food. As compared to land, the mix of public/private rights includes more public power in the case of water.

In addition to administrative duties, the public sector may exert explicit control or ownership over some portion of a watercourse, thereby exempting it from possible diversion. That is, the government may designate some water as state property. In the United States, the federal government surrendered crucial jurisdictional powers over water resources to the individual states on the formation of each state (Tarlock 1991, sec. 9.08[1]). This is the reason why different states were able to develop different approaches to water management. Nevertheless, the U.S. government retained some powers for the public interest. Many states have also reserved water through various mechanisms in order to advance public interests in primarily nonrival water uses.

To achieve federal objectives involving Indian reservations, national parks, national forests, wildlife refuges, wilderness areas, military bases, and similar exercises of federal authority, all of which are desirous of water for particular functions, courts have accepted the doctrine that the U.S. government possesses *reserved rights* to water (Getches 1990, 311). Because these federal rights are reserved, states do not possess the authority to interfere with them or authorize individual water rights that conflict with these reserved rights. On the other hand, in a prior appropriations system such as might occur in a western state, these reserved rights will generally have an assigned priority date established when the federal use was first authorized. Hence, if a block of public land is designated as a wilderness area in 1971, preexisting appropriative water rights remain senior to the water rights of the wilderness area. Since Indian reservations were generally established during the 1800s, these water rights are normally very senior.

A perplexing matter that still confuses water allocation is the absent quantification of many federal reserved rights. Any lack of resolution frustrates junior water diverters, state water management personnel, and water markets. If the establishment of an Indian reservation or a wildlife refuge implies the reservation of water, just how much water is that? The guiding principle is that the amount of water involved is limited by the federal purpose. For example, the reserved rights of a national forest extend only to water required for proper forest management, which does not include water in support of fish. But the question often remains, How much water is that?

In addition to federal reservations, states also employ various mechanisms to protect water from diversion (Shupe and MacDonnell 1993) because many experts and special interests believe that nonrival water uses are traditionally underserved. There are several instruments being applied now, and some of these institutions are young and evolving.

Box 4.1
National Audubon Society v. Superior Court of Alpine County

The "Mono Lake" Decision

Following application for a permit in 1940, the city of Los Angeles was granted rights to 100,000 acre-feet of water from Mono Lake, California's second-largest lake (Gillilan and Brown 1997, 152–153). Mono Lake receives inflow from several streams, but has no outlet. Its waters are naturally lost to evaporation, and the resulting saline condition has created a unique habitat, especially pertaining to the support of bird species. Los Angeles commenced use of 50,000 acre-feet immediately, transporting it three hundred miles to the city. Following the development of additional conveyances, the complete use of the 100,000 acre-foot permit began in 1970. These withdrawals resulted in a decline in the level of Mono Lake.

Some Californian college students, who commenced study of the lake in 1976, became alarmed about the extent of the lake's fall, and they established the Mono Lake Committee (Dunning 1993). As a consequence of their findings and activism, concern spread among environmental groups. A suit was filed in 1979 by the Audubon Society, Friends of the Earth, and the Mono Lake Committee. Among the suit's charges was the assertion that the state had mistakenly granted the 1940 permit because the state had a "public trust" duty that it had not performed. While the public trust doctrine historically addresses each state's role in managing tidal lands for the benefit of navigation, commerce, and fishing, courts have progressively expanded the scope of the doctrine to include habitat protection and nontidal lands.

In 1983, the California Supreme Court agreed with the environmental groups and directed the state water agency to reconsider the permit. In 1994, the agency ordered Los Angeles to suspend all Mono Lake diversions until the lake could recover to a specified elevation. The permit was modified to 32,000 acre-feet (Gillilan and Brown 1997, 153).

• When reviewing new applications for water withdrawal permits, the state may deny applications that will diminish remaining streamflows too greatly.

• A state legislature may issue a moratorium on new withdrawals from specified watercourses.

• A state may issue to itself or other agents water rights designated as instream flow rights. Such rights are normally quantified and possess a given seniority date. At the extreme, such rights can be viewed as minimum streamflow thresholds that are more senior than all other rights.

• States may allow interested agents to acquire water rights (on the market) and rededicate them to instream flow. This instrument as well as the prior one requires that the state first amend its list of beneficial uses to include instream flow. While modifications such as this appear to be compelling "no-brainers" and are easily accomplished, there are special interests who oppose this institutional change because they possess economic interests in maintaining water diversions at high levels. Agriculturally dependent businesses are an example.

• A water tax can be applied to all water market transfers with the tax "revenue" being redirected to instream flow. For example, a 5 percent tax applied to a 200 acre-feet/year transfer would mean that the buyer gets only 190 acre-feet and the remaining 10 acre-feet will now remain instream.[12]

• A state may participate in the water market, either buying permanent water rights or leasing them during low-flow periods, and then recommitting these rights to instream flows. This type of action has also been conducted by U.S. agencies (Simon 1998).

In addition to this assortment of tools, courts may also apply the public trust doctrine in novel ways, as was done in the Mono Lake decision. This approach allows long-standing water rights to be reduced or eliminated, without compensation to their owners. Hailed by environmental groups and loathed by water diverters, this tool either (a) establishes a "corrected" balance between rival and nonrival water uses or (b) threatens the development of private property in water rights, depending on which side of the fence you're on. From the standpoint of pursuing economic efficiency there may be truth in both views, depending on the situation. In terms of (a), water rights distributed during a prodevelopment era can overshoot the efficient balance of private and public rights. Moreover, the nonrival status of certain uses may

---

12. It should be acknowledged that such taxes cause the marginal value of water to be different for the two parties of a market transaction. In this example, if the seller is receiving $1,000/acre-foot, the buyer is paying $1,053/acre-foot. Economic efficiency requires equal marginal values, so there is some loss in social net benefits. Still, depending on the marginal value of instream water and the availability of other policy instruments (is there a better policy?), such a tax can increase the total value of water to society.

mean that "you can't get there from here" when it comes to relying on market trans-actions to repurchase overallocated rights. With respect to (b), exercises of the public trust doctrine cast a cloud of uncertainty over all water rights as well as the invest-ments in hardware that these rights encouraged. (Think about the Los Angeles capi-tal investments in water transmission facilities that were "stranded"—that became unusable—by the Mono Lake decision.) When a property right of any kind loses its dependability, it loses value, and the market's potential for achieving efficiency is eroded.

All things considered, the multitude of mechanisms for supporting nonrival water uses establishes quite an institutional patchwork. Cox's remark (cited earlier) about the crisis origin of many water rules and their lack of integration is clearly on target. Transaction costs are unnecessarily high. Our rules are falling short of what can be achieved. But the rules are maturing too. Perhaps greater attention to the economic features of these institutions will aid the maturation process.

4.9 Ground Water Law

As noted previously, most institutional innovation for water occurred for surface water situations because scarcity first occurred for surface water. Another factor slowing the development of ground water law is that ground water physics was poorly understood until the twentieth century, and ground water flow was regarded as mysterious. Although the principles of ground water movement are no longer mis-understood, except in courtrooms respecting archaic principles, it is expensive to as-semble the hydrologic information required for good planning decisions.

Ground water law contains many of the same variants as surface water law. This is to be expected, but there are differences as well. Some differences arise from the "stock" dimension of ground water resources, as compared to the "flow" character of surface water. A consequence is that dynamic efficiency is important for ground water allocation because water stored in aquifers can be depleted. Some aquifers have noteworthy annual recharge potential. Others have limited recharge, inferring that any pumping will effectively mine the aquifer's water.

Because ground water is usually depletable to some degree, the desire for dynamic efficiency asks that users balance the value of current use against the present value of future use. In accordance with the principles of chapter 3, every pumper should select a level of water use that equates MNB_0 and $MNB_1/(1 + d)$. Ideally, they will use the social discount rate in this decision making, but that is quite unlikely (the over-discounting market failure). A more fundamental problem than overdiscounting occurs if ground water users are not motivated to consider the opportunity costs of their current pumping. If the legal rules do not induce pumpers to consider

$MNB_1/(1 + d)$, they will set $MNB_0 = 0$, and conserve ground water inefficiently and inadequately.

Absolute Ownership: Weak Common Property in Ground Water

Not commonly used for water-scarce areas except in Texas, the *absolute ownership doctrine* assigns every owner of land overlying an aquifer the right to pump as much ground water as desired (Goldfarb 1984, 24). England and other countries as well as some eastern U.S. states also have experience with this rule. One cannot pump water for the single purpose of harming other ground water users, but landowners may use water for all other purposes and in any amounts they wish (Tarlock 1991, sec. 4.04). Also called *the rule of capture* because you own only what you can capture, the absolute ownership doctrine establishes a common consisting of all landowners overlying an aquifer. Landowners are not prohibited from pumping ground water and transporting it to be used on nonoverlying land (Goldfarb 1984, 25).

Because water table drawdown by any landowner induces aquifer flow toward the well and away from neighboring land properties, absolute ownership does not establish private property in ground water.[13] The amount of ground water each pumper can take is not quantitatively limited by absolute ownership. The absence of any notable constraints infers that this form of common property rule is so weak as to almost constitute an open access property structure.[14] As a consequence, conservation incentives are poor. Except for the possibility of moral consciousness, extremely low aquifer transmissivity, or large single-agent land tracts, landowners do not perceive any opportunity cost to their withdrawals other than pumping costs. Anyone choosing to forgo withdrawal of a unit of water is not guaranteed use of that unit in the future. Hence, absolute ownership encourages wasteful behavior of the $MNB_0 = 0$ type.

Reasonable Use: Common Property in Ground Water

Absolute ownership is derived from English common law, which is also the source of riparianism, but U.S. interpretations of common law and riparianism have usually indicated a preference for "reasonable" ground water use. Under the *reasonable use doctrine* (or American Rule) of ground water use, overlying landowners form an exclusive common (as in the case of absolute ownership), but any water use is con-

---

13. It can be said that absolute ownership is an aspect of private property in land (not water) in that land-ownership in an absolute ownership jurisdiction includes the right to access ground water. But this is a different matter than private property in ground water.

14. Indeed, it can be realistically argued that absolute ownership is a rarely seen example of open access. Yet when the practice of absolute ownership is closely examined, one finds that the deficiencies of this doctrine may have encouraged courts or legislatures to design accompanying rules that may check the worst excesses of absolute ownership. Also, only landowners are granted access so the full body of rules is not truly open access.

strained by a loosely defined reasonability test (Z. Smith 1989, 8; Tarlock 1991, sec. 4.05[1]). Water use cannot be "wasteful," and transport of water to nonoverlying property is allowed only when common members will not be harmed (Goldfarb 1984, 25). What is or is not reasonable is underdeveloped for ground water as compared to riparian principles. As compared to riparian surface water, reasonableness for ground water is less relative to the use of other common members. There is less emphasis on equitable sharing, but "the gap between the two rules is closing" (Tarlock 1991, sec. 4.05[1]).

As contrasted to absolute ownership, the additional criterion of reasonableness stiffens the rules and improves the prospects for achieving dynamic efficiency. But current tests performed for assessing reasonability do not achieve dynamic efficiency. It can be said that the reasonable use doctrine is a *dynamic improvement* over absolute ownership, but it does not take the rule set all the way to the goal of dynamic efficiency. Even if the "gap closes" and reasonability for ground water use came to be judged on par with reasonability for surface water, we would still have rules focusing on the allocation of water among current users. What of current use vis-à-vis future use? The practice of judging reasonability for surface water need not address this matter, but it is relevant for depletable ground water. Worse still, the prospects for improving reasonability tests in this direction seem remote. To do so would require that administering courts or agencies develop their economic training and perform complicated economic studies of dynamic efficiency.

Correlative Rights: Common Property in Ground Water

Correlative rights in ground water is a successive tightening of ground water law, relative to absolute ownership and reasonable use. Pioneered in California, the principle here is that the common composed of overlying landowners possess equitable shares that are prorated among users. Reasonability tests on par with those of riparianism are used. "The reasonableness of each overlying use is determined by comparing the requirements of competing overlying users and deciding whose use is more beneficial and in what degree. Correlative rights are not absolute but are rights to divert water subject to the reasonable needs of others and the availability of supply" (Goldfarb 1984, 25).

To address the matter of depletion over time, the correlative rights approach is to determine the "safe yield" of an aquifer and restrict annual total pumping to that amount. While safe yield computations tend to ignore economic principles, explicit attention to depletion is laudable, and it is conceivable that the difference between safe yield and dynamically efficient pumping levels may be small in some settings. The latter possibility has greater probability in a Californian context where aquifers often receive significant annual recharge. It is in cases such as these where safe yield computations are not far removed from dynamic efficiency.

While the intent of these provisions appears promising from the perspective of efficiency goals, it appears that correlative rights are unevenly applied in California. Only particular regions of California employ correlative rights in fact, and excessive ground water mining is rampant: "Management in some areas is often nothing more than the cumulative decisions of individual pumpers" (Z. Smith 1989, 59). As with all of the legal theories we are considering, there can be separation between the institutions that are purportedly used and the actual ones.

The Prior Appropriations Doctrine: Incomplete Private Property in Ground Water

Some states applying the prior appropriations doctrine for surface water have adopted the same system for managing ground water. There are notable exceptions such as California and Texas, as observed in the prior sections. States not using prior appropriations for surface water do not use it for ground water. The most important tenets can be applied in unmodified form to ground water. These include principles such as the quantification of water rights, the concept of seniority, and transferability; and they also include inefficient and dispensable elements such as beneficial use and forfeiture clauses. In point of fact, all of these features are generally employed for ground water in prior appropriation states, with the possible exception of transferability.

Given the efficiency advantages of prior appropriations in surface water settings, one might think that this doctrine would be attractive for ground water (assuming transferability). Unfortunately, the difficulties of depletion and the incomplete application of the doctrine confound prospects for dynamic efficiency. If we have established a system of quantified, prioritized (by time of first use), and transferable permits, when do we stop issuing new permits? Should we issue no additional permits beyond annual recharge? None beyond safe yield? What of the many aquifers having very low recharge relative to their stored water? Should rights be allocated to the stored water too?

Even if we momentarily ignore stored water, recharge can vary from year to year. If the ideals of prior appropriations are tightly applied, junior right holders should shut down their wells during low recharge periods. Operationally, this action necessitates an administrative estimate of recharge and a formal announcement of which right holders can pump. Thus far, administrative agencies have been reluctant to undertake such actions. In addition to the analytic obstacles in measuring aquifer recharge each year, the prevailing opinions of users are that "there's water down there, so why can't I pump it?" As observed by Tarlock, "There is seldom an absolute shortage. There is almost always water available for extraction at some level" (1991, sec. 6.04[1]). Until society is willing to firmly apply prior appropriations to ground water situations, the prospects for achieving efficiency will be poor. Firm application requires that everyone perceive "the water down there" as belonging to someone. If ground water is truly scarce, it should not be free for the taking merely because it lies beneath your land. Transferability is also needed lest scarce ground water supplies become bound to less valuable applications.

If our application of prior appropriations to ground water matures, there is still the uncomfortable matter of depletion and mining, which is not directly addressed by prior appropriations. Ground water depletion is the clear reality in the majority of aquifers under current institutions. Is that what we want? Dynamic efficiency supports a measure of depletion, but it must balance current marginal net benefits and discounted future marginal net benefits. The overdiscounting market failure implies individual agents go too far with their depletion decisions. Many observers believe that depletion is occurring too rapidly, and these beliefs are consistent with expectations stemming from any "tragedy of the commons" scenario. Such a tragedy is evident for prior appropriations jurisdictions because of poor enforcement. Assuming better enforcement, how might prior appropriations be extended to deal with depletion? While it has yet to find real-world application, a suggestion by Vernon Smith is worthy of our attention. (Smith is another Nobel Memorial Prize winner in economics, but this honor stems from his contributions to economics beyond the one acknowledged here.)

The Vernon Smith System: Advanced Private Property in Ground Water

One method to improve depletion speed is to define water rights specific to it. Smith suggests transferable ground water rights of two types, which he calls deeds (1977). Different deeds are established for an aquifer's renewable and stored components. Similar to surface water rights, the first type of deed entitles a user to a recurring amount of the aquifer's annual recharge. This deed might, for example, provide a particular right holder with the privilege to pump ten million gallons of water *each year*. Smith does not specify whether these type 1 deeds have seniorities or not, so we might like to attach seniorities if annual recharge varies substantially from year to year.

The second deed, ownable apart from the first, entitles a user to a fixed amount of the aquifer's stored water. This deed is depleted as it is exercised. If a well owner possesses a type 2 deed to fifty million gallons and uses five million gallons of it, the owner may still pump forty-five million gallons in future periods. Once the deed is exhausted, the user must cease pumping unless they own or purchase other deeds. Because type 2 deeds may be used at any time and there will be water available to fulfill them, there is no advantage to attaching any form of seniority to them.

Administratively, the Smith system requires that a public authority assess an aquifer's annual recharge and the amount of allocatable stored water. Then the authority distributes the two deed types among users, so that the total deeded quantities are less than renewable and stored water. Clearly, all pumping must be metered, but

Box 4.2
Cappaert v. United States

> In the unusual circumstances of *Cappaert v. United States*, the Devil's Hole National Monument in Nevada holds an underground cavern that is home to the desert pupfish (Tarlock 1991 sec. 9.08[2]). Ground water pumping by nearby ranchers threatened ground water levels and therefore the pupfish, so the U.S. government sued to restrain pumping. The Supreme Court decision sided with the government, saying that the government possessed a reserved right to ground water sufficient to guarantee a minimal pool level in the cavern. In essence, the establishment of the monument created a ground water right for the government, implying that latecomers could not commence any pumping that would deprive the monument's unique species.

all meritorious laws for scarce ground water scenarios involve metering. Presumably, most users would be granted both types of deeds, but the efficiency of the system does not require it. An owner of both deeds would logically employ the renewable deed first each year, with any additional pumpage coming out of the type 2 deed. Assuming available aquifer capacity, owners should be allowed to convert unused type 1 amounts into type 2 deeds.

At the margin under this system, water pumpers will make use of type 2 deeds, and all users will have to make decisions balancing the value of current use against the prospective value of future use.[15] No longer will depletion occur at someone else's expense. The resulting decision calculus will have agents performing $MNB_0 = MNB_1/(1 + d)$ trade-offs, using their private discount rates. Because both deeds are transferable, users will balance their individual MNB_0 (and therefore their $MNB_1/[1 + d]$ too) against the market value of the deed. Hence, we will approach the desired dynamic efficiency condition across all agents. While the market failure of overdiscounting and perhaps some externalities will still be present, a lot will have been achieved in terms of dynamic improvement.[16]

State Property in Ground Water

For the purposes of completeness as well as symmetry, we conclude this treatment of ground water law by acknowledging potential public uses of ground water. As with instream surface water, there are uses of ground water requiring that it be left in the aquifer. These instances are not common for ground water because it's in the ground where humans and humanly valued systems don't generally have natural access to it.

---

15. Unless users can "bank" their type 1 deeds by converting unused amounts into type 2 deeds, there's no incentive to underutilize type 1 deeds. Additional (marginal) pumpage will then have to be from type 2 deeds. If banking is sanctioned, users will consider their options more fully and balance the marginal value of type 1 and type 2 deeds, again implying that the value of type 2 deeds will be considered at the margin.

16. One of these externalities is the pumping cost externality noted earlier in this chapter. There are others that can arise, depending on aquifer circumstances. These shall be identified in chapter 7 when the marketing of ground water is more completely examined.

Although the desert pupfish scenario of *Cappaert v. United States* is atypical, it demonstrates that there can be pure ground water situations in which private rights will have to be limited in order to preserve or enhance nonrival values. When these situations occur, many possible policies can be undertaken, as were documented earlier for surface water scenarios. Ground water rights may be expressly assigned to a public authority; private ground water pumping may not be allowed unless it will not damage public values too much; ground water use can be taxed to motivate limited pumping; an authority can buy ground water rights for retirement; and so on.

More common are situations where ground water has nonrival value because springflow contributes to streamflows that support valuable habitats, aesthetics, and recreation. Because springflow amounts are determined by ground water levels that can be lowered by pumping, it is quite possible that the public sector may wish to reserve some portion of an aquifer for the widespread enjoyment of multiple nonrival users. Situations such as these arise because of the mutual interaction of ground and surface waters. Therefore, they are aspects of *conjunctive water management* that addresses the joint administration of surface and ground water while acknowledging their hydrologic connectedness.

4.10 Conjunctive Management

A common frustration for water managers and planners is the hydrologic interdependence of ground and surface water bodies, which is often in stark contrast to the institutions employed by governments. Water molecules flow quite readily from underground to surface water bodies and back again, and when they do, the allocative rules often change. Inconsistent institutions across ground and surface waters undermine the pursuit of efficiency. This is especially true for alluvial aquifers that are closely related to surface water flows, but the problem is not limited to these hydrologic conditions.

As an example of the problems that can arise, it is not unusual for a government to rely on private property managing for surface water and common property for ground water. Among other things, a prior appropriations jurisdiction purports to protect senior water rights against junior users. Junior water rights cannot be exercised unless supply is sufficient. The First Theorem tells us that this is a good thing. Because of this protection, a market will form to guide limited water to its most valued uses. Senior surface water rights are often not protected, however, against common property ground water rights. A ground water pumper may be allowed to commence or increase pumping depending on the legal doctrine. In many hydrologic circumstances, such an action will have negative consequences for surface water supply either by inducing ground water recharge from connected surface water or reducing ground water outflows to surface water. Both possibilities deprive some surface water user(s) of water unless it is in surplus. Efficiency is then thwarted because agents can satisfy their demand by exploiting the poor integration of water law. Ground water users can actually take senior surface water rights without paying. The unfortunate implications are numerous, but two should be emphasized:

· The possibility of taking water more cheaply than it can be purchased will encourage many agents to do so. As a consequence, these agents will use more water than suggested by efficiency precepts.

· The reduced security of surface water rights lowers their value to their owners and prospective owners, thereby reducing the potential to guide water to most valued uses and reducing the attractiveness of water market transactions.

Although these issues are sources of ongoing inefficiency, they have been sufficiently ubiquitous to encourage some reform, albeit slowly. Many water specialists have commented on these problems, so the lack of conjunctive management is well acknowledged. The problem is ordinarily rooted in the undeveloped state of ground water law as compared to surface water law, so the most important fixes must come from improvements to our ground water institutions. Progress has been slow, but there is some reason to be hopeful about achieving a better interface of our institutions. Greater attention to economic consequences can certainly help. If we are to harness the First Theorem for social benefit, we will need a consistent system of uncorrupted property rights.

4.11   Treaties and Compacts

Regardless of which property form (common, state, or private) is to be applied in water management, there are clear administrative benefits to resolving the amount of water allocable within any given jurisdiction. Because watercourses and water bodies often traverse political boundaries, each polity will not know how much water it commands until an agreement has been forged among hydrologic neighbors. This can be a difficult business. At the international level, conflict over shared water resources can even result in warfare, and water can also be a weapon of war (Gleick 2001).

If a government's water resource base is shrinking over time due to upstream development exterior to its jurisdiction, then there may be an overall loss in economic efficiency. That is, when upstream interests do not care about downstream losses, upstream marginal net benefits of water can be driven to zero, while raising marginal net benefits downstream. MNBs are not equated. When this happens, there are benefits to the upstream state, but the downstream state is injured even more.

The first step in resolving this problem is to divide the resource, so that each government knows its water budget. If the water supply is variable, then the terms of the agreement might guarantee each governmental party a percentage of the supply. Alternatively, one party might be entitled to receive whatever is left over after the other party receives its fixed entitlement.[17] Either type of agreement is called a *treaty* when it involves countries and an *interstate compact* when it involves U.S. states. Examples include the 1944 treaty between the United States and Mexico that apportioned both the Colorado and Rio Grande Rivers, and the 1922 Colorado River Compact that divided the river between "upper-basin" and "lower-basin" states. (Subsequent compacts divided Colorado River water among the various states.) Many similar compacts exist for other western waters (Bennett and Howe 1998), and future compacts are likely for eastern states now wrestling with water shortages.

Assuming these agreements are respected (that is, enforced), each jurisdiction can proceed to administer its water with the benefit of securely knowing its supply. Such knowledge can assist greatly by improving the basis of private water rights. By virtue of knowing its water supply, each government can allocate water rights without risk of overappropriation (assigning more private property rights than are physically available). In the United States, interstate compacts have the force of federal law, so enforcement is generally good. Occasionally, a state will sue an upstream state to force compliance with the terms of a compact. While such actions are costly and lengthy, upstream states become more careful managers afterward. On the international level, enforcement can be poor owing to the weakness of international governing institutions. Examples from the same treaty include the U.S.'s current frustration with Mexico's deficit release of tributary water into the Rio Grande (Texas Center for Policy Studies 2002) as well as, commencing harmfully in the 1960s, the U.S.'s deliveries of saline Colorado River water to Mexico (E. Ward 2003, chapter 3).

Following the successful negotiation of a compact or treaty, a second step in promoting efficiency is to allow interstate trade in any private water rights. Most governments are reluctant to take this step because of public outcries about allowing "our water" to be transferred out of state. The economic judgment is that barring market failures of some type, aggregate economic efficiency is advanced by allowing interjurisdictional transfers. On the other hand, it is probable that certain types of economically linked agents will be harmed by transfers.[18] On this basis, one can say

17. If the social goal of these agreements is to achieve aggregate efficiency, then the economic circumstances of each case can be used to decide between a proportional division and a fixed one. Bennett, Howe, and Shope (2000) show that the best generic division is to guarantee each entity a fixed amount of water up to a point of total supply and then an additional share of any surplus.

18. Using a common example, if irrigators in an upstream state sell their water to cities in a downstream state, there is likely to be some reduction in the agricultural output of the upstream area. Agricultural input suppliers and crop processors will then incur some reduction in income. While the farmers receiving funds for water will spend these receipts in other ways benefiting other people, there are still particular agents who lose as well as some who gain in the upstream state. This example does not represent a market failure, but it does indicate that specific upstream agents may have reason to be unsupportive of interjurisdictional trade in water. Further inspection of this matter will take place in chapter 7.

that allowing interstate trade as well as barring it are both efficient in the *neutral* sense.

These same issues and observations apply in ground water settings, but interjurisdictional agreements pertaining to shared aquifers are few. Again, the development of ground water institutions lags behind those for surface water, but there is good reason to negotiate treaties and compacts for aquifers as well. The pursuit of efficiency will be aided by such institutions, particularly in light of the need to keep MNBs in positive territory so as to advance dynamic efficiency. Too-rapid depletion is to be guarded against, and these agreements help.

4.12 Summary

The importance of institutional choice has required that we cover a lot of ground here. We have both surveyed institutional economics as it relates to water and overviewed key elements of water law. From the economic perspective, there are four variants of property that might be used for water: open access, common property, state property, and private property. Private property is of special interest because a resource being managed as transferable property will automatically cause a market to arise, and that market will produce a resource-conserving signal: price. In ideal circumstances, this market will achieve economic efficiency and, if applicable, dynamic efficiency. This achievement is attributable to the First Theorem of Welfare Economics.

When circumstances are not ideal, perhaps because of the presence of a public good, an externality, a natural monopoly, or overdiscounting, we can have a situation of market failure. Market failure means that we cannot fully rely on private property and the resultant market to attain efficiency. In these cases, efficiency can be advanced by private property in water, but we'll have to enact other policies to control the prospective market failures. Overall, it is critical to remember that the market system does not define what we are trying to achieve, but the market system, including water markets, may move things in the right direction—toward economic efficiency and dynamic efficiency.

When water managers and leaders are rallying attention to their missions, they are apt to mention the importance of water to our existence. Occasionally, one may say that water is "priceless." Such viewpoints simultaneously overlook the true problems and dismiss an all-important solution. Water is crucial for life, but so is food and shelter. Yet we do not talk of food and shelter as being priceless or in short supply. Modern societies have embraced the idea of managing food and shelter using markets—that is, "prices." Except for impoverished people, this system performs well, and we utilize a variety of welfare programs to upgrade the conditions of the poor, especially when it comes to food and shelter. Food and shelter are priced. They are consequently managed more transparently than water is. There is certainly a lesson here, even though unique aspects of water use limit the extent to which this lesson can be applied. The true problems have to do with the various market failures and the absence of prices for natural water, not the significance of water for sustaining our lives.

In the second part of the chapter, we reviewed various tenets of water law—not because they are perfect choices but to provide an economic interpretation of their roles and characterize their merits from this perspective. Examining the menu of surface water and ground water laws separately, all the property forms are represented except open access. For surface water, most important are the doctrines of riparianism (common property), eastern permits (state property), prior appropriations (private property), and correlative rights (private property). None of these institutions are rigidly established; they are evolving. Where water scarcity is increasing, rising dissatisfaction with riparianism is bringing about a transition to eastern permits. If these permits become recognized as transferable, we will witness an additional transition to private property. Prior appropriations is an especially interesting set of institutions because it has founded water markets with the capability to manage year-to-year variations in water supply. But it too is evolving, and in its current form it is accompanied by unnecessary rules fostering inefficiency, including beneficial use requirements, preferential use hierarchies, and forfeiture clauses.

The major doctrines of ground water law are absolute ownership (weak common property), reasonable use (common property), correlative rights (common property), prior appropriations (incomplete private property), and the Vernon Smith system (advanced private property). While some of these names and the underlying principles are derived from surface water counterparts, they are less developed for ground water. These represent opportunities for confusion as well as heightened inefficiency. The efficiency goals for ground water are more stringent than for ordinary surface water because of the added concern for depletion. Achievement of dynamic efficiency is the goal. All of the existing institutions are deficient in achieving the goal. They don't even try in most cases, leaving depletion decisions to individuals who do not reap all the rewards of conservation and who, therefore, are not fully motivated to behave in the public interest. The most promising institution is the theoretical one suggested by Smith, involving separate private deeds for ground water stock (water in storage) and annual recharge. Of the real-world doctrines, only correlative rights is attentive to depletion speed, opting to pursue safe yield rather than dynamic efficiency, but this can be a big improvement in managing depletion.

Due to important "in-place" and largely nonrival uses of water, such as instream flows for recreational and habitat support as well as bay and estuary sustenance, other institutions are applied to preserve or enhance water for these uses. Surface water diverters and ground water pumpers are not motivated to leave water where they find it, so society has formed rules for this purpose. Several examples of these rules were noted previously. They too are steadily evolving. One of the reasons society requires a mixed system of water management institutions, involving both private and public rights, is the need to allocate an efficient amount of water to instream and inground applications.

The marriage of surface and ground water institutions, as needed for conjunctive water management, is an unfinished business in all jurisdictions. Current institutions are incongruent and inconsistent. Therefore, backdoors for circumventing key rules exist, such as when new/expanded ground water pumpers effectively "take" surface water property from previously established water users. Efficiency cannot be achieved until institutions no longer subvert each other, and all incentives encourage people to behave as if scarce water had value.

Our treatment of laws in this discussion has been rather optimistic in that we have presumed that enforcement of these laws is assured. Unfortunately, what's on paper is often an idealistic interpretation of water law. The application of these rules is often incomplete, and enforcement is often lax. Since unenforced institutions are not in full social service, the solution for this problem is clearly evident.

4.13   Exercises

1. Attempt to identify one public good water use involving water supplied by an urban water utility. You must apply the two definitional requirements rigorously and correctly argue that the conditions are met for the water use you have selected. Repeat this assignment for an irrigation district.

2. When it can be applied, the First Theorem of Welfare Economics has been referred to as "the public use of the private interest." Explain the First Theorem in these terms.

3. Name the four generic property forms that can be established for any resource. Attempt to identify real-world, nonwater examples for each, explaining why your examples are suitable.

4. Suppose that your state has historically applied the riparian doctrine, and that twenty years ago the state initiated a requirement that surface water diverters and ground water pumpers register for permits. Each permit indicates an allowed annual quantity of water use. Originally, these permits were viewed as term permits in that they expire after ten years unless renewed by the owner. A group of water users is now suing the state, not because they object to the permit system, but because they want the permits to be (1) permanent and (2) transferable. The general environmental lobby agrees, but they also want (3) a ban on the issue of any more permits and

they want (4) all existing permits lowered by 20 percent. Critique these four policy elements from an economic perspective emphasizing the achievement of efficiency, and use your discussion to formulate a policy recommendation. Be clear about which policy elements are addressed by economic theory.

5. Describe how an efficiency-advancing combination of the prior appropriations doctrine and centralized planning might be designed for ground water depletion settings. Which of these two elements would end up deciding intertemporal and intratemporal allocations among agents? Compare this policy to the Vernon Smith system.

5 Policy Analysis

How should proposed rule changes be assessed?

A profound implication of the prior pages is that water shortages are typically an institutional deficiency, not a physical one. That's a difficult point to overemphasize. The physical environment provides all the water it can, and there is no more. If we cannot operate within this physically established water budget, then we have failed to select the right rules for water management. To say that water shortages are a perpetual condition is to say that we need to revise our institutions. This argument applies to demand management and supply enhancement strategies. As with demand management mechanisms (such as pricing, technology restrictions, and water use regulations), supply enhancement activities also need to be efficiently structured and encouraged by appropriately designed rules. Supply enhancements do not "materialize" new water. They alter the character of water in terms of when and where it is available, and they possibly alter its quality, but they do not create new water.

While the layperson's first thoughts about solving water shortages will stress supply enhancement alternatives, such enhancements are often costly, and most new project proposals have trouble advancing economic efficiency. To control costs, supply enhancements should be efficiently sized (scaled), efficiently timed, and efficiently selected. If good institutions are in place, only efficient supply enhancements will be pursued, and the rules will encourage the identification of all such enhancements.

Most supply enhancements are structural measures that can be called water projects. The peculiarities of *project analysis* are deferred to the following chapter. There, strong use will be made of the ideas developed in the present chapter—where the focus is on *policy analysis*.

Policies can be thought of as alternative institutions. Policy analysis for water resource problems is primarily about the economic analysis of institutional change. Society is always evolving its institutions, and we would like to investigate the merits of rule changes before they are undertaken. The same is true of prospective changes in the water rates that a utility or district might reestablish periodically. Rates can be thought of as simplistic rules: "you are entitled to receive water from us; you can choose how much; and here's how we will assess your water bill each period."

Given the economic fundamentals developed in chapter 2, single-period rule changes must offer positive net benefits if they are to advance efficiency. From chapter 3, multiperiod rule changes must provide positive net present value (summed and discounted net benefits) if they are to be dynamic improvements in efficiency. Hence, the key analytic requirement is the computation of net benefits. We performed some net benefit calculations in chapters 2 and 3. In this chapter, we will extend that work, add some rigor, and consider more advanced situations.

5.1   Two Policy Analysis Forms: Theoretical and Empirical

The economically trained analyst can conduct policy analysis on two levels: theoretical and empirical. Applying the institutional economics of chapter 4, an analyst may capably support certain policy reforms and protest other reforms on the sole basis of theory. Indeed, part II of chapter 4 was peppered with a large amount of theoretical policy analysis. As the various types of water law were introduced, economic theory was employed to characterize the pros and cons of each legal doctrine.

The success of theoretical policy analysis depends on (1) the completeness with which available theory is utilized, and (2) whether the audience of this analysis has sufficient understanding to grasp and accept the pronouncements. Not surprisingly, incomplete theory can give rise to incorrect assessments of policy. For example, a rudimentary understanding of First Theorem economics may lead the analyst to unwavering support of water markets while deriding all regulatory policies that are not market oriented. Such a perspective places too much faith in meeting the First Theorem's assumptions and fails to acknowledge the possibility that there may be important market failures to be addressed. When economists have differences of opinion on matters of theoretical policy analysis, it is usually because some are exercising economic theory differently or more completely than others. Sometimes, the differences arise solely from differing assumptions.

With respect to point (2) above, theoretical forms of policy analysis may be unconvincing to participants within the policy decision-making process. These people may not possess the necessary economic training to appreciate a theoretically founded argument. If analysts do not package this training along with their policy assessments (a tough task), the audience will remain skeptical. Decision makers are often predisposed to dismiss theoretically rooted analyses. They may distrust economics or favor status quo (existing) institutions over change. As noted in chapter 2, not everyone will benefit from economically efficient change, and those who might experience losses can be expected to raise objections. Readily available objections are "I don't understand or believe your theory," or "you economists are always disagreeing with one another, so who am I to believe?"

The clear advantage of theoretical policy analysis is the possibility of acquiring quick advice about policy, using only economic insight merged with common sense. Little or no data are required, and no programming or number crunching has to be conducted. In such cases, policy improvements need not be handcuffed by the expense and time delays imposed by quantitative analysis. Institutional advance can be accelerated.

Unfortunately, there are many cases in which theoretical policy analysis will not possess sufficient sharpness to offer a clear recommendation. Given that all policies are accompanied by both economic gains and losses, our theory may not have the power to know whether the gains exceed the losses. In other cases where theory is resolute, decision makers may not be convinced until they can see some "show-me" analysis containing numbers and "facts." Here, empirical policy analysis can be conducted. Whereas theoretical policy analysis can be conducted without empiricism, it does not work in reverse. Empiricism requires a sound theoretical foundation.

5.2 Empirical Policy Analysis: The Ins and Outs of Compensation Tests

Given the maximize net benefits efficiency criterion, a good policy change is one offering social benefits in excess of social costs. Hence, the empirical approach to policy analysis is to estimate the monetary value of prospective new benefits and compare it to the monetary value of prospective new costs. For anthropocentric reasons, all policy effects count, whether they are marketed goods or not. If the gainers of a prospective public action can hypothetically compensate the losers and have something left over, then that's a desirable course of action. This is called a *hypothetical compensation test*. If the policy is approved and undertaken, there will still be losers—compensation is hypothetical—but the socially aggregated net benefits will have been enhanced.

Thought of another way, we calculate the change in net benefits for every affected party and add these. If the aggregated net benefits are positive, then the policy is judged to be a good one.

An efficiency-improving policy occurs when $\sum \Delta \text{NB} > 0$.

Collapsing all policy effects into a single net benefit measure is simple, yet it may not capture everything of interest to decision makers. Decision processes can be sensitive to the distribution of net benefits—who gains and who is harmed, and by how much. For this reason, analysts may be well-advised to retain analytic detail in reported results. That is, instead of adding all computed ΔNBs and reporting the aggregate, it is good to report disaggregated findings: "Group A will experience losses of x thousand $ annually, Sector B will gain y thousand $ annually, and so forth."

In most water-related circumstances, these net benefit calculations will make heavy use of agents' water demand functions. Knowledge of demand will therefore be critical. As developed in chapter 2, residential and domestic consumers of water have value-sensitive demands for water. Business enterprises, motivated by profit, also have value-sensitive water demands.

Policy changes affecting people or businesses will alter the net benefits received by these agents through at least one of four primary mechanisms: *price rationing, quantity rationing, demand shifting,* or *supply shifting*. Forthcoming sections will deal with each of these policy types in turn. In the real world, some of these mechanisms may occur in unison, such as when a supply shift requires increased prices to cover new costs. By emphasizing the elements of such policy combinations, it will be possible to disentangle the various impacts on affected groups.

Figure 5.1 displays the initial, prepolicy circumstances for a group of water consumers. This group may include households, industries, or any combination of

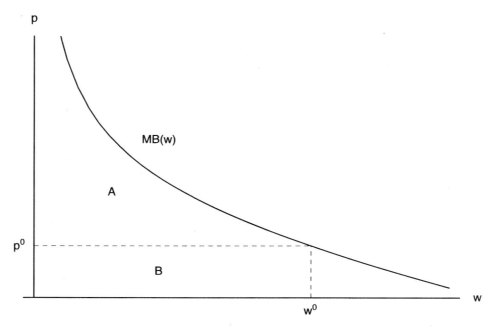

Figure 5.1
Baseline consumer welfare

water-using agents. While it could also be demand for natural water in a river, let's presume MB(w) is the group's collective demand for retail water supplied by a utility.[1] This utility meters water deliveries and charges p^0 per unit of water. In response, the consumer group chooses to take w^0 units of water. Total benefits received by water users is then the area under their demand, area $A + B$. Total revenue received by the utility is p^0 times w^0 or area B. Net benefits received by water users is area A. With this prepolicy setting in place, we can begin to evaluate alternative policy actions. First, however, some useful terminology is appropriate.

5.3   Consumer and Producer Surplus Measurement

If the demand group consists only of households, then area A of figure 5.1 can be unambiguously called *consumer surplus*. In our water context, consumer surplus is the net benefits of water consumption to households after they have paid for their water. With total benefits of $A + B$ and payments of only B, consumers have some benefits left over—what economists call consumer surplus. It is the availability of this surplus that motivates consumers to buy water. Without it, there would be no reason.

If the MB curve of figure 5.1 also contains business agents who are using water, then consumer surplus can also be an apt term for area A because these agents are consuming water as an input to a production process. These agents are buying water because it is one of the inputs enabling a profit to be made from the production and sale of some other commodities. In the marketplace for these produced commodities,

Box 5.1
Jules Dupuit, Father of Consumer Surplus

> The desire to value public works projects has long interested engineers as well as economists. The lineage of the consumer surplus concept traces to Jules Dupuit, "an engineer serving as an inspector of bridges and highways in France" during the mid-1800s (McKenzie 1983, 68). Dupuit debunked the idea that the total value of a good is its market price times the total quantity. He rationalized that consumers receive higher utility from the use of a commodity or service as its price falls. Also, as the consumer acquires more units of any specific good, they are assigned to less-valued applications. These facts had implications for valuing public projects in Dupuit's estimation.
>
> The idea of consumer surplus—that consumers receive a measurable benefit in excess of the price they pay for a good—has become important in economics. It is a key concept for both the policy analysis work of this chapter and the project assessment work of the forthcoming chapter. Dupuit possessed an early grasp of these ideas, and his examples include attention to increased water consumption spurred by falling water prices (Dupuit 1969, 258–259; reprint of translated 1844 work).

1. Recall from chapter 2 that the MB for natural water is obtained by subtracting marginal processing costs from the MB for retail water.

the sellers earn a ***producer surplus***, which is essentially the same thing as a profit.[2] Under a general condition, it can be mathematically shown that the producer surplus earned in these commodity markets is equal to the consumer surplus these business agents receive in the water "market" as water consumers (Just, Hueth, and Schmitz 2004, 63). That is, there is an equivalence, and it gives us two means of measuring the same thing: the benefits of water consumption as received by business agents. Moreover, this equivalence warns us about a potential double-counting mishap.

The prior observations reveal some overlap between the ideas of producer and consumer surplus, which render the two terms a bit redundant. At least that's the situation for retail water because it is often supplied by a nonprofit entity operating in a noncompetitive environment. The notion of producer surplus would not be redundant if a true market for retail water could occur. In such a circumstance, profit-motivated and competitive water suppliers would interact with consumers through a market. A supply-demand-balancing price would emerge. Consumer would earn a surplus defined as the area below the demand curve and above the price line. Producers would earn a surplus defined as the area above the supply curve and below the price line. Only the consumer side of this situation often applies, however, as noted early in chapter 2.

As a consequence, only the idea of consumer surplus may be fully applicable, and even that concept should be expanded to include the water consumption rewards (profits) to business agents. We will rely on the terms *consumer welfare* or *consumer net benefits* here, so as to limit any confusion arising from surplus terminology. Such welfare extends to all users of water.

5.4 Price-Rationing Policy

In figure 5.2, we contemplate a potential increase in the water rate from p^0 to p^1. Such an increase may be proposed to better match price with the marginal cost of water (to advance efficiency), ration a temporary water supply shortfall, or increase utility revenue. Whereas water users' net benefits are initially area a + b + c (= area A of figure 5.1), consumer net benefits will be area a after the rate increase. Therefore, the change in water users' net benefits for this proposal is − area (b + c).

---

2. Producer welfare measurement pertaining to altered policies requires the computation of *changed* producer surplus. This is essentially the same thing as changed profit, although there can be instances in which changed producer surplus (and welfare) is not identical to changed profit (Just, Hueth, and Schmitz 2004, 55). Such instances occur as a result of fixed cost obligations that cannot be avoided by a firm forced into nonproduction by a new policy. In such cases, which might result from a higher input cost, the nonoperating firm loses its profits *and* must still make payments toward fixed cost commitments. Here, then, the loss is prior profit plus fixed cost payments, which is obviously greater than the change in profit. In application, it must be said that economic empiricism rarely attends to this nuance, and analysts are typically content to think of changed profit as a suitable welfare measure.

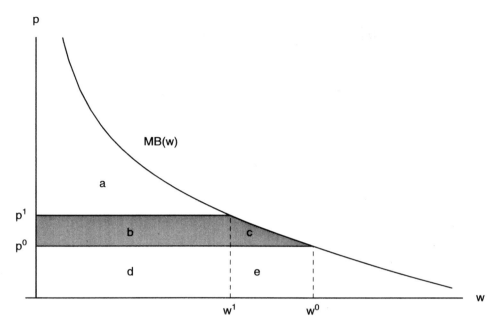

Figure 5.2
Effects of price-rationing policy

A second effect of this policy is to alter utility revenue. The utility sells less water than before, thus losing the revenue depicted by area e, but it gets more revenue for the water it does deliver, gaining area b.

The final effect of this policy is to lower the utility's production costs by lowering the amount of water it must process. To analyze and monetarize this latter impact, we will need to examine the utility's cost function. The dominance of fixed (capital) costs in most water utilities' budgets may imply that the change in production costs is small, at least from a mere accounting perspective, but we may also include all saved opportunity costs of water, such as the marginal value of natural water (λ in equation [2.30]) and the marginal value of depletable water (δ_0 in equation [3.14]).[3] For now, we will defer details on the analysis of modified production costs while continuing to acknowledge their relevance.

3. Some of these opportunity costs may lie outside the accounting stance of the decision-making body. For example, a utility resolving rate policy may be uninterested in the broader regional value of natural water if there is no water market signaling this value to the utility. On the other hand, even if an opportunity cost captures values lying exterior to the decision-making jurisdiction, the moral call to be good water stewards and acknowledge opportunity costs can be strong.

Table 5.1
Analysis of price-rationing policy (see figure 5.2)

	Consumer welfare	Utility revenue	Total change
Postpolicy:	a	$b + d$	
Prepolicy:	$a + b + c$	$d + e$	
Change:	$-(b + c)$	$+b - e$	$-c - e + \Delta\text{costs}$

These graphically depicted changes are summarized in table 5.1. The final row of this table collects the policy-induced changes, which are calculated by subtracting prepolicy net benefits from postpolicy net benefits. Whereas consumer welfare declines, this loss is partially offset by a rise in utility revenue.[4] Whether or not the total change in net benefits is positive depends on the change in production costs (Δcosts).[5]

Hence, the graphic investigation indicates that empirical policy evaluation will need to calculate the following integral:

$$-c - e = \int_{w^0}^{w^1} MB(w)\, dw. \tag{5.1}$$

If additional detail is desired, the separate impact on consumers can be calculated as

$$-b - c = \int_{p^1}^{p^0} MB^{-1}(p)\, dp, \tag{5.2}$$

where MB^{-1} is the inverted form of the marginal benefit function (solved for w). This latter measure is shaded in figure 5.2.

Whereas the preceding analysis infers that water rate increases are always bad for consumers, the analysis commences with a prepolicy scenario that may have become untenable. If the water utility faces changed circumstances requiring institutional change, then the appropriate analysis should compare the rate increase to other policy measures. One way to do this is to compare each conceivable policy response to the prepolicy scenario and then select the alternative with the greatest net benefits or the smallest sacrifice in net benefits. For example, if the utility is suffering from revenue shortfalls that may be recovered through nonvolumetric instruments such as increased connection fees or taxes, then the net benefits of these measures should be

4. It can be mathematically demonstrated that $+b - e > 0$ only when demand is price inelastic as is normally the case for water demand.

5. Applying the theory we have assembled injects these insights, however: $-c - e + \Delta\text{costs}$ is negative if the marginal cost of water is less than or equal to p^0; it may be positive if the marginal cost of water is greater than p^0; and it will be positive if the marginal cost of water is p^1 or larger.

Box 5.2
An Increase in Rates

City planners are proposing a 5 percent increase in all water rates. Prior to adopting this policy, the city council would like to receive information about the effects on consumers and the water department. We can rough out some quick and useful estimates using knowledge of an annual demand point and the price elasticity of demand. Suppose the water department delivers 180 million gallons per year while taking in $740,000 in revenue per year. Of this revenue, $520,000 is derived from volumetric (metered) charges, and the remainder comes from fixed fees such as monthly charges and late fees.

Analysis

A 5 percent increase in nonvolumetric rates will tend to produce an additional $11,000 for the utility, although it is conceivable that the altered behavior by consumers would lessen this amount slightly (e.g., fewer late payment penalties). This increase in revenue would also constitute an $11,000 injury to consumers. The average customer appears to be paying $2,889 per million gallons, so (180, $2889) can serve as a demand point for community water demand. Assuming an elasticity of -0.3 and linear demand, the point expansion method yields the demand function, $w = 234. - 0.0187 \cdot p$ or, in inverted form, $p = 12519. - 53.5 \cdot w$. Increasing the price to $3,033 will then yield a quantity demanded of 177.3 million gallons. We may now undertake the computations suggested by table 5.1:

$$\Delta NB_{consumers} = \int_{3033}^{2889} (234. - 0.0187p)\, dp = -25805$$

$$\Delta NB_{utility} = (3033 - 2889) \cdot 177.3 - 2889 \cdot (180 - 177.3) = 17731.$$

(Note that the integral area is the easily computed area of a trapezoid.)

In summary, it is estimated that water customers lose $36,805 worth of benefits due to the rate increases, and the water department gains $28,731 in revenues. Both amounts are annual. If this was the total picture, we would not recommend this policy. Yet the reduced water deliveries of 2.7 million gallons will lower the department's operating costs, so we will need the department to estimate the cost savings for us. Second, the rate-increase proposal may stem from a budget shortfall rendering the original rates infeasible. In this case, judgments about the new rates will have to be made relative to other budget-balancing policies.

studied too. Relative to the alternatives, the p^0 to p^1 rate increase may be welcomed by consumers in the sense that it offers reduced losses (higher net benefits).

Analytically challenging instances of price-rationing policy are situations in which a water supplier first begins to meter water and charge volumetrically. Early in their history, many water suppliers rely on flat rate fees, which are independent of water use, and customers are free to use as much water as they like. The prospective transition to water pricing is usually opposed by consumers, who have a hard time understanding how they will benefit. Using similar methods to those presented here, Hanke (1981, 1982) has evaluated the net benefits of commencing urban metering in Perth, Australia. Including the sizable cost of installing meters (one million dollars) and reading them regularly, the switch was estimated to produce aggregate annual net

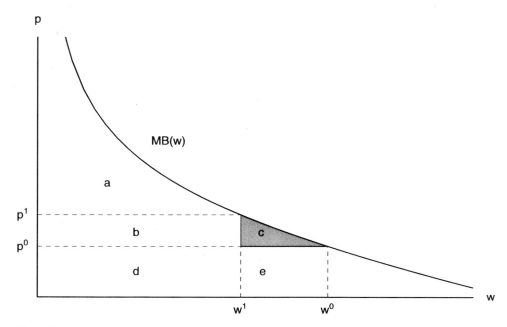

Figure 5.3
Effects of quantity-rationing policy

benefits of nearly one-quarter million dollars. Similar analyses have been performed for policy scenarios involving transitions to seasonal water pricing (higher summer prices) for locales that have been relying on nonseasonal rates (Renzetti 1992b) and to situations where a community might improve rates by adopting marginal-cost pricing (Feldman, Breese, and Obeiter 1981).

5.5   Quantity-Rationing Policy

A regulatory policy limiting the quantity of water demanded is diagrammed in figure 5.3. Presumably designed to confront a supply shortfall, this policy reduces water use by restricting user choice in some manner. Perhaps certain water uses are barred (such as lawn watering on certain days, car/sidewalk washing, or irrigating a low-value crop) or perhaps all users are told to cut back their usage by x percent. To aid comparisons, let's presume this policy reduces water use to w^1. The water rate remains at p^0.

In this policy, the utility clearly loses revenue represented by area e. Water users lose total benefits given by area c + e, and lose net benefits of area c *if and only if* we can make the following heroic assumption: all reductions in water use are

Table 5.2
Analysis of quantity-rationing policy (see figure 5.3)

	Consumer welfare*	Utility revenue	Total change*
Postpolicy:	a + b	d	
Prepolicy:	a + b + c	d + e	
Change:	− c	− e	− c − e + Δcosts

*For reasons discussed below, these columns contain overestimates of postpolicy net benefits and the changes in net benefits. That is, the losses in net benefits will be *higher*.

obtained by eliminating those uses on the (w^1, w^0) region of the demand curve, and all uses on the $(0, w^1)$ region are preserved. Otherwise, consumer losses will be higher (Brown and Johnson 1969; Turvey 1970). Unfortunately, "planners have no reliable way to set nonprice rules that allocate water to its highest-valued users" (Hanke 1978, 487–488). Barring or limiting specified uses of water is unlikely to promote efficiency because some users may attach high MBs to these uses. Percentage cutback decrees give users the option to decide on their least valued uses, thus providing some assurance that each consumer's losses will be minimized. Yet MB(w) constitutes demand for a group of users, and it is easily possible that some users should not curtail their water use for an efficient allocation of w^1. More generally, an equal apportionment of the shortfall is unlikely to serve efficiency. From an efficiency perspective, greater curtailments should come from low-value water uses, and it is unlikely that these are evenly distributed across the water-using population. The main consequence of these observations is that area c underestimates consumers' net losses.[6] The primary elements of the results are collected within table 5.2.

Writing table 5.2 findings in integral form, as in equations (5.1) and (5.2), is left as an exercise for the reader. Comparing the results of tables 5.1 and 5.2, it is seen that the total changes would be identical were it not for the bias in net benefit measures for quantity rationing. Hence, price rationing can always be expected to outperform quantity controls in terms of economic efficiency.

When the "Consumer welfare" columns of these tables are compared, it can be seen why consumers might be supportive of quantity rationing. On the surface, so to speak, area c is the lower bound to consumer welfare losses for quantity rationing. For price rationing, the loss is areas b and c. This is an incomplete, short-term perspective on the situation, however. In most regions water utilities are community

6. It may be possible to achieve better accuracy if demand can be partitioned into separate demands for differently impacted groups of agents and it is known how the quantity restriction will affect the different groups. For example, in an irrigation district context a policy forbidding the irrigation of pasture might be proposed. Instead of examining the demand for water across the district (MB(w) in figure 5.3), it may be possible to separate demand into two functions, pasture water demand and nonpasture water demand, depending on data availability.

owned, inferring that consumers ultimately feel the consequences of changes in utility revenue. For price rationing, the loss of area b constitutes a gain in utility revenue of the same amount. As long as the utility manages its funds efficiently, these effects offset precisely, and area b gets returned to consumers through the lowered revenue requirements of the community-owned supplier.

5.6   Demand-Shifting Policy

The third policy mechanism for affecting net benefits is demand shifting policy. These policies induce shifts or rotations of the water demand curve, as opposed to movements along the water demand curve as occurs with price or quantity rationing. Common demand-reducing policies include educational programs designed to apprise consumers of their conservation options (e.g., xeriscape information), the distribution or subsidy of alternative water use technology (e.g., free showerheads, low-interest loans for advanced irrigation technologies), and plumbing codes requiring the installation of water-conserving fixtures (e.g., low gpf toilets).

Demand-increasing policies are less common since most water issues involve scarcity. Communities do stimulate demand, however, when they recruit new commercial enterprises by lobbying businesses or offering tax incentives for businesses that locate locally. Demand also shifts outward naturally (without policy) due to population growth, income growth, economic development, climate change, and a host of other factors external to the policies undertaken by water suppliers.

An illustrative case is the demand-increasing policy associated with business recruitment. In figure 5.4, a utility is initially supplying w_0 units of retail water because it has set price at p_0. Observe that this price is based on the average cost of supplying water. A utility employing marginal-cost pricing can also be examined, but average-cost pricing better describes the great majority of water suppliers.[7] Initially, consumers are experiencing net benefits of area a + c. The utility is receiving no net benefits because it is employing average-cost pricing; total revenue $(p_0 \cdot w_0)$ exactly offsets total costs $(w_0 \cdot AC(w_0))$.

If the community decides to recruit additional water consumers, demand will be shifted from MB_0 to MB_1. The consequent welfare changes are indicated by table 5.3. It is seen that any positive slope in the average cost curve implies that preexisting consumers will experience losses due to recruitment. The new consumers will clearly experience gains, at least from a local perspective. Because recruited businesses may not be new enterprises and may have relocated from elsewhere, they may have experienced nonzero net benefits in their prior locale. Supporters of economic development policies such as recruitment incentives tout the income and employment

---

7. The unfortunate prevalence of average-cost pricing is more completely considered in chapter 8.

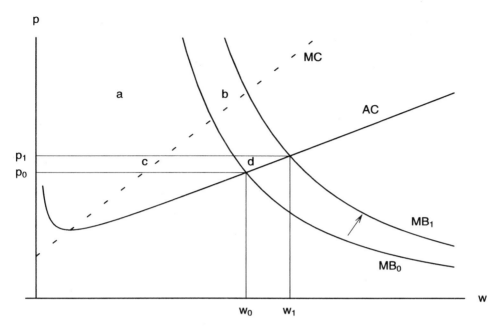

Figure 5.4
Effects of demand-expanding policy

Table 5.3
Analysis of demand-increasing policy (see figure 5.4)

	Preexisting consumer welfare	New business welfare*	Total change*
Postpolicy:	a	b	
Prepolicy:	a + c	zero	
Change:	− c	b	b − c

* Prepolicy and change entries in the latter two columns ignore the possibility that recruited businesses may have relocated from other regions and may have been receiving net benefits there.

benefits brought to the community by new businesses. Should these occur, preexisting consumers (or at least some of them) may be in receipt of additional net benefits. These benefits will be considered in section 5.10, where "Secondary Economic Effects" are discussed.

The results indicated within table 5.3 demonstrate that preexisting consumers lose welfare (excluding possible secondary effects) and recruited businesses gain. Omitted is the possible nonwater costs of the recruitment policies because estimation of these economic effects requires additional, nonwater information (e.g., drop in tax revenue, administrative costs of the recruitment).

While they will not be explored at this point, it is noteworthy that nonpolicy shifts in demand such as population growth can be handled using the same procedures discussed above, with new consumers substituting for new businesses. The drawing from a reservoir analysis late in chapter 3, as well as the forthcoming analyses of the next chapter, also address the modeling of a growing number of consumers.

Policy-induced decreases in the demand function must be more carefully scrutinized. It may be the case that policies for trimming water demand aim to do so without lowering the value consumers receive from their water use. At least that is the goal of many demand-reducing policies. Many of these policies attempt to alter the technology of water use, so that consumers can capture the same value of water service using less water. Some of these policies are purely educational, and inform consumers of new methods or technologies in an attempt to accelerate consumer adoption of such practices. In urban settings, native-plant landscaping promotion and advice involving leak detection/fixing, low-flow showerheads, and nighttime irrigation are examples. In agricultural settings, examples are "extension" programs that disseminate information or demonstrate alternative irrigation technologies (e.g., drip, surge, low-energy precision application [LEPA]) and alternative crop selections.

If these educational programs are well-founded, it is *possible* for water consumers to secure the same "water service" and value from their consumption using less water. Consumers can then save on their water bills, and the reduced demand conceivably allows the utility or district to supply water at a reduced price. Consulting figure 5.5, we see that consumer water bills totaled $p_0 \cdot w_0$ prior to the demand shift, and after the shift these bills total $p_1 \cdot w_1$. Hence, the gross gain to consumers is area $c + d + e + f$. If reduced water rates will not materialize because the AC curve is flat, the gain is area $e + f$. From these gains, we must subtract any costs consumers must incur to accomplish this shift in demand. Most important among these costs is any new equipment (especially water-using capital) necessitated by the conversion.

In figure 5.5, it would be a mistake to interpret area b as a loss in consumer benefits. This is not a loss because we are making the strong presumption that consumers are achieving the same benefits from their water, while using less water. To analyze other demand-reducing policies such as subsidies, rebates, or outright gifts of water-conserving equipment, we utilize these same methods, though less of the conversion costs is borne by consumers. Social costs are unaltered, however.

5.7   Supply-Shifting Policy

The fourth and final basic policy mechanism is that of supply shifts. Supply shifts can be accomplished through a variety of means, and they can impact consumers in multiple ways. Not surprisingly, the analysis of supply shifts is fundamental to project

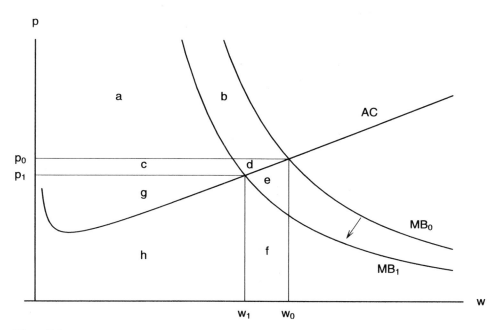

Figure 5.5
Effects of a demand-reducing policy

analysis in the forthcoming chapter. Many water supply projects shift supply outward, either lowering the marginal cost of each unit of delivered water or alleviating a supply constraint that had been truncating a supply curve. Supply can also be augmented by nonstructural approaches, such as purchasing or leasing water rights, or by entering into long-term contracts with water wholesalers. Increasingly relevant in water-scarce regions are the declines in water supply caused by policies that reshape rights to water. When water is fully utilized, as it is in many regions, policies that increase the water supply for one user group must also decrease the supply for another group. The same is true of water projects. New reservoirs storing water otherwise "escaping" downstream are most safely thought of as water reapportionments. It is often true that this escaping water is being used in a manner benefiting other people.

Supply increases and decreases can take on various forms depending on the nature of the policy. In this section we will examine policies that shift supply outward and policies that extend supply by relaxing a supply constraint. Supply-decreasing policies of these types can be treated as simple reversals of these cases.

Some supply-oriented policies make it cheaper for the water supplier to conduct business. Such policies lower both marginal and average cost curves. Examples include the procurement of a less expensive natural water supply, some new water

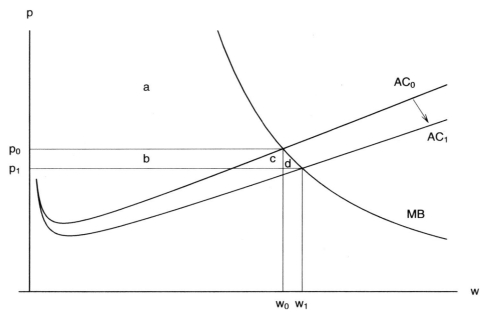

Figure 5.6
Effects of cost-reducing policy

treatment technologies, and the rehabilitation of ill-performing equipment (such as leaky distribution mains or canals). Other supply-oriented policies can extend the available water supply by alleviating a supply constraint. Examples include upgrades to water conveyances that are operating at maximum capacity and the procurement of additional natural water supply, either by purchase or project. Some policies have the ability to both lower costs and extend supply. The analyses demonstrated below will separate these two effects for clarity.

Let's begin with a cost-lowering supply shift such as that depicted in figure 5.6. Again, we can model such policies through the inspection of marginal cost functions, but the prevalence of average-cost pricing can make this a more interesting scenario. As noted previously, the use of average-cost pricing implies that there are no financial impacts on the supplier that need to be analyzed. As long as all costs are embodied in the average cost curves, including the cost of achieving the supply shift, all supplier-side welfare effects are already counted. In the circumstances of figure 5.6, consumers are initially experiencing net benefits given by area a. Subsequent to the supply shift, they experience net benefits of area $a + b + c + d$. Hence, the net benefits attributable to this shift is area $b + c + d$:

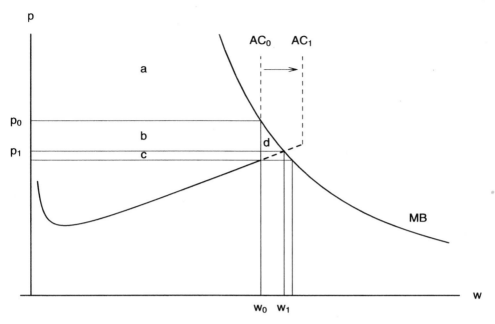

Figure 5.7
Effects of supply-extending policy

$$+b + c + d = \int_{p^1}^{p^0} MB^{-1}(p)\, dp. \qquad (5.3)$$

Less clear-cut is the analysis of supply-extending policies. In figure 5.7, we encounter an AC supply curve that is abruptly truncated at w_0 because of a supply constraint. An economically sound way to interpret the initial conditions is that the AC curve becomes vertical at w_0. If demand (MB) intersects initial supply (AC_0) in the nonvertical region of AC_0, there is no motivation for extending supply. But if the intersection occurs in the vertical region, there may be cause to expand supply, depending on whether the benefits exceed the costs.

It is important to be quite clear about the nature of the initial conditions, especially in terms of how the perceived "shortfall" is being managed. If the supplier prices water where AC_0 first intersects w_0 (the unlabeled, solid line below p_1), then consumers will wish to consume more water than is available. This is the economic depiction of prototypical water shortages. Yet if the supplier is managing the situation efficiently, so as to direct water to the most highly valued uses, then the initial situation is one where the supplier is charging p_0 per unit of water. In this case, price is determined by the intersection of demand with w_0. Moreover, consumers will receive net benefits illustrated by area a, and the supplier will receive net benefits given by area b + c because the supplier is receiving payments in excess of actual average costs.[8] Hence, efficient management produces net benefits of area a + b + c. Less-than-efficient management produces somewhat less net benefits depending on how the shortfall is allocated. (Apply the earlier discussion of price- and quantity-rationing policies.)

For concreteness, assume that the initial circumstances are efficient. This assumption may be unrealistic, depending on actual conditions, but it has interest because it is a requirement of federal project analysis in the United States.[9]

Suppose a prospective supply extension will allow the supplier to extend supply to an unconstraining quantity. Suppose further that the extension will simply move the truncation point rightward. Under these conditions, the postpolicy setting will have w_1 units of water being delivered to consumers at a price of p_1. In this case, the supplier has resumed the average-cost pricing of water, thereby eliminating all utility profits. The heightened water use of consumers at a lower price results in postpolicy consumer welfare of area a + b + d. Area b is thus effectively transferred from the supplier to consumers. These changes are summarized in table 5.4.

5.8 Overview and Analysis of Other Policy Types

An array of different policies have been evaluated conceptually in the prior sections. In doing so, we have emphasized four separate types of policy. Although a first reading of these policy investigations may suggest that the analyst must be familiar with a large set of possibilities, the unifying elements are simple, and they extend to all policy/project evaluations. The list that follows summarizes the major principles to be used:

1. A one-period policy is desirable (efficient) if the sum of changes in net benefits, summed across all agents, is positive. These agents include consumers, producers, and if relevant, governments and water authorities.

2. The change in net benefits for any given agent or group is computed by taking net benefits after the policy and subtracting net benefits prior to the policy.

---

8. If the supplier is community owned, then these gains will ultimately accrue to consumers.

9. The *Principles and Guidelines*, which dictates the methods of cost-benefit analysis for all U.S. water supply projects employing federal funds, requires that the initial conditions embody the efficient management of available water (U.S. Water Resources Council 1983). Although this provision is commonly overlooked in analysis, the reason for it is presumably to prevent federal funds from being expended to rectify problems that can be solved by better policy. Taken literally, this *Principles and Guidelines* provision imposes a need for the analyst to assume marginal-cost pricing, resulting in even greater efficiency than presumed in the ongoing analysis based on average-cost pricing.

Table 5.4
Analysis of supply-extending policy (see figure 5.7)

	Consumer welfare	Supplier profits	Total change
Postpolicy:	a + b + d	zero	
Prepolicy:	a	b + c	
Change:	+ b + d	− b − c	+ d − c

3. Net benefits are simply total benefits minus total costs.

4. Total benefits for consumers is given by the appropriately defined areas beneath demand (marginal benefit) functions. Total benefits for water suppliers is total revenue (price times quantity).

5. Total costs for consumers is total outlays (price times quantity). Total costs for water suppliers is acquired either by multiplying average costs by the quantity supplied or by computing the correct area beneath the marginal cost function.

Circumstances may arise in which the analyst is unsure about where to place a certain benefit or cost—in the sense of what stage of analysis it should be computed and to what agent grouping it should be assigned. Because the efficiency or inefficiency of a policy is merely the consequence of summed changes to net benefits, it is generally unimportant where an item is counted. What matters most is that every impact is counted and is not double counted. For example, the cost of performing a supply shift (in the prior section) can be quite sizable, as in the case of a new dam. This cost is a relevant change in net benefits and must be counted. It can be counted either by including it in the new average cost curve (AC_1) or it can simply be entered as a government expenditure, but not both.

Although there are policies other than the four featured in this chapter, including combinations of these four, the five principles enumerated above go a long way in the analysis of any conceivable policy. This includes reversals of any of these policies, especially the common situation of supply decreases stemming from water reallocations.

5.9 Incorporating ΔNB into NPV for Dynamic Policies

Many, if not most, policies are dynamic in character, meaning they unfold over time and have different effects in different years. It was established in chapter 3 that good dynamic decisions are ones for which net present value is positive, and these are called dynamic improvements. This is an extension of the static (one-period) requirement that aggregated changes in net benefits be positive. For policy-induced changes, the formula for NPV can be augmented to clearly indicate that we are targeting changes in net benefits, discounted to today's dollars.

Box 5.3
An Increase in Water Supply

An irrigation district is suffering a temporary water supply cutback. The Grain Irrigation District (GID) is a cooperative delivering water to its many farmer members. All farms in the district are diversified operations in that they grow several crops in rotation. GID delivers water five months each year and its total cost function for each month, expressed as a function of delivered water, is $C(W) = 60000 + 3W - 0.000003 \cdot W^2$. As is common, this function incorporates no value for the district's water right holdings.

GID generates most of its revenue with a \$30/acre annual fee on irrigated acreage, but it also charges \$4 per acre-foot of water delivered. All water deliveries to each farm are metered, and all farms pay both charges.

At the moment, the irrigation season is nearly complete, and there is only one more month of water demand. All acreage-based fees have been collected. Unfortunately, an aberration in the natural water supply is going to interrupt the coming month's water deliveries. Instead of satisfying demand with 50,000 acre-feet (at the \$4 rate), only 30,000 acre-feet are going to be available at farm gates, and management knows this to be true because of deficient upstream storage. Suppose there are only two management options. Either each farm will be allowed only 60 percent of its usual water, or GID will lease the 20,000 acre-foot shortfall from upstream irrigators. What's the maximum worth of an additional 20,000 acre-feet to GID?

Analysis

The question here concerns the value of a supply increment. What will occur without it? With crops already in the ground and nearing maturity, crop yields and farm revenues will be reduced by the shortfall. With the 40 percent curtailment, farm agents can be expected to use their portions in an internally efficient manner. This gives us some confidence that the losses will be minimized, implying that only the most marginal uses will not get served. (Allowing members to trade water with one another enhances this outcome.) A second point is that the elasticity of irrigation water demand will be high (more negative) this late in the season. Suppose that demand elasticity is -0.5 (it may be much higher).

There are two separate items to consider in evaluating the worth of leased water. One is the savings in GID's operating costs. The other is the value of water to irrigators. They are separate matters because the volumetric water charge of \$4 is not the marginal or average cost of delivered water. The cost savings is $C(50000)$ minus $C(30000)$ or \$55,200. The value of leased water to farmers is the area under their demand from 30,000 to 50,000 acre-feet. The constant elasticity demand form is $p = 10^{10}/W^2$ (point expansion method), so losses can be estimated as

$$\int_{30000}^{50000} \frac{10^{10}}{W^2} dW = 133333.$$

Subtracting cost savings from losses indicates that the district could benefit \$78,133 from having another 20,000 acre-feet of delivered water, so it should pay no more than that. Of course, due to conveyance losses in GID's canals, it will have to lease more than 20,000 acre-feet in order to deliver that much.

$$\text{NPV} = \sum_{t=0}^{T} \frac{\Delta NB_t}{(1+d)^t}. \tag{5.4}$$

If a policy will only exist for a year or if its ΔNB has the same sign year after year, it is acceptable to determine ΔNB for a single year. Otherwise, dynamic analysis should be pursued.

Application of (5.4) requires that a schedule of modified net benefits be determined, one for each period beginning with the current period, $t = 0$, and extending to the planning horizon, $t = T$. T may be defined by the expected lifetime of the policy, the traditions or rules of the authority, or the analyst. Clearly, the most important information required to compute NPV is ΔNB_t for every $t \leq T$. In performing this task, the principles underscored previously in this chapter are to be employed. It is not normally accurate to take ΔNB_0 and "inflate" it for future periods.

To compute ΔNB_t for a particular t it will be necessary to employ supply and demand functions for that t. This is less onerous than it first appears. Both supply and demand relationships can change over time, but with the exception of climate-induced shifts, they change steadily and can be benchmarked against current supply and demand functions. In accordance with chapter 3, inflation should be completely disregarded as long as the discount rate, d, includes no inflation component. If inflation is a component of the discount rate, the straightforward approach is to revise it (the discount rate) downward just enough to eliminate inflation.

Hence, changes in supply relations (AC and MC) are limited to changes in *real* (inflationless) costs. Except for the peculiarities of climate, such supply changes are easily forecasted in most circumstances because they are controlled by the supply authority. In the absence of any changes, MC_0 and AC_0 may simply persist over time. When they do change, the analyst will normally possess crucial information about when costs will change and by how much. For example, in the case of a supply-extending water project, the utility may be planning to sell bonds to procure funds for a three-year construction effort. Bond repayment obligations will immediately affect cost functions by known amounts, shifting the AC curve upward. In three years, on completion of the construction, the supply function will be permanently extended by a known amount of water, as in figure 5.7. Several years later, the repayment obligations of the bonds will have been completed, thereby shifting AC downward. All of these changes can be readily forecasted.

In the case of temporal movements in demand, the MB curve will generally shift outward over time in response to population growth and economic development. Such shifts can be projected based on recent experiences with demand growth or otherwise forecasted demand growth. Shifting the entire demand curve by a specified amount or a specified percentage is easily managed (as was done in the drawing from a reservoir example performed in chapter 3).

In cases where climate may reasonably be expected to perturb either supply or demand functions, there are alternative approaches for managing dynamic analysis. Four fundamental alternatives follow:

1. NPV can be computed from ΔNBs that are obtained from *expected* (average) supply and demand relations. The result will be *expected* NPV given the assumption that all future climate conditions will be average. This type of analysis is informative and readily accomplished. It may be remiss, however, for underappreciating possibly sizable swings in net benefits occurring during extreme climate conditions.

2. In addition to *baseline* analysis predicated on expected supply/demand, analysts may isolate specific "high" and "low" (or wet and dry) scenarios for additional evaluation. These added scenarios can be based on past experiences with supply and demand as they were affected by varying climate. Such analyses complement baseline findings by providing decision makers with a sense of how a policy's returns can be affected by climate. In particular, risk-averse decision making may be particularly concerned about the prospective policy impact during droughtlike conditions.

3. It is sometimes possible to compute NPV over the next $T + 1$ periods by assuming that climate during these periods will replicate known climate occurring over the past $T + 1$ periods. For this procedure to work, it must be possible to numerically link past supply and demand parameters with past climate.

4. If probabilistic information is available on climate—especially probability density functions for supply/demand drivers like precipitation, snowpack, or temperature—and the functional relationship between the driver(s) and supply/demand have been estimated, ΔNB can be computed via Monte Carlo procedures. In this case, the climate driver(s) are randomly and independently selected for each future t based on probability information, and the selection is used to compute each ΔNB_t. NPV can then be computed. Since this type of analysis is ordinarily performed on a computer, many iterations can be completed, and NPV can be computed for each. In this way, a range of possible NPVs can be computed, and the effects of unknown future climate on policy efficiency can be formally examined.

5.10 Secondary Economic Effects

Public discussion often emphasizes the economic development that may be enabled or injured by water policy impacting water-using commerce and industry.[10] For example, keeping water rates low is sometimes said to enhance economic development, bringing jobs and income to local residents. The same claims are commonly used to

10. Some of the material in this section is directly drawn from Griffin (1998).

support supply-enhancing water policies: "We need this water project in order to have the water 'necessary' to attract industry." Up to this point, we have only included the welfare of water users in benefit measurement. Should the benefits of added jobs and income be included as well?

It is well acknowledged that economically linked industries and households encounter *secondary economic effects* (or synonymously, indirect economic effects) when any industry changes its production level. Changes in output are accompanied by changes in employed inputs, including labor. Workers and input owners can therefore be affected. The altered revenue received by input providers (especially workers) modifies their expenditures, thus producing more secondary effects. The additional effects are again transmitted to other resource owners, resulting in continued "ripple" effects throughout an economy. Each successive ripple is smaller than the one preceding it. Combined however, these secondary effects can be larger than the first-round welfare effects, and it is common to hear about "economic multipliers" that capture summed secondary effects. But do any of these impacts translate into welfare changes that should be incorporated in policy analyses? That is, can the secondary economic effects initiated by water projects or policies be equated to secondary *welfare changes*? This question is at the heart of considerable confusion and misinterpretation in public discussion.

To better examine the "countability" of secondary economic effects, we can harness the notion of accounting stance, which was introduced in chapter 3. An accounting stance may be personal, local, regional, national, or global. Water districts and utilities normally have a local accounting stance, meaning that their decisions are based only on those policy effects that are experienced within their customer base. Federal water agencies normally have a national accounting stance; all welfare effects received by the nation's people are counted. With a local accounting stance it may be possible to count secondary economic effects, but such action should be carefully considered. As accounting stance broadens, it becomes less legitimate to count secondary effects.

Consider the example of a city utility facing limits in its natural water supply. Suppose that these limits are sufficiently serious that the marginal benefits of added natural water have become greater than the marginal costs of leasing water rights. Hence, it is efficient to lease rights unless there are cheaper options. Let's assume that leasing water rights is the cheapest mechanism for expanding supply. The issue is how much water to lease. With each leased unit, marginal benefits decline somewhat, so there is an optimal amount to procure, beyond which $MC > MB$. Is it legitimate to include secondary economic effects in marginal benefits? That is, if a commercial enterprise served by the utility uses more treated water as a result of the lease and also employs more nonwater inputs, are the added expenditures and subsequent ripples countable as benefits? Some of these secondary effects will occur within the community, so there may be impetus to count the local secondary effects.

The first thing to be recognized is that our presumed knowledge of water demand implies we know the direct benefits of leased water. The demand function tells us the marginal and total benefits for water users, including the expanding enterprise.

Second, the new expenditures of the business on other inputs are neither benefits for the firm nor can they be immediately interpreted as community benefits. Some of these expenditures may be directed to local businesses, workers, or other resource owners (e.g., landowners). The revenue and income received by these "locals" is not entirely a net benefit to them because they are giving up something of value and they may also experience production costs. But there must be some net benefit, for they would not otherwise willingly participate in the exchange. Hence, some portion of the original business's expenditures are local net benefits.

Third, in the same vein, some portion of the expenditures in later ripples will be net benefits for local agents. While the lion's share of net benefits may be received by businesses and resource owners external to the community, there will undoubtedly be "some" secondary economic effects that qualify as local welfare effects in that they are received by local people.

Fourth, if the utility chooses to act on these observations by including locally received, secondary welfare effects in estimates of marginal benefits, then it will be necessary to rent a larger amount of water (figure 5.8). But where will the funds come from? An expanding business will only pay a level indicated by its direct marginal benefits. The secondary-effect beneficiaries are receiving benefits not associated with their water consumption, so it seems impractical to charge them via a water price, even if they could be precisely identified. It appears the utility will have to use a different mechanism for funding the extra water. Candidates are increases in the monthly connection fees paid by all water customers and, if legally permissible, the general tax revenue received by the community.

Fifth, any dollars diverted from members of the community to fund the pursuit of secondary welfare effects were not idle. These dollars would otherwise be expended in some way, even if they are sitting in savings accounts. (Banks loan these savings deposits to people and businesses.) Certainly, these nonidle expenditures would be directed at a wide array of things, and many of these would be generating secondary welfare benefits of their own. Hence, there will be secondary welfare *costs* if the utility diverts these dollars into water policy undertakings. These secondary costs occur in diffuse form because the dollars were taken from many people engaged in many different consumption and investment activities. Is there reason to think that the secondary welfare benefits of water supply expansion exceed the secondary welfare benefits of nonwater activities? Put another way, is water "special" in terms of its ability to generate secondary economic effects? After much inspection by economic analysts

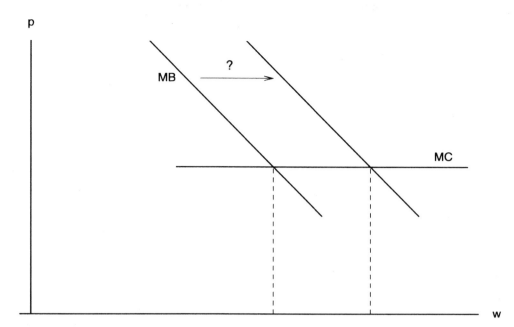

Figure 5.8
Do secondary effects shift benefits?

and theorists, the answer is no (Stoevener and Kraynick 1979; Young and Gray 1985; Hamilton et al. 1991; Mills 1993). There is nothing particularly special about water inputs that would differentiate them from the many nonwater inputs businesses employ and purchase. The secondary benefits generated by expansive water policy and projects are accompanied by secondary costs due to the redirection of monies toward water and away from other commodities. In any case, both the secondary welfare benefits and costs are difficult to calculate. As such, the advice of economists in such situations is to presume that secondary economic benefits are balanced by secondary economic costs—inferring that neither should be counted unless the utility can access funds outside its accounting stance.[11]

Last, the caveat within the prior point is crucial because it indicates a scenario in which secondary welfare effects are legitimately counted. To the extent that the

---

11. While this assumption is unlikely to be precisely correct, it is an expedient alternative to intricate economic analyses. Secondary effects are difficult to enumerate because it is necessary to possess a complete model of an economy's expenditure patterns. Simplistic, fixed proportions approaches such as input-output modeling have been successfully employed to estimate "multipliers" capturing the totality of secondary economic effects consequent to an expansion in any given industry. Nevertheless, these effects are not synonymous with secondary *welfare* effects for the reason that they identify gross effects, not net benefits (Cooke 1991; Hamilton et al. 1991, 1993; Hughes and Holland 1993; Young and Gray 1985).

financial costs of a specific water policy fall outside the accounting stance, it is practical to consider counting secondary economic effects. Still, care must be exercised so
that planning does not falsely attribute "specialness" to water as a generator of secondary benefits. If outside funds can be spent on anything the community wishes
(such as with hotel room taxes, severance taxes on exported minerals, and unrestricted gifts or grants), then nonwater endeavors by the community would also generate secondary benefits. If outside funds are only available for financing water
policy, as is clearly the case with federal subsidies of water projects, then secondary
benefits are countable for a local accounting stance. From a federal perspective, however, secondary benefits are not admissible for the reasons identified above. The
large-accounting-stance perspective is that secondary economic effects are merely
relocated economic effects, not net changes.

While the science of water resource economics has spoken clearly about the legitimacy of counting secondary effects and has identified the limited circumstances under which this should be done, the issue remains an inevitable part of the "noise" to
be faced in water planning. There will always be supporting interests for any given
water policy. These agents can be expected to forward any practical argument in support of their preferred action. Presently, political decision making is quite sensitive to
the promise of new jobs and income, or their loss. The average decision maker and
citizen does not possess the specialized knowledge needed to ferret out the truth of
these claims. Indeed, decision makers and citizens do think water is special. So it is
easy for people to subscribe to the claim that cheap and readily available water fos-
ters economic development in a unique way. These misunderstandings raise the burden of analysis and participation for economics-savvy water planners and analysts,
but they also open up an avenue whereby informed specialists can contribute in a
socially helpful way.

5.11 Incommensurables and Intangibles

The general procedures outlined in this chapter seek to condense all policy consequences into a single index, either $\sum \Delta NB$ or NPV.[12] Ideally, this index would then
be used to make a recommendation—either the policy is efficiency improving or it is
not. This procedure works well as long as all policy consequences are commensurable. A *commensurable* impact is an effect on human welfare that can be valued using
reasonable economic techniques. In the present state of economic science, however,
not all policy impacts may be commensurable.

It is informative to distinguish between two types of goods that are not commensurable: incommensurables and intangibles (Sassone and Schaffer 1978, 34). An *in-*

---

12. Some of the material in this section is directly drawn from Griffin (1998).

commensurable is a policy result that cannot be valued using reasonable techniques, but it can be physically measured. For example, a new program to price irrigation water higher, perhaps so that price is better aligned with marginal costs, may motivate some farmers to convert their earthen water canals to PVC pipe. The reduced leakage could dry up x acres of an artificial wetland that has evolved into a migratory pit stop for y thousand waterfowl. These effects, though countable, can be difficult to value. Similarly, this same policy may inspire other on-farm conservation techniques and consequently reduce some irrigation runoff that has been contributing x tons of salts to a natural water body, but again, what might the value be? Economists have made significant progress in valuing such things during recent decades, but each case can be unique.

An ***intangible*** is a policy impact that can neither be counted nor economically valued with reasonable efforts. For instance, a large hydroelectric project may improve national security through enhanced self-sufficiency in energy production and decreased exposure to political influence exerted by energy-exporting countries. But how can we measure or value the increment to national security? Either task represents a considerable challenge. Likewise, this same hydroelectric project might interfere with an indigenous people's traditional activity, such as harvesting fish during migratory spawning runs, with some consequential loss of cultural integrity for the group. Again, obtaining either physical or economic measurements of this impact is problematic.

The existence of incommensurables and intangibles means that some policy impacts will not be monetarized. Such impacts cannot then be included in any economic metrics such as the ΔNB or NPV. But at a conceptual level, this does not mean such impacts are irrelevant. They are policy consequences distinguished only in our ability to monetarize them.

In these circumstances, ΔNBs and NPVs are incomplete metrics. This is certainly not satisfactory, so it can be argued that the economic analyst should strive to monetarize all welfare effects to the extent possible, even if "reasonable guessing" is required (Mishan 1976, 407). Whenever a previously unestimated value is reasonably valued, the analyst has successfully converted an incommensurable or intangible into a commensurable.

When the valuation of noteworthy effects is not possible, the advice for analysts is to abandon a full reliance on whether $\sum \Delta$NB or NPV is greater than zero. *Regardless of what economic measures are computed and reported in the decision-making process, they should be accompanied by the reasonable disclosure of unmonetarized policy impacts.* This task can only be achieved by describing the unmonetarized impacts using available information and data. In the case of incommensurables, physical measures of the impacts can be reported. Intangible impacts should also be described even though physical measurement is infeasible. This body of impact information can be extensive for momentous policies. In such cases, it may be advisable to present the impacts using a large, many-page tableau whose cells contain descriptive text and physical impact measures (Sassone and Schaffer 1978; Yoe 1995).

5.12   Summary

There are many potential revisions of water policy in a world of rising water scarcity. Several types have been explicitly modeled in this chapter. Taken together, the examination of price-rationing, quantity-rationing, demand-shifting, and supply-shifting policies demonstrates the application of the economic techniques of policy analysis. The unifying principle of economic policy analysis is to improve aggregate economic efficiency. For one-period policies, this infers that the summed changes in net benefits must be positive. For multiperiod (dynamic) policies, the net present value attributable to the policy must be positive. In both cases, demand and supply information is normally required to complete the empirical work of computing welfare changes to all agents. For each agent grouping, prepolicy net benefits must be subtracted from postpolicy net benefits in order to compute the change in net benefits for the group.

Complexities for policy analysis arise when there are secondary economic effects that may be counted (depending on circumstances) or incommensurables/intangibles that cannot be counted (by definition). These topics are aptly represented by a sign that hung in Albert Einstein's Princeton University office, "Not everything that can be counted counts, and not everything that counts can be counted."

For secondary effects, it must first be decided whether they should be counted. In many cases, they should not be counted because they are offset by secondary effects occurring elsewhere. Yet it may be legitimate to count them in local accounting stances. It is not permissible to include secondary effects for national accounting stances such as those maintained by federal water agencies.

If incommensurables or intangibles constitute important policy effects, then analysts must decide whether to devote additional research to their valuation or be satisfied with their identification. If they remain unvalued, it must be acknowledged that economic measures are incomplete. In such cases, the reported economic measures should be accompanied by a fair disclosure of the unmonetarized policy impacts.

5.13   Exercises

1. A small water utility has rates consisting of a monthly connection charge of $25 plus a constant charge of $5 per metered 1,000 gallons. These charges are adequate to meet the utility's operation and maintenance costs, but they include no accounting

for natural water value. Presently, the two hundred customers consume 2.0855 million gallons (6.4 af) in a normal month. According to a new court ruling, the utility has been overstepping its water rights, and it really only has the right to 4.8 acre-feet per month. Because the utility can lease additional, senior water rights at a price of $160 per acre-foot, management has proposed a two-pronged policy: lease the full shortfall, and finance the added costs with either an increased connection charge for all consumers or an increased water rate. Analyze these circumstances and make a recommendation.

2. Draw a graph containing three curves: marginal benefits, marginal costs, and average costs. Make sure marginal costs are correctly related to average costs in your graph. (Marginal costs should intersect average costs where average costs are at their lowest level.) Starting from a prepolicy scenario involving average-cost pricing, identify on your graph the areas representing consumer net benefits and supplier net benefits. Suppose that a change to marginal-cost pricing is proposed. In a postpolicy scenario involving marginal-cost pricing, identify on your graph the areas representing consumer net benefits and supplier net benefits. What is the change in net benefits for consumers and the supplier, separately? What is the aggregated change in net benefits? What does your theoretical analysis tell you about the preferred method of pricing retail water?

3. Suppose retail water demand is given by $w_d = 70 - p$ and the marginal costs of retail water is $mc = 0.00125w_s^2$. (Invert the latter equation and substitute p for mc to obtain the supply function corresponding to marginal-cost pricing.) The water units in the prior relations refer to retail water. Currently, the supplier cannot fulfill the quantity demanded under marginal-cost pricing because natural water is in short supply. Suppose that only thirty-two units of natural water is available. Due to system leakage and evaporation, the relationship between natural water pumped and retail water received is

$$w_{rtl} = \frac{w_{ntrl} - 10}{1.1}.$$

What is the value of an action to increase natural water availability to forty-three units? Sketch an appropriate graph for this change and calculate the added net benefits.

4. If a water policy alters the profitability of a land-based production activity (like farming) by changing water rates or the available water quantity, and if the net benefits of this profit change are well measured, should we also include in net benefits the policy's effect on property values? (Reflect on appendix 3.A in chapter 3.)

5. A new supply-shifting policy of the state will have three direct effects in a specific river basin experiencing scarcity:

a. Supply will be shifted rightward for Upriver City; the net benefits of this shift to all of the city's water users has been estimated to be $5 million. The additional water use will result in the production of an added $2 million in output (market value). With a conservatively estimated multiplier of 2.3, secondary economic effects will amount to $4.6 million in the city.

b. Supply will be shifted leftward for the Downriver Irrigation District; the properly measured net "benefits" of this shift across all district irrigators is − $2 million. The value of farm output will lowered by $1 million in the district. The secondary effects multiplier for the farm sector is 2.5.

c. Between the city and the district is a river segment that will suffer some environmental degradation as a result of decreased flow. Some of these losses have been competently valued at $500,000. The remainder of the losses have not been valued.

Has this been a desirable policy for this river basin? Discuss your observations and reasoning.

6. The town of Agton's water utility engages in average-cost pricing. Across the community, the average consumer pays $1.60 per thousand gallons. In an average year, Agton collects just enough water revenues to cover all its costs of providing water. Annual water use averages 1.8×10^9 gallons. As the town's analyst, you believe that marginal costs would be $2 if marginal-cost pricing was in effect, and you estimate that average annual consumption would then be 1.7×10^9 gallons. Also, based on your knowledge of operating costs, every million gallon increase/decrease in water sales adds/subtracts $0.001 to/from marginal costs and $0.0005 to/from average costs.

Agton is courting a major industrial business, KCorp, and the mayor is hopeful that the business will choose to locate a processing facility in Agton. If it does, Agton has promised to charge KCorp no more than $1.50 per thousand gallons, and KCorp has told the town to expect it to take 0.2×10^9 gallons per year at this price. Analyze the effects of KCorp's arrival in Agton by taking the following steps:

a. Provide a relatively accurate illustration of the supply-demand situation, including shifting demands, AC and MC functions, and consumer welfare areas.

b. Calculate the complete impact of KCorp's water use on existing consumers.

6 Cost-Benefit Analysis

How should proposed projects be assessed?

Because water projects are instances of supply-enhancing policy, at least in their service areas, the methods introduced in the prior chapter are fundamental for project analysis. It is wise to consider project analysis in more detail, however, as it is crucial for several reasons. Water projects enjoy considerable public attention because there are many citizens and leaders who perceive projects as the prime solution to scarcity.[1] Large dams, with their concrete edifices countering gravity's force on staggering amounts of water, are very tangible evidence of human achievement, and in this sense they attract more attention than competing water policies. This attention is sometimes fanned by politicians, who earn voter recognition when they can secure project approval (and the subsidies that commonly accompany projects).

Ardent project supporters can include water agencies relying on budgets that are politically approved. More projects mean larger agency budgets and more opportunities for personnel. To a large extent, the support of agencies is natural given that they are well staffed by engineers who want to exercise their talents and training. The planning and construction of projects is a special challenge for these professionals. Nevertheless, we must be mindful that water projects can be hugely expensive for society. The sacrifices embodied in these expenses infer that projects displace other human endeavors, for our social budget is limited.[2] On the other hand, projects tend to be long-lived, so the benefit streams they generate may

---

1. This perspective is probably assisted by the fabled need for water mistakenly accepted by many people. As noted earlier, the necessity of drinking water is commonly overextended to include nondrinking water uses. In developed countries, per capita water use is many times larger than drinking water use. Because water policies commonly address marginal, rather than essential, water uses, the use of water for drinking is ordinarily unaffected and is therefore irrelevant to policy/project choice.

2. Not only are particular activities sacrificed as a natural consequence of project costs, but these costs may be concentrated on particular people. For example, Ortolano and Cushing's (2002) study of the Grand Coulee Dam in the western U.S. found that early settlers and indigenous people experienced large, uncompensated losses.

continue for many years, possibly even benefiting future generations. Still, who can say that alternative endeavors would not also benefit future people? All things considered, these are important issues, and there can be much at stake in deciding whether to undertake a project. With the inaccurate perceptions people hold about water, it is not surprising that there are cases in which demand groups think they need a water project only to find out that the costs exceed the benefits once the project is completed (Wilson 1997). When properly performed, economic analysis should be able to identify these many-million dollar missteps before they occur.

Recall that scarcity can be addressed in two broad ways: supply enhancement and demand management. The economic perspective is that we want to assemble the most efficient "package" of these measures. The efficient package varies from place to place depending on the economic circumstances, which in turn are affected by the hydrologic circumstances. If a new water project is part of this package, then it will supplant policy tools that would otherwise be deployed, including demand management policies. In this sense, then, other policies are in competition with water projects for redressing water scarcity. Absent a new water project, other policies will be called on or existing policies will be strengthened in some way. While these policies may lack the tangibility of a visible project, they can rival and exceed a project's contribution to social welfare.

The key question faced in this chapter is then this: What analytic techniques should be used to determine if a specific project is among the efficient package of water management policies? This subject is the domain of *cost-benefit analysis* (CBA) or, synonymously, benefit-cost analysis.[3] Fundamentally, there is nothing mystical about what we wish to accomplish in CBA. Following the ideals set out in chapter 3 and enlarged in chapter 5, net present value or another acceptable measure is calculated for the difference between without-project and with-project conditions. If NPV is positive, the project represents a dynamic improvement and is desirable. Easily said but performed with difficulty, CBA derives great importance from the huge expense some projects entail. Whole books are dedicated to this subject, so we will constrain attention to the larger matters in this chapter.[4]

CBA was arguably pioneered in the pursuit of a better framework for resolving decisions about national water projects. Although CBA is clearly applicable for all *accounting stances* (section 5.10) and a wide range of public investment decisions, its growth as a tool is intimately linked to national water projects, both U.S. and European. Political pressure for more and more water projects required the development

3. To avoid the implicit endorsement of benefit-cost ratio over net present value and other metrics, it is a good idea to use the term cost-benefit analysis.

4. For those wishing to examine this topic more deeply, important books have been authored by Gittinger (1982), Mishan (1976), Sassone and Schaffer (1978), Schmid (1989), and Zerbe and Dively (1994). The Sassone and Schaffer text is especially accessible to novices, and the Zerbe and Dively text is especially complete, although it is more oriented toward practitioners.

of a screening tool. CBA is that tool. Its usefulness for examining potential water projects in developing countries has caused it to be applied by international agencies. As we develop the accepted analytic principles of CBA, it is enlightening to consider the policy context in which CBA was developed in the United States.

6.1 Policy Background

The construction era for big U.S. dams was suspended in the late 1970s when President Carter called off water projects that were then in line for federal financing and construction. Though arguably a political act, it would seem that the seeds of this decision were sown much earlier by the decaying net benefits of new projects. Why did this happen?

Throughout much of the twentieth century, federal subsidization caused water projects to be prized by local and regional agents. Project benefits tended to be concentrated in the neighborhood of each project. To a large extent, costs could be dispersed across the nation. The wide dispersion of costs meant the average U.S. citizen lost little when a specific project was undertaken, while localized agents could gain a lot. Hence, a project that wasn't on most people's radar screens would be fervently pursued by potential beneficiaries. This atmosphere meant that the political demand for water projects surpassed the economic demand. As long as project approval and financing decisions lay in the political realm, projects would be more rapidly undertaken. This tendency gained intensity with the 1930s' New Deal era, when federal economic policy was to spend the U.S.'s way out of the Depression by employing people in public works programs.

Many of the water projects of the twentieth century were hugely successful and continue to generate benefits to this day. The early projects had unique advantages. The absence of water storage in undeveloped river basins, especially in the sparsely populated West, inferred that costs were low. The best dam sites were readily available, land was inexpensive, and the highly seasonal, natural water flows were unclaimed. The environmental costs were perceived to be low since environmental goods were then plentiful relative to demand. Economic development had not proceeded to the point where environmental demand for water was high, as it is today. Also, knowledge of environmental consequences was immature compared to today's. For example, we thought that fish ladders mitigated the barriers that dams presented to anadromous fish such as salmon, but this was a miscalculation.[5] On the benefit

---

5. Following considerable dam construction, the negative impact of dams on salmon numbers and the complete loss of some salmon runs motivated additional studies. Among other things, studies determined that dams slowed river flows that had traditionally transported salmon young (smolts) to the sea very quickly. The heightened travel time posed by reservoir "flat water" stresses the young and exposes them to greater predation by other species, and some perish in passage through hydroelectric turbines.

side for early projects, the relative absence of water storage in individual basins meant that initial projects yielded things that were unique and clearly valuable, especially a dependable water supply, some measure of flood control, and hydropower.

As water development proceeded, each additional project in a basin contributed more benefits, though in declining amounts. Population growth raised demand and therefore the benefits of the water projects, but other forces countered the rise in benefits. The products of water projects were no longer unique or even particularly scarce in some cases. Prior projects had provided a number of things, but all of these things have marginal benefits that fall as the available quantity grows. At the same time project costs were rising. Human settlement and economic development lifted land scarcity and value. With progress toward a full employment economy, labor costs rose. The remaining dam sites were less rewarding due to their less favorable topography and geology. Rising environmental costs, and rising environmental consciousness and activism, resulted from the progressive loss of "free-flowing" water and natural habitats. Water that was to be captured and stored by additional reservoirs was more likely to have become employed in some fashion.

Driven by political forces, development of water resources and the construction of water projects occurred at an inefficient pace. The United States continued on a water development trajectory that exceeded that indicated by dynamic efficiency, as generically depicted in figure 6.1. That is, the efficient amount of constructed water storage was clearly overshot by the time the Carter administration acted (t_0). In such a circumstance, it makes economic sense to suspend development operations until their economic attractiveness improves.

None of this automatically implies that it will become economically sensible to commence serious dam building again. Still, these arguments do illuminate what happened. The inventory of water storage facilities was produced too rapidly, and it takes a while for any inventory to be cleared. As rising water demand makes use of the excess inventory, increased scarcity legitimizes calls for new projects. Things change during the intermission, however. Not only does water scarcity rise; the scarcities of other resources rise as well, and new water projects will require the use of some of these resources. Institutions change too. Some of the new policies can address water scarcity in new ways, and the comparative advantages of supply enhancement efforts relative to demand management policies can shift.

At the same time, advancing technologies expand the range of alternatives by bringing out new options or making old ones more economical. Some of these options can spawn a new type of water project, as with reverse osmosis plants for desalinating unusable water or the lining of earthen canals with highly impervious, synthetic materials. Regardless of whether the proposed projects are traditional storage facilities or recent innovations, CBA may be applied to determine if they offer dynamic improvements.

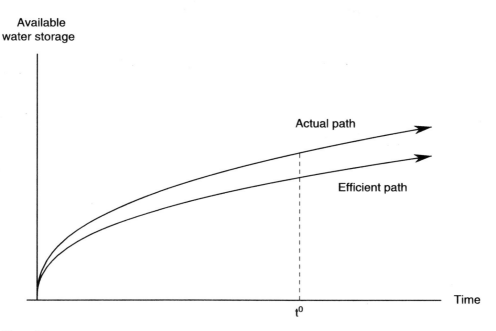

Figure 6.1
Water development trajectories

6.2   Required Economic Analyses: *Principles and Guidelines*

In U.S. water development agencies, as well as in selected lower-level jurisdictions such as states, CBA has been sanctioned as a required step in project evaluation processes. U.S. government rules stipulate that water projects making use of federal monies must be subjected to a CBA, and that project approval is contingent on the outcome. This requirement was initiated within the Flood Control Act of 1936, where it was stated that projects are economically acceptable "if the benefits to whomsoever they accrue are in excess of the estimated costs." This language is recognizable as requiring positive net benefits, yet it falls short of acknowledging a more appropriate test for dynamic efficiency, including the use of discounting, unless both benefits and costs are annualized.

From this humble beginning, the federal requirements for water project CBAs have steadily evolved, acquiring greater rigidity and standardization with each step. Early rules left substantial matters to be interpreted by the different agencies applying them. Inconsistencies arose, and there was ample room for agencies to inject their individual biases, which largely favored project construction. Major rule sets were established and later overwritten by official U.S. documents in 1952, 1958, 1962,

Box 6.1
Federal Discounting in the United States

By law in effect since the late 1960s, the discount rate used by U.S. water agencies has chased the market interest rates of U.S. Treasury bonds. Each year, the average yield of long-term Treasury bonds is computed and compared to the discount rate in use by water agencies. Long-term bonds are defined to be those with a maturity of at least fifteen years. If the average yield differs from the discount rate by .25 percent or more, then the discount rate is changed by .25 percent in the direction of the average yield (*Code of Federal Regulations* 18, §704.39). Hence, the discount rate used in water resource planning can be changed each year, but by no more than .25 percent. For water resource planning conducted during the October 2004 to September 2005 fiscal year, the announced discount rate was 5.375 percent (U.S. Bureau of Reclamation 2004). This rate has been in decline for a few years.

How does this stand with respect to the economically recommended practice discussed in chapter 3? By benchmarking against a long-term instrument backed by the financial power of the United States, the discount rate tends to capture the opportunity costs of long-term commitments and it does not incorporate risk elements. These are positive accomplishments. Nevertheless, the federal procedure does not add the social opportunity costs of capital arising from income taxation, and it does not net out the inflation component that is certainly embedded in Treasury yields. To some extent, these errors offset because they are working in opposite directions. One might argue that the inclusion of inflation is appropriate if planners are projecting benefits and costs in *nominal* (current year) dollars. Federal water planners use *real* dollars (e.g., 2005 dollars) in their CBA investigations, however. As a final observation, there is no lowering of the discount rate when long planning horizons are suggested by project characteristics and the welfare of future generations may be affected.

1973, 1979, and 1983 (Yoe 1993, 117–118). The 1983 rules, known collectively as the *Principles and Guidelines*, are still in force (U.S. Water Resources Council 1983) after they supplanted the *Principles and Standards* of 1973 and 1979. Today, the *Principles and Guidelines* (commonly called the *P&G*) are widely circulated, and the document is downloadable.[6]

Government rules for the conduct of CBA may depart from the disciplinary ideals set forth by economics. That is, there may be inconsistencies between the two. These gaps may be politically purposeful, engineered to elicit more or less favorable judgments of potential projects; or they may be caused by the maturing science of academic CBA—not yet realized or accepted by the authors of government rules. The *P&G* mostly mirror good economic recommendations. Over the evolving history of U.S. rules, it can be said that mandated CBAs have generally converged with economic ideals, although the application of these rules may still exhibit bias or otherwise undershoot required analyses.

An interesting and pervasive feature of the P&G and its predecessor is the separation of project impacts into four "accounts": national economic development (NED), regional economic development (RED), environmental quality (EQ), and other social effects (OSE). NED is portrayed as the pivotal account, and all commen-

6. ⟨http://www.iwr.usace.army.mil/iwr/products/reports/reports.htm⟩ or ⟨http://waterecon.tamu.edu⟩.

surable effects are to be properly monetarized in the NED assessment. Both marketed and nonmarketed goods are economically valued for inclusion in the NED account. Emphasis is clearly placed on the computation of annualized net benefits rather than NPV. Recall that ANB and NPV provide equivalent recommendations in assessing matters of dynamic improvement.

While exceptions are permissible in limited circumstances, proposed projects cannot be part of the federally recommended plan of action unless they offer, as compared to other policy options, "the greatest net economic benefit consistent with protecting the nation's environment" (U.S. Water Resources Council 1983, v). This goal is highly consistent with the objectives that we emphasized earlier: finding out whether projects are part of an efficient package of policy responses.

Observe that the quoted *P&G* statement assigns secondary status to the environmental quality account, which includes only unmonetarized effects on the environment—all monetarized environmental effects are included in NED. Unvalued environmental quality effects are to be quantitatively and qualitatively described using available techniques, which is a laudable approach for addressing incommensurable and intangible impacts (as mentioned in chapter 5). Note, however, that the stated goal of the *P&G* does not leave room for accepting reductions in NED net benefits if environmental quality can be enhanced. Hence, the primary avenue for approving projects that improve environmental quality is to monetarize the environmental benefits so that they are included in the NED account. The *P&G*'s predecessor was more open in acknowledging trade-offs between the NED and EQ accounts, and it allowed the approval of projects with low NED net benefits if the enhancements to EQ were great enough, subjectively speaking of course. This and some other differences between the *P&G* and the *Principles and Standards* demonstrate the political nature of governmentally required CBAs. Depending on the inclinations of the current administration, rules can be amended here and there to influence outcomes.[7]

The regional economic development and other social effects accounts have very low standing in the *P&G*. They are not absolutely required analyses, and they do not have significant bearing on project selection. Regional economic development includes only monetarized consequences affecting the project region. Therefore, it also includes everything in the NED account except for impacts on nonproject regions, thereby including transfer payments (e.g., subsidies and secondary economic effects) from the rest of the nation to the project region. The discussion of secondary effects in the prior chapter suggests that the minimal role of the RED account is theoretically justified. "Other social effects" is a sort of miscellaneous account,

7. President Reagan's administration (1981–1988) was less concerned with environmental protection than was President Carter's (1977–1981).

capturing incommensurable and intangible effects not relating to the environment. Examples include project impacts on local economies, quality of life, energy use, and future generations.

6.3 Envisioning CBA as More Than NPV

An essential observation, emerging both from the preceding chapter and the overview of the *P&G*, is that the goal of reducing all project impacts to a single dollar metric is unlikely to be achieved. The fact that some project effects will not be *commensurable* means that any computed CBA metric will omit some things. That is, NPV or any other economic measure will not encompass all notable project consequences. This becomes increasingly apparent for projects of size, due to the substantial variety of their effects as well as the scale of their effects. For this reason, it is improper to think of CBA as being analytically equal to NPV or any of its substitutes. CBA is about the determination and disclosure of all project impacts, not just those that can be measured in currency. Hence, CBA is more than the computation of NPV.

Critics of CBA sometimes contend that CBA omits selected project outcomes, but this is not a valid argument unless one narrowly equates CBA to an economic index when there are intangibles or incommensurables present. Again, CBA is bigger than NPV.

From a critical perspective, CBA does have shortcomings; they are primarily twofold. First, while the objective of CBA is to aid decision making by reducing all project impacts to common units, this objective is partly thwarted when certain project consequences are not valued. The degree of this problem depends on "how much" remains unvalued, and the problem can be partially or wholly remedied by devoting more effort (and resources) to the monetarization of project consequences.

The second possible problem is that CBA is a manifestation of the aggregate efficiency criterion. In CBA, project effects are monetarized and then weighted equally regardless of who is affected, unless the effects occur in different times periods. Impacts occurring in different time periods are addressed by discounting. Equal weighting of project impacts within the same time period can be argued to be ethically unfortunate when, for example, some effects are experienced by the poor while others are experienced by the rich. Within common project assessment circumstances, this weighting is sensible for the reasons set forth in chapter 2.[8] If, however, an envisioned social purpose of a water project is to remedy inequities in the social

---

8. The primary reasoning is this: failing to weigh monetarily measured project effects equally undermines the markets and price incentives that have evolved to advance economic efficiency in the allocation of all resources (the First Theorem). It is not normally prudent to dismiss these incentives just because we are now allocating socially owned resources (such as the government-collected tax revenues typically employed

distribution of resources, then a traditional application of CBA may fail to illuminate decision making.

For example, if a welfare agency (such as the World Bank) is contemplating participation in a rural water supply project for an impoverished community, the computation of NPV may be off target. In this situation, a social objective is to redirect resources and welfare to less-fortunate people and away from the more fortunate.[9] Elevation of economic efficiency is not the goal here, so CBA may be a weak decision aid. Certain principles of CBA may still be helpful, though. It is still feasible, for instance, to measure the welfare consequences of the proposed project and compare them to alternative, nonwater policies/projects for improving the target population's welfare.

6.4   A Spreadsheet in Need of Entries

Having established the big-picture context of CBA, it is possible to investigate the computation of economic metrics. The actual calculation of a CBA metric, such as NPV or annualized net benefits, is a small matter compared to the analysis required to determine the values of each benefit and cost. At the outset, it is useful to think of an empty spreadsheet that is in need of data entries. Such a spreadsheet is displayed in table 6.1. The two pivotal columns are the outlined schedules of benefits and costs over time. All other empty columns are functionally dependent on these benefits and costs as well as the selected discount rate. Summing the final (seventh) column tells us NPV. Dividing the sum of the fifth column by the sum of the sixth column provides the benefit-cost ratio. These two sums are the present value of benefits and the present value of costs identifiable as the numerator and the denominator of the benefit-cost ratio (equation [3.6]). Performing a numerical transformation on NPV, using equation (3.8), yields the annualized net benefits.

Where, then, do the crucial B_t and C_t entries come from? Fundamentally, they are acquired via the methods introduced in the preceding policy analysis chapter. Generally speaking, projects will modify the quantities of available resources—as in a *supply-shifting policy*. In most situations, benefits result from outward supply shifts. Inward supply shifts cause costs, but project costs also occur when project-required resources are purchased in the marketplace.

---

for project construction). To the extent that project impacts involve market failures such as externalities and public goods, it is important to employ socially corrected prices, but that is ordinarily a separate matter from the distributional one under consideration here. For the matter of weighting project impacts incurred by the rich versus the poor, it is normally desirable to weight dollar measures equivalently, which effectively assigns greater weight to a well-to-do person as compared to a resource-poor individual. Doing otherwise undermines the investment and resource application incentives that shape future social welfare.

9. Contributions to the World Bank come chiefly from the United States, Japan, and several member countries of the European Union (World Bank 2002).

Table 6.1
An incomplete CBA spreadsheet

Period	B_t	C_t	NB_t	$B_t/(1+d)^t$	$C_t/(1+d)^t$	$NB_t/(1+d)^t$
0						
1						
2						
3						
.						
.						
.						
T						
				$\sum = PV(Bs)$	$\sum = PV(Cs)$	$\sum = NPV$

A traditional water project will improve the supply of several goods simultaneously, depending on the intended manner in which the project will be operated. Some of these commodities will exhibit some jointness, in the manner described within chapter 2, in that the project will supply them nonrivally, at least to a point. Other project outputs are inherently rival. As an example of the latter, each unit of additional water supply may be allocated to one sector or another, not both. On the other hand, some project outputs are imperfectly nonrival, as with water supply and hydropower.[10] Because the estimation of project benefits will depend on the manner of project operations, it is normal to specify these operations—essentially specifying the quantity of supply shift for each output—prior to benefit assessment. It may also be practical to employ optimization procedures to resolve a set of benefit-maximizing outputs.

6.5   Obtaining the Benefits and the Costs

Before table 6.1's benefits and costs can be calculated, they must first be *identified* (Sassone and Schaffer 1978, 31–32). Water projects can be so momentous that it becomes difficult to first conceive of every possible benefit and cost category. Experienced agencies may formalize the "brainstorming" required for the identification process into a protocol designed to minimize the number of overlooked impacts. Clearly, quantification of specific benefits and costs cannot be undertaken until they are envisioned by planners. Many consequences of water projects are unintended. The story underlying the unanticipated costs situation in box 6.2 has been repeated

---

10. Reservoir releases for downstream water supply can jointly produce hydropower. Reservoir operations that maximize water supply benefits, however, are likely to be different from those that maximize the value of hydropower, largely due to differences in the preferred timing of water releases.

Box 6.2
Unanticipated Costs in the Missouri River Basin

Often, the consequences of water development are not well-known until after they have occurred, and in some cases these effects can become so worrisome that social efforts are undertaken to undo them. Consider the following summary remarks of a U.S. National Research Council committee examining opportunities for reversing damage to the Missouri River ecosystem. Clearly, water supply projects played a role here, both by changing the habitat directly and encouraging modified human activities within the basin.

Specific examples of twentieth-century changes in the Missouri River ecosystem include the following:

• Nearly 3 million acres of natural riverine and floodplain habitat (bluff to bluff along the Missouri River's mainstem) have been altered through land-use changes, inundation, channelization, and levee building.
• Sediment transport, which was the hallmark of the pre-regulation Missouri River (and was thus nicknamed "The Big Muddy"), has been dramatically reduced. Sediment transport and deposition was critical to maintaining the river system's form and dynamics. For example, before the 1950s, the Missouri River carried an average of roughly 142 million tons of sediment per year past Sioux City, Iowa; after closure of the dams, an average of roughly 4 million tons per year moved past the same location.
• Damming and channelization have occurred on most of the Missouri River basin's numerous tributary streams, where at least 75 dams have been constructed.
• The amplitude and the frequency of the Missouri River's natural peak flows have been sharply reduced. With occasional exception of downstream sections in the state of Missouri, the Missouri River no longer experiences natural spring and summer rises and ecologically beneficial low flows at other times of the year.
• Cropland expansion and reservoir impoundment have caused reductions in natural vegetation communities. These vegetation communities continue to shrink with the additional clearing of floodplain lands. The remaining remnant areas will be critical in any efforts to repopulate the floodplain ecosystem.
• Reproduction of cottonwoods, historically the most abundant and ecologically important species on the river's extensive floodplain, has largely ceased along the Missouri River, except in downstream reaches that were flooded in the 1990s.
• Production of benthic invertebrates (e.g., species of caddisfly and mayfly) has been reduced by approximately 70 percent in remnant unchannelized river reaches. Benthic invertebrates are an important food source for the river's native fishes and an important component of the river's food web.
• Of the 67 native fish species living along the mainstem, 51 are now listed as rare, uncommon, and/or decreasing across all or part of their ranges. One of these fishes (pallid sturgeon) and two avian species (least tern and piping plover) are on the federal Endangered Species List.
• In many reaches of the river, nonnative sport fishes exist in greater abundance than native fish species. The nonnative fishes are often more tolerant of altered conditions of temperature, turbidity, and habitat. Although some nonnative fish produce substantial economic benefits, nonnative species may also contribute to the declining abundance of native fish.

These ecosystem changes are not merely abstract, scientific measurements; they also represent the loss of valued goods and services to society (National Research Council 2002a).

in many regions of the world (World Commission on Dams 2000). Analytic teams must be vigilant because unintended project impacts are still project impacts in need of inclusion and evaluation.

Once identified, the various categories of benefits and costs may be prioritized prior to analysis. Some categories warrant extra attention because of the anticipated size of their valuations. Relative values may cause certain benefits or costs to be pivotal in the decision making assisted by CBA. Extra accuracy may be justifiable for these. Some categories may justify more immediate attention by virtue of the difficulty of their analysis. Difficulties may arise in either the complexity of analysis and/or the availability of suitable data. Not only may available economic data be in short supply; most economic assessments are also extremely sensitive to supporting technical information generated outside of economics. Hence, technical support from noneconomic disciplines is crucial.

Water projects can be accompanied by a diverse set of benefit and cost categories. From a water scarcity perspective, the main benefit is an increased water supply. Other major benefits may include enhancements to recreation, flood control, hydropower, navigation, water quality, and some aspects of environmental habitat. Valuing each of these requires that analysts possess or generate empirical knowledge about the demand for each of these commodities. Obtaining such demand information can be difficult, and some technical "resourcefulness" can be useful.

Major cost categories for traditional water projects include planning and design services, land, salaries and wages, construction materials and equipment, borrowing costs, and losses of a recreational or environmental nature. The analysis of costs is methodologically symmetrical to benefit analysis. The primary difference is that resources are being consumed, not produced. Unlike the things produced by water projects, however, many of the consumed things are common commodities and they are sold in the marketplace (e.g., fabricated steel, concrete, insurance, surveying services). In many cases, the amount of additional market production caused by a water project is too low to impact price very much. Thus, whereas the correct cost measure for market-obtained goods is area A in figure 6.2, this trapezoidal area may be well

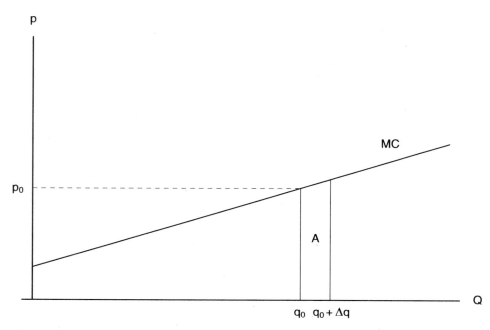

Figure 6.2
Valuing a cost increase

approximated by a rectangular area—the one simply obtained by multiplying the amount of the good used in construction, Δq, by its prevailing market price, p_0. Unless the scale of the project is large, this method works well for many costs. It can also be applied to evaluating hydropower benefits in some situations.

In the more difficult instances of cost assessment, the sacrificed good is not exchanged in markets. Recreation and environmental costs are prime examples. While water projects can augment certain types of recreational or environmental goods (e.g., water skiing, reduced turbidity), they commonly subtract others (e.g., white-water rafting, reduced native species). In these cases, the costs are properly based on the losses incurred by the users. While the theory here is easily relayed within figure 6.3, which identifies a project cost as area A, it can be difficult to obtain the required demand (marginal benefit) information. The importance of this topic justifies greater attention in chapter 9.

6.6 A Project Analysis Example: Applewhite Reservoir

Relatively simple extensions of fundamental policy analysis can be used to analyze water supply benefits. Focusing on the water supply dimensions of water projects, a

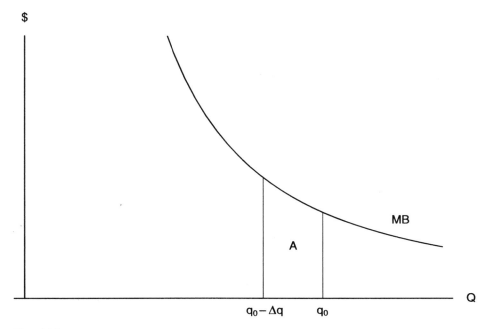

Figure 6.3
Valuing a diminished good

main distinction between policy and project analysis is that projects are more permanent. Whereas policies can be changed when society wishes, projects are largely irreversible. Hence, while some policies might be feasibly analyzed by finding their net
benefits under current demand conditions, a project will have to be analyzed using
present and future demand to find its net present value.

So water demand must be projected for project analysis. Typically, this is not difficult because it is normally acceptable to employ population projections obtained
from demographers who devote serious attention to this matter. One simple procedure for projecting residential water demand is to presume that it is driven by population growth. Equation (6.1) indicates how future water demand is related to current
water demand within this procedure. This is a practical approach for modern water
projects enhancing the supply of residential water.

$$W_t(p) = (1 + g)^t W_0(p) \qquad (6.1)$$

Here, g represents the periodic growth rate expressed as a decimal. (For example, a
population growth rate of 1.1 percent per year implies $g = 0.011$.) The index t serves
as an exponent when used as a superscript. W_0 is demand for the known population
in period 0. The nature of this relationship is illustrated in figure 6.4. Inverted de-

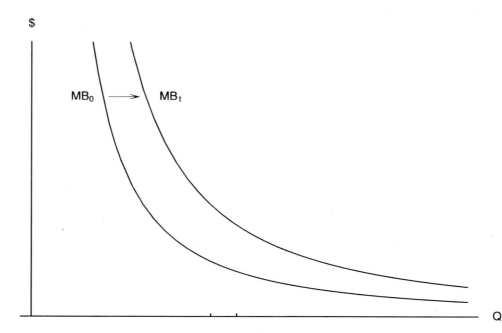

Figure 6.4
Growth-driven demand shifts

mand in the current period (MB_0) is shifted rightward over time by a multiplicative amount. (Can you use this figure to visualize the impact of population growth on the change in net benefits attributable to a water project?) You may recall that the approach of (6.1) was embedded in the dynamic problem of the drawing from a reservoir section in chapter 3 (note equation [3.18]).

To demonstrate how this demand-forecasting method can serve in project analysis, suppose that the following information is available for a specific, proposed water supply project:

- the schedule of project costs and the project's anticipated completion date;
- the water supply increase enabled by the project;
- the available water supply in the absence of the project;
- the current demand for tap water;
- the current costs of processing natural water into tap water.

The type of analysis needed for this scenario was suggested earlier by figure 5.7. The water project promises to shift out the supply of retail water by alleviating a natural water constraint. Depending on demand and price parameters, the project may produce immediate benefits or its benefits may not commence until population increases have raised demand further.

This analysis has been performed previously for a project proposed for San Antonio, Texas, and we will overview the crucial elements of this analysis here. As with other analyses presented in this text, there is a Mathematica file for this one at ⟨http://waterecon.tamu.edu⟩. (This file can be readily modified to examine other water projects.) The analysis conducted here is a month-by-month simulation of what would occur as a consequence of the project's construction. Net benefits are calculated for every month of a fifty-year planning horizon. Net present value is computed using these monthly net benefits.

Applewhite Reservoir was proposed as a modest-size water supply project.[11] For a projected expense of \$180 million, Applewhite would enlarge the city's water supply by 48,000 acre-feet per year. Because this facility would be locally funded, all the costs would have to be offset by higher water rates on the city's water consumers. Hence, the impact of the project on consumers would be twofold. On the one hand, a natural water constraint would be lessened; there would be more available water.

11. As no federal participation in this project was intended by the planners, no CBA was required and none was commissioned by the city. The city council approved this project, and land condemnation efforts were immediately undertaken. Construction of the earthen dam was well underway when citizen dissatisfaction about the project led to its cancellation. Because the city could not simply abandon the project and leave it in a semicomplete state, "cleanup" and revegetative measures were necessary before the dam could be fully discontinued.

On the other hand, the rates must be increased. Under these interesting circumstances, consumers will get to reveal their increasing demand for water while they are expected to pay for these benefits (no subsidies). Water price will rise because of the costs of the new reservoir, so individual consumers will use less water on average, but there will be more consumers over time. Roughly then, if the growth in consumer numbers outstrips the decline in water use per household, the project can generate net benefits and a positive NPV.

San Antonio planners expected to finance reservoir construction by selling bonds in the marketplace. Buyers of the bonds receive periodic payments until, essentially, they have the purchase price returned to them as well as some interest for "renting" their money. At the time of this proposal, the interest payments were expected to be 7.5 percent per year.

Based on the point-expansion method of identifying water demand, the current water rate and the current water consumption can be expanded using an assumed price elasticity. Because water demand in San Antonio is quite seasonal, monthly demand is used. Monthly price elasticities vary from -0.31 to -0.41 based on an earlier study of water demand across a large number of communities. Demand is most elastic (-0.39 to -0.41) during the summer months, when the marginal water use is normally lawn irrigation.

In the case of Applewhite, planners had already settled on a five-year sequence of water price increases to accompany and finance the project. Our analysis assumes that these same price increases will occur if construction is undertaken, and that they will stay in place until all borrowed funds have been repaid. Because water rates have been increasing even in the absence of development projects, we make the historically conservative assumption that real (inflationless) rates increase at 2 percent per year in the absence of Applewhite.[12]

Knowing the water demand function each month of the first year, the following simulation can be conducted beginning with the first month of the planning horizon.

1. Project the water demand (MB) function for the month using population projections.

2. Given total demand and the without-Applewhite water price, how much water do consumers want to consume?

3. Given total demand and the with-Applewhite water price, how much water do consumers want to consume?

---

12. As documented by Griffin and Chowdhury (1993), in the years leading up to the Applewhite proposal, rate increases had exceeded 2 percent per year. So this is a conservative estimate. An advantage for using programs such as Mathematica is that parameters such as this can be altered to determine whether a particular parameter is important to the eventual outcome (NPV).

4. Given the answers to 2 and 3, what amount of Applewhite's capacity (if any) will be utilized, and what is the change in consumer net benefits attributable to Applewhite (measured as an appropriate area beneath the MB curve)?

5. Given the with- and without-Applewhite water consumption quantities (2 and 3 above) and the differences in water rates, how much added revenue is generated under the "with" scenario? Subtract this from the outstanding debt after interest costs have been added for the current month.

6. Repeat this procedure for the next month of the planning horizon beginning at step 1. Reduce the with-Applewhite water rates to the level of the without-Applewhite rates as soon as all construction and borrowing costs have been fully retired.

Most aspects of this procedure are easily performed. Step 4 is the exception because the net benefits calculation requires some fundamental knowledge of policy analysis for supply-enhancing policies (chapter 5). Furthermore, calculation of the net benefit measure depends on the extent to which water rates or available water is limiting water consumption (Griffin and Chowdhury 1993).[13]

The selected discount rate used for this analysis is 4 percent. Figure 6.5 illustrates the findings of this analysis by plotting undiscounted and discounted ΔNB over the six hundred month period of analysis. Observe that the net benefits attributable to Applewhite are initially negative and become more negative during the first few years. What is occurring here is that rate increases to cover construction costs are harming consumers. Moreover, their reduced use of water is causing a situation in which they are making no use of the new reservoir. Eventually, however, the city collects enough additional revenue to fully retire all bonds, and water rates are dropped to without-Applewhite levels. At this point in time, during month 102 (four years beyond the city-projected time) the reduced rates encourage residents to begin some use of the reservoir.[14] At this point in time, net benefits turn positive and remain there. Net benefits beyond month 102 grow as residents progressively make greater use of the reservoir due to population growth.

Because net present value is the sum of discounted net benefits, we can visualize NPV by comparing the size of the gray area (negative present value) of figure 6.5 to the black area. The gray area appears to be larger, which is indeed the fact. NPV for

13. For the latter reason, an involved set of "which" programming commands is embedded in the Mathematica program for this example. These are basically the same as the "if-then-else" statements with which many readers are familiar.

14. It is not known how city planners performed their calculation, but they probably assumed that water consumers would not modify their behavior in response to heightened rates. Accurate analyses do not make this mistake.

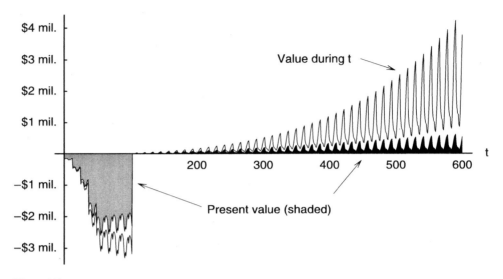

Figure 6.5
Applewhite net benefits (monthly)

Applewhite Reservoir is computed to be −$86 million. This project would therefore appear to be economically undesirable.

A major advantage of this analysis is that its computerization enables additional analyses that can generate important insights about alternative scenarios. Figure 6.5 shows that Applewhite's net benefits increase over time. Would a longer planning horizon result in a positive NPV? Since the reservoir's net benefits are decidedly negative during early periods, could things be improved by simply delaying the project a decade or so while buying the land now?[15] How might an altered pattern of population growth affect estimated benefits, and what would happen if unexpected water supply shortfalls arise in the absence of a new reservoir? These and many more scenarios can be evaluated when a flexible computer program is used.

6.7 Multipurpose Projects

Although this text is quite focused on water scarcity and the role projects can play in alleviating scarcity, water projects provide an array of benefits. Not only can water supplies be augmented for differing sectors, there are benefits and costs unrelated to

---

15. It is reported that the massively expensive Central Arizona Project was built eighty-six years too early, so such questions are important (Holland and Moore 2003). Not only can rescheduling reduce losses; it can also produce an economically advantageous water project.

water supply enhancement. Large water projects will typically contribute the following primary improvements:

- Water supply
  - Irrigation
  - Urban
  - Industrial
- Flood control
- Recreation
- Hydropower
- Navigation

All of these outputs are to be valued according to the theoretical material presented in this text. That is, there are demands for these improvements, and the added quantity enabled by a project provides benefits measurable by the correct area beneath the demand curve. There are features underlying some of these demands that make them unique, however.

Flood control benefits derive from maintaining a partially empty reservoir, so that it has the capacity to capture occasional flood waters, thereby averting downstream damages that would otherwise occur. Hence, these benefits are based on a probabilistic event, and benefits might be measurable as the value of the avoided negative consequences: property damage, deaths and injuries, lost business activity, and emergency responses. Flood control competes with the water supply feature of reservoirs because flood prevention is increased by lowering the stored water.

Recreation benefits are interesting in that some of them are dependent on the *flow* of reservoir releases, which enable downstream enjoyments for fishing, boating, camping, and so on. Other recreation benefits arise from the *stock* of water captured by a reservoir. This water also gives rise to fishing, boating, and camping types of benefits, although these flat-water activities differ from the flow-based ones. In all these cases, though, the idea of negatively sloped demand applies well.

Hydropower yields a clearly marketable commodity, and its value is well established by existing electricity markets. As expected, the demand for electricity is negatively sloped. Flexibility in the production of hydropower results from being able to turn it on and off fairly quickly, unlike other sources of electricity (thermal or nuclear plants). This means that hydropower can be employed to provide peak-load power, which is more valuable than base-load power. Although water released from a reservoir to serve as a downstream water supply also generates hydropower, the optimal timing of releases may be different for these two joint uses.

Navigation benefits emphasize the commercial value of moving commodities via water. Establishing commercial navigation or enhancing it by enlarging waterways or stabilizing water flow can promote additional traffic or shorten travel times. Generally, the benefits of navigation stem from the saved expense of alternative modes of transport, especially rail or truck, but it is also possible for new navigation possibilities to spur new commerce, rather than just the reallocation of existing commerce.

The possibility of measuring navigation benefits as saved "alternative costs" raises questions about the appropriateness of this technique, but the question is not unique to navigation. It is also practical to measure the benefits of water supply as the costs of alternative approaches for obtaining the same supply increments. But is it an acceptable approach?

6.8   Using Alternative Costs as a Benefit Measure

Through their association with project supporters, especially the project designers from whom important technical details are obtained, economic analysts can acquire and transmit a great many biases. Such biases typically result in benefit overestimation and cost underestimation. The analyst must guard against biases, but it is seemingly an impossible task to fully satisfy. Economic analysts must rely on non-economic specialists for extensive information, and economic analysts commonly do not possess the skills needed to reevaluate the information they are given. The problem of bias may be particularly acute in cost estimation, where it is harder to anticipate every conceivable cost, especially when the size of the project is large or the project is a technologically novel undertaking—implying that little experience is available for the accurate estimation of costs. As a consequence, cost underestimation can be said to be a "global phenomenon" (Flyvbjerg, Holm, and Buhl 2002). A recent survey found that "large dams have demonstrated a marked tendency towards schedule delays and significant cost overruns" (World Commission on Dams 2000, xxxi).

The economic analyst is also capable of injecting additional biases into project assessment. Some of these are subtle, perhaps too subtle to even be noticed by the analyst. They may arise from data selections or methodological selections. One methodological manner of "accomplishing" benefit overestimation is to employ the *alternative cost procedure* erroneously. This popular and readily performed measure of water supply benefits arises *if* a water development project will render unnecessary other expenditures devoted to the scarcity problem. If a water project will substitute for other expenditures, then the savings may rightfully be claimed to be benefits of the project. Often, this approach is a readily available method of benefit estimation, but its use requires careful consideration.

In the face of rising water scarcity, a great number of choices are available to decision makers at various levels. As discussed earlier, property regimes can be refined, prices can be improved, consumer behavior can be modified by incentives or regulations, or supply enhancements can be pursued. There are other alternatives as well. Any *efficient* measure will have, by definition, benefits in excess of costs. As such, the cost of any efficient measure is a lower-bound estimate of benefits. Therefore,

• if a water project displaces a measure that would be employed in the absence of the project, then the displaced measure's costs (called the *alternative costs*) can be used as a conservative estimate of project benefits;

• it would constitute double counting to count as project benefits both alternative costs and the benefits of the alternative measure.

Potential misuse of the alternative cost technique arises when analysts pose alternatives that will not be adopted in the absence of the project (Young 1996, 41; 2005, 103–104). It is difficult to be visionary about the measures that will be deployed as scarcity increases. Project analysts, as well as project supporters, can be misled in their perceptions about what will be done in the absence of a proposed project. In this setting, it is always possible to identify costly alternatives that appear reasonable, yet are not reasonable in relation to their prospective benefits and overlooked options. For example, it may be argued that in the absence of Applewhite Reservoir, businesses may be forced to shut down, the desalinization of brackish ground water may be commenced on a large scale, or an expensive interbasin conveyance facility may be constructed. Each of these alternative measures derives some support from the *need*-based thought patterns that permeate public opinion in matters of water. While it is possible that one or more of these alternative measures are legitimate in that they would truly be pursued, it is economically important to also consider policies capable of addressing scarcity more cheaply. This includes demand management policies such as improved pricing and social innovations in improved institutions such as those noted in chapter 4. That is, it is fallacious to pose alternatives that society will come to reject (or regret) once the costs of costly options are publicly and privately confronted. To pose such alternatives in conjunction with the alternative cost procedure only serves to overstate project benefits and justify inefficient projects. Clearly, then, analysts using the alternative cost procedure have a tough duty to fulfill.

As a logically related principle, the benefits of a project are bounded above by the costs of an alternative measure capable of supplying the same benefits (Steiner 1965). For example, suppose a water project will provide two types of benefits, such as water supply and hydropower, and there are two alternative measures (such as a desalinization plant and a wind farm) capable of supplying the same products. In this case, the benefits of the water project cannot be greater than the combined costs of the alternatives. If we want to use the summed costs of these two alternatives as the measure of benefits, however, we must verify that there are no cheaper options, and we must provide a reasonable argument for why beneficiaries value the gains this much. That is, it should be reasonable to expect that in the absence of the project, the beneficiaries will build the desalinization plant and the wind farm.

As another example, observe that the Applewhite proposal promised to provide 48,000 acre-feet annually for $180 million. That works out to $3,750 per acre-foot. If water rights in the region are transferable and the city can buy all it wants for $1,500 per acre-foot, then the water supply benefits of this project can be no greater than $72 million plus any transaction and conveyance costs necessary to put water market purchases on par with the project.

6.9 The Costs of Borrowed Funds

When undertaken by governments receiving general tax revenue, projects can be built using legislatively appropriated funds. In these cases, the legislature dedicates a portion of tax revenues to project construction. Yet the expense of project construction can also lead to borrowing by project builders, due to the mismatched timing of costs and repaid benefits. Although other approaches are possible, borrowing is typically conducted by selling bonds: fixed-length obligations (ten years, for instance) to repay the lender on expiration of the bond. There is an array of bond instruments of varying character, with various terms designed to be mutually attractive to borrower-sellers and lender-buyers. Repayment may be periodic (especially quarterly) or one time. Bonds may be uninterruptible, they may be paid off early at the seller's option, or they may be "called in" by the buyer. After they are purchased, most bonds are transferable, meaning that the buyer may sell acquired bonds to other individuals. Hence, buyers may recover their investment without waiting for the bond to mature. This flexibility is valued by buyers, thereby raising their willingness to buy bonds and lowering the implied rate of interest. A good resource for more information on the various characteristics of bonds as they relate to water supply systems is the text by Raftelis (1993).

Implicit to all bonds is compensation for temporary use of lenders' funds. This compensation is a form of interest rate, and it constitutes an added cost of project construction. Many bonds for constructing water projects are sold by governmental authorities, and this may enable the buyer to exempt bond-derived income from taxation. As a consequence, buyers are willing to pay more for tax-exempt bonds, driving the implied interest rate lower and allowing government issuers to benefit from lowered interest costs.

The principal and interest costs incurred for any water project is a project cost in the period in which it is to be paid. To avoid double counting, construction costs are not separately registered. For example, suppose the funds to enable a $10 million construction expense in year 0 are acquired by selling $10 million worth of bonds in year 0. The agreed terms are that the seller will repay the buyer $1.1 million annually beginning in year 1 and ending in year 10. In this case, the CBA should set aside the $10 million expense and include the annual payments as the appropriate project costs.[16] This method properly incorporates both capital outlays and borrowing costs in the CBA. In the event that borrowing costs are precisely equal to the discount rate, it will make no difference whether the repayment schedule or the construction cost schedule are used in the CBA.

6.10 Financing Projects: Implications for CBA

Aside from borrowing costs, CBA and financial analysis of projects have tradition-ally been viewed as separate matters. That is, CBA has been performed without re-gard to "where's the money coming from" questions. For project analysis by federal authorities, financing questions have normally centered on the allocation of costs to various purposes. Because project beneficiaries are ordinarily expected to make some contribution to project costs, and because these contributions are expected to be grounded in facts, it is important to "allocate" all project costs to particular pur-poses. This ***cost allocation*** process partitions all project costs across project purposes, which are then matched to specific beneficiary groupings. Historically, different levels of federal subsidization, stated as percentages of the costs to be repaid, have been allowed for different purposes (e.g., municipal water supply, irrigation, or recre-ation). Beneficiary groups have often been allowed to "borrow" these assigned costs from the government, sometimes for long periods and at low rates of interest. Indeed, U.S. project beneficiaries have traditionally received greater subsidy through these favorable loan terms than they have from their less-than-100-percent cost repayment responsibilities (Wahl 1989).

In the more modern era, the ongoing reduction of federal subsidies and the general public desire for financial responsibility is causing economic analysis (CBA) to be more closely related to financial analysis. As a prime example, if a particular group of beneficiaries (e.g., a city or an irrigation district) are expected to sacrifice a portion of their benefits to offset project costs, then it is possible that these payments and the manner in which they are collected will affect the measurement of benefits.

If its share of allocated costs is large relative to benefits, a benefiting group may withdraw its participation due to the confounding effects of small net benefits for the group, divisive issues about the distribution of water and obligations among group members, and difficulty resolving an internal, fund-collection instrument for meeting the repayment obligations. For example, a group of farmers may support a

16. The implied interest rate for these terms are given by the solution for i in the equation

$$10 = \sum_{t=1}^{10} \frac{1.1}{(1+i)^t},$$

which is 1.77 percent.

new project capable of augmenting irrigation supplies, but if the farmers have to pay the full costs they may withdraw their support. Even if the farmers believe that their benefits exceed their costs, they may be unable to settle on a mechanism for collecting revenue and repaying their assigned project costs.

Furthermore, different repayment collection devices may alter the net benefits to be received from the project and thereby affect the CBA. For instance, an organization might be able to collect their repayment obligations through alternative mechanisms: (1) a property tax assessment on all landowners in the service area, (2) a lump-sum assessment on water users independent of their water use, or (3) an increase in metered water fees. Each option has different implications for how much project water will be consumed. Hence, the benefits will be affected. Approach (1) spreads the costs across project water users and nonusers, thereby enhancing the rewards to water users and assuring that they make high use of the cheap water (which is not a good thing). Approach (2) can be accomplished with added acreage fees for irrigators and added monthly "meter" charges for urban users. In these cases, the marginal price of water remains low, thereby encouraging high utilization of project-supplied water, but the added nonvolumetric fees can spur some water users to decline participation. That is, some business agents, especially irrigators, may believe that the lump-sum assessment is greater than the prospective benefits of an extended, cheap water supply. Such responses have implications for the benefit measurement procedures used in CBA. The third approach to defraying costs allocated to a group has a direct affect on the marginal price of water to members. Because members have water demands, not needs, there will be a response to the increased price. The decrease in quantity demanded serves to limit received benefits, thereby having a clear effect on benefit measurement, as demonstrated in the Applewhite analysis.

6.11   Cost Allocation by Separable Costs-Remaining Benefits

Given that cost allocation is relevant to CBA, how is it conducted? Because this is not an easy question, different answers are possible. Difficulties arise because any given water project will usually provide multiple benefits and many project costs are not the clear result of any single purpose. For example, for a water reservoir enhancing multisectoral water supply, navigation, flood control, hydropower, and recreation, how are the costs of inundated land to be assigned? These land costs are the collective result of all these purposes. The same can be said for most aspects of the most expensive structural element: the dam itself.

Because joint costs such as land and the dam are attributable to all purposes, how should they be allocated? A first response might be equal apportionment, but that answer is not sensitive to the fact that benefits vary across the different purposes. Thus, equal cost allocations are not normally equitable. Nor do they turn out to be efficient. A second possible response is to prorate costs on the basis of water use—the more water received, the higher the allocated costs. This answer is not sensitive to the water demand exhibited by different purposes and will reduce participation by beneficiaries for whom marginal benefits are low even if they can make a positive contribution toward joint costs.

The most widely used method of cost allocation is a procedure descriptively called *separable costs-remaining benefits*. It is commonly abbreviated as SCRB (pronounced "scrub"). In its first step, *separable costs* are determined for each group of project beneficiaries. This is accomplished by taking the total project costs and subtracting the total costs of an imaginary project in which the group/purpose is absent. For example, the separable costs of hydropower are all the costs attributable solely to the presence of this purpose in project design, including turbines, generators, and electrical transmission and control facilities. It is efficient and generally regarded to be fair to allocate to each purpose its separable costs. If a purpose cannot take responsibility for its separable costs because its benefits are inadequate, then that purpose should be omitted from the project.

Unfortunately, the sum of separated costs across all purposes will be less than total costs. A second step is thus applied. *Remaining benefits* are calculated for each purpose by subtracting its separable costs from its estimated benefits. Then, all *nonseparable costs* (total costs minus all separable costs) are prorated across the beneficiaries on the basis of their remaining benefits.[17] Nonseparable costs are often called joint costs too. If group A has three times the remaining benefits as group B, group A will contribute three times more to nonseparable costs than will group B. As long as a project can pass a cost-benefit test, it is mathematically assured that the summed remaining benefits will exceed the nonseparable costs, thus assuring that SCRB's second step (the remaining benefits proration) will leave each beneficiary grouping with positive net benefits. While this property of the SCRB procedure aids the social pursuit of net benefits and is therefore consistent with dynamic improvements, its justification rests on an equity foundation. Hence, its acceptance is partially contingent on fairness arguments that may be contested by some parties.

Table 6.2 contains a demonstration of the SCRB procedure for an unsubsidized project benefiting three groups. The present value of all costs is $100 million, as shown in row 1. The estimated benefits for each sector are given in row 2, and these are also expressed as present values. Though not directly shown in the table, in the absence of urban water supply purposes the project will cost $92 million rather than $100 million. Hence, the urban sector's separable costs are $8 million. This result is

---

17. By extension, this procedure can be applied to situations where some costs are nonseparable among a subset of project purposes. In such cases, there can be intermediate steps in which semi-nonseparable costs are allocated among the responsible groups/purposes.

Table 6.2
Separable costs-remaining benefits in application

	Urban	Hydropower	Recreation	All
			-$1,000-	
1. Project costs				$100,000
2. Benefits	$50,000	$40,000	$30,000	$120,000
3. Separable costs	$8,000	$17,000	$2,000	$27,000
4. Remaining benefits (2 − 3)	$42,000	$23,000	$28,000	$93,000
5. Nonseparable costs (1 − 3)				$73,000
6. Percentage of remaining benefits	45.16%	24.73%	30.11%	
7. Assigned nonseparable costs	$32,968	$18,054	$21,978	$73,000
8. Allocated costs (3 + 7)	$40,968	$35,054	$23,978	$100,000
9. Net present value (2 − 8)	$9,032	$4,946	$6,022	$20,000

entered in row 3. Similar computations reveal the separable costs attributable to the other two sectors.

Only table entries for rows 1–3 are exogenous to the table. All other entries are computed using information from these three rows. The remaining benefits are the differences between row 2 and row 3 entries. The summed separable costs amount to $27 million, implying that the remaining costs are nonseparable. In rows 6 and 7, the nonseparable costs are allocated on the basis of row 5 and 6 information. The finalized cost allocations for each sector are provided in row 8.

It is important to acknowledge that the proration of nonseparable costs might be performed well, from an efficiency perspective, using other procedures. By definition, nonseparable costs are jointly "caused" by all project participants. Therefore, there are weak precepts for deciding how these costs should be allocated. From an efficiency basis, it can only be said that each group's share of the nonseparable costs is bounded above by the group's remaining benefits. If more than that is allocated, the group is motivated to withdraw its participation. This would constitute an efficiency loss because the group does have a positive contribution to make toward nonseparable costs. Given this, using the table 6.2 example, an equal apportionment of the $73 million in nonseparable costs across the three sectors would not be advisable. (Examine the table to see why this is true.) All things considered, the SCRB procedure is well suited to the task even though its implicit concept of fairness is not the only feasible path.

6.12 Summary

CBA represents important economic work because water projects are a well-touted mechanism of relieving water scarcity. Political pressure favoring water projects can be enormous—due in part to the relative distribution of benefits to costs. Such pressure is not relevant to how economic analysis is conducted, but it is a key reason why analysis is conducted. Any given project can be expensive, so assessing each project's net worth is a good idea. The theory here tells us that a project constitutes a dynamic improvement if its net present value is positive. Absent positive NPV, a project is demonstrably not part of the efficient package of scarcity-addressing measures. It is always worthwhile to think of CBA in these "part of the efficient package" terms. Because there are many alternative strategies to solve water scarcity, we wish to select the best ones and discard or postpone the others. For this reason, governments such as the United States require CBA when their money is to be used in construction, and some governments have established rules regarding the proper execution of CBA.

The computation of NPV or its equivalents is a simple matter once all the distinct benefits and costs are assembled. Therein lies the challenge. Clearly, the estimation of demand is a crucial step for such analysis. The calculation of individual benefits and costs is an extension of the framework developed in the prior chapter. Projects promise water supply enhancements, hence the central benefits are measured as an area beneath natural water demand curves. This method is closely examined in the prior chapter.

Because certain things sacrificed or produced by projects may defy attempts to value them—what were called incommensurables and intangibles in chapter 5— some costs and benefits will be neglected by NPV. In such cases, which are common, NPV becomes a partial indicator of project worthiness, and it is no longer advisable to accept/reject projects solely on the basis of NPV. Here, the warning given early in chapter 1 applies: economically provided guidance is weaker than we would like. The consequences are that analysts must persevere in reporting all project impacts, including those external to NPV, and decision-making processes should extend consideration beyond NPV. These consequences inject an inevitable degree of subjectivity into project decisions unless strong efforts are devoted to monetarizing all significant benefits and costs.

6.13 Exercises

1. The marginal benefits of water for a given population in year 0 is given by $mb = 20 - 3w$. If the annual population growth rate is 1 percent and population growth is the only shifter of demand, what is the marginal benefit function in year 5?

2. Suppose that a new dam is proposed to alleviate an urban scarcity problem. No benefits other than water supply are conveyed by the project. The dam will capture an additional five thousand acre-feet of water every year for a current cost of $2,000 per acre-foot. That is, the present value of project costs is $10 million. Suppose that

discounted and summed project benefits measured as the areas under users' MNB curves are $20 million. If state law permitted the transfer of water rights, it is expected that such rights would trade for $1,000 per acre-foot. Unfortunately, state law does not allow such exchanges to occur. Should this dam be built? Would you modify your answer if this dam scenario is repeated throughout the state?

3. If the present value of a project's construction costs are $400, what alternative split(s) of these costs between the two beneficiaries can be economically justified? The gross benefits received by users 1 and 2 are $350 and $150, respectively. Their separable costs are $50 and $70, respectively. Provide a full explanation.

4. The Kettle Irrigation District (KID) wants to assess the economic merits of a canal rehabilitation project promising to reduce conveyance leakage. Currently, KID withdraws 50,000 acre-feet of river water in a typical year so as to deliver 20,000 acre-feet to farm gates. Although this indicates an average conveyance loss of 1.5 af for every 1.0 af delivered, engineers believe that the marginal conveyance loss is much lower (0.2 af lost per 1.0 af delivered). For the sum of $3,600,000 divided equally over three years, a private contractor will refurbish KID's canals during three consecutive winter off-seasons. The worst canals will be addressed first. Considered independently, the three phases are projected to reduce leakage by 5,000, 4,000, and 3,000 acre-feet, respectively. These accomplishments will have finite lives, however. Each is expected to degrade linearly following each season, so that each repaired canal will return to its present condition after ten years of service. For example, the first phase will reduce leakage by 5,000 af during its first year of operation, but it will save only 4,500 af during its second year. After ten years, conveyance losses will not worsen further. Using a 6 percent discount rate and a twenty-year time horizon, assess this project and make recommendations after applying the following information to evaluate benefits. The district estimates its water production costs at $5 per acre-foot (mostly for energy), but farmers are charged $8 for every acre-foot they receive. KID has an ample water supply during most years, but during one year out of five there are climate-caused shortages. During these dry years, KID allows trading among its farmers, and these lease prices generally hover around $10 per af (excluding KID's delivery charge). KID has never allowed direct trading between its farmers and nonmembers, but there is an active water market in the basin. During most years, regional lease prices approximate $50/af, but they triple during the one out of five dry years.

7 Water Marketing

To what extent can markets solve scarcity problems?

Two scarcity-addressing strategies dear to water resource economists are water marketing and water pricing. *Marketing* is a management policy for natural water, whereas *pricing* pertains to partially or fully processed (retail) water. In this chapter and the next, economic advice pertaining to these two institutions is closely examined. Water marketing is tackled first, in recognition of the considerable attention and reforms relating to this institution during the past quarter century. As with all scarcity strategies considered here, the crucial question is this: What is the potential role of this policy *among* the set of efficiency-enhancing tools? No single tool is a panacea.

Water marketing is a well-celebrated device in the literature of water resource economics. Economic theorists and practitioners have expressed great concern about the "missing" water markets that once resulted from the seemingly irrational legal restrictions pertaining to the trade of water rights.[1] Although these restrictions have been relaxed in many regions, reform efforts continue.

Economic promotion of water marketing is the direct product of the First Theorem of Welfare Economics. The First Theorem favors the use of transferable property rights to manage important resources. We market all kinds of raw resources fundamental to economic development—timber, minerals, oil—so why not water? We market all sorts of humanly essential commodities—housing, food, medicine—so why not water?

The guidance of the First Theorem—remembering that its assumptions must first be met—is that no institutional form can do a better job of advancing economic efficiency than markets. In chapter 4, the First Theorem was cautiously applied to

---

1. While there is no shortage of earlier literature interested in the use of water marketing (Ciriacy-Wantrup 1956; Hartman and Seastone 1970; Milliman 1959), a wealth of economic literature favoring transferable water rights began to emerge during the 1980s. Fervent examples of the latter include Anderson (1983a, 1983b). Other useful readings include El-Ashry and Gibbons (1986), National Research Council (1992), and Wahl (1989).

water resource issues. There we saw how water's uses and attributes, primarily its flow character, perplex straightforward application of the First Theorem. Things are not as rosy as we would like. There are obstacles to overcome. In particular, private water rights must be carefully defined, well administered, and thoughtfully limited if water markets are to serve society. It is not enough to simply define water rights and "let the market work." The concept of a "free market" advancing economic efficiency is too superficial in most situations. Continued public sector participation is required if water markets are to improve economic efficiency. Moreover, agent behavior must be restrained.

The goal of this chapter is to consider the potential role of water marketing in greater detail. We will investigate some of water marketing's history and its terminology. A generic structure for approving water market transactions will be outlined. Some specific, currently operating markets will be visited to inject some useful concreteness and to see how water markets actually work. Most of the discussion will emphasize surface water circumstances, but ground water will receive attention too. Ground water marketing is rarer, and a concern is the added complexity of setting ground water depletion rates. Several types of ground water externalities can also be hurdles.

7.1   The Instruments of Water Marketing

The pricing of retail water to customers and the *privatization* of water processing facilities do *not* constitute water marketing. In addition, whereas some water marketing arrangements may involve or even necessitate complementary agreements for money pertaining to the use of water storage or conveyance structures, such agreements are properly regarded as infrastructure marketing, not water marketing. *Water marketing* means the exchange of natural water rights by willing buyers and sellers. Water markets are enabled by the full or partial adjudication of natural water resources among agents, with the crucial characteristic of transferability included. As long as individual agents possess private property in natural water, they will be able to exchange water for money or other property. Ideally, these rights are severed from the land on which they are originally used, meaning that water can be exchanged separately from land. Such water rights are necessarily quantified, so that a solid basis is established for monitoring water use and enforcing water rights. Unless enforcement is consistent and accurate, water rights can be circumvented, and the incentive to trade will be injured. People don't buy things that can be readily taken from them or that "can be had for the taking."

When water rights are fully transferable and contracts between parties are respected by law, a large variety of marketing instruments are feasible. In fact, the available instruments are really only limited by the imaginations of the transacting parties, unless government disapproves. When one visits actual water markets, a variety of marketing terms is encountered, depending on regional customs. Because water marketing is not universally practiced, the rules and jargon vary across jurisdictions. In the interest of consistency, the following basic definitions are adopted here:

• A permanent exchange of a water right is a water right *sale*.

• A water right *lease* or *rental* occurs when the owner retains permanent ownership while allowing another agent to temporarily use a right, normally during one year. Lease markets are often quite local because the temporary nature of the exchange makes it impractical to overcome the higher transaction costs commonly associated with nonlocal transfers.

• A water right **option**, sometimes called a **dry-year option**, is a contingent contract between a buyer and a seller. Ordinarily, the buyer pays an *option price* at the time of contract signing for the seller's agreement to a contract that will last multiple years (normally at least ten years). The contract terms will specify the circumstances in which the buyer can exercise the option to use water owned by the seller. These circumstances may be defined by a prespecified physical trigger, such as the flow in a river or the amount of surface water in a reservoir, which if too low will permit the buyer to exercise the option. If the buyer exercises the option to the water and temporarily interrupts the seller's use, the buyer must make another payment, called the *striking* or *exercise price* (Michelsen and Young 1993). The latter payment may have been prespecified in the option contract or the means of its determination may have been prespecified (such as compensating a farmer for lost earnings based on the season's expected crop price and cropping expenses to date).

• Water right **banking** occurs when a public intermediary, such as a water district or state agency, leases water from owners for the purpose of leasing it to other water users. Bank-supported sales are also possible, but leasing is prevalent. Water banks can be useful devices for addressing social concerns or legal constraints regarding water transferability wherever these issues foil the direct exchange of water between agents. The goal of such banks is to assist in the reallocation of water from low-value uses to higher-value ones. The bank's management may specify fixed lessee and lessor prices (not necessarily the same prices) or it may establish either price through auctioning. This representation of water banks excludes situations in which water right owners place a portion of their water in a storage account solely for their later use. It also excludes government operations facilitating water right trades through the use of announcements, promotions, and matchmaking services.

Another instrument is worth observing so that it may be disqualified as marketing. A water right *delivery contract* is a multiyear agreement between a water-using agent (usually a city, a district, an agency of government, or a manufacturer) and a water supplier (such as a water utility, district, or authority). The contract agreement stipulates a pricing arrangement and the obligations of each party, possibly including water quantities to be regularly delivered to the buyer. In addition to water storage or conveyance by the supplier, such contracts may require further processing of the delivered water. Because the supplier has undertaken investments, especially for storage, improvements to natural water have been made. Hence, contracts go beyond the mere marketing of natural water and are more closely related to retail water pricing even if the processing is incomplete.

Water marketing is best done after rights have been quantified. As detailed in chapter 4, quantification of transferable surface water rights can proceed in two directions depending on how the variability of water flow is addressed. Under the prior appropriations system, rights can be specified volumetrically (e.g., fifty acre-feet per year or three hundred cubic meters annually) or as a maximum sustained flow (e.g., three cubic feet per second), and each right has a specific priority date. When flows in a watercourse are insufficient to satisfy all existing appropriative rights, the most junior rights cannot be exercised at all. Under a system of correlative shares, each right constitutes a specified portion of the available flow. In this case, deficiencies in watercourse flows are shared equally across all water users.

In comparing these two systems' alternative assignments of water supply risk, one must remain mindful that these rights are tradable. Hence, in a prior appropriations context, agents holding junior rights need not remain junior. Being junior becomes a matter of choice after water rights are initially assigned (adjudicated). A junior owner can make exchanges for more senior rights, perhaps by offering money along with the junior right or trading a large junior right for a smaller, more senior one. Rights can normally be broken into smaller rights, injecting even more flexibility into exchange opportunities. Any agent may be motivated to assemble a portfolio of water rights of differing seniorities. Thus, the possibilities are many. If a junior right is not served because of an inadequate natural water supply, then that is the expected consequence of a low-value right. A high level of service cannot be expected from a low-value resource.

Although the equal standing of correlative shares insinuates fairness in apportioning shortfalls, not all water uses have the same tolerance for risk. For some municipal and industrial uses, shortfalls can cause serious losses. The same can be said for high-value, irrigated crops such as orchards and vegetables. Agents involved in such risk-averse activities want an ensured water supply. In a prior appropriations setting, they can trade for a more senior water right. In a correlative shares setting, the primary recourse of risk-averse agents is to accumulate additional shares. The unfortunate economic result, both privately and socially, is that these shares will be idle during normal flow periods. As long as accumulated shares can be leased to other users during normal years, however, the efficiency losses of this system can be substantially alleviated. Dry-year options are also a useful approach for managing risk under a correlative rule structure.

Due to their differing approaches to water supply risk, the choice between prior appropriations and correlative shares can have efficiency ramifications. The prior appropriations doctrine is better suited for situations involving heterogeneous user types, either in a multisectoral context or the sense of user variety in a single sector (Howe, Schurmeier, and Shaw 1986b). On the other hand, the correlative share system is easily operated, and it performs well when agents are homogeneous, such as occurs in many irrigation districts where farmers are producing similar crops. Each style of water rights has its comparative advantages. These advantages are reduced when the possibility of water rights leases and options are introduced to supplement the possibility of water right sales. That is, the two water right systems have more similar economic consequences when leasing and options are feasible.

7.2   The Upside: Unlocking the Resource from Low-Value Applications

In regions where water marketing is a novel instrument and scarcity is significant, the social rewards of allowing water marketing can be high. Whenever property rights do not foster transferability, water tends to stay in its original uses. This is not a good thing in an expanding economy with new technologies, new commodities, new enterprises, and additional people. If we contrast privately motivated transferability to the reallocative opportunities of state-run administrative procedures or common property regimes, such as riparian rights, the social preference is usually apparent (Livingston 1995).

The main opportunity for reallocating riparian rights is to stiffen the reasonability criteria over time or, in a permit system, to lower permit sizes. By progressively tightening what is reasonable water use, agents will be required to use less water, and water will be consequently made available for new uses and new people. A regulatory or judicial system for deciding these things will have to be conducted. It will be expensive to operate. Old users will not be happy about tightened rules and they will resist. They will adopt water conservation technology with hesitation because it is expensive. They will abandon aged water uses slowly because they only experience the losses, not the benefits. To evolve the reasonability criteria and reasonable permits over time, water administrators and jurists will focus on "representative" users within a given class of water-using agents. Water use limitations or regulations will be based on examinations of these representative water users. The onus of these decisions will lie with the government. Even if the government's judgments are efficient for the average corn irrigator and the average household, efficiency for nonaverage agents will be elusive.

By contrast, a water market motivates both old and new water users to assess their water use strategies in relation to the scarcity value of water. Old users will have a positive perspective on the gains of reallocation because they can benefit too. Agents who are not representative members of their water-using group can respect their unique circumstances. Rather than having obstinate agents trying to obstruct reallocation, established right holders will collaborate in efforts to uncover alternatives, including new techniques and conservation options. If an old agent is getting $40 in net benefits out of their most marginal water and a new agent could get $200 out of the same unit of water, there's a clear opportunity for a trade. The main matter they have to resolve is how to split the $160 in gains. Both will gain, so the old agent becomes an agent for change instead of against it.

In some circumstances, allowing water trades will be slow to motivate reallocation. The most significant of these occurs where irrigation districts supply water to farmers, but the end users do not hold title to the water rights. Individual irrigators might then welcome trade and reductions in their water use, yet be unable to do it. Although districts have an obligation to advance the interest of their clients, and water marketing is a serious strategy for accomplishing this, it's a troublesome path for districts even when it is socially desirable. If the district transfers some of the water rights it holds, some irrigators within the district will need to curtail their water use. How are these responsibilities to be assigned? How are the water marketing receipts to be divided? What happens when farmers queue up, each wanting to share in the rewards? Called the "compensation problem" by Rodney Smith (1989), it is necessary to invent new procedures for water market participation when districts possess the water rights. This situation becomes even more complex for districts when they consider the implications pertaining to the shared conveyance losses as well as the internal reuse of seepage and runoff (Miller 1987). District employees, including the manager, have a hard time seeing the personal benefits of water marketing, so they are unlikely to exploit the idea. Furthermore, in some districts neither the irrigators nor the district have the right to transfer water rights because the rights are officially owned by the government. The latter condition need not be viewed as permanent in light of opportunities to convert state property into private property, but it is a tough hurdle to overcome.

7.3 Basic Water Trade and Value Theory

If water rights are private property and two agents are so motivated by differences in their marginal water values, they can trade. Suppose that agents 1 and 2 own transferable rights to annual water withdrawals, given as $\bar{w}_1$ and $\bar{w}_2$. Either $\bar{w}_1$ or $\bar{w}_2$ may be zero, but not both. Suppose further that agents 1 and 2 have linear marginal net benefit functions, given as follows:

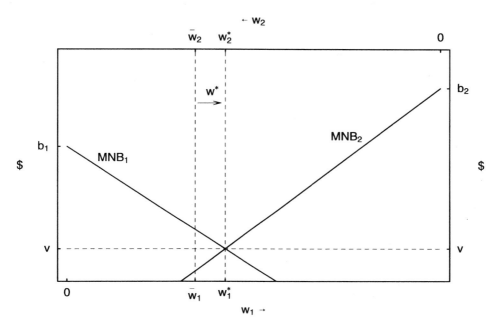

Figure 7.1
Water trade and value theory

$$MNB_1 = b_1 - m_1 w_1 \quad \text{and} \quad MNB_2 = b_2 - m_2 w_2. \tag{7.1}$$

Recall that these marginal net benefits for retail water tell us the marginal benefits of natural water. Substituting $\bar{w}_1$ and $\bar{w}_2$ into these two equations results in each party's current marginal value of natural water, and indicates whether there may be trade opportunities. If $MNB_1 \neq MNB_2$, there are mutually gainful trade possibilities unless the transaction costs are preventive. Setting such transaction costs aside until the next section, suppose that $MNB_1 > MNB_2$, as in figure 7.1. In this case, agent 2 should lease some water to agent 1, not because it is economically efficient, but because it is privately rewarding. (Privately rewarding can also turn out to be socially rewarding, as the First Theorem informs us, but the agents don't care about social rewards, which is the beauty of the thing.)

How much water should these agents trade, and what price might they settle on? If there are no obstructing transaction costs, these two agents can maximize their individual benefits by consuming water to the point where

$$MNB_1 = MNB_2, \tag{7.2}$$

which is a single equation in two unknowns. Let's call the unknowns w_1^* and w_2^*. The second equation needed for the solution is

$$\bar{w}_1 + \bar{w}_2 = w_1^* + w_2^*. \tag{7.3}$$

Once (7.2) and (7.3) are simultaneously solved, the amount to be leased is $\bar{w}_2 - w_2^*$ (or $w_1^* - \bar{w}_1$). Label this amount w^*. At the margin, each unit of water will be worth the same to each agent after execution of the lease. Hence, $MNB_1(w_1^*) = MNB_2(w_2^*)$ is a good benchmark price for the leased water.

Alternatively, any lease terms that acceptably divide the rewards of this lease to both agents are also practical. Except for the money arrangement, the gains received by agent 1 are

$$\int_{\bar{w}_1}^{\bar{w}_1 + w^*} MNB_1(w_1)\, dw = b_1 w^* - m_1 \bar{w}_1 w^* - 0.5 m_1 w^{*^2}, \tag{7.4}$$

and the losses to the seller are

$$-\int_{\bar{w}_2}^{\bar{w}_2 - w^*} MNB_2(w_2)\, dw = b_2 w^* - m_2 \bar{w}_2 w^* + 0.5 m_2 w^{*^2}. \tag{7.5}$$

Any lease price v will work as long as it more than compensates the seller for the sacrificed water value, and it does not offset all of the buyer's gains. Hence,

$$b_2 w^* - m_2 \bar{w}_2 w^* + 0.5 m_2 w^{*^2} < vw^* < b_1 w^* - m_1 \bar{w}_1 w^* - 0.5 m_1 w^{*^2}, \tag{7.6}$$

which reduces to

$$b_2 - m_2 \bar{w}_2 + 0.5 m_2 w^* < v < b_1 - m_1 \bar{w}_1 - 0.5 m_1 w^*. \tag{7.7}$$

The relative bargaining abilities of the two parties will determine v within the range given by (7.7). In a many-agent setting, offers from other agents will narrow this range and further promote the achievement of a lease price that is equivalent to MNBs.

An important question concerns the relation between the lease value of natural water and the value of a permanent water right. The mathematical background for answering this question is given in appendix 3.A of chapter 3. As with land rights, a permanent water right gives its owner a perpetual flow of economic benefits. If the value of this service is v in every period, then the value, V, of a permanent water right is given by the present value of this service flow:

$$V = \sum_{t=0}^{\infty} \frac{v}{(1+d)^t} = v \cdot \frac{1+d}{d} \quad \text{or} \quad V = \sum_{t=1}^{\infty} \frac{v}{(1+d)^t} = v \cdot \frac{1}{d}. \tag{7.8}$$

For example, with a real discount rate of 4 percent and a constant service value, the value of a permanent water right is twenty-five or twenty-six times its lease price. At 2 percent, the permanent right's value is fifty or fifty-one times its lease value.

The basic relationships between the lease price and the sales price observed by the equations in (7.8) illustrate a fundamental point. Yet the equations may be crude in some settings. Lease prices will vary from year to year depending on the climate, so the idea of a constant v is not realistic. Thus, the relation captured within (7.8) applies most accurately when v is an average lease price across time. A further complication is presented by rising scarcity. Rising scarcity implies a marginal value of leases that is trending upward over time, even when expressed in real (inflationless) terms. Fortunately, (7.8) can be readily modified for these situations.[2] There may also be other factors leading to discrepancies not accounted for by financial identities such as (7.8). Some water users are especially appreciative of high reliability in their water supply, and they may value the dependability of a permanent water right beyond its mere service flow. Even so, (7.8) serves as an interesting benchmark.

Often, the analyst will encounter situations in which differing trades are available (or have already been conducted), but comparisons are frustrated by differing terms. Payments may be one time, now or later, or they may be recurring. The amount of water involved may be variable or fixed, or deliveries may not commence until some future date. Given the variety of terms, is it possible to condense the varied elements into a single expression of market value? A useful approach is to calculate the *equivalent single price* by dividing the present value of all financial terms by the present value of all water terms (*Water Strategist* 1997). The numerator of this ratio is computed from the schedule of monetary exchanges while the denominator is computed from the schedule of water exchanges.[3] The denominator of this computation is measured in units of water, so the ratio indicates dollars per unit of water. The equivalent single-price yardstick can also be used for comparing other scarcity-addressing measures, such as conservation investments and supply-shifting policies. Yet, because evolving scarcity means that water will have rising value over time, equivalent single price is not a perfect measure.

7.4 Modified Theory in the Presence of Transaction Costs (Optional Topic)

The existence of transaction costs can pose a serious hurdle for agent traders. This is especially true in water markets (Colby 1990b; Archibald and Renwick 1998). Traders can regard these costs disdainfully, as they may have little regard for the

---

2. For example, one may place a growth term such as $(1 + g)^t$ in the equation's numerator and construct a different result. Unless $g \geq d$, the value of a permanent water right will still converge to a finite value.

3. For a similar concept emerging from an engineering economics perspective, see the discounting of water quantity introduced by Walski (1984) when he originally defines *equivalent flow rate*. To apply either concept, it is necessary to contemplate the discounting of water quantities, whereas discounting is normally confined to economic prices and values.

Box 7.1
Calculating the Equivalent Single Price

A nearby water district has made the following proposal to a growing city: "If you retire our current debt of \$25 million, and starting next year, take over all maintenance and replacement costs for our system in perpetuity, you can take possession of half our water rights starting next year." The annual costs of this arrangement appear to be \$230,000 (in real dollars), and half the water district's rights amounts to 15,000 acre-feet annually. How does this offer compare to the city's typical payments for leased water, which are currently \$100/acre-foot.

Analysis

The equivalent single price of leased water is easily computed; it is \$100/acre-foot. If a 5 percent discount rate and an infinite planning horizon are used, the equivalent single price of the district's offer is given by

$$\text{ESP}_{\text{proposal}} = \frac{25000000 + \sum_{t=1}^{\infty} \frac{230000}{1.05^t}}{\sum_{t=1}^{\infty} \frac{15000}{1.05^t}} = \frac{25000000 + 230000 \cdot 20}{15000 \cdot 20} = \$98.67/\text{acre-foot}.$$

So the district's proposal approximates the current price of leased water. Serious consideration of this offer may be warranted if the rate of appreciation in the lease price is expected to outpace inflation, and the city can get enough benefits out of this 15,000 acre-feet to offset the costs (i.e., is NPV > 0?). It may easily be the case that 15,000 is a large amount relative to the city's normal leasing activity. Hence, whether NPV > 0 may hinge on the city's plans for extracting benefits from its excess natural water supplies during the early years after this proposal is accepted. Of course, the city should also regard the district's asking terms as negotiable.

market failures guarded against by some transaction costs. In locations where market exchanges are novel or infrequent, transaction costs can be especially high due to a lack of familiarity either by market participants, their legal representatives, or the administrative agency. In general, the impact of transaction costs on water market participants can assume three forms:

1. The tradable amount of water rights may be administratively limited, prohibiting agents from exchanging as much as they would like.

2. There may be additional costs for the traders to pay, for legal and technical services, administrative fees, or taxes; and these costs depend on the amount of water being exchanged. These are variable transaction costs.

3. There may be additional costs for services, fees, and taxes that do not vary with the amount of water being exchanged. These are fixed transaction costs, and they are commonly more significant (larger) than variable transaction costs.

The problems posed by the first form are easy to understand. If the tradable amount is less than w^*, the quantity that agents 1 and 2 wish to rent, then they will trade up to the limit. MNBs will not be equated. Some modifications to (7.4) through (7.7) will be required to understand the market pricing behavior. Market gains to agents 1 and 2 will be lowered, but we cannot say that economic efficiency is harmed unless we know that this specific transaction cost does not serve to curb a market failure.

Variable and fixed transaction costs (points 2 and 3 above) are relatively easy to model using the prior framework. Let the dependency of *marginal* transaction costs on transferred water be given by the function $VC(w^*)$. This is equivalent to $VC(\overline{w}_2 - w_2^*)$. These variable transaction costs prevent the equilibration of MNBs. Let FC denote the fixed costs of engaging in a transaction of any size. A candidate for the optimal amount of leased water is given by the simultaneous solution of the system,

$$MNB_1(w_1^*) = MNB_2(w_2^*) + VC(\overline{w}_2 - w_2^*) \quad \text{and} \quad \overline{w}_1 + \overline{w}_2 = w_1^* + w_2^*, \qquad (7.9)$$

for w_1^* and w_2^*. Recall that $\overline{w}_1$ and $\overline{w}_2$ are the initial water right holdings by the two agents. The first equation of (7.9) is similar to (7.2), but it contains a new term on the right-hand side. The difference between the two agents' marginal value of water, evaluated at their initial holdings levels, must be adequate to offset the marginal transaction costs. This will lower the amount of water leased in common situations.[4] Moreover, it is entirely possible that the optimal lease will actually be $w^* = 0$ unless the gains of trade are sufficient to offset all transaction costs including the fixed ones. For this reason, the gains attributable to the candidate solution to (7.9) must be computed and then compared to the summed transaction costs. In the following expression, net gains to the two agents are on the left side; all transaction costs are on the right:

$$\int_{\overline{w}_1}^{\overline{w}_1 + w^*} MNB_1(w_1)\,dw_1 - \int_{\overline{w}_2}^{\overline{w}_2 + w^*} MNB_2(w_2)\,dw_2 \overset{?}{>} FC + \int_0^{w^*} VC(w)\,dw. \qquad (7.10)$$

If this inequality checks out correctly, then the candidate solution given by (7.9) is indeed the best trade. Otherwise, "no trade" is the preferred option for the agents, and the presence of transaction costs completely thwarts mutually advantageous marketing. Again, however, this may be a socially desirable result if the transaction costs are acting to control market failure. Although transaction costs are not the only barrier to be overcome by potential traders (Young 1986), it is a significant one.

---

4. This claim presumes that MNBs and marginal transaction costs are declining functions of water quantity. Other circumstances are imaginable, however, and some may give rise to solutions to the prior system of two equations that are not truly optimal trades because they are local, not global, solutions or because they do not satisfy second-order conditions (chapter 2 appendix).

7.5   A Typical Exchange Framework

An earlier chapter alluded to real-world water markets operating in a "mixed system" constituting a governmentally regulated market. Property rights to surface water can be exchanged, but some protection against market failures is installed. There is heightened regulation of these markets. Hence, water right traders cannot always do what they like. If such a system is operating optimally, the trade constraints serve to limit some type of market failure, such as return flow externalities or recreational public goods.[5] How do governments actually oversee water markets, and are regulators effective in promoting economic efficiency?

Figure 7.2 contains a generic depiction of water market oversight as conducted by western states in the United States (Chang and Griffin 1992; Colby 1995). This is an interesting model of water marketing because it starts to illustrate where the pitfalls lie. The emphasis here is on permanent trades. The process is initiated after two parties have determined that they wish to conduct a trade. There are multiple steps to the process, especially the following:

1. Prospective traders, particularly the current owner, must submit a formal application to the appropriate state agency. Traders may pay professionals for assistance in this stage and then retain these professional services for forthcoming stages.

2. The state agency will review the application for completeness and technical accuracy, perhaps requesting resubmission or additional information.

3. Based on established agency protocol, the agency will select potential third parties to notify. Those notified are then given the opportunity to consider the exchange and lodge protests. Notified agents may include all possible third parties or a subset.

4. The agency will conduct a hearing and then rule on the proposed exchange. If there are no unsettled protests, the agency is more likely to approve the exchange without modification. In the event of protests, the agency will seek a ruling consistent with the relative rights of all parties. Agency procedures may require that impacts on other third parties be considered, regardless of whether these parties protested or were notified.

5. The agency ruling is final unless it is appealed and subsequently modified by judicial review. Any party affected by the agency's ruling may have grounds for appealing the agency's decision through legal suit.

Steps 3 and 4 of this process are especially interesting due to their prospective effects on water market efficiency. The notification stage can be practiced narrowly

---

5. Recall from section 4.3 that the use of water for nonrival purposes (recreation, habitat, etc.) may give rise to understated market demand if "users" can gain without paying due to nonexclusion.

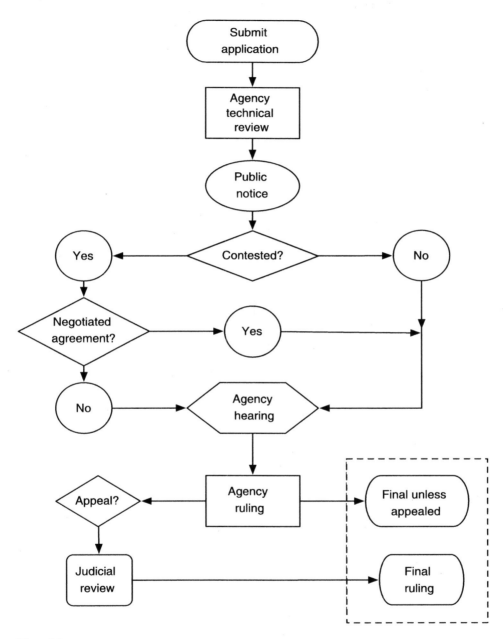

Figure 7.2
Typical oversight of vater sales

or widely, depending on state rules. States customarily assign high standing to third-party water right holders. As a result, notification may be extended to all water right holders downstream of the uppermost transactor (the buyer or the seller) on the watercourse. Alternatively, agency protocol may be to eliminate some of these right holders from the "notify list" on the grounds that the proposed exchange is not expected to affect them. A second category of water users, instream water beneficiaries, may not be notified unless they possess instream water rights. Instream rights are novel in some states and nonexistent in others (Gillilan and Brown 1997). These rights entitle their owners to a specified flow along a segment of a watercourse and may have a seniority date like other appropriative rights. If notification is not extended to all third parties, then the possibility of inefficient transfers increases, unless the agency can perform third-party protection in the absence of protests.

In step 4, the agency assembles both written and oral statements regarding the legitimacy of the proposal. The general objective of the hearing is to determine whether the transfer may do harm to *recognized* third parties. In general, transfers are not approved if injury can be reasonably expected. Regardless of how senior the traded right may be relative to rights possessed by third parties, negative effects are not allowed. If the transfer can be modified in a manner not harmful to third parties, then the agency may rule in favor of a modified exchange, perhaps a smaller one or one that places constraints on the water buyer regarding the exercise of the right. In some states, a second agency (often fishery oriented) may represent instream flow stakeholders or the administering agency itself may be charged with this responsibility. In many jurisdictions, regard for instream flow maintenance or bay and estuary inflows is relatively immature, having arisen only in recent decades. Proposed trades can easily affect patterns of streamflow, thus making instream flow protection an important concern, as demonstrated in the forthcoming section.

7.6 The Downside: Guarding against Market Failures

Due to the flow character of water, there are many conceivable externalities to water marketing, even in the best of circumstances. Some of these third-party effects are negative; others are positive. From an efficiency perspective, we wish to encourage water trades that enhance net benefits, all effects considered. Trades offering negative net benefits are not desirable. As accurately stated by a National Research Council report on western water marketing, "The goal is not to promote transfers per se but to use them to accomplish better overall water management" (1992, 3). That is, the First Theorem establishes conditions under which markets are useful means to an end (efficiency), but marketing itself is not the goal.

One important step in controlling third-party effects is to focus on the ***consumptive use*** of the right being transferred. Original water rights quantify allowed *diversions* of water because such quantities are easily monitored and enforced. But if traders are permitted to exchange diversion quantities, there will usually be substantial impacts on other water right holders. For this reason, the previously described approval processes are normally quite diligent in denying transfers that would raise consumptive use. Yet that is insufficient protection against all externalities.

To better examine some of the consequences of water trade, carefully consider the pretrade scenario diagrammed in the upper-left quarter of figure 7.3. In this basic setting, there are three offstream water users (diverters) located consecutively along a river. The column left of the river indicates annual water flow within each segment of the river, consequent to the diversions and return flow of each water user. The right column identifies diversions (−) and return flows (+). To render the setting as conducive to marketing as possible, each user is assumed to have an identical consumptive use ratio. Each agent consumes 25 percent of its diversions; this 25 percent is not actually lost—it goes somewhere else. In the absence of equal consumptive use, the oversight authority would have to limit transfers to the consumptively used portion of a water right (Western Water Policy Review Advisory Commission 1998, 6–28). In the pretrade scenario, observe that instream flows are smaller in reaches of the watercourse immediately below the users' points of diversion.

Now suppose that differences in their marginal water values encourage users A and C to identify a mutually attractive trade. C wants to sell one hundred units of its water right for a price that A is willing to pay. This is an "upstream" transfer, and upstream transfers are more likely to harm third parties than are downstream transfers. If allowed, the regime of river flows and water use will be modified into the post-trade 1 scenario of figure 7.3 (upper-right quadrant). For ease of examination, the circled numbers represent possible third-party benefits and the boxed ones are possible third-party injuries. Note that there are no impacts farther downstream, as the exiting flow is unchanged. On the instream flow side of the ledger, flows are lower on four segments and higher on one. Indeed, the flow is impossibly negative on one segment, implying that agent B will not be able to make full use of its water right. Hence, agent B is a third-party loser if this trade is approved.

All regulated water markets should be able to identify the injury to B's right and would therefore reject a transfer larger than eighty units of water. If A and C still want to conduct a hundred-unit trade, they shall have to include B in their bargain. If A's and C's net gains are not sufficient to compensate B for the loss of five water units, they will have to forgo this part of their exchange. Efficiency will thus be served.

Even a transfer of eighty units, however, would harm the flow on four segments while improving the flow on one segment. The flow on one segment would even be nonexistent. Although this segment may be short in length, its emptiness disrupts the environmental "connectedness" of the river and serves as a barrier to life-forms

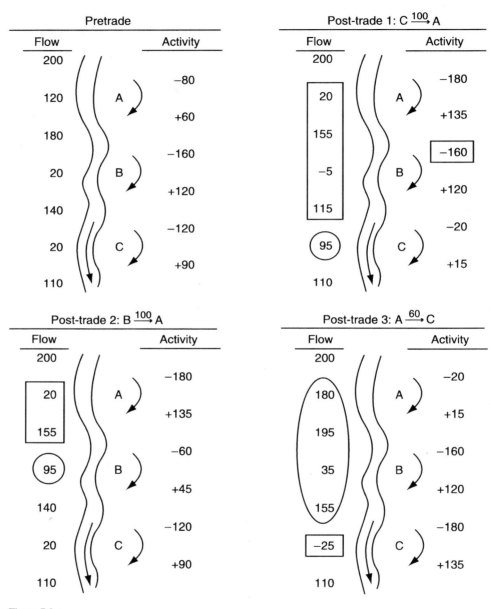

Figure 7.3
Some third-party complications
Note: Decreases from pretrade are boxed, and increases are circled.

that otherwise travel the river or derive sustenance from it. There are other environmental consequences valued by humans as well. This may be a sizable loss if it is allowed to occur.

Whether or not such a transfer would be approved depends on whether instream flow rights exist and whether they would be harmed, *or* in the absence of any instream flow rights, approval will depend on whether the regulatory process devotes any attention toward flow maintenance. If third-party protection does not foster instream flow protection and enhancement, the water market system will fail to achieve efficient results.

Even if regulation is extended to instream flow, what should be done exactly? Whether or not such a transfer should be approved depends on the net benefits to A and C as well as across these five river segments. We can certainly trust A and C to judge their personal participation in this trade, but what are the net benefits to instream flow users. Some of these uses are nonrival, so there are multiple users' values (added "vertically," as in figure 2.13) to contemplate in resolving the net instream flow benefits of this transfer. We can expect to find negative net instream flow benefits here. Four segments are harmed—one dramatically. How are we to weigh these losses against the presumed gains to A and C? What side agreements might A and C be able to create so as to mitigate the third-party effects and obtain transfer approval? The real-world prospects here are weak due to the nonrival character of instream flow values (Colby 1990a; Anderson and Johnson 1986). It's no wonder that upstream transfers can be especially problematic in scarce-water settings.

What if this transfer could be rendered "less upstream" by having agent A obtain the hundred water units from agent B instead of C? The post-trade 2 scenario captures the physical impacts of this trade. There are no external effects on offstream water users, and there are fewer effects on the pattern of instream flow. Again, however, one segment is highly and negatively affected. Whether the damages here exceed the gains to trade is hard to ascertain without additional comprehensive information. But at least the damages are reduced in comparison to the C → A exchange. Is the alternative B → A exchange more efficient than the C → A proposal? That's hard to know. It depends on the value of water to B and C, and it also depends on the value of instream flow along three river segments. All in all, that's tough to figure out. And agent A may want to buy from C anyway, perhaps because of an inexpensive lease offer. There's a big regulatory challenge here.

To see how things get reversed for downstream transfers, study the final post-trade scenario in figure 7.3. It is not possible to inspect a hundred-unit transfer because A's right is smaller than that. So let's presume a sixty-unit transfer from A to C. As is typical, no offstream water users are harmed by the downstream transfer of consumptive use rights, so this type of third-party consideration is alleviated. Instream flows are increased for four river segments, but one river segment has an impossibly negative flow. Hence, this trade is too large to be feasible. Physically, it is only practical for C to buy 26.667 units of water rights from A and still be able to withdraw it.[6] Such a trade would deplete all the water in a single segment, again raising issues about social costs relative to social benefits, perplexed again by the nonrival character of instream flow values. Whereas downstream transfers greatly reduce negative marketing externalities, they are not eliminated.

These sorts of scenarios occur with some frequency in the literature of water marketing. Institutional solutions are available, but they are not "silver bullets" because many situations are unique. As noted by Gould in his careful work, "Markets perform best when dealing with homogeneous products, but appropriative rights are far from homogeneous" (1988, 22). The flow character of water creates all kinds of noteworthy interrelationships among a watershed's water users. Thus, all water rights, not just those of the prior appropriations type, have varying conditions—all attributable to the flowing character of water.

7.7   Can the Downside Be Fixed?

Is there anything that can be done about these problems or are there situations in which these problems are minimal? The answer to both questions is yes, but the solutions are not costless and the conditions are not widely met.

Where water market externalities include streamflow effects, an elaborate system of incentives could be erected so that traders are forced to factor instream flow effects into their deals (Griffin and Hsu 1993). Coupled with the ordinary practice of alerting offstream right holders about proposed transfers, this system would accomplish two efficient things. It would discourage inefficient transfers caused by negative externalities, and it would lead traders to seek out transfers producing positive externalities. Both are required if efficiency is to be achieved. Operationally, however, this system requires a major change in current institutions, and it will be difficult to obtain the information needed to set excellent incentive levels, which will vary across both watercourses and their segments. Additionally, each incentive would be functionally related to the amount of water in each segment because it reflects the scarcity of instream flow. If we can be content with relatively stable yet imperfect incentive levels, this system becomes very practical, but it requires a major institutional reform.

---

6. Observe in the pretrade scenario that there are only twenty units in the river after C has exercised its rights. It can only augment its withdrawals by twenty units plus any upstream consumptive use it can retire upstream through trade. Given that consumptive use is 25 percent everywhere, the maximum purchase C can make is given by the solution to $x = 20 + 0.25 \cdot x$. Any transfer in excess of x will not be fully beneficial to C.

Alternatively, the state can establish minimum streamflow standards for each stretch of every noteworthy watercourse and then reject all transfer proposals that would broach these standards. Such a system would protect against the most harmful externalities, but it would not eliminate all negative impacts on instream flow. Nor would this approach provide any encouragement for transfers that enhance stream-flows. How might we improve on this minimum-streamflow approach? We could take the additional step of allowing ownership of instream flow rights, and also allowing agents to buy offstream rights and convert them to instream flow rights—a good idea—but such possibilities are already achievable by imaginative agents.[7] The real problem is that much of the value of instream flow is derived from nonrival uses. Instream flows give us recreation, biodiversity, scenery, waste assimilation and transport, and commercial navigation. Each of us may benefit, but the public good nature of instream flows (nonrival and nonexclusive) gives us the opportunity to benefit without paying (free riding). Hence, the market demand for instream flow will universally understate true demand. The operations of instream flow user groups can be a positive force, and evidence clearly indicates that market action in support of streamflow is occurring (Landry 1998; Loomis et al. 2003), but such activity should not tempt us to think efficiency is being achieved.

In terms of isolated situations where these problems may be miniscule, excellent candidates are found among agents that share manmade conveyance structures. Once water is removed from its originating watercourse at a given location, thereby establishing a specific regime of downstream flows, and this water is placed in a conveyance serving a multitude of users, the subsequent transfer of water among conveyance users may have little or no effect on the watercourse. In these circumstances, the potential for externalities is greatly diminished. Transaction costs can be consequently lessened, with positive implications for achieving efficiency through marketing. Indeed, the most successful water markets resemble this situation. In some locales, there are shared facilities that deliver water to both agricultural and urban interests. These are particularly attractive opportunities for water marketing.

7.8 The Worldwide Extent of Marketing

The marketing of water is neither novel nor new. Centuries ago, it was practiced along English rivers (Scott and Coustalin 1995) and within at least one irrigation

---

7. For example, agent-groups interested in instream flow such as rafting businesses, kayakers, and sport fishermen can "sponsor" downstream transfers. By identifying potential upstream sellers and downstream buyers of water rights, and injecting additional funds into the deal, it is possible for these agent-groups to encourage transfers that enhance flows. With the proper contractual protection regarding future transfers of the transacted water, such deals convey instream flow waters to the sponsors without the sponsors actually owning any water rights.

district in Spain (Maass and Anderson 1978, chapter 4). Water marketing is also conducted in various countries. One recent book documents the use of water marketing in Chile, India, Mexico, Pakistan, Spain, and the United States (Easter, Rosegrant, and Dinar 1998). Some of these countries have modified their laws recently in order to activate the desirable attributes of water markets (Ahmad 2000; Kloezen 1998). Australia has also delved into water marketing through new policies (Sturgess 1997). Undoubtedly, regional water value has initiated many trade markets, not all of which have been documented. It is interesting that water marketing exists informally, or in black market form, in some regions where it is not sanctioned. Such examples are testaments to the worth of natural water and the potential differences among traders' marginal value of water.

7.9   Leading U.S. Markets

History shows that the creation of water markets can be more accidental than planned. For whatever reasons, institutional arrangements and conditions have emerged here and there that have been consistent with transferable rights in water. In the presence of adequate scarcity, these rights initiate a market. These markets are not normally "declared" to exist by some authority. They simply arise. Furthermore, the most active markets in the United States have benefited from special circumstances that have reduced transaction costs. Lowered transaction costs lower the burdens to be overcome by buyers and sellers, thereby furthering their incentives to participate. Here, we will examine some of the most notable U.S. water markets. All of these lie in the West, because eastern, riparian-based laws have been unsupportive and scarcity is lower, at least thus far.

Northern Colorado Water Conservancy District

The mismatch between the location of water users and the location of water has been a long-term challenge for Colorado water planners. Colorado's highly populated "east slope," including Denver, has important surface water flows in the Arkansas and South Platte basins. The east slope, however, is separated from a most important surface source. Between the east slope and the Colorado River basin lies the Continental Divide within the Rocky Mountains.[8] Ever since the displacement of native people, west slope population and development has been low relative to that on the east, so the state has had a long-standing interest in moving Colorado River water to

---

8. The Continental Divide is the line of highest elevation running north-south through much of the Americas. Precipitation east of the divide flows easterly, primary toward the Atlantic Ocean and the Gulf of Mexico. Precipitation west of the divide runs toward the Pacific Ocean.

the "right" side of the Continental Divide. In addition, the two interstate compacts pertaining to the Colorado River assign considerable rights to Colorado. These factors have inspired many proposals for interbasin transfer projects, and numerous facilities of this type have been constructed in Colorado. Some of these facilities are part of the Colorado–Big Thompson Project (C–BT). Unique project features have given rise to one of the nation's longest operating and most significant water markets.

The Northern Colorado Water Conservancy District was created by Colorado in 1937 (⟨http://www.ncwcd.org⟩).[9] Its original functions were to take on the repayment responsibilities of the C–BT and manage the resulting water supply. Project construction and financing were performed by the U.S. Bureau of Reclamation. The repayment obligations were quite favorable to the district, implying a high degree of federal subsidy, but the most momentous aspect of the project was the flexibility of the created water rights (Howe, Schurmeier, and Shaw 1986a). When the project's facilities became fully operational in 1957, 310,000 acre-feet of west slope water were available to water users on the northern east slope. Originally, the lion's share of this water was committed to irrigation.

A unique feature of project water is that all of it is new to the east slope. This raises a question regarding the ownership of return flows, which are also new to the east slope. The selected legal rule was that there are no return flow obligations associated with this new water. That is, the district owns these water rights and all the return flows resulting from the exercise of these rights. A second unique feature emerged from equity concerns about the burden of repayment ($25 million). Because many irrigators in the east slope service area already possessed adequate water and did not want to pay for additional water, it was decided that project users would receive water "allotments" and pay an annual fee for each allotment. This allotment practice effectively assigned shares of C–BT water to individual users, and these shares became transferable property. In a typical year, a share entitles the owner to 0.7 acre-feet, but this amount can vary substantially from year to year. Because downstream entities benefiting from C–BT return flows have no enforceable claims to these return flows, the transfer of C–BT allotments within the conservancy district is easy to do. The notification and hearing stages of the generic transfer process diagrammed previously are averted entirely.

The interbasin transfer feature and the method of collecting repayment funds therefore resulted in the creation of a new water market. Initially, the market value of these shares was low, and some owners actually abandoned them to avoid a $1.50 per year assessment fee. During the 1970s, east slope population growth and some

9. A full historical account of the district is provided by Tyler (1992).

degree of speculation caused a rapid rise in value, temporarily peaking at over $2,000 per share in 1980 (in 1985 dollars) (Howe, Schurmeier, and Shaw 1986a). The market value of these shares later began to rise again, and they have traded at several times the 1980 peak in recent years. Clearly, this is a valued property right. Cities have become important owners of shares, and they are known to acquire shares well in advance of putting them to use. When cities have excess C–BT rights, they generally lease them to farmers. An active rental market exists, and it is aided by the district office, which operates a "bulletin board" service (now on its Web site).

Howe, Schurmeier, and Shaw (1986a) argue that this market is a noteworthy enhancement of *regional* economic efficiency beyond the domain of C–BT water. Even though C–BT water is only 17 percent of the region's surface water supply, the transaction costs of transferring it are unusually low. All third-party return flow considerations are circumvented because return flow beneficiaries have no rights. "Thus, C–BT water is the 'easily saleable margin' of water and plays a disproportionately important role in the efficiency of water use" (196). Howe, Schurmeier, and Shaw acknowledge that the absence of third-party protection does not mean that there is an absence of third-party effects, but they reason such effects should have a neutral-to-positive impact on regional net benefits. Their reasoning cannot be automatically extended to other areas.

The Lower Rio Grande Valley of Texas

Within the state of Texas, four different water rights doctrines are practiced—two for surface water and two for ground water (Griffin and Characklis 2002). The applicable doctrine depends on the region. One of these four doctrines was judicially established. In the Lower Rio Grande Valley of Texas, the drought of the mid-1950s underscored the failure of a confused system of water administration, which at the time included aspects of riparianism, Spanish land grants with implied water rights, and prior appropriations. The confusion led to a legal suit of considerable importance, taking about fifteen years to complete (Chang and Griffin 1992). When this case finally concluded, the court had disentangled an array of competing water claims and established a coherent apportionment of the valley's water resources. Witnessing this cumbersome transition, the legislature decided to take a different path for the rest of the state's surface water. Thus, the Water Rights Adjudication Act of 1967 coalesced all surface water rights, except those in the Lower Rio Grande Valley, into a prior appropriations system.

The court-performed adjudication of Lower Rio Grande water did not establish priority dates for water rights, as used by the appropriations doctrine. Nonmunicipal water users were assigned shares of the annual flow of the Rio Grande, rather than specific amounts. Hence, drought years would result in proportionately lowered water allocations to all users. The judge felt that municipal water rights deserved a higher degree of certainty than the prevalent irrigation rights, so he established a "municipal reserve" of 50,000 acre-feet. This reserve approximated the level of municipal water rights in normal flow years.

The allocation of available water works in the following fashion. Inflows to the two upstream storage reservoirs are tallied each month. If inflows are sufficient, the municipal reserve is reset to its maximum level (now 225,000 acre-feet), inferring that all municipal water rights have a guaranteed year of full deliveries. If additional inflows are available, they are prorated across the water accounts of all nonmunicipal water right shareholders. All water use by all right holders is monitored, and water accounts are debited each month for the water they use.

Ever since the court apportionment, valley water rights have been transferable. Because of rapid population growth in the region, most permanent transfers of rights have been from agricultural to urban uses. The unequal standing of these two types of rights means that an irrigation *share* of flows must be converted to a *fixed* amount of a municipal right. Every several years, the "watermaster" overseeing this process raises the municipal reserve level so that it is in line with the increased municipal rights.

There is an active market for rental water, especially among irrigators. The rules do not allow the leasing of urban water to irrigators because that would subvert the priority devoted to urban rights. Since the allocation system insulates municipalities from water shortfalls, nearly all risk is assigned to irrigators. In times of drought or treaty failure, irrigation water is in short supply, and its marginal value rises.[10] Inflows must reach dire levels before municipal water rights are curtailed. As a consequence, lease prices for irrigation rights are more variable than municipal lease prices (Characklis, Griffin, and Bedient 1999).

Like the northern Colorado market, the Lower Rio Grande system is endowed with a unique character that eliminates attention to return flow externalities. The valley is the final segment on the Rio Grande before the river enters the Gulf of Mexico. Diversions of water from the Rio Grande generally do not reenter the river, nor do they yield significant benefits for third parties. Hence, the notification of affected parties and the subsequent hearings are averted. Transaction costs are low as a result.

This market has performed a social service in a semiarid region of substantial population growth. Most of the water rights now held by cities were acquired in this market. As in the Colorado market, cities tend to acquire rights well in advance of actually using them. While it cannot be proven that this market maximized economic

---

10. A 1944 treaty between Mexico and the United States specifies allocations of the Colorado River and the Rio Grande to each nation (U.S. Statutes at Large 1944). Lax enforcement in the tributary regions of Mexico has recently caused chronic water supply shortfalls in the Rio Grande basin. But the United States is not the only harmed party to this treaty. In the Colorado River basin, the United States has been previously deficient in its obligations to deliver sufficient water of usable quality (Wahl 1989, chapter 9).

efficiency, it is easily shown that efficiency has been improved (Chang and Griffin 1992).

Although return flow externalities are not worrisome in this region, market activities have progressively concentrated any water supply shortfalls on a shrinking pool of irrigators. Because each transfer converts a variable share to a fixed amount, the variability of the converted share is reassigned to the entirety of the remaining irrigators. This constitutes a new externality that grows in significance as the size of the municipal reserve grows, detracting from the achieved efficiency of the valley market. This problem is easily corrected; future transfers could omit the conversion of a share to a quantity, effectively meaning that urban buyers acquire exactly what the owner has to sell. This institutional revision has yet to be undertaken.

Visitors to the region will observe that the system is not appreciative of instream flow maintenance. River flow can become precariously low as a consequence of intensive use, with unfortunate implications for water quality. Water marketing is not at fault, though. The historical assignments of water rights did not do a good job of reserving rights for this purpose.

In recent times, lower Rio Grande water rights have sold for approximately $1,500 per acre-foot. This is much lower than the market-indicated value of water in northern Colorado. One of the lessons is that the value of water can be greatly different from place to place, depending on relative scarcity and the allowed rights of action. Also, whereas all U.S.-side surface water in the lower Rio Grande is marketable, the ready transferability of C–BT water is unique in its region—meaning that there is a premium attached to these rights.

California

Because water is a heavy commodity relative to its marginal net benefits, its marketable value may not be large in comparison to its transportation costs. A result is that most water markets are local, although some are regional. This is because a convenient natural or manmade conveyance is required to move water from the seller's to the buyer's location. Hence, markets commonly operate along a river or within a district in which water users share conveyance facilities. Local transfer also lowers externalities and transaction costs, as mentioned earlier.

A notably large water market is the one that has arisen in California. By virtue of an extensive system of canals and storage facilities (portions of which were heavily subsidized), California possesses an unusual ability to *wheel* water about the state. (Wheeling is the movement of water from agent A to agent B using a different organization's infrastructure.) This expansive system provides the means of moving the larger water supply of northern California and the Colorado River to the southern and coastal areas of the state. As in other western states, most water development was originally oriented toward irrigated agriculture, so irrigators possess the greatest

Box 7.2
Water Marketing to the Max: The Owens Valley Buyout

A storied event in terms of western water transfers, California history, and engineering feats occurred a hundred years ago when L.A. officials covertly purchased land and the associated water rights in Owens Valley, nearly 240 miles away. Los Angeles was then a city growing rapidly (from 100,000 to 200,000 people in a few years), and its water supply had long been problematic. Working secretly so as to avoid inflaming the purchase prices or causing an outcry, Fred Eaton (a prior water superintendent of Los Angeles) established sales contracts with many Owens Valley residents under the guise of seeking ranch land. He then transferred these contract opportunities to the city.

When the acquisitions were publicly announced in 1905, William Mulholland was the city's water superintendent. He had labored long on various city water projects and policies, including the installation of meters (Mulholland 2000, 83–85). To transport the Owens water to its new owners, a large aqueduct was constructed under Mulholland's direction, and this project's many challenges were not overcome until 1913. Owens Lake, the saline water body into which the closed-basin river previously terminated, was thus deprived of inflows. Initially, some irrigation rights remained in the Owens Valley, but the city resumed land purchases during the 1920s. Los Angeles would eventually come to own 95 percent of the valley's farmland and 85 percent of its towns (Reisner 1986, 104). Various segments of the aqueduct would later be dynamited by valley residents, but the city just rebuilt them. This infusion of water initiated great opportunities for Los Angeles while sapping those of the Owens Valley. Without this early transfer of water, the area's history would have evolved quite differently, and there would be far less consternation about present-day water marketing in California.

entitlements to water. A great deal of Californian water development was undertaken and paid for by the U.S. Bureau of Reclamation. Unlike the C–BT arrangement where the receiving district is the official operator of the multipurpose project, even though the Bureau owns the water (Michelsen 1994, 974), in California the Bureau is the owner-operator for most of the water it delivers to irrigation districts under projects authorized for irrigation purposes. Other Californian water developments were state financed. And of course, there are numerous instances of district and private water development. As a matter of state law, developed California water rights are limited by beneficial use and reasonability criteria. Another pertinent factor is that California has evolved an unusual mix of water doctrines, capable of perplexing water marketing (Kanazawa 1998).

Rigidities in these institutional arrangements have historically limited the transferability of California water. Irrigators are quite attached to the low contract rates they pay for Bureau water (volumetrically priced). Theoretically, these irrigators should be able to reach agreeable bargains with thirsty cities, but there have been barriers in the way:

1. Irrigation districts do not own much of the water rights, although they are entitled to continued contract arrangements with the Bureau.

2. Bureau-established water prices are always favorable to irrigators because the Bureau excludes the social value of natural water and makes other omissions as well.

3. If irrigators publicly display a strong willingness to lease/sell water, their subsidized contracts with the Bureau could be politically jeopardized.

4. Irrigators' willingness to use less water could be interpreted as a reduction in beneficial use and therefore water rights.

With respect to 3 and 4, when continued access to water depends on anachronistic concepts such as beneficial use, water entitlements are deficient because they are not clearly quantified. Hence, irrigators approach such marketing "opportunities" with hesitation. If they agree to lease their access to water, they may end up with reduced future rights. Progress toward marketing then requires that assurances be developed in order to entice sellers to the bargaining table.

With this institutional baggage in place, California entered a multiyear drought during the late 1980s. As water in storage was progressively depleted, rising scarcity created an atmosphere in which institutional change became feasible. When scarcity became sufficiently dire in 1991, state law was revised to declare water transfer to be a beneficial use (Coppock, Gray, and McBean 1994). Transferability was immediately put to use in the form of a water bank. In the following year, federal law was also revised to allow the transfer of Bureau water by contract recipients.

During the 1991 Drought Water Bank, the state's Department of Water Resources (DWR) leased over 821,000 acre-feet of water at the stated price of $125 per acre-foot (Coppock, Gray, and McBean 1994). The DWR resolved this price, announced it, and accepted water from willing lessors at this price. The DWR leased this water to willing buyers for $175 per acre-foot, with the higher price intended to offset conveyance losses (estimated at 25 percent) and administrative costs. Approximately 390,000 acre-feet was leased out, with another 250,000 acre-feet stored for future use. (Unexpectedly high rainfall changed marketing conditions almost as soon as the bank commenced operations.) According to an analysis by Howitt (1994b), using the techniques of chapter 5, the 1991 bank was an economic success—producing over $100 million in net benefits (omitting transaction costs).

After this bright beginning, California water marketing slowed as a result of wetter weather and public concern for the local economies of water-exporting regions (Yolles 2001; Hanak 2003). During some recent dry years, market activity has rivaled that of 1991, but concern for the welfare of water-exporting regions remains widespread (Hanak 2003; Johns 2003). Research found that the 1991 bank had a negative effect on water-exporting locales (Howitt 1994a; Dixon, Moore, and Schechter 1993). Such information is aggravated by the well-known fate of the Owens Valley and seriously dampens Californian enthusiasm for water markets. When farms idle land so they can lease water to others, they reduce their purchases of productive inputs such as seed, fertilizer, machinery, and labor. They also have less farm output to be transported, marketed, and processed. That's disliked by farm input suppliers and farm output processors in particular, and by rural businesspeople in general. These agents object to water marketing. They say that water is essential to their communities' economic welfare and that it is important to retain water locally for future development. Viewed another way, local communities are expressing the idea that rights to water are not solely private, and that these rights have public obligations. Sensitive water planning will consider these objections, and the Californian system is a sensitive one.

This is a new kind of third party to water marketing. Wherever it is legitimized as a valid concern, a serious barrier to nonlocal water marketing is created. On the other hand, these third-party effects bear an uneasy resemblance to the secondary economic effects that we barred from *nonlocal* consideration in the policy and project analysis of the prior two chapters. Which viewpoint is the correct one? The pervasiveness of this question within the water marketing debate makes it imperative that we answer it accurately.

7.10 The Grounds for Area-of-Origin Protectionism

The promise of water marketing is a better equality of MNBs across all water users—that is, economic efficiency and the greatest possible social benefits from water use. Thus, the rewards of marketing are highest when the divergence between MNBs is greatest. Most often this occurs when agriculture's MNBs are low relative to urban/industrial MNBs. *Inter*sectoral water trades are therefore the most socially rewarding. *Intra*sectoral trades are potentially useful too, but they tend to produce less net benefits per unit of water.

Intrasectoral water trades do not have deep implications for secondary economic interests. An agriculture-to-agriculture water trade means that the same sorts of complementary inputs will be purchased (seed, fertilizer, etc.) and the same sorts of off-farm processing will happen. These trades should not be harmful for the local economy. Even better, these intrasectoral trades are likely to enhance the competitiveness of local producers in regional markets, thereby contributing positive secondary effects to the area economy.

Conceivably, intrasectoral trades can be between distant partners, but such exchanges are uncommon, so the concern does not arise often.[11] The greatest apprehension of local interests in water marketing is the prospect of nonlocal, intersectoral water marketing. The issue here is remarkable in that it appears confined to water.

---

11. With respect to ag-to-ag transfers, the transaction costs of nonlocal trades are commonly large in relation to differences between agricultural MNBs. Water sales among cities are rare since utilities are seldom interested in selling water, but leasing can be common.

There are locales serving as sources for timber, ores, coal, oil, and fish, yet host communities are not objecting to the extraction and shipment of these resources to other regions. How is water different?

The difference is that there are jobs rooted in the collection of nonwater resources, and many of these jobs will be performed in the producing region (Colby 1988, 740). There may even be local employment for some resource processing after the cutting, extracting, or catching is done. Therefore, the removal of resources other than water creates economic opportunities within originating regions. These opportunities are sharply reduced for water that may only generate employment for a small number of intermediaries and, in a few cases, temporary jobs in the construction of new conveyance facilities.

What is the economic thinking on this matter? Should water marketing be constrained whenever local economies stand to lose?

The Area-of-Origin "Problem"

An *area of origin* is a region serving as a water marketing exporter. If residents and nonwater resource owners within an area of origin have a governmentally sanctioned claim to water-driven benefits, then either interregional water transfers have to be prohibited or a compensatory policy mechanism has to be devised. If trades are prohibited, then an important policy tool is damaged. If transfer approval requires compensation of these third-party interests, then a new cost is imposed on sellers or buyers, lessening interest in trading. In spite of this disadvantage, some U.S. states have taken the latter approach (Deason, Schad, and Sherk 2001, 184).

The central economically linked third parties of this debate are agriculturally dependent businesses and labor. These interests perceive reduced water employment as reduced economic opportunity. Yet, the economic impacts on these agents can be small when water is strictly obtained from low-value farm operations. Furthermore, water marketing leads to a regional influx of dollars, and these monies generate secondary economic effects, too. Unless the new monies are not applied within the area of origin, the water-driven negative effects might be easily dominated by the money-driven positive effects. Still, recognition of both sides of this exchange may not placate agricultural businesses and labor unless it can be expected that the new monies will be applied in agriculturally oriented pursuits.

There are crucial trade-offs to be faced here, and they can have momentous implications for marketing's range as a scarcity-fighting mechanism. Depending on how sellers use their water marketing receipts, areas of origin can suffer economic losses as a consequence of water markets. While the loss may be small in relation to a local economy's size, fewer goods may be sold and the tax base can be reduced when water is exported. Thus, rural communities may be negatively affected third parties, even though it is difficult to call this relationship an externality.[12] On the opposite side of the transfer, there is an opposing *area of receipt* in which more goods will be sold and the tax base will be enlarged as a consequence of a water market transfer. Without empirical analysis, it is tough to know if the receiving area's gains are lower than the originating area's losses, but the greater direct value of water to the receiving area is a hint that the secondary benefits are greater as well. In any case, how should any secondary losses of the area of origin be weighed against the secondary gains of the area of receipt?

Our fundamental objective, aggregate economic efficiency, tells us that area-of-origin concerns—like secondary economic effects—"count" only for local accounting stances. For broader accounting stances, negative secondary effects are offset by positive secondary effects occurring within areas of receipt. For a regional accounting stance, the offset may be partial. At the federal level, the offset is likely to be complete. In the Californian scenario, because the area of receipt is also in the state, the offset is likely to be complete. Hence, the recommendation of economic efficiency is to forget about third-party protection relating to area-of-origin impacts. Any protection will reduce the net benefits the state receives from its water endowment.

Yet California's deliberations have gone in the opposite direction. Progress toward new rules has been slow. In jurisdictions other than California, debate about the transferability of water also includes this anxiety, even when prospective importing regions also lie within the jurisdiction's accounting stance.

Resolving the Problem

How can we come to understand the realities of public concern for areas of origin in relation to the guidance of economic theory? There are at least two answers.

The first answer is that it is not necessary to align public debate or decisions with economic recommendations. Rules about the transferability of water are politically resolved. As such, they are resolved by political forces. So if agents from areas of origin argue on behalf of their interests and if they are successful, then they will have politically transformed the duty/privilege mix of water rights (see section 4.5). In so doing, the local community's right to economic gain from water use will be enhanced

12. We must be careful about equating these third-party effects to externalities. Externalities are an important class of market failures because they prevent markets from achieving efficient results. It has long been acknowledged that there is a class of externalities called *pecuniary* externalities that exist because of the efficient actions of markets (Baumol and Oates 1988, 29–31). These are not market failures. Proper market performance will initiate price changes that affect producers and sellers of goods, either positively or negatively. Pecuniary externalities are viewed as good things because they enhance efficiency, while the other class of externalities, *technological*, prevent markets from achieving efficient results. When economists discuss externalities today, they are implicitly referring to technological externalities. The secondary economic effects pertaining to areas of origin are a form of pecuniary externality. There is no failure in the First Theorem of Welfare Economics in the case of pecuniary externalities.

and the rights of water users will be lessened correspondingly. Areas of receipt will be losers under this transformation, and the summed net benefits of water use across the broader polity will be lower, as compared to a rule set where secondary economic effects are inadmissible third-party impacts. Conceivably, economic development occurs elsewhere if water transfer rules are too strict (Clyde 1989, 444). Areas of origin may gain generally, but the owners of water rights will sacrifice for it. Also, the inertia of water rights will have been raised. The latter point greatly concerns some observers given the burdens of scarcity and the need for policy tools (Gardner 2003).

A second answer is that we possess a second efficiency criterion, and it allows compassion about area-of-origin protection. Neutral economic efficiency was discussed in chapter 2, where it was noted that this criterion declines to weigh the economic benefits of different agents. From this concept emerges a spectrum of economic allocations (and rules). Third-party protection of areas of origin can be one of them. While summed net benefits across the greater jurisdiction will not be maximized, the economic result may be efficient in a neutral sense. In this situation, the benefits provided by water are lower, and they are distributed differently. This concept is depicted generally in figure 7.4, where the welfare of each region is measured on the two axes. Absent any protective rules for areas of origin, trade among water users can bring the total economy to point A, where net benefits are maximized. With area-of-origin protection, the result is not aggregately efficient, but it can be on the

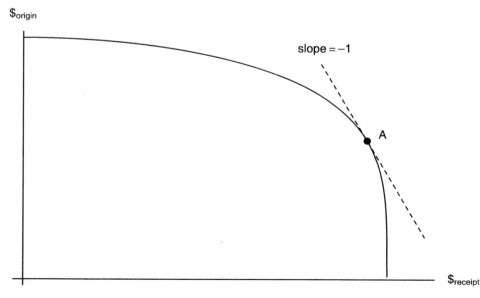

Figure 7.4
Compared efficiency outcomes

frontier of neutrally efficient results—to the benefit of the area of origin and the detriment of the area of receipt (relative to point A).

Armed with either of the efficiency perspectives, the rational policy commentator can remark favorably or unfavorably about area-of-origin protections: either it is a matter of aggregate efficiency or equitable distribution, the latter being something for society to resolve for itself. But caution should be applied. The second path impedes a tool that can be a powerful ally for the solution of water scarcity. While the National Research Council report's collective opinion expressed sensitivity about areas of origin, it was also properly observed that "although water transfers can bring negative effects, it is important to recognize that a dynamic, growing economy depends on processes that allow declining industries and firms to be displaced by growing firms and industries" (1992, 50). All available policies for effecting area-of-origin protection will obstruct some trades and even raise the transaction costs of successful water trades, with harmful aggregate effects.

All in all, it is clear that this issue tests both economic theory and the wisdom of public decision making. Fortunately, there are many circumstances in which this problem is moot, especially in local markets where buyers operate near sellers. The highlighted Colorado and Texas markets are examples.

It can also be concluded that rule choices are once again delimited by *accounting stance*. An area-of-origin jurisdiction can efficiently choose to limit water transferability, if the jurisdiction possesses such authority. An upper-basin state or province can understandably establish rules favorable to marketing *within* its boundaries while disapproving outward transfers. In doing so, it may run afoul of national interests and even national law, but the desire is understandable. In addition, from the accounting stance of nations, it may be efficient to bar natural water exports to other nations or negotiate compensation for secondary economic effects. Such actions may not be tenable under free trade agreements (Anderson and Landry 2001), but they are understandable for a national accounting stance contemplating only water allocation and not the trade of all goods.

7.11 The Ground Water Challenge

Although the theoretical ideals of surface water marketing have been fruitfully realized in many regions, ground water marketing is lagging, as ground water institutions commonly do. The challenges are greater, and the information is lower, owing to the underground location of this resource. Keeping in mind that the social objective is to advance efficiency, we can distinguish two scenarios:

1. aquifers that are essentially unconnected with managed surface water;
2. aquifers that are hydrologically interconnected with managed surface water.

The second case involves a problem excluded from the first, which is challenging enough. If transferable ground water rights are to coexist with some form of surface water management, the ground water rights should not subvert the surface water system (and vise versa). Indeed, ground water institutions should interface well with surface water rights. In interconnected cases, it is occasionally true that lax ground water rules undermine transferable surface water rights, as noted in chapter 4. If ground water users are allowed to pump water and thereby induce ground water recharge from associated surface water, then that is an imposition on surface water users and surface water rights. A good interface would also include a method for allowing ground water users and surface water users to transfer water among themselves. Administering such a system requires some hydrologic expertise, but it can and has been done (Balleau 1988; Gisser 1983, 1025).

As with surface water, the earliest ground water institutions associate usage rights with landownership. We noted in chapter 4 that many governments maintain rules in which ground water cannot be traded apart from land. This is quite a burden for achieving ground water marketing, yet water's scarcity value can lead to circumstances in which land is traded primarily for its ground water access. Such instances are known as ***ground water ranching***. In its usual conduct, a city utility will reach beyond city borders to acquire land underlain by attractive ground water resources. It is economically unfortunate that land must be reallocated in order to allow water transfer, thus risking the misallocation of land. Yet the city may be able to put the land to good use, perhaps by leasing it to others. In some instances, cities have purchased irrigated lands, built infrastructure to convey pumped ground water to the city, and leased the land to the original owner for the purpose of dryland agricultural production.

A second form of ground water marketing is sometimes allowed in jurisdictions where water rights are attached to land. Buyers can *contract* with landowners for the use of land for ground water exploitation. Such contracts are usually long-term, as the buyer intends to install expensive wells and conveyances requiring the assurance of longevity.

While it is fortunate that the legal attachment of ground water rights to land can be overcome through ranching and contracts, such approaches do not correct the common property nature of unquantified ground water rights. Wherever ground water rights are not specified in terms of usable quantity, the many users having access to the aquifer do not have true private property in ground water. They may have private property in land, but their water rights are a type of common property, to be shared with other members of the common. Absent quantification, other rules (such as tests of *reasonability*) will have to be used to manage common property ground water.

An economically highlighted method of escaping common property and installing private property in ground water is the two-deed Vernon Smith system discussed previously. In this system, users can transfer their ownership to either the annual *recharge* of an aquifer or the *stock* of depletable water in the aquifer. Any particular user may own one or both deeds. Both deeds are fully quantified, and all water pumping is metered so that these property rights are well respected. Ground water marketing under this system can do a good job of allocating the resource among competing interests. Accommodations for new, more valuable uses of water can therefore be achieved. There are, however, some market failures to consider.

Potential Market Failures

For the most part, ground water-specific market failures arise only in situations where an aquifer is being mined (depleted), meaning that pumping exceeds recharge. For aquifers where pumping is well matched by average recharge and the aquifer is merely serving as an underground reservoir or conveyance, efficient surface water institutions such as markets apply well. Problems may occur, however, when ground water is not regularly renewed by natural recharge. While potentially numerous, the market failures peculiar to the marketing of depletable ground water are often empirically small. A small market failure will not impinge "much" on the market's ability to achieve our efficiency goal—dynamic efficiency, in this case. Still, we must be clear about the potential problems before recommending transferable ground water rights for a given aquifer. A listing of the relevant market failures include the following:

Overdiscounting Market Failure   When market participants apply personal discount rates exceeding society's discount rate, depletion will occur too rapidly.

Pumping Cost Externality   Pumping by well operators lowers the water table and raises the pumping costs of other users.

Well Interference Externality   Each users' pumping will create local *drawdown* and a *cone of depression* in the vicinity of the users' well. If this local drawdown affects the wells of nearby well operators, their pumping costs will be negatively affected beyond the typical pumping cost externality.

Spatial Externality   Aquifers are typically thinner along their periphery, implying that well owners in these areas may find that their wells have dried up if the water table gets low enough (Anderson, Burt, and Fractor 1983, 231).

Saltwater Intrusion Externality   Some coastal aquifers are hydrologically connected with saltwater, and the pumping of freshwater induces saltwater movement into areas once containing freshwater (Gonzalez 1989). If there are wells in the "salted" area, their productivity will be lost. This problem can also occur in noncoastal areas.

Land Subsidence Externality   The hydrologic pressure of in-place ground water may support overlying land, so its removal can cause the land surface to drop irreversibly, with losses to land value and structures built on the land. Losses may also be caused by the increased flood potential of lowered land.

All these externalities increase with pumping, so they combine with the overdiscounting market failure to imply one thing: a market resolved rate of ground water depletion will be too fast. The questions are, how fast, with what consequences, and what are the available policy remedies?

The first two of these market failures are the most ubiquitous, so they warrant first inspection. Overdiscounting and pumping costs are natural to consider jointly because they occur simultaneously. When well operators are deciding how much to pump in the current period, they can either ignore the future impact or consider it. The impact is real, so if good institutions are in place, the well operator will consider it. More pumping now must be balanced against declines in the water table, which imply greater future pumping costs and possibly greater future investments in the well. These future costs enter today's decision making after they are discounted by the decision-making agent. If the discount rate is socially wrong or the pumping costs are underestimated, pumping in the current period will be too great. Summed across all agent-pumpers, overdepletion will occur. Unfortunately, private discount rates are too high (chapter 3), and the rational agent will only consider the impact on future personal pumping costs, not the future impacts on all other well operators. Theoretically, then, the influence of the overdiscounting and pumping cost market failures are qualitatively clear (Burness and Brill 2001). But are they quantitatively significant?

The quantitative extent of these problems depends on aquifer characteristics as well as the number and behavior of agents. If there is but one pumping agent, the pumping cost externality disappears altogether because all costs are self-inflicted. As well operators become more numerous, the externality grows in severity. A worst-case scenario occurs when the number of well operators is very large.

Some quantitative insight can be achieved by reviewing the empirical work of Gisser and Sánchez (1980), who modeled a New Mexico aquifer being used for irrigation. Using a basic lumped-parameter aquifer model with pumping costs that are linearly dependent on water table elevation, Gisser and Sánchez solve for two usage paths. One path is portrayed as the "no-plan" one, where pumpers are so numerous that they have no regard for future impacts.[13] The other path is the dynamically efficient one, using a discount rate of 1 percent, which displays a high regard for future

---

13. Gisser, Sánchez, and some other authors call the "no-planning" approach "competitive," which is unfortunate because it seems to blame inefficiency on the forces of competition rather than market failures. This is false, but it can be occasionally suffered in light of its tradition in the literature of ground water depletion (Burness and Brill 2001, 21n).

effects because it is so low. Their analysis can be replicated, using Mathematica to solve the embedded differential equations and map the results. Figure 7.5 displays water usage and water table elevation over a several-hundred-year period. While this aquifer should be regarded as unique, in light of its high storage and high recharge relative to aggregate pumping, the results are intriguing. Moreover, the availability of a ready model to explore other scenarios is useful. (Readers are warned that the long-term productivity of this particular aquifer does not extend to all aquifers.)

In the Gisser and Sánchez results, we see that unplanned paths are not strongly different from optimal paths. No-plan pumping is higher than optimal pumping. The consequence is that the no-plan water table is always less than optimal and future pumping costs are always too high. The theoretically predicted disparities are visually apparent, but they do not appear to be sizable. Since the goal here is to maximize net present value attributable to ground water use, how does each path compare for this measure? In this situation, unplanned NPV is only about 0.3 percent less than optimal NPV—a small difference. Based on these findings, the pumping cost externality and overdiscounting do not appear to be issues worthy of attention, but there are important conditions in the Gisser and Sánchez model that may not be universal.[14] Further testing of different circumstances often find little difference between the rewards of no-plan and optimal pumping schedules, but the result does not always appear (Koundouri 2004). Hence, careful consideration of individual aquifers may be commendable prior to installing the two-deed transferable right system or other legal systems.

Moving to the remaining ground water externalities, well interference is a consequence of wells being too close to one another. In such cases, models like the one posed by Gisser and Sánchez do not incorporate all the important relationships (Zimmerman 1990). It appears that distributed parameter models are needed if these location-specific impacts are to be modeled. Most jurisdictions require wells to be approved before drilling, for the primary purpose of limiting such negative relationships (Emel 1987). Such policies predate the development of transferable ground water in most areas (because this externality is not unique to water markets). They are likely to be an adequate remedy for the problem.

Spatial and saltwater intrusion externalities are of the same nature and effect. Given the "right" conditions, if water pumpage is sufficiently large, the usefulness of certain wells will be permanently lost. Only the owners of these wells are likely to care about this consequence, so pumping by others will tend to be inefficiently high.

---

14. Because the unplanned case does not assign any weight to future pumping costs, it can be interpreted as an instance of an infinite private discount rate. Hence, any model solution using a discount rate between 1 and ∞ percent must lie between the paths illustrated in figure 7.5.

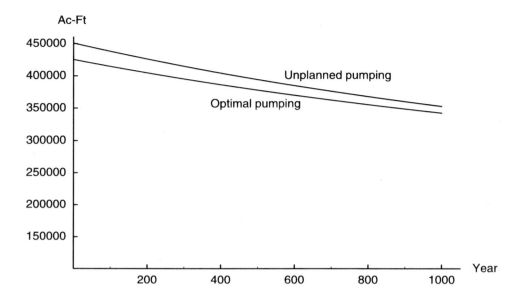

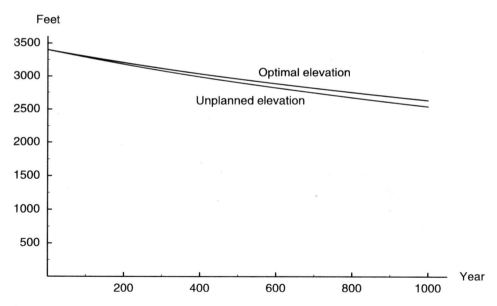

Figure 7.5
A pumping cost externality

As in the case of depletion, the main economic worry is not necessarily that these wells are lost. The problem is they are lost too soon. The maintenance of a high water table to forestall saltwater intrusion or keep peripheral wells in operation can be a high cost to pay in terms of the sacrificed productive value of the ground water in storage. Economic scrutiny might conclude that the costs are too large relative to the gains. Of course, these are not problems specific to ground water marketing. Indeed, should owners of unusable wells still possess water rights, then they can gain some benefits by marketing the rights (Anderson, Burt, and Fractor 1983, 240). In any case, if the prevention of intrusion and the protection of peripheral wells is desirable, then the initial allocation of ground water rights should not establish more salable rights than is consistent with these goals.

Finally, there is the problem of land subsidence to consider. In usual circumstances, the problem of subsidence is not known before it begins to occur. Moreover, once acknowledged, it is hard to predict where and when it will occur. It may strike broadly across an aquifer's area, or may cause problems here and there. It may impact valued structures or idle land. Because of its unpredictability, the value of losses may be hard to anticipate. So the usual economic advise of equating marginal costs and marginal benefits is difficult to apply. As with the immediately prior externalities, ground water marketing does not exacerbate these social problems relative to alternative ground water management institutions. Indeed, it helps to minimize the costs of externality control by creating a forum in which limited and valued ground water use can be allocated to its most valued applications.

Does Ground Water Marketing Make Sense?

These potential market failures raise concerns about the merits of ground water marketing, but the marketing of scarce ground water may make considerable sense relative to alternative institutions. The in-use alternatives described in chapter 4 include absolute ownership, reasonability criteria, and correlative rights. These alternatives do not sidestep these problems. Only the latter doctrine makes a concerted attempt to manage depletion. Hence, whereas overdiscounting and the pumping cost externality are legitimate concerns about ground water marketing, transferable rights in ground water are apt to outperform common property regimes. In addition, the yet-to-be-used, two-deed system provides the public with a direct mechanism for managing declining aquifer levels: the adjudication of the stored water deed. If water table levels are in need of protection, possibly because of one or more of the externalities discussed above, then a clear option is to allocate very little stored water (perhaps none of it) to private agents. In such circumstances, the transferability of deeds to recharge water will be even more important, owing to the increased overall scarcity of water.

7.12 Summary

What marketing can and cannot achieve depends on the starting place. In many instances, that starting place is dominated by common property institutions that have lived beyond their usefulness. There is much that can be improved in such circumstances by moving institutions toward transferable water rights. But there are stumbling points to be carefully observed, lest we trip in policy design. One must be mindful that the goal is to achieve efficiency, not water marketing. Water marketing is only a means to achieve the goal.

Unlike typical commodities, water frustrates efficient marketing because of its flow character. This renders water different from the resources to which the First Theorem of Welfare Economics applies well. Flow infers that all water transactions produce third-party effects. Return flow externalities are a significant hurdle for water markets. Moreover, there are a number of nonrival water uses that are underserved by pure forms of water marketing. While promarketing advisers assure us that nonrival user groups do occasionally participate in water markets, the important issue is whether their participation results in greater efficiency than alternative institutions.

Managing all these things efficiently is a considerable challenge and compels us to construct a mixed system of rules—some market oriented, some not, all intertwined. A highly regulated market is the consequence. Unavoidably, the transaction costs of market operations become significant, thus limiting the social effectiveness of water exchanges.

Close consideration of these matters reveals both policy remedies and locations where potential market failures are minimal. An operational overview of three important water markets reveals not only the inner workings but also the scenarios where water marketing is an especially good social strategy. Clearly, water markets are unique tools, and they are bettered by good crafting and fortuitous circumstances.

Current public debate over the prospective trade of water is sometimes misguided—expressing grave concern about the private ownership of something so dear, and not thinking about the extension of that argument to other dear goods like food and housing. There is a bit of merit in anxiety pertaining to area-of-origin economic effects, however. When water leaves rural areas, as it sometimes does under water marketing, there are negative consequences for economic activity in the area of origin. These effects are offset in an area of receipt, so an accounting stance including both areas would perceive positive net benefits. Distributional concerns favoring the area of origin can lead to protective rules barring nonlocal trades or establishing some sort of compensatory mechanism. Prohibitions designed to aid areas of origin are helpful to those areas, but significant (and generally greater) costs are experienced elsewhere as a result of such protections, and the overall social performance of water marketing is damaged.

Ground water is a special case in that ground water rules should foster coordination with hydrologically associated surface water and there is the matter of depletion to address. The two-deed system is promising in these respects. Although there are several types of externalities to be controlled in some fashion, they are not generally worsened by ground water marketing relative to other institutional frameworks now in place.

7.13   Exercises

1. Suppose linear MNBs for two agents, as depicted in figure 7.1. Suppose that these natural water demands are specified by

$$MNB_1 = b_1 - m_1 w_1 \quad \text{and} \quad MNB_2 = b_2 - m_2 w_2,$$

together with $(b_1, b_2, m_1, m_2) = (32, 25, 1, 0.5)$. Water units are acre-feet per year, and monetary units are dollars. Additionally, agent 1 owns twenty af and agent 2 owns fifty af of water rights. Assuming no other agents, what is the optimal amount of water for one of these agents to lease to the other? Except for the financial terms of the lease, what value does the seller lose and what value does the buyer gain? Illustrate these results by drawing a replication of figure 7.1 that is reasonably accurate for the data of this problem. What are the net (aggregated) gains? If this water is leased on a per acre-foot basis, what range of prices might be used? What price equilibrates MNBs? Using the latter value, a discount rate of 10 percent, and assuming all conditions to be steady over time, what is the market value of a permanently transferred acre-foot? How much money might each agent be willing to pay their separate attorneys to guide a permanent exchange through the state-run approval process?

2. You are an irrigation district manager who has assembled some information on demand and supply within your system. You believe retail demand this coming year will be $w = 95005p^{-0.8}$, and your total costs will be $C = 7.2 \times 10^4 + 8.23 \times 10^{-9} w^3$. Both of these functions are expressed in units of natural water. What is the maximum amount you should be willing to pay for a four thousand unit lease if you already have rights to sixteen thousand units?

3. In recent years, water lease prices have been rising 3 percent annually even though inflation has only been 1 percent. Presently, a water right to a hundred acre-feet can be rented for $7,000. Given this information, compute and explain a sales price for a hundred-af right. Use a 6 percent real rate of discount and a twelve-year planning horizon. Repeat the computation for an infinite planning horizon.

4. Compute the equivalent single price of conserved water for phase 2 of the canal rehabilitation project in chapter 6's exercise 4. In this phase, assume that Kettle Irrigation District pays $1.2 million in year 2 for the specified schedule of future water savings.

5. Private trade in water rights is prohibited by law in your state. Yet the state water agency has won a judicial ruling affirming the following legal interpretations. First, water right owners can contractually surrender their rights, but only to the granting water agency, and the agency can offer financial incentives for such surrenders as long as they are formally called "water development projects" and are the cheapest available projects. Second, the agency can establish reasonable fees when it grants "new" permanent water rights. Given that 70 percent of water diversions in the state are for irrigation and growing cities are very desirous of heightened water availability, the agency has decided to use these legal interpretations as grounds for a bank to be run by the water agency. How would you separately counsel bank administrators about setting surrender incentives and permit fees if your goal is to promote economic efficiency?

8 Water Pricing

How should prices be set?

As compared to water marketing, which is feasible only in jurisdictions allowing it and is practiced only among natural water handlers, water pricing is a far-reaching instrument. A great many agents pay a price for the water they use. The price of water is a statistically strong determinant of water demand even when the price elasticity of demand is low. Although it is not the only determinant, it is the only administratively controlled factor consistent with freedom of choice by water users. As a consequence, pricing is a serious tactic for combating scarcity, and it is a prime *demand management* strategy. The potential of pricing as a policy tool is revealed by a basic, market-instilled notion: "If demand exceeds supply, then price must be too low." In the science of economics, it is price that balances supply and demand, so if supply $\neq$ demand, then price requires fixing. While this observation is helpful, at least at a primitive level, the idiosyncrasies of water delivery require that economists refine the idea, as we shall soon see. Isolating marginal costs in light of several complexities is a challenging business. Moreover, this basic observation leaves important questions unanswered:

• If price is typically too low to control scarcity, are there systematic reasons why this occurs or why it should occur?

• If price is wrong, what is the procedure for determining the right price?

• If we improve price so that demand and supply are better balanced, what are the consequences for water-using agents?

• All things considered, can the clients and owners of water supply organizations rally in support of improved pricing or must their disapproval obstruct this policy instrument?

This chapter is devoted to these questions. To begin, it is a good idea to review the background established previously.

• Efficient pricing is normally equivalent to marginal-cost pricing. Because the maximization of net benefits yields the advice MC = MB and because rational, water-using agents will choose their water use so that MB = water price, we must find MC to get the optimal price. Nevertheless, the determination of a best water price becomes more complex with deeper inspection, as we shall see.

• Applying the delineation of the prior chapter, water pricing relates only to processed water, although the degree of water processing may be incomplete, such as occurs when a reservoir-owning authority sells water to area cities. We are not investigating the pricing of natural water. The actual processing may be slight, perhaps involving only storage or conveyance, but some processing is occurring.

• In chapters 2 and 3, we found that delivered water price should include the value of natural water. This opportunity cost may only be revealed as a Lagrange multiplier, differently obtained in situations of renewable supplies such as surface water (equation [2.30]) or depletable supplies such as ground water (equation [3.14]).

• Because competition is normally absent in a given service area, as is appropriate for a natural monopoly, there is a single water supplier in each locale.[1] Retail water price cannot be determined by competitive forces. In all situations, the supplier either sets its own prices freely or establishes water price in an administratively regulated framework. Client-owned suppliers such as irrigation districts and public utilities are usually the least regulated, for the simple reason that client-owners are not apt to be self-abusive in setting price. Privately owned utilities are more heavily regulated in order to offset their intrinsic monopoly power; left to their own discretion, they lean toward prices exceeding efficient ones so as to increase profitability.

With these principles firmly in place, let's consider the specialized nomenclature of water pricing.

8.1   The Terms of Pricing

In common terminology, *water price* is a volumetric price placed on metered water. A water *rate* is often the same thing as a water price. The term water *rates*, expressed plurally, typically refers to the entire package of charges applied by a water supplier. Indeed, any given supplier may simultaneously apply an extensive array of charges, with good reason. To begin with, water rates almost always include two categories:

---

1. Recall from chapters 2 and 4 that competition is unwanted in the provision of retail water. Duplication of water treatment, storage, or delivery infrastructure would cause costs that would surmount any advantage to competition.

• *charges that depend on the amount of water used*, where the per-unit charges may vary according to the type of use, the amount of use, the time of use, and so on;

• *charges that are not based on water consumption* such as new connection fees, "meter" charges, or irrigated acreage charges.

The facts that rates include water and nonwater charges, and that the prices vary with an assortment of factors is an immediate complication of the issue at hand. Ideally, to foster good scarcity signaling the water charges will be independent of the nonwater charges, but all elements of the rate package affect the supplier's revenue. Because the adequacy of revenue to cover the supplier's costs is an important concern, elements of the rate package are interdependent. Increases in one charge may allow another charge to be lowered. As a consequence, any study of the "best" water price is obligated to consider other elements of the rate structure. Just as importantly, the pursuit of efficiency should take full advantage of all available pricing tools.

Water-Based Charges

In non-U.S. settings and the academic literature, water rates are sometimes called *water tariffs*. Yet the word tariffs can be interpreted as "taxes" in economic jargon, so we shall avoid the tariff reference from this point forward. Although governments may be responsible for setting both taxes and water rates, there is an important distinction to be respected. Taxes are revenue-collecting mechanisms that enable governments to perform varied functions (maintain streets, build schools, operate the government, defend the borders, fund welfare programs, etc.). Water rates are charges for the measured delivery of a valued commodity. This is not a tax. It is the cost of a service, and it is good to encourage an appreciation of this fact through one's choice of terminology.

The term *rate structure* may address whether the per-unit price of water decreases, stays the same, or increases with the amount of water consumed. Figure 8.1 portrays the three available rate structures. The uppermost rate structure depicts decreasing block rates. For each customer, price is constant within every "block," but as metered consumption increases into the next higher block, price falls. The first block in this schedule exists from w_1 to w_2 units of water, and each water unit in this block costs the consumer p_1 dollars. While it is often true that $w_1 = 0$, some suppliers grant each consumer a small amount of water consumption, free of any volumetric price. If water consumption lies within a higher block, all units of water are still billed at the rate applicable for their block. Hence, the metered water bill for w units of water is not $p_2 \cdot w$. It is $p_1 \cdot (w_2 - w_1) + p_2 \cdot (w - w_2)$. It is also notable that the "marginal price" faced by this consumer is p_2. Different consumers served by this system may then face different marginal prices.

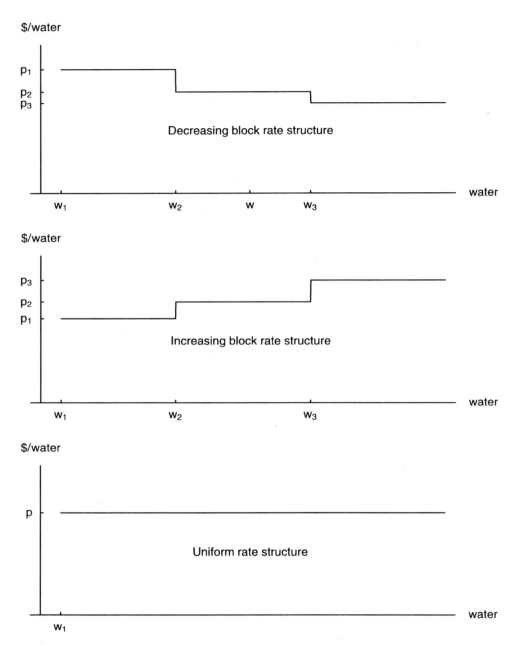

Figure 8.1
Three types of metered water rates

Historically, decreasing block rates were favored, although this has been changing as the economic circumstances of utilities evolve (Organisation for Economic Co-operation and Development 1999, 56). Three reasons explain the long-standing preference for decreasing block rates. As noted previously, the natural monopoly status of suppliers is due to the declining average costs of providing water. Said another way, greater systemwide deliveries lower the per unit costs for everyone, so stimulating consumption with a lower price for large water consumers might seem appealing. Second, it is widely assumed that large water users such as businesses and industries are more steady in their water use in that their peak-hour and peak-day water use is not dramatically greater than their average water use. In contrast, it is typically presumed that small water users such as households contribute more to peak water usage. Because system capacity is both expensive and constructed to meet peak demands, it is arguable that residential users are causing higher average and marginal costs for the utility. Third, decreasing block rates are favorably viewed by suppliers because they stabilize revenue in the presence of climate-impacted demand. With decreasing block rates, a greater proportion of revenue is derived from the initial units of consumed water, and these units are less likely to be affected by climate.

The opposing rate structure is naturally termed *increasing block rates*, although inverted block rates is also an encountered term.[2] Motivation for the adoption of increasing block rates comes from two sources. First, increasing block rates are often claimed to enhance water conservation because large water users are "penalized" for their behavior. Sometimes, one even encounters claims that increasing blocks are commendable on the basis of marginal-cost pricing, but that is an errant interpretation.[3] Second, because larger water users tend to be wealthier water users in residential settings, there may be a perceived degree of "fairness" associated with increasing block rates. Yet industrial users faced with increasing block rates may think it unfair (Goldstein 1986, 56). In developing countries, increasing block rates may enjoy considerable support because the basic water uses undertaken by the poor are internally subsidized by this rate structure (Boland and Whittington 1998).

For both decreasing and increasing block rates, the number of blocks is two or more. With a single block, the rate structure is called *uniform* or *constant*. Uniform rate structures are generally favored by the economic efficiency criterion when

---

2. Use of the term inverted underscores the tradition and dominance of decreasing block rates until recent years.

3. Just because the schedule of marginal costs is typically increasing as water deliveries increases does not mean that the pricing schedule should increase as well. The individual water user is just one of many users. Together, all users determine the system's current marginal costs. Individually, they have little influence. From another perspective, consider a marketed commodity other than water. In spite of rising marginal costs, everyone faces the same price, as should be the case.

water use can be well measured. The reasoning is simple. At any given minute, on or off-peak, marginal consumption by all consumers has the same impact on supply costs. That is, all currently operating consumers are responsible for the same current marginal costs. There is a measurement problem, however. Meter reading is not performed constantly. At best, using current technology, meters are read monthly, so water managers only know each agent's total use for the month. The schedule of the agent's particularized water use within each month is not known, so it is impractical to charge the agent an appropriate time-dependent marginal cost for each unit of consumed water. (The rate would be higher during hours of peak use.) For this reason, temporal characteristics of the agent's water use must be inferred from the metered quantity. Usually, this inference has been resolved on the basis of sector (residential, commercial, etc.) and ultimately metered water use, with low-volume users presumed to have greater peaking impacts. Hence, until time-dependent rates become more practical, applying a single uniform water rate to all customers is not a bulletproof economic recommendation in all settings. It does apply well, however, when peak-hour and peak-day marginal costs are not markedly different than off-peak marginal costs.

Rate structures other than decreasing block, increasing block, or uniform are sometimes discussed (American Water Works Association 1984, 61–63), but they have not achieved much application. Nor are they likely to.

One method of time-dependent pricing is supported by contemporary metering practices. Monthly meter reading allows water prices to vary by month. Thus, as a utility moves through the year, encountering low-to-high water supply conditions relative to demand, it is feasible to apply month-specific prices. This is called *time of year pricing*. While such a system has not gained complete favor, it is more efficient than keeping prices fixed for an entire year.[4] Many urban suppliers now employ a simplified variant known as *seasonal pricing* in which separate winter and summer rates are applied. Winter rates apply for part of the year, and summer rates make up the rest. Summer rates are justifiably higher because much of the supply system is only used during the summer. Given that there is idle system capacity during winter periods, it is clear that the purpose of the idle capacity is to provide summer service. It is therefore economically appropriate to assign these costs to the summer period, resulting in higher summer rates. The summer value of natural water is also higher in most regions.

---

4. The rate revision process is typically an annual affair, and approved rates are commonly locked into place for the duration of the coming year or longer. Arguably, the pronouncement of different rates for each of the forthcoming twelve months would be viewed as unnecessarily complex in light of the need to keep rates understandable by clients. Furthermore, all agent's meters are not read on the same day as the service area is divided up into different "cycles" in order to make economic use of meter-reading labor. This adds complexity to the matter of resolving monthly rates.

Essential Nonwater Charges

While there are minor nonwater charges that are components of water rates, two nonwater charges are especially important. Both of these charges are rationalized by the capital intensity of the water supply industry, which has even greater capital requirements per dollar of product than the electricity, telephone, or railroad industries (Beecher, Mann, and Landers 1991, 23).[5] Both of these charges are focused on the many "points of use" at the end points of the water delivery system. Water managers refer to these end points as the number of "connections" or "meters" in their system.

The first of these fees is the ***meter charge***, which is usually paid every billing period. This fee can also be called the minimum charge or the service charge (American Water Works Association 1991, 34). When irrigators are charged on the basis of irrigated area (acreage), this fee functions much like a meter charge for each acre. Because it is not based on water consumption, the meter charge serves as a *flat rate* if it is not accompanied by a volumetric charge. Modern rate systems, however, incorporate both the meter charge and a water price. Historically, the meter charge component was employed in the absence of a volumetric charge. Irrigation districts have a strong propensity to rely on the acreage charge for revenue generation (Michelsen et al. 1999). Suppliers enjoy the revenue stability resulting from meter charges, and overall costs are lowered because meters do not have to be installed or regularly read. Yet the presence of a zero price for water provides a perverse incentive for consumers in light of the value of processed and possibly scarce water, variable operational costs (e.g., energy, treatment chemicals), and the value of the physical capital needed to obtain, store, treat, and deliver this water. For these reasons, both meter installation and meter-reading efforts have been accepted as worthwhile undertakings in most modern systems (Organisation for Economic Co-operation and Development 2003).

The combined application of a water charge and a nonwater charge also coincides with economic recommendations for declining-average-cost industries. In the technical economic literature concerning "two-part tariffs," the dual application of a meter charge and a volumetric charge enjoys extensive theoretical support (Brown, Heller, and Starr 1992; Kahn 1988; Ng and Weisser 1974).

The second significant nonwater charge is the ***connection charge*** that modern utilities place on new connections to the delivery system. Also called a buy-in charge, a tap fee, an impact fee, a hookup fee, and a system development charge, this is a

---

5. Observe, however, that all the basic resource inputs of these industries tend to be priced by the marketplace. When we consider the intrinsic opportunity cost of natural water and begin including it in calculations such as capital intensity per dollar of output, the water industry's rank may change.

one-time fee for each new point of water use, such as a new home (Herrington 1987, 53). Note that this charge applies to new service locations, which is not the same thing as a new client. (An old client can relocate to a new connection.) Once paid, this charge is subsequently capitalized into the value of the new point of use. For example, it is embedded in the cost of a new home.

In water-scarce regions, the forced growth of a water supply system (forced by economic and population development within the service area) can be responsible for sizable increases in water demand. Where is this water to come from, and who should pay for it?[6] New infrastructure will have to be constructed for containing and moving this water, and new infrastructure can be expensive in the modern era. Again, who is to pay for it? If "old" connections are expanding their usage, then it is clear that old connections should pay. To the extent that growing use is due to an expanded number of users, however, the situation is different. Economic doctrine indicates that developers should pay these costs and pass them along to new connection buyers. These added costs are the marginal costs of the new connections and the new homes or businesses, and efficient pricing requires that prospective owners face the correct marginal costs. Absent such a mechanism, new development will have to be subsidized by existing customers, thus causing a breakdown in economic signaling. Growth will occur too fast in water-scarce regions and too slow in water-rich areas. This point looms large when one considers the current locations of the harshest water problems and the long-term role of underpricing in accelerating these problems.

If we embrace the argument, why should existing customers get to enjoy cheap connections just because they were here early? it is equitable for existing connections to share the costs imposed by new connections (Herrington 1987, 53). This equity-based perspective maintains that new connections should not be distinguished from the old ones and that water supply expansion costs should be recovered through volumetric charges on all users (Organisation for Economic Co-operation and Development 1999, 44).[7]

The opposing equity argument is more weighty, however: Why should existing customers have their positions eroded due to an externality imposed on them by new customers who choose to locate in a water-scarce environment? Modern econo-

6. In the western United States, some city utilities require developers to acquire water rights and transfer them to the utility before new connections can be finalized. In locales without such requirements, connection charges amounting to several thousand dollars are not unheard of.

7. Recent Organisation for Economic Co-operation and Development (OECD) literature espouses lumping old and new customers together, but this argument clashes with the "user pays principle" also being supported for the pricing of water by the OECD (1999, 31–32). If the old system is adequate for the old customers, then new customers are the "users" of required system expansions. As a related matter, if new connections are to be owned by long-standing customers who are moving, it should be recognized that moving customers are selling homes that embed value for their service connections.

mies are replete with situations where early resource users are allowed to enjoy "appreciation" of their assets. For example, newcomers pay dearly for land and homes in places where they were once cheap (because they were not very scarce). Foresight in resource use is supported by society as a means to encourage more valued development. Once it is seen clearly, the water supply situation is no different. Hence, connection charges can be said to "add equity to the financing and pricing system" pertaining to water (Raftelis 1993, 73) as well as adding efficiency.

In summary, water *rates* employed by any given supplier might incorporate a volumetric charge for water, a recurring meter charge for every client, and if the service location is a new one, a connection charge. All of these components are justifiable in the sense that they advance economic efficiency. These are the three primary tools of water pricing.

8.2 The Customary Objectives of Rate Setting

One of our tasks is to find out why water is systematically underpriced by suppliers. That water is underpriced is widely evident—quantity demanded frequently exceeds supply (Rogers 2002, 3). Why is this condition prominent? An important answer arises when one examines the objectives pursued in rate-making practice. Some objectives actually promote this outcome, albeit indirectly.

The literature pertaining to rate setting typically identifies multiple goals to be pursued (Boland 1993; Ernst and Young 1992; Herrington 1987). The commonly observed goals are as follows:

Revenue Sufficiency   Enough revenue should be collected to offset all costs.

Economic Efficiency   Rates should maximize water consumers' net benefits or maximize net present value across all water consumers.

Equity and Fairness   Consumers with equivalent characteristics should pay equivalent rates, and rates should be perceived as fair by customers.

Simplicity   Rates should be easily understood by clients.

Legality   Rates should be legally acceptable.

This is not a complete listing of goals appearing in prior literature, but it captures a sufficient number of them. Because each goal injects a unique perspective, there is no single system of rates maximizing every goal for a given supplier. Indeed, each goal may generate a unique rate structure, so there is internal conflict among them. The key issue is whether the nonefficiency goals are sufficiently important to be allowed to foul efficient water use. Hence, they warrant deeper investigation.

Revenue sufficiency is paramount in the mind-set of water supply managers. Managers are understandably interested in "breaking even" and running a financially solvent operation. Moreover, large capital installations are commonly funded by issuing bonds, and interest rates on bonds are sensitive to the financial status of the supplier (which determines their "bond rating"); the greater the ability to generate revenue, the lower the interest rates that are ultimately enjoyed by customers. Concern regarding revenue sufficiency is quite apparent in a periodically updated American Water Works Association (1991, 2000) manual for water utilities. All rates are cost based in these guidelines. Other goals are hardly acknowledged.

An emphasis on revenue sufficiency promotes the idea of average-cost pricing. If the average costs of supplying water are computed and if everyone pays exactly the average cost for every unit of water they consume, then collected revenue will equal total costs. But average-cost pricing is not the same as marginal-cost pricing, so there will be an efficiency loss (proved by a chapter 2 exercise) that is widely acknowledged (Mettner 1997). Ordinarily, average costs are less than marginal costs, so the quantity demanded will be too high with average-cost pricing. Yet revenue sufficiency is a compelling goal. Its importance means that any system of economically efficient rates may have to be adjusted to produce a balanced budget for suppliers. Conceivably, some loss in efficiency is a possible outcome, but careful attention can produce revenue-adequate and highly efficient rates, as we will find later.

Equity and fairness are difficult objectives because they are malleable in practice and mean different things to different people (Jones and Mann 2001). Clarity here can be hard to achieve. For example, one equity precept is that customers causing equal costs for the water supply system should pay equal rates. This seems like a good idea. Some commentators on such a directive may ask if these equal consumers have equal income, though. Such questions inquire about the affordability of water for all consumers, and introduce other perspectives on fairness.

Indeed, there may be a large variety of customer characteristics relevant to the fairness of rates even when these characteristics have no cost impacts not captured by metered water use. Is the customer elderly, on a fixed income, a small start-up business, a relocating firm, living in a wealthy suburb, a member of an indigenous population, the owner of a swimming pool, irrigating valuable citrus or ordinary corn, and so forth? Such considerations have the potential to undo efficient pricing. As an institutionalized example, the U.S. Bureau of Reclamation still performs ability-to-pay analyses of farmers receiving water from its projects, and subsequently limits charges to farmers' ability to pay, thus exacerbating the overuse of water in the western United States (Wahl 1989, 33). The varied potential interpretations of fairness and the injury such issues portend for efficiency renders the general fairness goal quite troublesome. As a consequence, we shall not promote it here. In circumstances where fairness is a critical concern, such as in less-developed countries where access to water is ill developed, efficient pricing may be a premature tactic anyway (see Whittington 2002b for additional ideas).

Simplicity in rate design is commendable from an economic perspective. The idea behind efficient rates is to motivate all consumers to behave efficiently—to consume water up to the point where price is the same as marginal benefits. For this to work, rates must be understandable enough for consumers to know what the price of water is. Uniform rates receive high marks here. Most urban water consumers do not understand more about their bills than what is expressed by the idea that higher consumption causes a higher bill. They do not know the different block prices, the block definitions, or which block they are usually in. Uniform rates inject some degree of proportionality into bills and remove the need to be aware of blocks, thus contributing to the true purpose of economic rate setting.

Legality is a compelling request as well. Suppliers must abide by all laws pertaining to rates. Rates are commonly regulated, and rate changes must be acceptable to oversight agencies. Yet at the level of examination here, it is understood that legal rules may be based on outdated doctrines that are no longer suitable for water management (such as average-cost pricing). Sometimes, then, a good action is to adopt a policy that changes the law.

Given the variety of these objectives, there is ample room for conflicts. Pursuing these objectives jointly will entail trade-offs and compromises (Boland 1993). In the end, some measure of efficiency will often be sacrificed, and water will be systematically underpriced. That is, an important reason for underpricing is the wide range of goals that are blended into the rate-making process. Water managers have often been blamed for this problem, due to their single-minded focus on one goal (revenue sufficiency) and reluctance to depart from traditional ways of pricing.

An especially problematic set of goals in terms of obstructing efficiency is the various visions of equity and fairness. Some perspectives on equity and fairness support efficient pricing, but many do not. In addition, we should understand that average-cost pricing is not the only method for achieving a balanced budget, and we should seek out efficient pricing options that also produce sufficient revenue for a financially solvent operation. We should also become better aware that it is often impossible to design rates that are simultaneously efficient and equitable and so on, regardless of how desirable that outcome would be. It is an unfortunate fact that shortage and scarcity become more likely when efficiency is compromised in favor of other goals.

8.3 Accounting Practice

Insight and respect for the problems of pricing emerge quickly when studying accepted accounting practices for setting water rates. Managers' overriding concern for revenue sufficiency has created a major niche for accounting-based tools and guidance. The abridged procedures reviewed here are more fully developed in the careful descriptions provided by the American Water Works Association (1991,

2000) and Raftelis (1993). These are nice resources for examining the accounting, not economic, basis of water pricing.

A common example of noneconomic accounting is directions to divide costs by the number of service units (especially the volume of water or the number of connections)—that is, average-cost pricing. Average-cost pricing is only economically acceptable when it well approximates the signaling performed by marginal-cost pricing. The approximation is sometimes good, but it should not be presumed. Moreover, there are other paths by which accounting oversights can contribute to water underpricing (Moncur and Fok 1993; Moncur and Pollock 1996). The several problems faced here are challenging, even before accounting advice is modified to improve efficiency.

There are three general steps in rate-making practice, as overviewed in figure 8.2, which is slightly modified from Raftelis's original illustration (1993, 134–135). In step 1, revenue requirements are projected for forthcoming periods. The future costs are estimated, including allowances for the depreciation and replacement of current infrastructure. This can be a demanding task, but it is a required part of rate-making practice, whether water is scarce or not.

The goal of step 2 is to distribute projected costs across various client groups. These groups include not only the sectoral groupings identified in figure 8.2 but also any delineations that are cost relevant. For example, the location or elevation of some customer clusters may impose greater costs, either for specific transmission lines, pumping energy, or water leakage.

A key feature in the traditional practice of this step is to recognize the differing impact of customer classes on supply system capacity, as noted previously. Traditional rate-making practice has therefore allocated system capital costs across user classes while making adjustments for peaking demands. This is one avenue by which decreasing block rates have been justified, although we should remember that suppliers are predisposed to favor decreasing block rates because such a structure stabilizes revenue.

In the final step, rates are "designed" based on the cost allocations of step 2. Responsible groups must incur their allocated costs in some rate form. Note that Raftelis's graphic includes a meter charge and a volumetric water charge, but does not consider the one-time connection charge for new service locations. Design is an apt word for the latter step, but designing truly commences in step 2. There are many choices to be made in terms of "how" rates are to appear, even before the actual quantification takes place. Should multiple blocks be included? Should the meter charge depend on the diameter of the pipe going into each client's location? Should apartment dwellers face the same rates as residents of single-family homes? Should various commercial establishments and industries be distinguished on the basis of their wastewater quality? And so on. Because rate design is limited by the detail sought in step 2, these steps are not purely sequential; some aspects of rate design

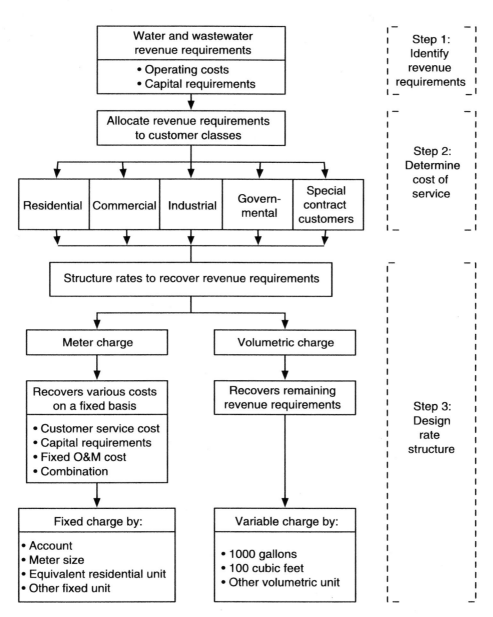

Figure 8.2
Cost of service and rate-setting schematic
Source: Raftelis (1993, 134–135).

must be envisioned so that sufficiently detailed information is available for step 3. There may be some feedback as well. If the rates that are initially resolved during step 3 are different from the current rates, then it is possible that demand will be affected, thereby altering the costs of step 1.

8.4 The Economic Theory of Pricing

The accounting-based process, beginning with the "identify revenue requirements" step, must be more carefully conducted if we are to achieve marginal-cost pricing. With rising scarcity, the old principle of projecting total costs and dividing them by water quantity is a policy failure. Management can and should do better. It is important to determine marginal costs as well as to incorporate scarcity values in price signals to consumers. Interestingly, if retail water were supplied by competitive forces, scarcity would be priced into the final product, but competition is not viable for retail water, so planners must figure this out without market assistance.

There are two sorts of scarcities to attend to here. There is the scarcity of the infrastructural capital used to harness and deliver water, and there is the scarcity of natural water. Either or both may be applicable. In each case, the economic recommendation is to identify marginal costs and incorporate them in rates. The general economic recommendations for the three primary pricing tools are as follows:

1. Growth in water supply infrastructure may be partly spurred by growth in use by existing system connections, but it is largely caused by growth in the number of service connections. Using the methods outlined below, new connection charges should include the marginal costs of harnessing, treating, and transporting the additional water supply. Without this important signal, the location decisions made by agents will be inefficient, with negative implications for water use and conservation.

2. Regardless of whether the rate structure is block or uniform, water price should include the marginal value of water. Such values are not ordinarily full accounting costs for the supplier (as shown in equations [2.30] and [3.14] for surface water and ground water, respectively), but they are the social value of natural water, and efficient use will not be achieved by omitting these values. Furthermore, if these additions are insufficient to offset expensive infrastructure growth (item 1), then this cost is also applicable to existing water users, and including this value in water price has merit too. The summed modifications of water price may be sizable, but they are warranted. In settings where these changes might induce "rate shock," a multiyear phase-in period may be desirable, and the recommendation that follows will have greater significance.

3. An accounting consequence of including natural water value in the price is that rate revenue will tend to exceed the supplier's costs. To eliminate this profit for pub-

licly owned suppliers or to reduce the profit to ordinary levels for privately owned suppliers, the excess revenue can be returned to customers in the form of lowered meter charges. There are other internal options, such as funding water conservation education or conservation devices, but such mechanisms may cost more than they are worth.[8] Strict economic advice should be followed before engaging in such revenue-spending efforts. External outlets such as road improvement or computers for schools may have emotive appeal, but they will often be objectionable on efficiency, equity, or legal grounds.[9]

These principles are sufficiently momentous to warrant closer inspection, including examples. For similar perspectives, see Herrington (1987) and Warford (1997). It is helpful to first revisit a key element of our economic theory now that we have seen that the cost of water provision is not solely dependent on the amount of water supplied.

Adopting a New Vision of Cost Determinants

To begin with, our fundamental economic notion of supply cost determinants needs improvement. The earlier theory maintained that costs are functionally dependent on delivered water amounts. This is deficient and in need of redevelopment. Accounting-based treatments indicate that there are many *fixed* costs of water supply that are, at best, loosely related to how much water is delivered. The clearest case is the large amount of infrastructure that "stands ready" to deliver a wide range of water amounts. While the energy costs of running this infrastructure are well related to the amounts of water passing through it, the costs of maintaining this infrastructure are not. As a more interesting example, all urban water delivery systems experience a certain amount of leakage. This loss of water is a cost. To a large extent, this cost is not functionally determined by the amount of delivered water. Instead, it is functionally determined by the existence of a pressurized, ready-to-serve distribution system of specific extent and character.[10] In unpressurized situations such as irrigation canals, leakage might be better determined by water deliveries.

---

8. Properly priced water induces consumers to adopt worthwhile conservation measures and reject others. Unless a particular mode of conservation is economically efficient for a majority of agents and has not been already adopted by these agents, a subsidy program risks being either unfair to early adopters or inefficient. Still, it is conceivable that many consumers are not aware of advantageous conservation measures, and this may justify conservation education for as long as the program produces net benefits.

9. In terms of efficiency, we do not wish to devote more resources to nonwater activities than maximizes net benefits or net present value. In terms of equity, it is arguably improper to "tax" water users for the purpose of funding nonwater endeavors. For the latter reason, there is now legal guidance prohibiting cross subsidization of utility-provided services in many jurisdictions.

10. It is easy to get misled here. For example, economists and other analysts have often modeled water leakage in urban systems as if it was a function of water use. In the same vein, water managers express water losses as a percentage of metered water deliveries. But in pressurized systems, most leakage will occur even if no one is consuming water, so it is not functionally determined by consumption.

Based on accounting principles and the pricing tools at our disposal, the following cost function is a better choice:

C(# of new connections, water delivered systemwide, # of connections),

or in shorthand

$$C(\Delta N, W, N). \tag{8.1}$$

This representation is more accurate than the one introduced in chapter 2, but it still regards only accounting costs. Consequently, its eventual pricing recommendations must be enhanced.

Pricing New Connections

The crucial question to be answered for assessing the new connection charge is this: For a given number of new connections (such as the 150 new connections expected for a given utility during the coming year), what is the difference between the present values of systemwide capital costs *with* those connections and *without* them? (This is similar to the separable cost determination of the SCRB method considered in chapter 6.) The reason for examining a present value difference is that there may be two kinds of capital costs impacted by the new connections: immediate ones and future ones. Looking only at $\partial C / \partial \Delta N$ from the first period's (8.1) is not a full disclosure of the impacts of the new connections.[11]

In ordinary circumstances, the immediate costs will compose the majority of the present value difference and will be the easiest to estimate. The immediate costs include conveyance capital for new or expanded transmission and distribution lines, new water control or monitoring equipment, new meters and account establishment, new wells or water pumping plants expressly needed for the new connections, and new water acquisitions or development.

In some circumstances, differences in future costs may also be noteworthy, thereby justifying an examination of a present value difference. Future considerations may affect the new connection charge positively or negatively. On the one hand, the addition of these connections will have the tendency to shift forward (sooner) the entire schedule of water development. For example, a renovation of a wastewater treatment plant will now be commenced six years from now instead of seven. Or a canal-lining project will be undertaken next year instead of the following one. On the other hand, all the new capital installed for the new connections is new. Unlike existing facilities and pipelines serving existing connections, the new stuff will last longer and incur less rehabilitation costs in the immediate future, thereby lowering the new connections' financial load on the water supplier, at least for the immediate future.

---

11. This observation dates back at least to Turvey (1969, 290).

Once the present value difference is estimated, it may be acceptable to determine the new connection charge by dividing the difference by the number of new connections. Alternatively, different consumer classes can be legitimately assigned different charges, as is illustrated in the analysis of Lippai and Heaney (2000). It is conceivable, however, that the marginal new connection will have a different impact than the average new connection. Close inspection during the procedures described here should disclose whether average costs might misstate marginal costs significantly. By repeating these computations each year, it should be possible to maintain a suitably accurate new connection charge.

Pricing Water: The Volumetric Component

Maximizing systemwide net benefits subject to a current limit in the availability of renewable water (as in equation [2.26]) while using the new cost function, (8.1), and realizing that agents adjust their use so that their marginal benefits equals the price, the following pricing advice for water is obtained:

$$p = \frac{\partial C}{\partial W} + \lambda = \frac{\partial C}{\partial W} + MVW, \tag{8.2}$$

where λ is the Lagrange multiplier capturing the social value of natural water or the *marginal value of water* (MVW). Equation (8.2) shows how to establish water price in an economic way, as opposed to an accounting way. The two major differences are the evaluation of a derivative rather than an average and the inclusion of water's value in a natural state.

If the water supply originates from a depletable water supply in some manner, such as from ground water or possibly a reservoir containing a tight supply over the next several periods, the appropriate procedure is to set the price so that it maximizes net present value. This was demonstrated by equations (3.13) to (3.15). As compared to (8.2), a similar pricing recommendation emerges for depletable water:

$$p = \frac{\partial C}{\partial W} + \delta_0 = \frac{\partial C}{\partial W} + MUC, \tag{8.3}$$

where δ_0 is the Lagrange multiplier representing the value of in-place water in the current period. In the technical economic literature of depletable resources, δ_0 is known as marginal user cost (MUC) (as discussed in chapter 3). (Remember that this value will grow over time at the rate of discount, according to equation [3.17]. δ_0 was also computed for an example empirical setting in chapter 3.) The marginal user cost is also calculable as the *future value of depletable water discounted to today*. It is most readily obtained through the numerical solution of a dynamic optimization problem, such as that conducted within equations (3.13) to (3.15). An example of this

Box 8.1
Computing New Connection Costs

Big City expects to add twelve hundred connections in the forthcoming year on the southern and eastern edges of the city where several different residential developments are occurring. Eventually, however, the city expects to serve six thousand new connections using the transmission lines and distribution facilities it is undertaking for the upcoming twelve hundred connections. Hence, it is sizing facilities for the six thousand rather than the twelve hundred. While most of the new connections are single-family homes, some are multiunit dwellings and some constitute light commerce (restaurants, gas stations, etc.). The utility's tradition is to capture the different loading tendencies of different sectors by using a block rate structure, and the utility has decided to continue with this approach. The three developing areas on the eastern side are more expensive to serve due to an environmentally sensitive area that must be traversed by a long transmission main. All of the new facilities will be internally financed from the existing rate revenue, but the costs will prohibit accelerated retirement of the utility's issued bonds. The utility is paying on several issues of bonds, which originated in different years with different effective interest rates. Were it not for these expansion projects, the most costly bonds would be retired first and their interest cost is 6 percent annually.

Analysis

The distinctions present here require that the analysis be partitioned. All of these developments require transmission facilities, but the eastern ones are $400,000 more expensive than the others. Since this $400,000 is an immediate cost and will serve two thousand connections, new connection charges in this area must be $200 greater than the others. This $200 is an average cost, rather than a marginal cost, but location decision making by new households should be little affected by the distinction.

Big City resolves new connection charges using a ten-year planning horizon unless there are outstanding reasons for extending the time frame. The capacity expansion plan with and without the six thousand connection developments are given by the second and fourth columns of the following table. All units are expressed as thousands of dollars.

Year	With costs	Present value	Without costs	Present value	Change
0	$38,000	$38,000	$27,000	$27,000	$11,000
1	$29,000	$27,358	$27,000	$25,472	$1,887
2	$30,000	$26,700	$30,000	$26,700	$0
3	$32,000	$26,868	$32,000	$26,868	$0
4	$64,000	$50,694	$64,000	$50,694	$0
5	$58,000	$43,341	$58,000	$43,341	$0
6	$38,000	$26,789	$38,000	$26,789	$0
7	$38,000	$25,272	$38,000	$25,272	$0
8	$58,000	$36,390	$39,000	$24,469	$11,921
9	$56,000	$33,146	$72,000	$42,617	−$9,470
				Total:	$13,352

The $400,000 in extra expenses for the east-side transmission line is omitted from the data because only its beneficiaries will repay this sum. The present value columns contain the present value of the immediately leftward column, using a 6 percent discount rate and the appropriate number of years.

Box 8.1
(continued)

> The key information is in the rightmost column, which is the difference between with and without present values. Accordingly, a $13,352,000 increase in costs is the result of increased service for six thousand connections, and these new connections are jointly responsible for the increased capital costs. Efficiency dictates that these new costs be collected from these connections. Spread equally across the six thousand enabled connections, the new connection charge is $2,556 with a $200 surcharge for the east side. Alternatively, rather than allocating the increase equally, it might be allotted differently, such as by the type of use (commercial, residential) or the meter size in an effort to better reflect differential capital causes. Note that charges for forty-eight hundred connections will not be collected until the future, thus warranting a 6 percent increase per year in the $2,556 (or like) figure. This is justifiable because Big City management is taking advantage of an economic opportunity. If it does not provide for the forty-eight hundred future connections now (by "oversizing" transmission and distribution), they will be even more expensive when they are requested.

Box 8.2
Obtaining the MVW in the Presence of a Water Market

> Some of the expenses that Big City is incurring in box 8.1 are for water rights. The city's continuing preference has been to purchase rather than lease these rights. Presently, the market value of reasonably senior rights is approximately $2,000 per acre-foot. How should Big City price its delivered water in the interest of motivating efficient use and appropriate conservation?
>
> **Analysis**
>
> The fact that the city's purchase of these rights (and previous rights) may have been recouped through new connection charges is of no consequence to metered water rates. The retention of these rights exacts an opportunity cost (they could be released and sold), so *all* of the city's inventory of water rights has a value indicated by the current market value. These water rights are nondepreciating assets. An infinitely lived asset worth $2,000 per acre-foot has an annual value of $113.21 per acre-foot (applying a 6 percent discount rate), which is equivalent to 35¢ per thousand gallons. (Use equation [3.26] of the chapter 3 appendix and the unit conversions preceding chapter 1.) Hence, 35¢ per thousand gallons should be added to the calculated cost of service as long as no natural water costs are accounting costs used to calculate the cost of service. Regardless of whether the rate structure is uniform or block, this MVW should be applied to all users and blocks. If marginal conveyance losses are nonzero, the 35¢ figure should be increased appropriately.

sort of work, with a focus on identifying MUC, is that performed by Moncur and Pollock (1988). Another real-world example will be shown in chapter 11.

For mixed water supplies that are simultaneously employing both ground water and surface water, the pricing recommendations of (8.2) and (8.3) should be equivalent (Griffin 2001, 1345).

As a third, economically driven revision of water pricing, it is entirely possible and potentially desirable that there will be time spans in which water supply infrastructure will be inadequate to provide the quantity demanded, even under the prior pricing advice. This will be particularly apparent for growing water suppliers faced with large capital costs of expansion. Recall that capital investments in water supply should be timed so that they achieve dynamic efficiency. That is, we should be timing expansion so as to maximize net present value.[12] Building facilities too early sacrifices net present value and should be avoided.

Water supply systems tend to grow in spurts to take advantage of "scale economies" at the time of construction. Once underway, it is often inexpensive to enlarge things a bit. Thought of simply, "When you're digging the ditch, it doesn't cost much more to lay a bigger pipe in it." Hence, when the next expansion is undertaken, excess capacity will exist for a while, until additional demand growth exhausts this capacity and calls for the next expansion. The timing of these periodic expansions may have significant implications for the net benefits that clients receive from their supply system because these expansions are capital intensive and expensive. Put another way, delaying a project by a single year saves the system a value equal to the lump-sum cost of the project times the cost of borrowing funds.[13] The latter term is usually indicated by the rate paid on bonds.

Following the economically recommended schedule of investment may then cycle the water supply system through times of plenty (excess capacity) as well as shortage (fully employed capacity). During the latter periods, the quantity demanded may outstrip the quantity supplied. In these restricted times, there is a need to efficiently ration the limited capacity of the system. Economic advice is to increase the water price by an amount called the ***marginal capacity cost*** (MCC):

$$p = \frac{\partial C}{\partial W} + MCC. \tag{8.4}$$

MCC's inclusion will exactly balance supply and demand, and it will cause limited water to go to its most valued uses. Indeed, the recommendations of MCC-inclusive pricing and optimal project timing or "stalling" go hand in hand because optimal scheduling over time is dependent on optimal allocation within each period. Any failure on one side of this arrangement will perturb optimal action on the other side. Because MCC emerges from the desire to achieve efficient scheduling of *future* expansions, it is "forward-looking" and not illuminated by past accounting costs made for water supply capacity (Turvey 1976, 158). A numerical example of using MCC to stall investment and thereby achieve an economic gain is presented by Jones et al. (1984, 18–21).

---

12. Recall that this is a stricter criterion than requiring dynamic improvements (i.e., NPV > 0).

13. For example, if the applicable bond rate is 4 percent (in real, inflation-deducted terms) and a $20 million project can be delayed with no increase in completion costs other than inflation, the cost savings will be $800,000. It does not matter much if this is a multiyear construction effort; all expenditures are delayed one year. If this delay does not cost the beneficiaries more than $800,000 in lost benefits (using chapter 5's techniques), this is a welcome delay.

Box 8.3
Finding MVW or MCC to Balance Demand with Supply

Little Town is experiencing an unexpected shortfall in water supply as a consequence of a well collapse. While two remaining wells are fully operational, it's now August, and water is in high demand. It will take one month to complete and link a pipeline to a neighboring community that is willing to sell their surplus surface water supply at cost. Eventually, new deep wells can be drilled. In the interim, Little Town's capacity to produce water must be allocated as best it can. With an normal August quantity demanded of 100 million gallons, the community must get by on 70 million with its two wells operating continuously.

Analysis

This situation is not economically different from a climatic abnormality causing demanded quantity to exceed available supply. Most communities faced with this situation will embark on emergency rationing measures, beginning with heavy restrictions on outdoor water use. This type of policy can work, but it neglects the differential preferences of people and therefore does not dedicate water to its most valued uses. It also involves enforcement costs. Some people attach a high value to specific outdoor uses, while other people have little regard for their outdoor use. Some indoor and commercial uses have slight value (as long as pricing encourages their continuation). A more efficient option is to handle the shortfall through pricing. Little Town uses a summer rate of $4 per thousand gallons. If demand elasticity is gauged to be -0.6, then a 30 million gallon demand response (30 percent) requires a 50 percent increase in price. The new rate of $6 should be well publicized so that consumers can rethink their water use activities. This path has the extra advantage of yielding additional revenue for the corrective expenditures that are planned and also distributing the expense on the basis of customers' water valuations.

Interestingly, because the situation involves scarce capital (two wells), the additional $2 is called MCC. If the situation were one of scarce water and ample capital, the analysis and results would be unchanged, but we would call the $2 MVW.

An interesting aspect of marginal capacity cost is its movement over time (Dandy, McBean, and Hutchinson 1985). It can go up or down from year to year, unlike MVW and MUC, which tend to strictly increase over time. During periods of restricted supply and growing demand, MCC will steadily rise from one year to the next, but it drops on completion of each supply enhancement. Some thought has been devoted to finding ways of smoothing year-to-year variations in MCC (Swallow and Marin 1988; Beecher, Mann, and Landers 1991), but to do so defeats efficiency somewhat. Combined with the prior findings, we conclude with the following advice for economic pricing:

$$p = \frac{\partial C}{\partial W} + MVW + MCC \quad \text{or} \quad p = \frac{\partial C}{\partial W} + MUC + MCC. \tag{8.5}$$

The first equation of (8.5) applies for renewable water, and the second applies for depletable water. If natural water is not scarce, then MVW and MUC will be zero. If the supplier is operating with excess capacity, then MCC will be zero. If there is constrained infrastructural capacity yet the inclusion of natural water value (MVW or MUC) in price reduces the quantity of water demanded, then MCC will be reduced—to zero, if excess capacity is created by the demand response.

These recommendations, especially the ones pertaining to water value, presume the normal scenario in which there are little to zero accounting costs relating to natural water costs embedded in $C(\Delta N, W, N)$. In some urban settings, occasional water market purchases or ground water ranching activities mean that this is untrue. Consequently, *some* of the natural water used by the supplier may be properly priced to end consumers. The dictates of efficient pricing means that *all* delivered water in these jurisdictions should include a natural water value (Howe 1993, 5), but we do not endorse double counting. So some care must be exercised. Suitable practice is illustrated by box 8.2, which also demonstrates the great advantage of water marketing in disclosing water's regional value.

Should efficient pricing policy be markedly different than existing policy, implementation of (8.5) can be progressively approached over a period of years. As water suppliers ramp toward water prices that include 100 percent of opportunity costs, consumers should be able to transition more smoothly. Other benefits of phasing may be that water managers can gain information about demand responses and may be better able to achieve prices that balance marginal benefits and marginal costs with less under- or overshooting of the estimated opportunity costs in (8.5).

Pricing Existing Connections: The Meter Charge

The final water rate component to be determined is the meter charge. A purely economic recommendation is to charge ongoing connections on the basis of what they cost at the margin—that is, $\partial C/\partial N$. This will implicitly include obvious account-related costs such as meter reading and billing as well as a portion of the administration and distribution costs. Still, there is a low-cost opportunity to sidestep this advice and thereby achieve a balanced budget for the supplier. That is, revenue sufficiency can be achieved with little loss in efficiency. This is an especially important opportunity in light of pricing recommendations for new connections and metered water, which can lead to excess revenue. That's most apparent when water prices include opportunity costs for which there are no corresponding accounting costs.

The meter charge recommended here is obtained as estimated costs minus estimated revenues (including volumetric charges) and divided by the number of active connections/accounts.[14] The costs can include some amount of acceptable profit for privately owned water suppliers. In extreme circumstances involving high MVW/

---

14. It is possible and perhaps desirable to refine this approach. For example, differentiating connections on some basis, such as sector, is economically acceptable as long as the distinguishing feature is not driven by water use. For example, basing the proration of excess revenue on the basis of water use would undo the incentives created for water-using behavior.

MUC/MCC, it is conceivable that the meter charge will become negative. Such an anomaly, however, does not present problems in application or results.

Overall, the advantages of this approach are that:

• revenue sufficiency is achieved;

• the potential financial burden of efficient, scarce-water pricing on consumers is off-set in full or part, depending on each consumer's water use;

• consumers are treated as shareholders in that they have a claim to the net benefits produced by the water supply system;

• low-income consumers, who are typically low water users, may have lower bills as compared to traditional pricing methodology.

Given that this system draws more of its revenue from volumetric charges and less from meter charges, the potential disadvantages are that:

• consumers should become better educated about their water-using behavior and how their bills are computed;

• high water users will see larger overall water bills.

One may ask, What's the point of charging more for water, but giving the money back with a different element of the rate structure? Indeed, there is no point if consumers do not understand billing methodology. But if water price is higher and people understand that, then they will attempt to adjust their water-using activities appropriately. After all, they are not getting *their* money back; they are receiving their share of the *system's* surplus.

There can be an "income effect" associated with modifications to the meter charge. If more efficient water rates entail lower meter charges as well as higher water price, then the reduction in meter charges is equivalent to an increase in consumer income. If a portion of the income increases are spent on water, then water demand is increased, thus partially offsetting the reduction in the quantity demanded. Available evidence is that the *income elasticity* of water demand is positive, yet too low to have much impact (Dalhuisen et al. 2003). Economic theory tells us that the positive income effect cannot be as large as the negative price effect. Nevertheless, it can be appropriate to account for the income effect when resolving efficient water rates. Whereas it is still efficient to return the rewards of better pricing with reduced meter charges, a slightly larger increase in water prices may be necessary to offset the income effect.

8.5 Specifying Seasonal Volumetric Rates

Having laid out the fundamentals, the high economic functionality and popularity of seasonal rates merits a deeper explanation. Only the volumetric component of rates

Box 8.4
Pricing Scarce Water in a Water-Marketing Irrigation District

In today's scarce-water environment, the Grain Irrigation District (GID) sees an opportunity in the possibility of leasing its water to a town downriver. The individual members of GID do not own explicit water rights because those rights are officially held by the district. Still, the members would like to reap some benefits from the appreciating water assets owned by GID. Leasing seems most practical because it is a temporary commitment that can be discontinued if the experiment misfires. Because the idea of distributing membership "dividends" for the leasing of water is too novel, the district's board of directors has decided to use the lease receipts to refurbish some aged, leaky canals during the off-season and lower members' water rates in the immediate season. The agreed lease arrangement is that the district will receive $50 per acre-foot for 10 percent of its water supply of 250,000 acre-feet. $1,000,000 of this single-year income of $1,250,000 will be allocated to the renovation project, and the remainder will simply be revenue. GID wishes to update this season's water rates to take advantage of the new income and motivate members to make good use of their 90 percent water supply. The benchmark for this season's rates is given by last year's rates: $40 per acre and $4 per acre-foot. Last year, 130,000 acres were irrigated by GID's members, and they used 260,000 acre-feet in a high snowpack year in which an abundant water supply was predictable. This year's mountain snowpack appears to be far less promising, which is why the town wishes to shore up its water supply using the water market.

Analysis

First, it is recommended that the renovation project be subjected to economic inquiry. This project should be rejected unless it has a positive NPV for the district. There's no use spending money just because some of it is laying around. Assuming it is a sound investment, the membership's total water bills must be lowered by $250,000 to offset the new revenue. That action will induce a high number of irrigated acres, but quantity demanded must be no higher than 225,000 acre-feet.

As one approach, the new lease arrangement identifies a $50/af water value rather than a $4/af one. If the rate is raised to $50, however, farmers may be likely to forgo irrigation this year. Moreover, if an open market existed here—one where individual farmers possessed individual water rights—more water would exchange hands at a reduced price. Hence, $50 is not a believable marginal value in this case.

To generate a more viable approach, we can assume high acreage this season, perhaps as great as last season. That is, the rate subsidy produced by the infusion of $250,000 can spur an elevated number of irrigated acres. Perhaps it is best to presume that there will be 130,000 acres and then resolve a volumetric price that is consistent with a total use of 225,000 af. Using last season as a starting place, and assuming a demand elasticity of -0.8, the volumetric rate must increase by $0.67. [(35/260)/0.8 times $4.] Last year, the volumetric component produced $1,040,000 for GID. With the changes, it is expected to produce $1,050,750 this year. With the $250,000 in lease revenue, the $10,750 in extra volumetric revenue, and $70,000 in saved pumping costs, GID can break even by lowering the acreage fee by $2.54. (Sum the three increases and divide by 130,000.) Hence, an arguably good rate pair is $37.50 per acre and $4.67 per acre-foot. To help generate efficient behavior, it is even a good idea to offer $2.54 per acre to producers who decline to irrigate this season.

The analyst can be reasonably confident about every aspect of this work except the presumed demand elasticity, which is a key element. Given the immediately available information, it is difficult to be comfortable about the true rate responses of these irrigators. Relative to typical values of agricultural water, $4.67/af is still a low rate, so demand elasticity may be low in this region of the demand function. Therefore, sensitivity analysis should be performed by repeating the analysis with other feasible elasticities (to see how much error there may be in being wrong), and additional information may be pursued for this important parameter (survey some farmers before the season starts?).

is useful to vary seasonally. There is not a significant seasonal change in scarcity that can be signaled by a new connection charge (which is long-run in computation) or a meter charge.

As with the base rates just discussed, it is useful to start with the accounting costs. In the summer, $\partial C / \partial W$ is greater. It can be seen and predicted which system elements are useful only during the summer. These costs should be allocated to the summer months. They should not be merely averaged across expected summer water deliveries; there should be attention given to whether the last unit of summer water —the marginal one—is more expensive than the average one. This may well be the case if the marginal unit of water is more expensive to procure. If there are dynamic aspects to this inspection, then it is advisable to conduct an analysis like the one recommended for calculating the new connection charge.[15] Find the difference between all costs' present value in with- and without-summer-months scenarios. The extra costs are attributable to summer water use and should be embedded in its rates. Having done all this, it is still possible that system capacity or available water is too deficient to meet quantity demanded. In such cases, which are more likely during summer months, the summer water price should be augmented by MCC or one of the natural water values (MVW or MUC), as appropriate.

8.6 Wastewater Charges: A Complication

Often, water-supplying utilities and districts are also responsible for treating the wastewater effluent that is emitted by water-using agents. This is especially true in urban settings. Irrigation districts may also undertake improvements and encounter variable costs for the disposal of irrigation return flows, however, so wastewater costs can be applicable to irrigation as well. The primary features of water pricing carry over to wastewater pricing in that it may be sensible to apply three distinct charges to every agent: a volumetric charge for the amount of wastewater discharged, a recurring fixed charge for each service period, and a start-up fee for defraying the capital costs of initial service.

The interesting complication presented by wastewater is that it is difficult to measure the load that individual agents place on the wastewater management system. The return flow of irrigation can be diffuse (also called "nonpoint"), thereby frustrating measurement. In urban environments, sewage emissions flow into unpressurized pipes and are conveyed from the point of emission by a gravity-dependent process into the collection lines of the wastewater authority. Agent-specific measurement of

---

15. The examples are numerous. A new well might only be employed during the next three summers, but population growth may cause it to be used every winter starting four years from now.

emission volumes or weights is sufficiently difficult (though technically feasible) that it is not economically practical. Because pricing wastewater services is contingent on measuring wastewater emissions, there is a problem to be overcome. We wish to price something that cannot be individually monitored.

For these reasons, wastewater treatment authorities have adopted the practice of inferring wastewater loads from metered water consumption. Such indirect measurement of wastewater is not a perfect system, but it remains the preferred option. Under the theory of "whatever goes in must come out," this appears to be a good system. But there are at least three issues:

1. In urban settings, a large amount of water might be used outdoors and would therefore not enter the sewage system. This is especially true during summer months when lawn and landscape irrigation takes place. During the summer, other outdoor water-using activities might be elevated as well (car washing, pool use). Since these water uses do not burden the wastewater system, it would be improper to charge a wastewater fee for them.

2. There are wastewater loads that do not originate from metered water consumption, such as occurs when urban agents purposefully channel their roof or drain gutters into the sewage system.

3. The wastewater discharges of agents are heterogeneous in terms of water quality. When different agents are emitting different water-borne contaminants, they are imposing different demands and costs on the waste treatment system. This can be especially problematic when varied commercial or industrial establishments are issuing varied contaminants. Charging for wastewater service on the basis of metered water use will not capture these differences (Rogers 2002, 14).

Addressing these problems presents a challenge that can be partially met. A substantial correction for outdoor water use can be accomplished by employing the *winter-averaging method* for pricing residential sewerage services. In this now-popular practice, metered water use over consecutive winter months (e.g., November, December, and January) is averaged for each agent, and the agent's rest-of-year sewer bills are based on this average. This procedure excludes the extra-outdoor water consumption due to outdoor water use during nonwinter months.

The remaining two issues have not been handled as satisfactorily.

Options for pricing storm waters channeled into sewers are available, but they are rarely pursued and the normal approach is to ban such activity. For example, knowing measured roof area and local precipitation allows easy computation of wastewater load. But water suppliers may not be aware of which clients are doing this, and there is sure to be conflict over the institution of drainage prices, especially when the current price is zero. Phasing in such a rate is possible and justifiable in areas where waste treatment costs warrant it. Otherwise, agents may be enjoying a service and receiving benefits that are less than the socially incurred costs (implying an inefficiency).

Options for the differential effluent pricing for different agents depend on the authority's ability to distinguish these agents by classifying them or quantitatively evaluating their wastewater quality. Classification by business type might be feasible if the utility can acquire such information inexpensively. Alternatively, it may be practical to "spot check" effluent quality periodically and levy a volumetric charge consistent with the treatment costs. Quality parameters can include characteristics "such as biological oxygen demand (BOD), chemical oxygen demand (COD), suspended solids (SS), ammonia, and phosphorus" (Raftelis 1993, 179).

8.7 Summary

Of all the tools available for solving water scarcity, better pricing is the most under-utilized relative to its potential. Establishing better pricing is a serious goal, and its complexities require serious effort. There are three elements of the rate structure that are both crucial and interdependent. One of these is the volumetric price of water. The other two are the new connection charge and the recurring meter charge.

Although we overviewed the accounting-based work that is fundamental to rate setting without going into great detail, this work is pivotal for finding scarcity-appropriate rates. In the interest of achieving efficiency in water use, the economic revisions of accounting methods are to emphasize marginal supply costs and incorporate natural water values in the volumetric rate component. Both improvements are important, and the latter one is a key economic prescription. Natural water values include the values of renewable (surface) water and depletable (ground) water. The first is termed the marginal value of water and the second is termed marginal user cost. They are equivalent in application and different in computational origin (efficiency versus dynamic efficiency). In addition, if there is scarcity associated with some element(s) of water supply infrastructure, then a third value should be part of rates. It is called marginal capacity cost. Properly computed and included, these additions solve water-scarcity conditions by motivating appropriate conservation.

The new connection charge is an important component of modern rate structures because it helps recover significant costs from causal agents and contributes crucial signaling. The message of this component will vary from area to area depending on intrinsic scarcities, both of water and infrastructure. Where scarcities are lower, the signal to potential new agents will be more inviting. Where scarcities are high, the message will be an incentive to locate elsewhere. This instrument can make an important contribution in a world of varying water scarcity. It is a valuable service to urge people and businesses to locate where resources are least scarce. Moreover, it is important for the overall economy that the output prices of water-using businesses reflect the full costs of production, including natural water.

As counseled here, the meter charge serves as a budget-balancing measure. Whereas the typical formulation of rates—driven by the revenue sufficiency goal—does not signal water scarcity or achieve economic efficiency, smart use of the meter charge can support both efficiency and revenue sufficiency objectives. This is not a traditional use of meter charges, but it is endorsed by contemporary instances of water scarcity. The recommended modifications of the two other rate elements will often cause revenue to exceed the water supplier's accounting costs, so we require a sound method of dissipating this excess in a manner not harmful to efficiency. Lowering the meter charge is a simple approach to this problem. Many consumers do not understand how their bills are formulated. Hence, a crucial requirement in all of these prescriptions is to educate consumers. Bill computation should be lucid in all cases.

While the impact of these ideas depends on the starting place—what rates are now in each locale—the overall affect is to raise net benefits above current levels. The policy analysis methods of chapter 5 warrant application to each case, to gauge the net gains and possibly who wins and who loses. The usual situation will be that the average client gains while large water users experience larger water bills. Overall, once the policy implications of better pricing are well comprehended, the majority of clients should be supportive. Moreover, many of those who will pay more will also be supportive if they can be assured there is sound science underlying the changes.

8.8 Exercises

1. Invent and diagram (as in figure 8.1) a completely specified multiblock rate structure. Or contact a water utility to obtain theirs. (If the utility's rate structure is uniform, get wastewater charges too.) You must provide both a clear diagram and a corresponding equation for bill computation. The equation should include a particular meter charge.

2. The Southern Irrigation District (SID) enjoys a 365-day growing season, but it has no storage facilities to use in conjunction with its surface water rights. SID's water rights are correlative and entitle the district to 20 percent of the river flow throughout the year. Water rights are owned by the nonprofit district, not the owners of the 10,000 acres in its fixed service area. The district funds its operations using a $15 per acre annual assessment on all acreage, irrigated or not, and a $10 per acre-foot charge on metered water deliveries (currently 28,000 af/yr). Assume no conveyance losses.

There is an active regional water market among private, water-owning agents and towns. SID does not participate in this market. Summer water is leasing at $163 per acre-foot whereas there is no market interest in winter water rights.

Can you recommend policy revisions that would be welcomed by typical land-owners? Attempt to integrate proper terminology into your suggestions. Be as specific as possible.

3. Ground water is being depleted so rapidly in Highflat County that the economic merits of an expensive, yet unbuilt surface water project are rapidly getting better. The Shallow Reservoir project still has a negative net present value, however (no incommensurables or intangibles are relevant). Careful analysis indicates that at the current pace of change, Shallow Reservoir will pass a cost-benefit test in another five years, when project costs will be $15,000 (real, current dollars) per perpetual acre-foot of natural, undelivered water. The optimal time to build Shallow Reservoir is calculated to be in ten years, when project costs will be $16,000 per perpetual acre-foot. Can you make a specific recommendation for a beneficial action to occur this year? What effects will this policy have on the future project and why?

4. Due to local political interventions, a growing town cannot establish efficient connection charges. Growth-driven production costs are recovered through water rates. The current policy is to annualize capital costs over ten years at an 8 percent real discount rate. These costs are then assigned to each of the ten years. Recovery is made via increases in volumetric water rates using average-cost pricing. Because the town has different winter and summer rates, analysts applying this averaging process pay attention to capital's relative use across seasons.

Counting the associated permitting costs and linkage capital, a new well to be installed next year will cost $200,000. During the first five years, this well will only be used during the summer (in progressively larger amounts). Demand will be sufficient for the well to be partially used during the winter of year 6 as well as all summer. Commencing in year 10, the well will be in full-time winter operation.

a. Undertake the steps you can to resolve rate changes for next year. Explain the additional steps and the needed information. If nothing else changes, how will rates change in year 2?

b. List and explain the opportunities you see for accomplishing a more efficient pricing policy.

5. Drycreek Suburb is fully utilizing its available water supply. There is neither a shortage nor any surplus. Prospects for an increase in water supply are quite poor because cities in the region have obtained all water rights except those dedicated to environmental uses. There have been no problems with the fixed water supply, for the suburb has had a constant population for many years. Drycreek operates its own water utility. At the present time, utility revenues match costs exactly, as long

as the utility continues to exclude water right values from its accounting costs. The utility currently serves ten thousand connections receiving two billion gallons annually. Each of these ten thousand clients pay a monthly meter charge of $30 and a uniform rate of $2 per thousand gallons. Demand elasticity is thought to be in the -0.4 to -0.6 range.

Development interests are willing to convert some neighboring desert into a residential area if Drycreek will annex the property. If this happens, the utility must serve an additional one thousand connections without an increase in natural water supply. Developers have offered to separately pay for all necessary new capital, including all additions and improvements for storage, pumping, treatment, and conveyance. The additional property tax base is somewhat attractive to Drycreek, so leaders are contemplating the proposal.

a. If a new rate structure is the only approach for coping with the expanded number of clients, what are your quantitative recommendations for it? Explain your work.

b. Apply appropriate techniques to measure the impact of this development on existing consumers. (Hint: First decide which policy type from chapter 5 this is.)

9 Demand Analysis

How do we obtain marginal benefit functions?

The preceding chapters underscore the serious role that water demand plays in scarcity, policy and project analysis, markets, and pricing. For these reasons, it is often desirable to estimate water demand. The word estimate is good to keep in mind, for demand is not known with certainty until it is actually here, and even then only the *quantity demanded* will be revealed. Hence, the rest of the demand function, which might have occurred if different conditions or prices were in place, will not have been unveiled by agent action. So evidence about the full demand function arises bit by bit. Evidence trickles in as human behavior is observed through measurement. The observed quantity demanded provides knowledge about the true nature of water demand, but the disclosure of demand can be slow relative to planners' desire for it.

In some cases, even human choices pertaining to water demand are not well revealed. A common example is the water that gets used by people while it is still in a watercourse (for recreation, scenery, fishing). In such cases, people "use" whatever water is there, without paying for it or deciding how much water to put in the watercourse. So little demand information is readily apparent in these situations. Most of these cases arise when water takes on *public good* attributes. Recall from section 4.3 that the economic definition of public good is not based on ownership. It occurs when a water use possesses the technical characteristics of *nonrivalness* and *nonexclusiveness*. Also, remember that the distinction between whether water is being used rivally or nonrivally affects the technique for adding the demand of individual agents or sectors to arrive at total demand (see section 2.8).

The end result of these several considerations and complications is that water demand is never fully known, no matter whether water is being used as a private or public good. But demand can be well estimated if the appropriate methods are followed. To learn about demand-estimation methodology, one must delve more deeply into the realm of applied economics.

Earlier, the water demand functions of single producer or consumer agents were observed to be functionally dependent on many economic variables, especially the price of water. This allows us to write it as w = D(p; ...) as in equations (2.7) and (2.10). Or it can be drawn in two-dimensional water-price space (figures 2.4 and 2.6) if we can pretend that all other determinants are fixed for the sake of highlighting the price relationship. The reason for emphasizing price is not to say that other factors, such as climate or population, are less significant determinants or irrelevent. The reason is to take advantage of price's role in scarcity management, policy analysis, and project analysis. Knowing how demand depends on price enables useful instruments and important analyses pertaining to water scarcity. These are some of the crucial items that economics brings to the water management table, but they cannot be completely enjoyed until demand's relation to price is first discovered.

The demand function can also be inverted, or solved for p, so that p is on the left-hand side of the equation. The custom is to replace p with MB to explicitly acknowledge that marginal benefits have been identified: $MB = D^{-1}(w; ...)$. This function can be called the marginal benefits function or the demand function because both forms contain identical information. If price is absent, then it is improper to claim that *demand* has been estimated. In such unhappy circumstances, one is confined to terms like quantity demanded, use, "needs," or requirements. The latter two terms are especially unfortunate as they cultivate a misinterpretation of the scarcity issue, but all four terms limit the sorts of management advice that can be generated.

9.1   Demand Is More Demanding Than Value

The form of the marginal benefit function makes it clear that we require a "schedule" of how MBs change as water use changes. Hence, it is typically deficient to only know the total benefits of a given level of water use. For example, it might be analytically determined that recreationists on a given lake value their aggregate, water-based experiences at $1 million annually, to the credit of the lake. In this case, we know only the total value of the total amount of water in the lake. While this information may have been costly to obtain (because such research is not cheap), it does not help water management very much. Unless we are contemplating the elimination of this lake or its original construction where there is no lake, knowing a total value is not particularly helpful.

Similarly, knowing a single marginal value does not enable the same level of managerial power as does knowing the function. For instance, we might observe that water is generally leasing for $60 per acre-foot in a vibrant regional water market in which lots of water rights are being transferred. That's great evidence that the marginal benefits of water under current supply and demand conditions is $60, at least to those involved in trade.[1] But if we are contemplating a policy measure that will substantially alter supply or demand, how are we to do the type of analyses recommended in chapter 5? We need functions for that, not points. The same is true of project analysis.

In the published literature there are ample reviews of the marginal value of water in different sectors. When considering such data it becomes easy to gloss over the fact that the marginal value of water is not really a constant. It changes. Not only does it change over time but it changes as water use in a given application changes. As always, marginal benefits are functionally dependent on w. The same is true of instream uses as well (Gillilan and Brown 1997, 104–109).

If it can be determined how the total or marginal benefits vary with water use, then we are onto something quite useful. Knowing B(w) or B(w; other things) allows differentiation to determine MB(w), and of course integration allows us to reverse course to get B(w) from MB(w). Hence, total benefit information can be obtained from the right marginal benefit information and vice versa. This enables all kinds of helpful decision making.

For example, if the marginal benefits schedule/function for lake water is known, then allocative and scale questions can be addressed: "How much water should be maintained in the lake this summer versus creating hydropower with some of it and/or releasing it for irrigation or retention in a downstream reservoir for recreation there?" That is, the efficient use of water can be well examined. It also becomes practical to answer questions about the value of each unit of water: "Given that there is X units of water flowing into the lake this month and Y units discharging, leaking, and evaporating, what is an appropriate lease value for a fifty acre-foot addition?" Or we could assess the value of a dam-raising project that would add to the lake size. While these are merely examples, addressing most of the interesting questions necessitates demand information for all the relevant parties/sectors.

9.2 The "Requirements" Approach

There is a long history of interest in water demand estimation, but most so-called demand projections do not succeed because they lack economic literacy. The well-rutted tradition of water resource planning is to project water resource "requirements" instead of demand. Unlike true demand, requirements do not embed scarcity-sensitive parameters, which is increasingly erroneous in light of the growing

1. It is also possible that other factors or traditions are guiding price formation and that market prices are not a good indicator of marginal benefits (Young 1996, 28). Further inspection by well-informed analysts is still useful (Ward and Michelsen 2002).

scarcity of infrastructural capacity as well as water scarcity. To be successful, demand must be perceived as value/scarcity sensitive. As reported in response to "need"-based terminology (see section 2.3), a great deal of water use occurs in low-value applications or is discretionary in some sense, *and* water policy and projects do not contribute to basic human needs for water (with the possible exception of developing-country settings). As a consequence, terms such as needs and requirements are inaccurate, and the extension of these terms to water management fails to illuminate the real issues.

In the misguided requirements approach to demand estimation, analysts project the amounts of water to be used by individual agents or sectoral agent groups, typically *without accounting for rising scarcity*. Even when variable scarcity is eyed, analysts usually produce high, baseline, and low scenarios, or offer a "conservation" scenario in which less water is to be used if some nebulous package of water-saving measures is enacted. This demand projection methodology is ordinarily driven by population growth and, sometimes, exogenous growth in economic activity. Finally, all the water requirements of various sectors are summed to "find out" what has actually been *assumed*: "future demand is greater than supply," inferring that supply must be increased. The result is an assumed one because water use behavior is projected without accounting for rising scarcity.

Economists have long been critical of the requirements approach, in part because it blocks off half the equation for managing scarcity. The only envisioned option is to increase the water supply. "By using these 'requirements' forecasts, the water manager's range of choice is artificially constrained and water resources can be misallocated. This is clearly seen by realizing that the use of a requirements forecast forces water planners to consider only the supply side of demand-supply relationships. They assume that the demand is given, and consider only adjusting supply to meet this demand" (Davis and Hanke 1971, p. 3-2). Given that there are two classes of scarcity strategies—supply enhancement and demand management—and given that we may wish to choose from both groupings for the sake of advancing efficiency, it is misleading to omit the demand side. Moreover, the omitted side contains the information needed to assess the benefits of any additions to supply.[2] Sticking with the requirements approach is always easier for analysts because it requires less information, but it also constrains management options. Such restraints are problematic in the new era of water scarcity. Traditional choices involving supply enhancement are increasingly expensive and have reduced relevancy as the physical availability of water becomes tighter. In the end, we must increase decision-making awareness of

---

2. The requirements approach implicitly places an infinite value on supply enhancement, but that is not believable.

the ultimate fallacy of focusing on supply enhancement in a world of physically and economically limited water.

Part I: Demand Methodology

Several methods for estimating water demand are available. Possessing alternatives is useful because

• certain methods are conceptually compatible with particular water uses and not with others;

• for some options, the necessary data may not be available or the data may have lower "quality" relative to those available for other methods;

• the application of multiple methods may be able to verify or vilify each other's estimates of demand.

Table 9.1 lists eight distinct methods that possess some capability for determining water demand. In the forthcoming sections of this chapter, each of these techniques will be developed. Later, major sectoral classifications of water demand will be individually considered in order to review popular methods and the accumulated empirical evidence.

9.3 Point Expansion

The point expansion method was introduced in chapter 2, and it has been applied to numerous examples in the text since then. Although credit for the earliest application of this method is hard to determine, its application in water resource contexts dates at least to James and Lee (1971, 314–315). The technique is easy to apply, and it is "functionally capable." This means it can obtain an entire demand function estimate, as opposed to just a single value for a single quantity (or vice versa). To use this method, a point on the demand function must be known and the price elasticity of demand (or its slope) must be given or assumed. The first of these informational inputs is commonly available. Price elasticity, however, must be exogenously obtained. That is, elasticity must be provided by another method.

Because the single point "anchors" the obtained demand function, the only purpose of the elasticity measure is to extend the demand function, in two directions, away from this point. Given that elasticity is a single parameter, it can be used to produce only a single parameter for the demand function. The same is true for the contribution of the single demand point. Hence, the only viable options for the resulting demand function are two-parameter functions, especially the linear and constant elasticity forms:

Table 9.1
Methods of demand estimation

Technique	Functionally capable	Data/input types	Sectoral specialities
1. Point expansion	Yes	A known (w, p) and an exogenous elasticity	Potentially useful for all sectors, but elasticity must be generated by another method
2. Residential imputation (single-activity analysis)	No	Output amount and price, and a cost-of-production budget	When water is a large input to production, especially irrigation
3. Math programming (multiple-activity analysis; linear or nonlinear)	Yes	Multiple activities (i.e., outputs/prices and budgets for each)	When water is a large input to production, especially irrigation and possibly industry
4. Production function (estimation or simulation)	Yes	Experimental data or physical relationships	Irrigation, hydropower, individual manufacturing processes
5. Statistical regression (direct estimation)	Yes	Behavior (agent level or aggregate) under administered prices; market transactions; or metadata	Urban/residential, industrial/commercial
6. Contingent valuation	Yes	Survey data from consumers	Urban/residential, recreation
7. Hedonic pricing	No*	Market transactions of land and/or water	Recreation, irrigation
8. Travel cost	No*	Survey data for recreation participants	Recreation

* Adaptable, but in the author's opinion, it tests the limits of commonly available data.

$$w = mp + b \quad \text{or} \quad w = kp^{\varepsilon}. \tag{9.1}$$

The latter form may also be called log linear or log-log because a logarithmic transformation of the right-hand side produces a relationship that is linear in p. Both of these functions are easily inverted for p (marginal benefits).

It should not be presumed that water demand actually exhibits linearity or constant elasticity across the full range of w and p. That is, these two functional forms are assumptions used by the method, but they may not correspond to actual human behavior in situations far from the point of expansion. Human behavior makes its own road maps, and is unlikely to follow anything as uniform or strict as linearity or constant elasticity. We have considerable confidence that demand will possess negative slope in all cases and a positive second derivative (upward concavity) in most cases, but that's about as much structure as can confidently be imposed. As demonstrated in chapter 2, applications of either form may exhibit considerable differences if we use demand ranges far from the known point. Differences will appear both in projections of w for a given p, and for valuations, either marginal or total, for a given w. These differences suggest that errors between the actual and predicted amounts may also be large away from the known point.[3]

With these caveats in mind, the point expansion method can still be a powerful technique for estimating demand. Prior examples in prior chapters are clear indications of this power. Moreover, as observed in the final column of table 9.1, this method can be potentially used for all sectors of water demand (e.g., residential, commercial, recreation, hydropower, etc.). Again, however, this method is not internally capable of supplying the elasticity information itself.

9.4 Residual Imputation

Although it is a relatively simple method with limited immediate power for isolating demand, *residual imputation* is the foundation of more powerful approaches and thus deserving of close attention. Residual imputation and its extensions only work in production settings—that is, where water is used in the production of other goods. Young (1996, sec. 3.3.1, 4.1.2; 2005, sec. 3.4–3.7, 3.10) provides the best available discussion of this method, which is fundamentally the careful examination of a single production activity in which water is employed as a production input. It is founded

---

3. If the external elasticity estimate arises from statistical procedures such as regression, then these procedures may also produce additional statistical information about the "quality" of the estimate (standard error or confidence interval). One can employ this additional information to similarly find confidence intervals for applications of the resulting demand function (Griffin and Chang 1991, 214–215). For example, we can use chapter 6's techniques to economically value a proposed height extension of an existing dam and then calculate a 95 percent confidence interval for this estimated value.

on the idea that in a broad market economy, each production input (or its owner) will be paid according to its marginal value in production. Therefore, if we know how much of every input is necessary to produce a given level of output(s), and if we know the values (prices) of all outputs and inputs except one, then we have the information necessary to assess the unvalued input. Knowing the quantity of this unvalued input and the net profitability enabled by this input, then we also know its average value. Knowing the average value is not the same as knowing the marginal value, and we still only have a point value, not an entire function, but it is a beginning that can be built on.

For example, we may visit with the manufacturers of canned peas and collect lots of information relevant to the value of water to these producers. Suppose that these manufacturers do not buy water because they provide their own water through the exercise of their water rights (surface or ground water rights; private or common property). We can determine their water production costs by close inspection, but that will only give us a lower bound for the producers' value of water. (Water must be worth more than its production costs, for producers would not spend that much otherwise. But how much more?)

To perform residual imputation, the following analysis is possible. For each one hundred cases of canned peas, we can determine (1) canned pea value (one hundred times the wholesale case price), (2) the amortized costs of all plant production facilities and land devoted to pea processing per hundred cases, (3) management costs per hundred cases, (4) returns to financial equity per hundred cases (the profit due to owners or shareholders), and (5) the amounts and prices of all purchased inputs such as worker hours, raw peas, electricity, preservatives, and salt (again, per hundred cases). *If* we have performed this inspection without omitting any input except water from consideration and *if* we have valued everything correctly, then (1) minus the sum of (2) through (5) can be claimed to be the economic contribution of water to this production process. Hence, the *residual* profit can be *imputed* (assigned) to the lone remaining input. If we divide this residual by the amount of water used for one hundred cases, then we have identified the average value of water in this production activity.

A lot of things can go wrong here. We could forget or be ignorant about some input(s). The result would be that our residual would be attributable to water and the other input(s), and we would overestimate the value of water. Or we might misstate the value of output by mispricing it or thinking that our formulated production activity produces a hundred cases when it really doesn't. Or we might misestimate the true costs of some input, with obvious consequences depending on the direction of our error. Or we might be in error about the amount of water used, with potentially serious implications for the final step. In practice, these four error types are apt to overestimate the value of water, due to the tendencies to overlook minor inputs and employ optimistic assumptions about the production technology. Hence, it is arguable that residual imputation is a "bounding exercise," as it tends to determine an upper bound for water value. Using conservative assumptions at each step is therefore advisable.

In other applications, the manufactured product may be sufficiently unique or underestablished that it is not possible to collect data from producers. In such cases, we might "engineer" a prospective budget for a likely firm and then apply this technique to our budget. The same error types apply, but they become more worrisome as a result of our reduced information base. As noted by Young, "Because of the arithmetic of the process, any degree of error in forecasted revenue from incorrect output forecasts will be magnified several times in the residual" (1996, 35). For this reason, it is a good idea to use residual imputation only in cases where water is used in large quantities, as noted in the final column of table 9.1.

As described, residual imputation is a procedure for finding a point, not a function. In general, this point may be (w, average benefit) rather than (w, marginal benefit), but there are at least two available paths for conducting this work so that (w, MB) is a more confident result.[4] Instead of developing these paths as a central pursuit, let's see how residual imputation underlies more advanced approaches for obtaining a demand function.

9.5 Activity Analysis and Math Programming

To generate even more information, residual imputation can be applied to settings in which more than one activity is analyzed. An initial possibility consists of two overlapping, yet alternative activities. A close examination of this opportunity yields insight that is applicable to yet more extensive analyses.

Activity Pairings

In the case of two activities relying on similar sets of production inputs, there are a couple of approaches that can be followed. In the *first method*, we construct a third

---

4. If our production activity focuses on the last units of output produced, such as the last one hundred cases produced annually, we have made some progress toward obtaining a marginal valuation. If, however, one hundred cases is a significant portion of the agent's total production, then there may be little basis to claim that the result approximates a marginal value. As a second option, if we will be applying our determined point together with an exogenously determined elasticity, then we can mathematically use the total imputed value instead of the average imputed value, together with linear or constant elasticity demand and the presumed elasticity, to compute a fully consistent demand equation. The mathematics of this technique are provided in the appendix to this chapter. One of the interesting aspects of this approach is that it demonstrates how poorly average value may approximate marginal value in the instance of linear demand.

activity that is a simple difference between the first two.[5] For example, suppose that the same farm or group of farms can grow cotton as a dryland (rain fed only) or irrigated crop. The irrigated operation (activity 1) is expected to produce more cotton and more revenue per unit of land area than the dryland operation (activity 2), but there will be other differences as well. One has irrigation equipment to acquire and operate, and the other does not. Accompanying the greater water use of the irrigated crop will be larger amounts of other inputs as well (fertilizer, pesticides, land preparation, management advice, harvesting effort, etc.). But some of the inputs are similar across the two activities, and we may have had a hard time valuing these for the residual imputation of each activity. Two important examples are the value of the land and the value of the owner-operators' personal or family labor. If these difficult inputs are present in near-equal amounts in both activities, however, then we can focus on the differences and sidestep an examination of the difficult inputs completely.

In particular, subtracting the net income of activity 2 from the net income of activity 1, after accounting for all differences in revenue and costs, tells us the contribution of the added irrigation water over and above dryland production. The resulting information is similar to the results of residual imputation: a *point* that relates a specific amount of water to a total value enabled by the use of this water. The straight application of residual imputation to the irrigated activity yields the same type of information, but by using a second, overlapping activity as a basis of comparison, we have simplified the analysis and possibly achieved better accuracy. But we still have a point instead of a function, so more work must be done.

As a *second method* of processing the information from two alternative production activities, it can be assumed that the agent or agent group will make a selection between them based on the price of water. This helps us to move toward the identification of a demand function, rather than just a demand point. Suppose that activity 1 uses more water and produces more net income than activity 2, but that activity 2 achieves more income per unit of water. Both activities may use similar amounts of a limited productive capacity such as land, machinery time, or managerial ability, so there are limits to how much of both activities can be conducted. Furthermore, increases in one activity imply that the other must be correspondingly lessened.

The analysis becomes more concrete when mathematics is applied. Define each activity in such a way that it uses one unit of production capacity, such as one acre of land, a hundred hours of time, or ten thousand cubic feet of factory space. Let A_1 denote the number of units of activity 1 to be conducted by an agent. A_2 is the number of activity 2 units. Production capacity is limited to be no greater than K, so $A_1 + A_2 \leq K$. Suppose that the wetter activity yields π_1 units of net income (if water

---

5. This approach has been called the "change in net income" method (Young 1996, 54–55).

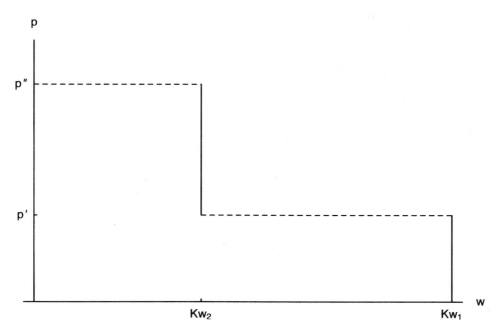

Figure 9.1
Two-activity responses to water prices

is free) and uses w_1 units of water. Similarly, let activity 2 yield π_2 units of net income (if water is free) and use w_2 units of water. Lastly, the wet activity provides more income when water is free: $\pi_1 > \pi_2$, and the average income per unit of water is higher for the dry activity: $\pi_2/w_2 > \pi_1/w_1$.

With either priced or limited water, the agent's economic problem is to choose a mixture of activities so that net income is maximized. Figure 9.1 displays the solution for priced water. At a zero price of water, the agent can generate a profit of $A_1 \cdot \pi_1$ by using $A_1 \cdot w_1$ units of water. Here, only the wet activity is optimal, so $A_1 = K$ and $A_2 = 0$. As the price rises above zero, the 100 percent dependence on activity 1 remains in force, but total profitability falls and the profit advantage of activity 1 declines. As the price rises further, there comes a juncture where the agent is indifferent between the two activities because they are equally rewarding. This price point p' occurs where

$$\pi_1 - p'w_1 = \pi_2 - p'w_2$$

or

$$p' = \frac{\pi_1 - \pi_2}{w_1 - w_2}. \tag{9.2}$$

At p', any combination of the two activities adding up to K total units is equally profitable. For higher prices still, the drier activity is preferred and the total use of water is Kw_2. (Observe that p' is given by a ratio of "differences" that makes it resemble a derivative.)

As the price rises higher still, profitability diminishes. Eventually, there is a water price for which profits go to zero. This occurs at the choke price point p'' where $p'' = \pi_2/w_2$. At prices higher than p'', the agent conducts neither activity and demands no water.

There's yet another way to look at this, and it generates a similar picture. Suppose the agent does not pay for water but must allocate their limited water supply across these two activities. For each potential level of water supply, the agent will want to choose the combination of wet and dry activities that result in the greatest income.

Think about what occurs as this water supply increases from zero. At $w = 0$, the addition of some water would allow the agent to commence water use, and the scarcity of water would cause the agent to use it where it is most valued, in activity 2. Here, the marginal value of water is $p'' = \pi_2/w_2$ because every unit of water allows $1/w_2$ units of A_2 to be conducted and each unit of this activity is worth π_2.

The same is true as the water supply rises. Initially, all water is committed to activity 2 and generates the same net benefits per unit of water. This flat level of marginal benefits is traced out in figure 9.2. As water supply rises further, however, activity 2 reaches a maximum because it is bounded by capacity. At this point, $A_2 = K$ and water use is Kw_2. For a water supply higher than this, it becomes optimal to begin replacing activity 2 with activity 1. This is because activity 1 is more profitable and water is more plentiful now. The replacement operation must obey some simple constraints. Denote the increase in activity 1 as ΔA_1 and the decrease in activity 2 as ΔA_2. Capacity cannot be exceeded, so $\Delta A_1 = \Delta A_2$. The summed changes in water use must equal the change in supply, so $w_1\Delta A_1 - w_2\Delta A_2 = \Delta w$. Combining these two constraints algebraically and presuming $\Delta w = 1$, so that the impact of a one-unit increase in water supply may be studied, it is seen that

$$\Delta A_1 = 1/(w_1 - w_2). \tag{9.3}$$

Net benefits are changed by both the addition of some units of activity 1 and a loss of activity 2. Specifically, $\Delta \text{Benefits} = \pi_1\Delta A_1 - \pi_2\Delta A_2$, but activity 1 is increased in equal amounts to the decrease in activity 2, so

$$\Delta \text{Benefits} = (\pi_1 - \pi_2)\Delta A_1. \tag{9.4}$$

Substituting (9.3) into (9.4), the net benefits of a one-unit increase in water supply is determined for situations in which $w > Kw_2$:

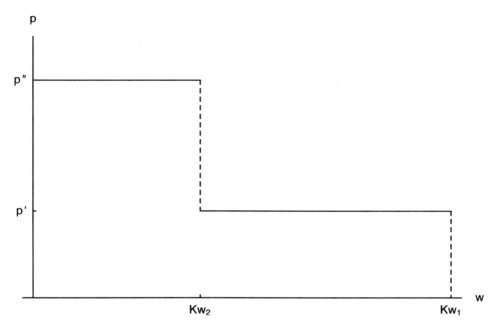

Figure 9.2
Two-activity responses to water availability

$$\Delta \text{Benefits} = \frac{\pi_1 - \pi_2}{w_1 - w_2} = p'. \tag{9.5}$$

This is the marginal benefits of water supply throughout the second segment of water supply, and it is also depicted in figure 9.2. For still higher levels of water supply, with more than Kw_1 units of water, no added benefits are generated because the agent is operating at capacity with the most water-using and profitable activity available. Because there a capacity restriction that is more constraining than water, the value of more water is zero.

Reflecting on this, both figures 9.1 and 9.2 address optimal water use in a two-activity world, and there are important similarities. Indeed, it is the differences that are subtle—the exchange of dotted lines for solid lines. The second depiction is a bit more popular because it explicitly inquires about and exhibits marginal benefits. That is, inverse water demand in an arbitrary, two-activity production setting is shown. In a two-activity scenario where each activity has an established water requirement, the resulting demand function is a step function with only two steps. Demand has the anticipated negative slope only to the extent that the right step is below the left one. Elsewhere, the slope is zero or undefined. Having a "requirement" within each activity is unfortunate, but at least there is an exterior alternative offered in the other activity. This suggests that the inclusion of more activities would be welcome.

The intuition developed here extends directly to broader models in which many activities are included and each individual activity possesses a presumed water requirement. If there are a hundred water-using activities modeled, then it is possible to obtain an aggregate demand function consisting of a hundred steps, with a discontinuity or jump separating each one.[6] Demand will be downward sloping in a gross sense, but flat within each segment. Each activity has, at its heart, a residual-imputation origin in which a net benefit is matched to a level of water use and other resource-consuming requirements as well. Because we cannot get more out of such modeling than we put in, these invariable activities impose some rigid structure on the water demand estimate. Hence, there are flat spots in demand, by methodological assumption rather than by fact.

Consider also that there are really many ways to produce any given commodity. Fundamentally, more or less water can be used if less or more of other inputs are used. The construction of a single activity to represent each commodity is therefore a rough approximation at best. Greater refinement occurs when different activities are posed for the same good, such as when there are multiple activities for canned peas or irrigated cotton, each with its own net benefits and resource requirements. Of course, this added detail comes at the cost of added analytic effort, so there is a trade-off to be faced by the analyst.

Mathematical Programming of Multiple Activities

Two general methods of evaluating activity pairs were presented in the prior section: one looked at the difference, and the other considered the optimal choice between the two options under different water prices or water supplies. The second method has some promise in elucidating demand functions, but it is normally desirable to consider more than two activities. Having multiple activities presents some analytic challenges, but computerized optimization approaches can help out by making optimal selections for us. This defines the class of ***mathematical programming*** or operations research approaches to estimating demand.[7] Four steps are required: a group of water-using activities is identified, their economic and resource-using characters are quantified as individual activities, an optimization model selects economically optimal activity levels as either water price or water supply is varied, and the model's

6. It is also possible that some activities will be "bested" by others, inferring that some activities are not economic relative to others and there will be less than one hundred steps.

7. This technique is sometimes called the engineering approach to water demand estimation, in recognition of its close attention to the many processing details by which water and other inputs are transformed into products (Kindler and Russell 1984, chapter 2; Bain, Caves, and Margolis 1966, 178).

results are reassembled to identify overall water demand. All types of mathematical optimization models are applicable to this approach, so the analyst may need to spend some time making choices about methods and software. The immediate methodological options are linear programming, quadratic programming, and other nonlinear methods.

Our focus is finding water demand, but because demand is implicit to math programming models, and because water supply and hydrologic relationships can be added too, it is often the case that mathematical programming is used to perform policy and project analysis. That is, both the supply and demand sides can be modeled by mathematical programming. This opportunity will not concern us more until chapter 11, when demand and supply are brought together in empiricism.

Math programming is particularly adept at determining water demand in production settings, but it is not a preferred method for household demand. Production settings are better oriented to activity identification. The range of potential applications is large, however, and published examples are available for each of these situations:

• a single firm with production options for its outputs (such as a farm that can potentially irrigate corn using different water amounts or flood, sprinkler, surge, or drip technologies);

• a single firm with different potential outputs, all of which may use water as an input;

• a homogeneous regional sector with different product or technology choices;

• multiple sectors, each as an individual activity or several/many activities, in a region or watershed;

• multiple sectors across multiple regions.

The policy or project setting will normally suggest which of these orientations is appropriate.

Using linear programming, let's examine how this approach works in the presence of variably priced water. Suppose there are J water-using activities to choose from, each with its own rewards (net benefits) and resource uses. A_j represents the amount of activity j, and j ranges from 1 to J. Let d_{1j} be activity j's use of limited productive capacity, such as available land, and C_1 be the fixed capacity constraint. Hence, we must enforce the constraint

$$d_{11}A_1 + d_{12}A_2 + d_{13}A_3 + \cdots + d_{1J}A_J \leq C_1. \tag{9.6}$$

On the right-hand side of this constraint, C is subscripted with a 1, and the d parameters are double subscripted to invite the inclusion of other constraints involving other production inputs, interinput relationships, or interoutput relationships. Such constraint packages are common in linear programming specifications underlying water demand, but they are not needed for the general presentation here. The assumption that every activity is nonnegative in quantity is implicit here, but it is important.

Each activity also consumes water in the amount of w_j (possibly zero) per unit of A_j. In this case, the total amount of water used will be

$$W = w_1A_1 + w_2A_2 + w_3A_3 + w_4A_4 + \cdots + w_JA_J. \tag{9.7}$$

This constraint is similar to that of (9.6) and is usually an ordinary part of the constraint package.

There may be other considerations of significance, but for simplicity let's suppose that the only other consideration is the payoff of each activity. Suppose that the jth activity yields net returns of π_j, inclusive of all revenue and costs except for water purchases. This means that net benefits across all activities and water pricing are given by

$$NB = -pw + \pi_1A_1 + \pi_2A_2 + \pi_3A_3 + \pi_4A_4 + \cdots + \pi_JA_J. \tag{9.8}$$

Because the latter function represents what we wish to maximize, and because it and the constraints (9.6) and (9.7) are linear in form, we have established the following linear programming problem:

$$\left.\begin{array}{l} \text{Maximize } NB = \pi_1A_1 + \pi_2A_2 + \pi_3A_3 + \pi_4A_4 + \cdots + \pi_JA_J - pW \\ \text{subject to} \\ d_{11}A_1 + d_{12}A_2 + d_{13}A_3 + \cdots + d_{1J}A_J \le C_1 \quad \text{and} \\ w_1A_1 + w_2A_2 + w_3A_3 + \cdots + w_JA_J - W = 0. \end{array}\right\} \tag{9.9}$$

Once the π, d, C, and w parameters are established by the analyst, the problem given by (9.9) can be solved by computer for various levels of p. By varying p in specific intervals across some interesting range of water values, a step function for demand can be obtained, like those illustrated in the prior two figures.

It bears repeating that this method is an outgrowth of residual imputation and therefore subject to the same issues. Several brands of errors are conceivable, and each one can have crucial implications for the estimated demand function. Given the possibilities, it seems best to reserve mathematical programming for cases in which water is a quantitatively significant input to production processes, as is also recommended for residual imputation.

The application of nonlinear programming methods, including quadratic programming, can offer improvements in accuracy, but the general approach is unchanged. Accuracy improvements result from a better representation of true production relationships and constraints. Not many technological relations are actually linear in form, which presumes pure proportionality in all activities. For example, doubling

Box 9.1
Demand from Linear Programming

The typical farm operating in a region of interest has five different crops that can be irrigated. As a first step to analyzing demand, we might be content with a five-activity linear program. (Later, we might include limited-irrigation activities in which water use is lower, but yield or cost sacrifices are involved.) With one thousand irrigable acres, the first constraint is

$A_1 + A_2 + A_3 + A_4 + A_5 \leq 1000$.

The fourth and fifth crops are normally grown in rotation from year to year. Hence, crop 5 is grown on the same land where crop 4 was the prior year and vice versa. To support this rotational norm, we might require $A_4 = A_5$. After accounting for expected rainfall, the five activities use 4.0, 3.4, 2.7, 2.6, and 1.6 units of irrigation water, respectively. Except for the cost of water but including the on-farm costs of applying water, the net profits stemming from each unit of each activity are $100, $90, $75, $70, and $50, respectively.

The fully assembled linear programming problem is as follows:

Maximize $NB = 100A_1 + 90A_2 + 75A_3 + 70A_4 + 50A_5 - pW$

subject to

$A_1 + A_2 + A_3 + A_4 + A_5 \leq 1000$,

$-A_4 + A_5 = 0$, and

$4A_1 + 3.4A_2 + 2.7A_3 + 2.6A_4 + 1.6A_5 - W = 0$.

If this problem is solved once for every integer value of p beginning at zero and ending at thirty, and if the (W, p) ordered pairs are saved from each solution, the resulting thirty-one points can be graphed as they are in figure 9.3 to visualize the demand function. Although there are five available activities and all are employed for some choice of price, there are only four steps (plateaus) in this function (instead of five) due to the effect of the rotation constraint.

any linear action doubles the costs, the returns, and the water use. Exercised judiciously, the unfortunate presumptions of linearity can be sidestepped by the careful selection of constraints and by breaking up nonlinear relations into "piecewise" linear ones, but nonlinear methods are also applicable. A more detailed examination of these alternatives is not warranted given their added complexities and the fact that they are extensions of the points already introduced here.

9.6   Production Functions

Mathematical programming makes headway in estimating water demand because it commences with basic activities, which form the basis of a water-using technology or set of technologies. Each activity can be likened to a well-chosen spot on the continuum of production options. If many activities are included, then we are more likely to do a good job of "building out" the technology with these many points. There's a more satisfying option that may be available. Instead of working with these discrete

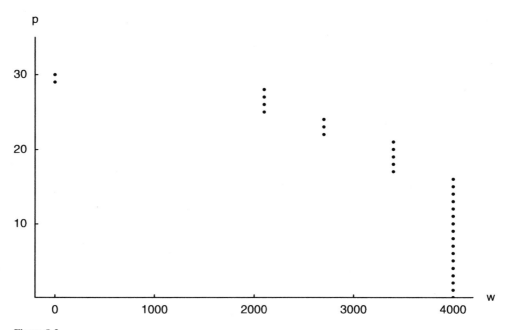

Figure 9.3
Linear programmed demand

points, it may be possible to determine the continuous relationship underlying the technology. The production function repeated here,

$$y = f(w, x_1, x_2, \ldots, x_n), \tag{2.1}$$

was the keystone of chapter 2's production theory for a water-using business agent. If it is possible to estimate how output depends on water and nonwater inputs in such a continuous way, then this can be the basis for estimating water demand. Once in our possession, the conversion of (2.1) into water demand is simple. Applying (2.6), f is differentiated with respect to w and set equal to p/p_y, the price of water divided by the price of the output. The result can be manipulated into a form like either $w = \cdots$ or $p = \cdots$, and the task is complete. (Recall that this procedure is demonstrated in section 2.3 (box 2.1) for two different production functions.)

Hence, another way to estimate demand is to first estimate the production function. How can this be done? There are two notable approaches: *estimation* and *simulation*. Opportunities to use them are not widespread.

In the first, there must be experimental data in which water use is controlled and measured, other production inputs are controlled, and then the resulting output is measured. If these data cover a suitable range of water use, then it is possible to statistically estimate the production function using regression analysis. That is, one or more functional forms for the production function are fitted to the data. For example, a two-input square root function would be

$$y = \alpha_0 + \alpha_1 w^{0.5} + \alpha_2 x^{0.5} + \alpha_3 w^{0.5} x^{0.5} + \alpha_4 w + \alpha_5 x + \sigma, \tag{9.10}$$

where the two inputs are water and x, the α's are parameters to be estimated by a procedure such as ordinary least squares, and σ denotes the error term. There are many functional forms that can be selected, and there are many criteria that may be relevant to the selection. It is commonly advisable to use forms that are not too "rigid" in the sense that they impose too much structure on the data, and it is also a good idea to perform this analysis with more than one functional form (Griffin, Montgomery, and Rister 1987). For instance, the linear form is usually a poor selection because it "maintains" (i.e., imposes) constant marginal productivity of water without allowing this assumption to be tested. As another example, the Cobb-Douglas form with which all economics students become quite accustomed, $y = \alpha_0 w^{\alpha_1} x^{\alpha_2}$, is rigid relative to the alternatives, including simplistic options like the quadratic and square root forms.[8]

Although it is no longer a common activity, agricultural researchers have conducted extensive field experiments in which carefully measured water is applied in different quantities to different plots of a single crop. This type of information is conducive to the estimation method. Many such estimates are collected in Hexem and Heady (1978), and one of these serves as the basis of an exercise problem following chapter 2. Vaux and Pruitt offer a nice, agronomically grounded discussion of this approach (1983).

In the second setting in which production functions can be applied to get water demand, the production function is not estimated from data. It is *simulated* through expert knowledge of the physical relations that underlie the role of water in product formation. Depending on the nature of the production process, knowledge of the governing physics, biology, or chemistry may allow for scientific specification of the production process, especially the contribution of water in differing amounts. In this case, the production function might be expressible in a form such as (9.10). Or the production function may be implicit to a multirelation computer model that seeks to estimate production consequences for a range of inputs and settings. When

---

8. Among other things, regardless of the information embedded in experimental data, the Cobb-Douglas form imposes zero output if any input is zero, constant sign of the second derivative with respect to any input throughout the range of input levels (constant concavity), and constant elasticity of substitution between inputs (Griffin, Montgomery, and Rister 1987, 221).

embedded in a complex simulation model, the combined effects of many intramodel relationships may treat water as a continuous variable even though it cannot be expressed as simply as (2.1). Or the relationship may be noncontinuous such as when water use is only allowed at prescribed, alternative levels. Such discrete (non-continuous) models reveal less information about demand and are more aligned with the demand-revealing abilities of math programming models than production functions. Simulation does not generally rely on optimization, however.

Although some correlation or regression analysis may be used for resolving model coefficients, many simulation models do not have a strong statistical basis. If they did, they might be better classified as an estimation model. That would commonly be a good thing because statistical information also tells us things about the quality of the parameter estimates and overall fit. Absent this information, simulation models can appear "ad hoc" or "made up" unless model components are well justified and documented.

Hydropower is a good example of a sector for which water demand can be well simulated. There is a strong physical basis for knowing how a given water flow with a given hydraulic head produces power when it passes through turbines and spins electricity-producing generators. Indeed, this type of modeling can even be improved through the estimation method, since actual generator operation makes it possible to observe the electrical output of hydropower facilities under different water release conditions.

Bioagronomic models have become popular approaches for simulating agricultural output under different input scenarios, including irrigation. Part of the attraction of such models is that they address more issues than just water use, and they have become highly used for their ability to track the water-transported pollutants of agriculture such as sediment, nutrients, minerals, and pesticides. Depending on the detail and effort committed to the economics of water use within such a model, the internal depiction of water demand may be a strong one, allowing water demand to be identified, or the emphasis on water quality may imply that the basis of water demand is rather weak when applied to scarcity matters.

9.7   Direct Statistical Regression

Relative to an alternative procedure, the aforementioned techniques are not good candidates for identifying the water demand of households. Household water use can be highly varied across these agents, so the identification of representative "activities" can be challenging. Fortunately, water demand can be estimated directly when the proper data exist, and this is an especially good approach for obtaining residential and urban water demand. Indeed, the direct estimation of water demand is a viable approach for at least three circumstances. These three are best delineated by their data sources:

1. *Consumption behavior*, or consumer responses to supplier-established prices of retail water;
2. *Market transactions* of natural water;
3. *Meta* data emerging from prior estimates of demand.

Each of these opportunities will be discussed in turn. The second and third types of direct estimation are much rarer than the first in terms of published applications.

The first type owes its popularity to the wide availability of data. Millions of agents are served by water suppliers that set rates and then meter water use for billing purposes. As long as the supplier does not constrain agent behavior other than by setting water rates, these agents' subsequent behavior presents demand information pertaining to retail water. If, however, water rates are accompanied by other forms of rationing—such as water use restrictions, water supply shortfalls, or limited water pressure—then metered behavior will identify something less than actual demand and will be statistically inferior.

With the appropriate data in hand, the goal is to directly estimate the demand function as it was originally postulated in chapter 2:

$$w = D(p; \text{ other demand determinants}). \tag{9.11}$$

Assuming suitable data, this method proceeds by postulating a set of measurable exogenous variables that includes the water price,[9] choosing one or more candidate functional forms for the demand function, D, organizing the needed data, and applying statistical regression procedures to estimate function coefficients from the data and interpret the findings.

There are analytic matters to be resolved at each of these steps. The exogenous variables should be conjectured to be the most influential determinants of water demand, but they must also be measurable without too much difficulty. The choice of functional form will be important for the same reason as in production function analysis: we prefer to use a relatively flexible form in order to "let the data speak" instead of imposing a specific structure by using a rigid function. Collecting the requisite data can be time consuming, and there are many "levels" of data that may or may not be appropriate depending on what is available and the ultimate goals of demand

---

9. The possibilities are extensive here, but the emphasis must be reserved for the most important factors, lest the "degrees of freedom" needed for statistical confidence be lost. For example, most studies of community water demand focus on water price, demographic descriptors such as income or property value, and climate variables. If the demand sector is the producer of other economic goods, then the inclusion of other input and output prices may be warranted as well.

estimation.[10] The choice of regression procedure, such as the use of ordinary least squares, can also be challenging for the novice practitioner. Similarly, the interpretation of regression results can also lead to numerous questions by inexperienced analysts.

The economics subfield called *econometrics* concentrates on statistical matters and has developed a wealth of experience with demand estimation. It has been found that there are many considerations of importance in demand estimation. Consequently, water planners can obtain good counsel from econometric experts. Most of the issues to be encountered are generic, in the sense that they also emerge in nonwater issues and are therefore well-known to econometricians. A few are peculiar, though.[11]

As a reminder about the kind of information attained once retail water demand has been estimated, the analyzed behavior has to do with consumer selection of retail water amount in response to retail water price. Hence, we will possess the means to assess the value of retail water to consumers, and we can also project retail water use under differing supply/price/scarcity conditions. Yet information about the value of natural water necessitates the adjustments suggested in chapter 2 in order to arrive at marginal net benefits and thereby begin to isolate the demand for natural water.

The second direct method for estimating water demand uses water market data (Gray and Young 1984; Young and Gray 1972). Wherever a water market operates, every trade of water for money generates a quantity-price data pair. If enough trades are reported so that a sufficient quantity of data are generated, then it is possible to estimate natural water demand directly. The accepted economic procedure is to estimate market demand and supply *simultaneously* because both forces come together to conclude in a market-resolved quantity-price pair, (W, p). One agent's willingness

10. *Microdata* consists of data from *individual* connections within a water supply system. *Community (or district) data* is aggregated across each water supply system for a given time period. Either microdata or community data can be "cross-sectional," meaning different data points for different agents or agent-groups operating in the same time period; "time series," meaning different data points for the same agent or group operating in different time periods; or "pooled" or "panel," meaning that the final data set has both a cross-sectional and time-series character. Microdata from a single supply system is not a feasible basis for direct water demand estimation because there is no usable price variability in the data. Time-series microdata from a single system is an improvement, but not a significant one in and of itself. Hence, the most useful studies of water demand involve cross-sectional data, often also with a time-series component. Time-series data are viewed as appropriate for analyzing short-run demand, when consumers have committed themselves to particular behavioral norms and particular water usage capital such as lawn size and water-related fixtures/devices (e.g., dishwashers, toilets, pools, lawn sprinklers). Cross-sectional data are considered to be more informative regarding long-run demand because of the different incentives and traditions faced by agents in different places with different scarcities and prices.

11. A basic assumption of regression analysis is that exogenous variables, such as price and climate in the present case, are independent of the dependent variables (water use in our case). If block rates are in force, however, then price depends on usage. This fouls the applicability of ordinary least squares regression procedures somewhat (Griffin, Martin, and Wade 1981; Terza and Welch 1982; Renzetti 2002b, 22–26). Alternative regression procedures are available to address the "simultaneous" determination of price and quantity, and they may lead to statistically different regression parameters (and different elasticities too).

Box 9.2
Regression of Demand from Consumption Behavior

After assembling data from several sources, a fairly complete set of data exists for 30 towns and cities. These data cover three years of monthly consumption by an average household. For each community and most months, you have recorded water use, water price, average personal income, and climate information, among other things. If the data set was complete, you would have 1,080 separate observations (30 times 36), but some missing information causes the data set to only have 1,031 observations. (Both the extended data [221 communities times 60 months] and the data subset used here are available at ⟨http://waterecon.tamu.edu.⟩) The collected information is sufficient to examine several other variables, nonlinear expressions of demand, and more advanced regression techniques, but you might first estimate the linear version of $W = D(AP, I, C)$ where:

• W is the month's water "production" (pumpage into the water supply system) for the entire community, minus all industrial water use, divided by the number of days in the month as well as by the community's entire population;

• AP is the month's water and sewer bill divided by W (hence, the average price) for an average household using W gallons of water per person per day;

• I is the annual personal income in thousands of dollars per capita for the community;

• C is a climate variable postulated to affect water use (defined as the month's average daily temperature times the number of days in the month not having a significant rainfall).

The estimated demand equation, with p-values given parenthetically, is

$$W = \underset{(0.001)}{32.81} - \underset{(0.000)}{26.64}\,AP + \underset{(0.000)}{9.590}\,I + \underset{(0.000)}{0.07253}\,C. \quad R^2 = 0.46.$$

All four coefficients have high statistical significance according to the low p-values and have the expected sign (right?). R^2 is not high, which is a common result for cross-sectional data.

Inserting the data set's average values for I and C, and graphing the inverse of the estimated equation, yields the demand function exhibited in figure 9.4 (graphed only for the range of observed AP in the data). More information on these data and some of their applications are reviewed by Griffin and Chang (1990).

to sell is determined by their preferences and options; another agent's willingness to buy is similarly affected by their preferences and options; and a transaction is the result. Omitting one side makes it possible to misstate the price responsiveness of the other side.

A basic water demand/supply system is given by (9.12):

$$\left.\begin{array}{l} w^d = \alpha_1 + \alpha_2 p + \alpha_3 g + \eta \\ w^s = \beta_1 + \beta_2 p + \beta_3 p_y + \mu \\ w^d = w^s \end{array}\right\}, \tag{9.12}$$

where η and μ are normal error terms, and w^d and w^s (identical data), p, g, and p_y are data components. This three-equation system consists of linear water demand, linear water supply, and an obligatory equilibrium requirement for demand and supply. Any of the available statistical regression procedures for simultaneous equations can be applied so that all six parameters (α_1 through β_3) are estimated (see Kennedy

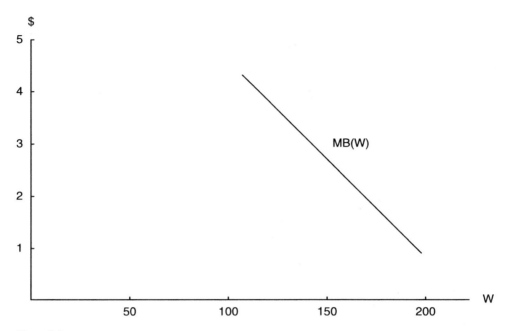

Figure 9.4
Regressed demand

2003, chapter 10; Pindyck and Rubinfeld 1991, 288–302; or any statistics or econo-metric text discussing linear systems). Linearity may be an overly strong assumption, in which case the basic model suggested by (9.12) may require respecification and more advanced statistical methods.

For technical reasons stemming from regression requirements, this method's de-mand and supply equations must contain at least one exogenous variable other than the water price.[12] Candidates for the additional variables are many, but they must have logical impacts on demand or supply, and data must be available. In this case, we are investigating the determinants of natural water demand and supply, and the market is likely to be dominated by the sale (or lease) of agricultural water to urban entities. An urban effect on demand might be a measurable index of growth, g, such as the population growth rate or the acreage of rezoned land. An influence on supply might be the prospective profitability of crop production or simply the price of an important agricultural commodity, p_y.

The third direct estimation method is called meta-analysis. It novelly uses data com-prised of the specifications and results of prior statistical studies. For example, there

---

12. Kindler and Russell (1984, 34–37) provide a brief, water-based discussion of these points.

are lots of published "consumption behavior" studies of urban water demand from different countries, different communities, and different time periods. Each of these studies assembles water use, water price, and other data, and then estimates one or more demand functions. Meta-analysis treats each such previously published demand function as a single data point. Relevant aspects of each data point include the resulting demand elasticity, which functional form was used, data characteristics (e.g., household or aggregate? monthly? cross-sectional? block rates?), and study location. Other aspects of each data point might also be incorporated if they are widely available across prior studies and if they are postulated to have a meaningful impact on elasticity findings.

Then, regression procedures are used to estimate linear or nonlinear representations of the following function:

$$\varepsilon = F(\text{functional form, data level, region, etc.}) + \sigma, \tag{9.13}$$

where σ is the usual regression error term. Many of the exogenous variables of meta-analysis may take on binary ("0" or "1") values. For example, a simple functional form variable may be "0" if the study elasticity was produced by a linear function and "1" for a constant elasticity function if those are the only two forms used.

In water scarcity settings, the most apparent application of meta-analysis is to see how elasticity estimates are affected by study settings and study choices. Econometricians may be interested in this type of analysis because it may identify the more crucial variables and thereby indicate where future research should be heading. Water managers may be interested in the outcome of (9.13) if no original study of water demand has been performed in their area, and they want to avoid the time and costs of such a study. Rather than perform meta-analysis themselves, water managers may be content to examine prior metastudies as an aid for selecting a demand elasticity or, better yet, an acceptable range of elasticities for local conditions.

9.8   Nonmarket Valuation Techniques

The final three methodologies of table 9.1 are collectively classified as *nonmarket valuation techniques*, in recognition of their usefulness for valuing goods that are not normally traded in marketplaces or purchased in consumer-selected quantities. They are novel avenues that may be applied to modify an otherwise incommensurable or intangible good into a commensurable one. In many situations, it is a public good that is being valued by these tools, although these methods are applicable for both private and public goods. As noted earlier, some water uses constitute public goods, meaning that the water use is both nonrival (your consumption of water for a certain use does not detract from the amount of water available for like users) and nonexclusive (it is prohibitively expensive to exclude agents from this use activity).

Recreational and environmental uses of water often display these two properties, albeit impurely. Nonmarket valuation techniques are most often applied to value environmental goods (such as water quality), recreational experiences (such as sport-fishing activities), or the preservation of unique places or species. It is common for recreational activities or destinations to have a river or a lake as a central feature, so these techniques often involve water resource values.

In many applications, each of these three techniques is used to determine a *total value* for a given resource, such as the total annual value of recreation at a specific lake or the annual value that society attaches to the continued existence of an endangered fish. But we are not especially interested in total values here, as noted earlier in the chapter. We wish to discover demand—how the marginal benefits change as the amount of water used in the activity changes. Alternatively, if it could be determined how the total value is functionally related to the amount of water used, then a derivative could uncover the marginal benefit function that is truly desired.

Of these three techniques, *contingent valuation* has the best capacity to produce the functional information needed to conduct policy or project analysis. For this reason, it receives greater attention in the following sections. For reasons of completeness as well as understanding their capabilities, the methods of hedonics and travel costs are also considered. The latter techniques are of more limited usefulness because they emphasize a single, total value for a discrete amount of a valued public good. It is certainly possible, however, that knowing a single total value might be useful for isolated analyses of water scarcity. It is also conceivable that modifications of these two methods might improve their suitability for estimating demand, so we shall attempt to indicate these possibilities too.

These three techniques are more firmly in the domain of economic expertise, so it will be necessary to limit detail. The remaining discussion is intended to convey a sense of how these things operate and what they can achieve. Readers wishing to invest more heavily in these methods will be well served by Young's chapter 4 (2005).

9.9 Contingent Valuation

The *contingent valuation* (CV) method relies on a survey of agents' preferences, conducted either personally (face-to-face) or remotely (especially by mail or telephone). This technique is classified as a *direct, hypothetical* method of nonmarket valuation (Mitchell and Carson 1989, 75–90; Freeman 1993, 23–36). It is direct in that valuation is not inferred from "demand-associated" evidence; agents are asked to provide specific details about their values.

For example, agents could be asked if they would pay $5 more (yes or no) to go boating on a specific lake if the lake's summer water level was always at least x_1 feet high as opposed to the usual minimum of x_0 feet. By proposing different fees to different respondents and by varying x_1 as well, demand-revealing data are generated. The subsequent statistical analysis can estimate the demand for X if enough data are available. Because knowledge of lakeside topography informs engineers about the relationship between X and water quantity, the boating demand for lake water is estimated. (Again, as with all of the methods listed in table 9.1, unknown demand is being "estimated.")

CV loses some reliability and credibility because of the hypothetical nature of survey question(s). Respondents generally know that they will not be required to pay the survey-proposed fee. Hence, respondents may not provide accurate answers, and they may even misreport purposefully so as to distort decision making in a personally favored direction. In a less strategic vein, some respondents may simply be unfamiliar with their valuation of the good because they are unaccustomed to paying for the good or even thinking about its intrinsic value. Respondents may even object to the whole idea of paying fees and consequently submit a "protest response" in some manner (e.g., saying no to any proposed payment, no matter how small, or terminating the survey). CV experts heed the warning that you can get "hypothetical answers to hypothetical questions" (Cameron 1992, 302). This requires that analysts be careful in survey design and survey administration practices.

Experienced CV practitioners are well apprised of the biases and pitfalls.[13] The 1989 Exxon *Valdez* Alaskan oil spill created a pressing legal problem because many environmental losses occurred as a result of this incident. U.S. liability law clearly dictated that compensation had to be paid. What was unclear was the level of damages, so the various factions hired specialists to study the damages as expert witnesses for the forthcoming court cases. Contingent valuation became a key technique in this work and for a new law meant to lower the frequency of oil spills (Portney 1994). The ensuing dialogue among economists spilled into the valuation literature, creating intriguing and productive debates.[14] This close scrutiny of CV has enabled improvements in the methodology. But these improvements also "raise the bar" in the sense that more work has to be performed to apply the method correctly.[15] It is no longer an accepted practice to merely ask agents what they are willing to pay for some commodity and then accept the answers as useful.

13. Hanley and Spash (1993) offer a succinct introduction to the mechanics of the method as well as some of CV's better-known issues.

14. These circumstances are well described by Portney (1994), and two companion papers do an excellent job of debating the opposing positions (Diamond and Hausman 1994; Hanemann 1994). These three papers are "must reads" for anyone attempting to gain insight on the valid application of contingent valuation.

15. The 1993 *Report of the NOAA Panel on Contingent Valuation* is available online at ⟨http://www.darp .noaa.gov/pdf/cvblue.pdf⟩. The first two of the six authors received Nobel Memorial Prizes in 1972 and 1987, respectively.

In recent years, experimental economics has been fruitfully applied to study the relationships between "actual" and hypothetical values with the goal of improving the reliability of contingent valuation.[16] A great deal has been accomplished, and the procedure continues to grow in complexity and specialization. No silver bullet has been uncovered for converting potentially hypothetical values into actual values, but techniques for getting good hypothetical values are being refined. One of the upshots is that this is not a method that can be well performed by novices. It's a good idea to retain experts if CV is to be used to estimate nonmarket water demands for water planning. Moreover, planners should keep in mind that CV is a costly procedure to apply because good surveys are expensive to conduct (Harrison and Lesley 1996).

Typical CV empiricism seeks a total value for a discrete amount of a good or group of goods, rather than seeking demand. For example, a study may attempt to value the marine life (shellfish, otters, birds, fish, etc.) that was extinguished or injured in an oil spill.[17] As a more common type of undertaking, a CV study might assess the value of a natural stretch of "wild" river to kayakers and rafters, or the value of a lake that is "cleaner" in some dimension as compared to a baseline. In each of these settings, the amount of the good is established and the analysis is attempting to establish a total value for the good(s), rather than the demand for variable quantities of the good. Depicted graphically as in figure 9.5, the typical CV study estimates the area given by $A + B$ or B, rather than attempting to resolve the marginal benefit function, MB.

It is possible to move beyond this basic pursuit, however, by varying x_1 in the survey instrument, as noted above. Also, x_1 might be naturally variant, as occurs when recreationists are surveyed at different times, and water levels or flows are different at different survey times (Duffield, Neher, and Brown 1992). CV can be thoughtfully combined with other tools so as to obtain marginal values. For instance, Johnson and Adams (1988) manage to value instream flows contributing to angler success in a recreational fishery. From a statistical perspective, more data are required to estimate demand ($MB(X)$) than a single value (A or $A + B$). Hence, a greater number of surveys must be applied. Varying x_1 may also test the ability of respondents to accurately discern their personal preferences and deliver consistent results.

Water-based applications of CV extend to rival goods as well as nonrival goods. For example, CV methods can be applied to examine residential water demand (Tho-

---

16. See, for example, Blumenschein et al. (2001), Brown, Ajzen, and Hrubes (2003); Cummings and Taylor (1999); List and Shogren (2002); Loomis et al. (1996).

17. Recall from chapter 1 that economic precepts are anthropocentric, inferring that marine life has no self-appointed value in human decision making. Yet humans do experience gains and losses on some perceived level as a consequence of rises and falls in our environment. It is those human preferences that we seek to value.

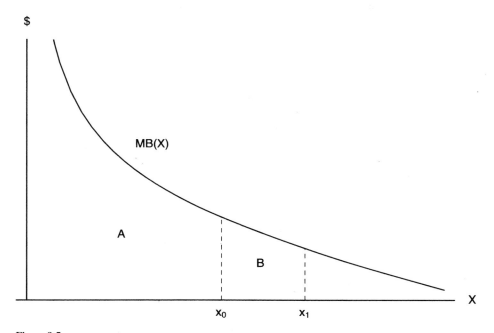

Figure 9.5
Demand estimation versus valuation

mas and Syme 1988). Whereas CV can also be utilized to value an indeterminate modification, such as "more water conservation" (Rollins et al. 1997), such findings have weak practicality. For reasons relating to project analysis, primarily in developing countries, households have been surveyed for the value they attach to the establishment of piped water service.[18] Such service may be confined to trucked water or communal spigots, where residents dispense water into containers to be carried to their homes. Or the service may provide taps for each household. Usually, such studies consider the establishment of water delivery services in locations where little delivery infrastructure exists. As a variant, households may be surveyed regarding the worth they attach to increased water service reliability, which can be notoriously poor in undeveloped regions of the world. Finally, using CV methods to value modified water service "reliability" is sometimes performed in developed countries.[19]

18. An educational exchange about this approach also contains pointers to some of the available literature (Merrett 2002; Whittington 2002a; Lauria 2002). Also, see McPhail (1994); Raje, Dhobe, and Deshpande (2002), Pattanayak, Yang, Whittington, and Bal Kumar (2005).

19. Although the topic of economic uncertainty is not carefully developed in this text, due to the added complexity it requires, climate-induced shifts in water supply and demand imply that scarcity has a probabilistic dimension. Viewed in this way, new projects and policies alter the *probability* of water supply short-

9.10   Hedonic Pricing

The method of *hedonic pricing* (HP) examines data on the market price of some commodity, where the commodity has one or more variable, yet identifiable quality(ies). If the price of individual trades can be observed and if the qualities of the good being traded can be observed as well, then it may be possible to perform hedonics so as to value the important qualities. This method is often practical for sales of land. If one of land's characters involves linked water rights or access to water, then it may be possible to see how water affects land value, thereby explicitly valuing water. That is, "water access value" or "water use value" might be inferred from land value. Hedonics is sometimes performed on wage rates over differing occupations in order to examine how workers value their exposure to different dangers or toxic risks. But land values are of greater interest for water evaluation by hedonic methods.

The hedonic pricing method is classified as an *indirect, observed* method of non-market valuation (Mitchell and Carson 1989, 75–90; Freeman 1993, 23–36). It is indirect because the valuation being sought (e.g., water) is inferred from the values witnessed for another commodity (e.g., land). It is observed rather than hypothetical because the data are created by actual market transactions.

In application, the analyst collects information on the market price of individual land sales and the several/many individual characteristics of each trade. Then price is regressed against the characteristics to see if price is well related to these characteristics. It is necessary to presume a specific functional form (or two or more), generally expressed as

$$p_{land} = f(w, char_1, char_2, \ldots), \tag{9.14}$$

where the water variable, w, can be indexed in a variety of ways depending on the circumstances.[20] It can be argued that the linear form is a poor choice for f (Hanley

---

falls. In other words, the real impact of these measures is to influence the reliability of a given water supply relative to demand. Hence, it can be useful to study the value that households place on reliability, and there is a growing literature in this area (Barakat and Chamberlin 1994; Griffin and Mjelde 2000; Howe and Smith 1993, 1994; Koss and Khawaja 2001; Lund 1995). Much of this literature employs the contingent valuation method.

20. Possibilities for measuring "water" include the following: "Is the land parcel riparian or not?" "How many meters is the parcel from a recreational lake's shoreline?" "Is the land irrigated or dryland?" or "How many water rights are conveyed with the land?" Rather than having land price on the left-hand side, we might have observable natural water prices from a water market, thereby allowing investigation of the determinants of water price, perhaps with features like seniority, size, or classification on the right-hand side. There may be other possibilities, and consideration of prior literature is important (Hartman and Anderson 1962; Crouter 1987; Kulshreshtha and Gillies 1993; Lansford and Jones 1995; Loomis 2003; Mendelsohn and Dinar 2003).

and Spash 1993, 76). Once the estimation is complete, the most immediately interesting finding is $\partial f/\partial w$. Theoretically, this is the contribution of water to the value of land. This partial derivative is the market-implied value of the water variable, but unless the form of f is highly restrictive (e.g., linear), this derivative will also be dependent on the levels of other characteristics. In some cases, the water variable may be defined as a binary variable (such as "has water rights or not," "is riparian or not," "has lake view or not"), so the analyst ends up with something more "lumpy" than a partial derivative here.

As with the residual imputation method, the primary results of HP can be sensitive to the omission of key variables. If (9.14) omits a determinant of land price, then the effect of the omitted term will be "spread across" the remaining variables, including water. While the tendency may be for the omitted variables to inflate the resultant water value incorrectly, collinearity among the many included and omitted variables perplexes interpretation. On the other hand, there is nothing about HP that prevents the inclusion of unrelated characteristics (to p_{land}), with more unfortunate consequences. In the end, it is hard to express high confidence in the estimated (9.14) and its computed water derivative unless data are ample, and water is an important and independent feature of the transferred property.

If we wish to extend this technique so that it yields a demand function for the water variable, then more work is needed. Water price is not an element of (9.14), so additional information must be injected (Freeman 1993, 387–391; Hanley and Spash 1993, 76–78). When these difficulties are combined with issues stemming from data availability and omitted variables, it becomes hard to rely on HP for generating water demand functions. Whereas HP can often estimate a value such as B in figure 9.5, the estimation of MB is an unlikely achievement. Even when it is possible to estimate MB with this method, it is unlikely to possess much credibility.

9.11 Travel Costs

Different people traveling to a specific recreation site are traveling different distances. The differing distances mean that these people are effectively paying different "prices" to enjoy the same amenity. That's a reason visitation declines with distance. Travel costs, which are a crucial price of using the recreational site, include both the expenditure of money and time.[21] By measuring the quantity of agents' site visitation and their travel costs, it is possible to estimate their inferred demand for that site.

---

21. There are other relevant costs too, such as entrance fees, licenses, and equipment, but travel costs are noteworthy because they impose different prices on different agents, thereby permitting a glimpse at the demand function.

This is how the ***travel cost method*** works. It is most commonly applied to ascertain the value of recreational sites. If the site in question is popular because of a water-based activity (fishing, skiing) or water amenity (scenery, tranquillity), then there may be grounds for extracting a water value from this information.

Like hedonic pricing, the travel cost (TC) method is classified as an *indirect, observed* method of nonmarket valuation (Mitchell and Carson 1989, 75–90; Freeman 1993, 23–36). It is indirect because values are inferred from agent behavior rather than being directly expressed. It is observed rather than hypothetical because the data are generated by actual behavior.

As with other methods, there are problems to be surmounted when applying this method. The conversion of travel time to travel costs is an evolving economic issue, with many complications. If a trip includes multiple destinations, then some procedure is needed to allocate travel costs across the separate destinations. Other issues are well acknowledged and reviewed in the literature (Cameron 1992, 303; Freeman 1993, 448–456; Hanley and Spash 1993, 86–91).

To employ the travel cost procedure so as to reveal the demand for water, the usual travel cost demand must be expanded to include a water-impacted measure of the site's quality. A basic form of the statistically estimated function would then be

$$v = f(p_v, W, \text{other things}), \tag{9.15}$$

where v is the number of visits to a particular site, p_v is the full price of visitation including all fees, costs, and travel costs, and W is a water or water-determined measure of site quality (Freeman 1993, 446–447). For example, W might be the area or height of a lake, or it might be the number of fish caught per day. As long as the relationship between W and actual water quantity is well-known to analysts (an additional informational requirement), knowledge of (9.15) can permit the marginal benefits of water to be calculated. Unfortunately, the estimation of (9.15) is not often possible because the inclusion of W strains the data that are realistically available. W may be relatively constant within a given recreational season, meaning that the variability of W necessary to conduct regression may only be available across different seasons. This requires time-series data, which are not common for travel cost studies. Moreover, there may be many times-series variables besides W to include in a time-series travel cost model. Lastly, it is important for W to be a relatively significant factor to recreationists, who must also have knowledge of W, or at least expectations about it, before committing to trips. In aggregate, these requirements are taxing, and they limit the ability of TC to estimate water demand. Whereas discrete values such as the areas illustrated in figure 9.5 might be achievable or TC might be combined with a method like CV (Freeman 1993, 461–462), TC itself is not an especially promising approach. For example, Ward (1987) combines TC and CV to investigate instream flow demand for boating and fishing.

Part II: Empirical Demand Findings for Three Sectors

9.12   When Considering Prior Empirical Studies …

In light of the relative difficulties of these methods, most water resource practitioners would love to rely on point expansion—if only someone could tell us what elasticity (or slope) to apply. Ideally, we would have a definitive listing, perhaps even a table, where we could look up a demand elasticity for any situation. That is not a realistic hope, at least not yet. Water resource scenarios are too diverse, and they are ever changing too. For one thing,

1. scarcity-induced change continues to move agents to new regions of their demand functions, higher on demand curves, where elasticity may be different than what has been found previously.

Other matters also perplex attempts to resolve clear "rules of thumb." Here are some of the major ones:

2. Because demand is sensitive to price, sector of use, climate, cultural and social norms, nonprice policy (such as water use regulations), income, and so forth, elasticity is quite possibly sensitive to these factors as well. As noted earlier, human behavior is unlikely to emulate a constant-elasticity road map.

3. Whenever demand or supply is seasonal, as is normally the case, demand elasticity is likely to exhibit seasonality too. The relevance of supply is that seasonal supply (MC or AC) will affect where supply equals demand (MB), thus causing elasticity to be evaluated at a different point on the demand function. Unless we are setting aside the economic goal of efficiency, then, elevated scarcity during hotter, drier periods will drive demand elasticity higher, at least as long as there are low-value water uses that can be curbed (e.g., sidewalk washing and large lawns in household settings or pasture/hay irrigation in agricultural settings).

4. It is necessary to distinguish between demand elasticity in the short run versus demand elasticity in the long run. This is not actually an "either-or" selection as there are gradations to be recognized. In the long run, demand is more elastic (more negative) because consumers have more choices at their disposal. In the very short run, water users have highly fixed technologies in place. That is, their water-using *capital* or *durables* are relatively immutable from an economic perspective (Dubin 1985; Wirl 1997). This includes household items such as appliances, pools, lawns, and landscaping (Griffin and Mjelde 2000) as well as industrial and agricultural capital. Whereas a change in water price will leave these items unchanged in the short run, in the long run agents will reconsider and possibly alter their durable base. (Think

of the immediate effects of soaring gasoline prices during the 1970s versus the long-term effects on the types of cars purchased by consumers.)

5. Prior empirical studies of water demand have been conducted with noisy data. All of the techniques reviewed in this chapter share this condition. This common characteristic can be improved but not eliminated. A consequence is that elasticity results are noisy too. Even when they are analytically determined, elasticities should be thought of as random variables for which we only know an expected value. When a statistical technique is involved in finding elasticity, it is possible to know more than the expected value; perhaps a statistical "variance" and "confidence interval" about this expected value can be estimated as well. Even when a nonstatistical technique such as mathematical programming is used to identify demand and possibly demand elasticity, however, it is still accurate to perceive the results as imperfectly known. These techniques have parameters, perhaps hundreds of them, that are "known" with varying degrees of imprecision, which are then imparted to the results.

Thought of pictorially, each panel of figure 9.6 includes a baseline (bold) demand curve obtained by the point expansion method. Presumably, the illustrated point is reasonably well-known from recent conditions, and the presumed elasticity ($\varepsilon = -0.45$) has been imported, perhaps from studies conducted for other regions and/or earlier times. If we can be honest with ourselves about this framework, the three panels of figure 9.6 indicate areas of caution for our demand applications.

Perhaps due to issues 1–4 above, there may be some doubt about the precision of the chosen elasticity measure. In the upper panel of figure 9.6, two competing demand curves are included. Their elasticities are -0.2 and -0.7. If one of these demand functions is "truer" than the presumed demand function, then further analysis may mislead us, especially if modeled conditions will involve quantities or prices far from the initial point.

Issue 4 above can be especially important in the manner just depicted, especially if the analysis at hand involves a long planning horizon combined with high growth in scarcity. The short- versus long-run issue can also have quicker relevance if scarcity has been rapidly changing in recent years. Such changes would hopefully elicit new policy and price signals to agents, causing them to reconsider their current water-using capital. In the middle panel of figure 9.6, the original point of demand expansion is in error for forthcoming periods because agents are transitioning to a lower demand through changes in durables and technology (i.e., conservation investments). It may be that households are changing their landscaping to native plant species, farmers are switching irrigation technologies or moving to dryland production, or industries are modifying production processes to recirculate more water. Due to the signals of higher scarcity and the responses, the original point lacks permanence.

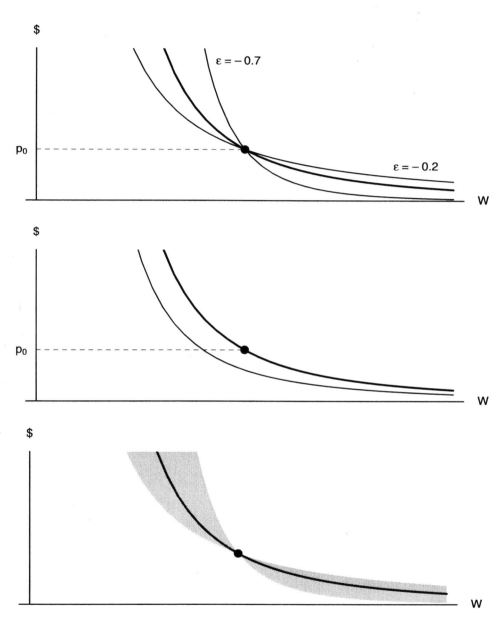

Figure 9.6
Estimation and projection errors

The final panel of figure 9.6 reminds us of the imprecision with which all methods estimate demand. There may be a high probability that demand lies within the darkened range, but it is impossible to say exactly where with certainty. For near-current conditions such as at p_0, our demand estimate may be tightly known, whereas the range can be quite wide under future conditions where scarcity is markedly different than it is now.

A prime upshot of these considerations is the usefulness of sensitivity analysis for demand parameters. Once baseline analysis has been performed using the baseline demand function (or *functions* if there is more than one), analysis can be reperformed using alternative demand parameters. Such work reveals the sensitivity of results to imperfectly known demand, and injects useful caution regarding policy, pricing, and project decisions.

With the prior advice in mind, we can consider some of the empirical evidence researchers have generated about water demand. Needless to say, there are many available studies, and they employ a variety of techniques. There are many important nuances within these studies. Regions are different. Time periods are different. Data are assembled from different sources. Variables and functional relationships are defined in different ways. In some cases, we can consult existing reviews rather than originally reviewing the many studies and their distinctive elements.

9.13   Residential Water Demand

Residential water demand is the easiest to consider because it is so directly studied by prior statistical analyses of consumption behavior. This does not mean that analyzing residential water demand is easy to do. Indeed, there are interesting challenges to be faced by analysts wishing to do this sort of work. Renzetti's (2002b) book on water demand summarizes these issues well.

One can obtain a quick overview of empirical findings by consulting the meta-analyses performed by Espey, Espey, and Shaw (1997) and Dalhuisen et al. (2003). These researchers have collected information from many studies for further statistical analysis. In terms of the assembled price elasticities, the work of Dalhuisen et al. is the most exhaustive, and they further compile these studies into a downloadable spreadsheet.[22] This spreadsheet lists 314 price elasticities for residential water demand, gleaned from 64 distinct studies released from 1963 to 2001. No attempt to prioritize or qualify these studies is performed, but we should recognize that a gradation of care and thoroughness exists across these individual research works. The range of price elasticities is surprisingly wide, extending from -7.47 to $+7.90$.

22. See ⟨http://www.feweb.vu.nl/re/master-point/database.html⟩.

Frankly, some of these studies' findings are unacceptable. Either because of poor quality data or statistical issues, not all of the reported price elasticities are believable.

On the one hand, highly negative price elasticities are hard to accept given the relative importance and affordability of water for most modern households. It would seem quite rare for a 7 percent increase in water price to motivate households to reduce their consumption by more than *one-half*, as indicated by the -7.47 elasticity $(7\% \cdot (-7.47) = -52.29\%)$. Hence, the most negative elasticity estimates of this sample are too extreme to be applied in typical settings.

At the opposing end of the spectrum, the possibility of positive demand elasticity (upward-sloping demand) is also hard to comprehend. Two possible explanations are either data measurement errors or price being collinear with important omitted variables. Compounding problems are possible too, such as the "simultaneity" issue arising from regression analysis in the presence of block rates. As a more practical matter, if water rates are low in a given study area, then consumers may not be paying enough to notice the price. In the latter case, it is conceivable that price elasticity would not be statistically different from zero. It is thus possible for statistical studies to produce a slightly positive price elasticity estimate. But price elasticities greater than $+0.1$ are odd, and they encourage further investigation in this author's opinion.

An acceptable procedure for culling the Dalhuisen et al. collection of price elasticities is to omit outliers at each end of its spectrum. Excluding both the highest and lowest 5 percent of the price elasticities narrows the range dramatically because of the small number of outliers. The resulting elasticities vary from -1.233 to $+0.01$, with only one slightly positive elasticity. Across these 282 "observations," the average elasticity is -0.3835. If we count the number of elasticities lying in each 0.1 interval extending from -1.3 to $+0.1$ and graph the results, figure 9.7 is obtained, which also indicates the mean with a dashed line. Given that some of the studies represented here are rather dated, it is possible that the distribution depicted in figure 9.7 has shifted leftward in recent times, meaning that today's average would be a little higher. Hence, modern price elasticities for annual water use are likely to lie in the -0.35 to -0.45 range. Examining the Dalhuisen et al. results more closely, it can be argued that long-term residential price elasticity may be approximately 0.3 or more points higher (e.g., -0.7), but 0.2 points higher would be a conservative estimate. Furthermore, although the Dalhuisen et al. results can be referred to for greater differences, in my opinion monthly price elasticities (with seasonality) differ from the annual estimates as follows: winter price elasticities are about 0.1 points lower (closer to zero and less responsive) and summer price elasticities are 0.15 to 0.2 points higher. Of course, regional disparities imply that these generalizations will not fit all situations.

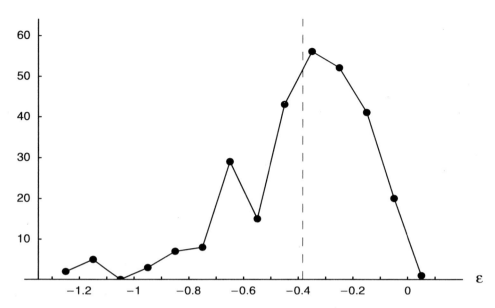

Figure 9.7
Counts of residential elasticity estimates

A crucial matter not to be overlooked here is the overwhelming evidence that demand is price responsive. Except for a few results out of hundreds, it would appear
that people do not "require" a fixed amount of water independent of price. Fundamentally, then, the economic concept of demand applies for water just as it does for
all other commodities and resources. And although one can always cite a couple of
studies that do result in very-near zero or even positive demand elasticity, equal attention to the extremely negative elasticities should tell us something about the vaga-
ries of statistical analysis as well as the noise that arises in a world of incomplete,
imperfect data and omitted effects.

9.14   Industrial and Commercial Water Demand

Due to comparative data availability, industrial and commercial water demand is
much less studied than household or agricultural demand. The data deficiencies include price and quantity information as well as other demand determinants. Our
base economic theory of chapter 2 tells us that business water demand is a function
of output and input prices as well as water price (see box 2.1). If we are to distinguish
the role of water price from other effects and thereby isolate the marginal benefit of
water in production activities, we must disentangle the effect of water price from the
other influences.

Small commercial operations such as restaurants, laundries, and car washes commonly obtain their water from city utilities. Because such water is priced and metered, it would seem practical to subject this demand to statistical analysis. Like other businesses, however, the water demands of these operations are affected by other factors, especially things that affect the levels of production activities. Water use data will therefore vary in response to a variety of things, which will confuse the identification of water price's role. To make progress, we must acquire good data on a number of things.

Large industrial users tend to supply and process their own water; they are "self-supplied." They often exercise their own water rights. They frequently make their own expenditures to convert natural surface or ground water into the processed water they desire. Water use is commonly unmetered or unreported because it is not required. Self-suppliers ordinarily face no "price" for their water use.[23] Whereas these business enterprises do experience costs of water withdrawal and processing, they may not record these costs separately from their other incurred costs. Even when the appropriate data are recorded somewhere, analysts do not have ready access to them. These facts limit the applicability of regression techniques for discovering demand. Yet with enough ingenuity, progress can and has been made.

For these reasons, there are limits to what regression analysis can practically achieve here. Mathematical programming is often called on as a technique for studying water demand in these situations. Math programming analysis, though, tends to identify a discontinuous version of demand (as shown earlier). Because of dramatic differences in the way water is utilized in firms producing different goods, programming studies distinguish industrial classifications. This is difficult analysis to do correctly, especially when it is dimensioned by a large number of dissimilar, water-using businesses producing dissimilar goods.

Renzetti has provided two reviews of available evidence pertaining to industrial water demand. One is contained in the aforementioned book on water demand (Renzetti 2002b, 38–46). The second is his introductory chapter for a book that reprints previous articles on industrial water demand (Renzetti 2002a). Prior studies are few, and most are dated. Math programming analysis is sometimes performed without noting elasticity. For a general perspective on these results, table 9.2 lists some of the primary studies cited by Renzetti along with the date of their publication. For further information, the interested reader should begin with the individual papers of the Renzetti (2002a) compilation.

---

23. Acknowledging this fact is not the same as supporting it. Recall from earlier chapters, especially chapter 8, that the value of natural water should be faced by any water-using agent. In locales having a viable water market, agents do tend to face the opportunity cost of the natural water they use, regardless of whether they pay a per-unit fee for it. Yet in the absence of such markets, this signal is also absent. In the latter cases, the only means of inducing efficient consumption behavior may be to meter water withdrawals and apply a natural water charge. This is especially true of scarce ground water scenarios because ground water institutions have yet to cause agents to perceive an MUC-inclusive opportunity cost.

Table 9.2
Studies revealing industrial or commercial demand elasticity

Author/sector	Price elasticity of demand
Rees (1969)	
Chemical	−0.96
Food	−3.3 to −6.7
Drink	−1.3 to −4.1
Nonmetallic metals	−2.5
Turnovsky (1969)	−0.47 to −8.4
De Rooy (1974)	
Cooling	−0.89
Process	−0.35
Steam	−0.59
Ziegler and Bell (1984)	
Chemical	−0.98
Renzetti (1992a)	
By two-digit Standard Industrial Classification	−0.15 to −0.59

One must worry about the accuracy of dated elasticity estimates for contemporary circumstances. New research in this area is occasionally forthcoming (such as Moeltner and Stoddard 2004), but progress is slow. Another concern is that some industrial uses have tended to employ water in a weakly consumptive, flow-through manner, as for cooling. Under these conditions, demand elasticity may be quite negative since there may be inexpensive means for curtailing water use with little loss in productive value. If a particular application of water is weakly consumptive, such as flow-through cooling water in a region where the raised water temperature is not ecologically damaging, then the use may take on a highly nonrival character—justifying continued low pricing and sustaining a highly negative elasticity.

9.15 Agricultural Water Demand

Agricultural water demand is a well-studied topic, as befits the dominant water use in most water-scarce regions. Typical agricultural water demand studies are of the mathematical programming variety. Although examples of hedonic methods exist in the agricultural literature, they have not been suggestive of water demand.[24] Meta-

---

24. By assembling sales records for agricultural lands, some of which are irrigated and some of which are dryland, it is possible to statistically examine the contributed value of irrigability (Darwin 1999; Mendelsohn and Nordhaus 1999; Mendelsohn and Dinar 2003). Because the profit advantage of irrigated lands should be capitalized in land value, if not separately capitalized in the value of separable water rights, it may be possible to extract water *value* with such studies (applying equation (7.8)). Water *demand* estimation is more elusive, however, as noted in the earlier section on hedonic pricing.

analysis has been recently applied (Scheierling, Loomis, and Young 2005). The prevalence of math programming is the result of poor data availability for statistical analysis. It is interesting that most math programming studies *embed* agriculture's demand response to limited supply, but these studies are not focused exclusively on the identification of demand. So they do not tend to report simplistic things like demand elasticity. Popularly investigated topics include what crops are most profitable to grow under differing water availability scenarios, which irrigation technologies are most profitable, and what crops/technologies and sectoral water allocations should be regionally undertaken in a multisectoral economy with limited water.

Sometimes, a math programming study of irrigation will identify some of the (w, MB(w)) points on the demand function, much like the points that were displayed in figure 9.3. Examples include careful studies by Bernardo et al. (1987, 1988) that use an agronomic simulation model to provide the coefficients of a math programming model. When demand points are tabulated by studies such as these, the formula for computing elasticity between two points,

$$\varepsilon = \frac{\Delta w}{\Delta p} \cdot \frac{p}{w}, \tag{2.12}$$

can be applied even when the study does not report elasticity.[25] In doing so, one generally finds that agricultural water demand is very price inelastic (negative and close to zero) when water is plentiful (for large quantities or low marginal value). As the available water shrinks (or its marginal value increases), the price elasticity rises and eventually becomes elastic ($\varepsilon < -1.0$). Hence, profit-maximizing irrigators do not curtail their water use much (in percentage terms) when a very low water price increases. Yet as the water price continues to rise, the quantity demanded responds more highly. For still higher prices, the percentage change in quantity demanded can exceed the percentage change of price. Unlike residential demand, irrigation water demand will often exhibit a choke price—a price threshold above which the quantity demanded is zero. Overall, these findings tell us that agricultural water demand is generally not a constant elasticity function.

The demand points tabulated in the Bernardo et al. studies allow seventeen elasticities to be computed. They range from -0.006 to -0.57, and pertain to a single, representative farm in the northwest region of the United States. The variable elasticity

---

25. The results reported in the discussion below use the formula

$$\varepsilon = \frac{w_2 - w_1}{p_2 - p_1} \times \frac{p_2 + p_1}{w_2 + w_1}$$

for computing elasticities from neighboring demand points. Hence, the selected (w, p) point of (2.12) is midway between the two demand points, (w_1, p_1) and (w_2, p_2).

Table 9.3
Studies revealing irrigation demand elasticity

Study	Method[1]	Price elasticity	Type[2]
Bernardo et al. (1987)	MP/rep. farm	−0.10 to −0.57	arc
Bernardo et al. (1988)	MP/rep. farm	−0.006 to −0.57	arc
Howitt, Watson, and Adams (1980)	MP/state	−0.19 to −2.23	arc
Kulshreshtha and Tewari (1991)	MP/district	−0.05 to −3.09	arc
Amir and Fisher (1999)	MP/district	−0.19 to −0.49	point
Nieswiadomy (1985)	Stat/GW	−0.8	log-log
		−0.29, −1.24	point
Ogg and Gollehon (1989)	Stat/GW	−0.07 to −0.26	point + log-log
Moore, Gollehon, and Carey (1994)	Stat/GW	+0.03 to −0.1	point
Bain, Caves, and Margolis (1966)	Stat/district	−0.64	log-log

1. MP = math programming; stat = statistical analysis of water use and price data; rep. farm = representative farm; district = district level MP or statistical data for multiple districts; and GW = ground water.

2. Arc = arc elasticity, computed between two demand points; point = elasticity computed at a particular point on the demand function; and log-log = elasticity is constant along the obtained demand function.

stems not only from a range of water availability scenarios and implied values but from differing water sources and irrigation technologies as well. Table 9.3 contains this information along with similar findings for the other studies reviewed here.

Other studies may first use math programming to generate demand-revealing points as above and then do additional work with these points, such as connecting them, computing elasticity across neighboring quantity-value pairs, or fitting a function through them.[26] Each such study involves a particular irrigated region, involving potentially unique climate, soils, and agricultural market conditions (i.e., prices and subsidies). By themselves, the computed demand points of each of these studies illustrate a negatively sloped step function of the general appearance given in figures 9.1–9.3, though conceivably with far more steps (see also, for example, Kelso, Martin, and Mack 1973, 124–125; Kindler and Russell 1984, 142–143). For the math programming studies of table 9.3, the range of determined elasticities is wide, and it is dependent on where on the demand function we measure elasticity.

The results of Howitt, Watson, and Adams (1980) infer unique demand elasticities for irrigation.[27] If we use their results to compute more elasticities than they tabu-

26. Some of these studies omit the minus sign when reporting/discussing demand elasticity. This is not unusual in mainstream economics as the negative demand response to price is presumed. Omitting the negative sign can lead to confusion, however.

27. Other studies formally reviewed here support the finding of low price elasticities at low prices. The unique character of the Howitt, Watson, and Adams results is sometimes found in other studies, though. For example, Oamek (1990, 121–130) examines the potential sale/lease of water rights by irrigators of the

late, demand is elastic ($\varepsilon < -1.0$) for the lowest prices. Then demand becomes quite inelastic as price increases. At the highest evaluated prices, demand is still inelastic, but elasticity is becoming more negative again (more elastic). Eight elasticities—ranging from -0.19 to -2.23—are computable from their results.

Kulshreshtha and Tewari (1991) regress a line through their math programming demand points, reporting that a linear function fits better than some other functional forms. Their demand elasticities follow the usual pattern, as do most other studies noted here (very inelastic at low prices and more elastic for higher prices). Listed elasticities between pairs of demand points range from -0.05 to -3.09 (231).

Amir and Fisher (1999) formulate a math programming model that they use to investigate demand within several Israeli irrigation districts. They also regress a line through their data points.[28] After evaluating elasticity at a single price for different districts, elasticities ranging from -0.19 to -0.49 are tabulated.

Similarly constructed math programming models investigate irrigation's response to changing energy prices. Such studies also disclose water demand because energy price can be thought of as a surrogate for water price. When ground water is used by irrigators, profits are sensitive to energy costs. In such cases, energy costs may be the primary variable cost of water. As energy price rises, the quantity of ground water demanded falls. So math programming studies of these situations also yield step functions relating energy prices to water use (Gardner and Young 1984; Taylor 1989).

Nieswiadomy (1985) uses the dependence of ground water demand on energy price to create a data set capable of supporting statistical analysis. Using water table measurements to infer annual water use and defining an energy price for one acre-foot of water, irrigation water demand is statistically estimated for a specific study region. For the high-energy price period of the data set (1973–1980), irrigation demand is demonstrably responsive to price for the two models estimated—a linear function and a log-log form. Demand elasticity is only identified for the log-log form. It is -0.8 throughout the data range.[29] Recall that constancy of elasticity is maintained (forced) by the log-log form. Nevertheless, if the linear form's estimated slope is

---

Colorado River basin and reports findings consistent with high elasticities at low prices. Because irrigators' supply of water rights mirrors their demand for water, these results are comparable. Oamek does suggest that his low crop prices may be a reason for irrigators' willingness to supply a large amount of water at low water price. (Recall the important manner in which output prices influence the firms' demand for water inputs; see equation [2.6]).

28. In regressing a line through their demand points, Amir and Fisher appear to include all their demand points in the regression's data set. Recalling figure 9.3 above, if there are points that are vertically aligned, then the lower points understate water's marginal benefits and should be excluded.

29. A later paper by Nieswiadomy (1988) uses these same data to estimate a cost of production function (for agricultural products). One result is a reported "output constant water demand elasticity" of -0.25. This is a different sort of elasticity than the one that interests us.

used along with the average data tabulated in the paper, an elasticity of -0.29 emerges for 1973 (cheaper energy) and -1.24 for 1980 (expensive energy). Further inspection shows that both of these elasticities increase with rising price.

Also relying on pumping costs to reveal something about irrigation water demand, two additional studies use data from surveys of U.S. farmers. Ogg and Gollehon (1989) examine the relationship between quantity demanded and average pumping costs (price), and obtain price elasticities of -0.07 (linear form), -0.17 (log-log form, instrumental variable estimation), -0.18 (quadratic form), and -0.26 (log-log form). Unfortunately, the intraregional variability of per acre water use in the 1,927-farm data set is exceedingly low, causing the reader to wonder if ground water-using farmers are accurately reporting their water use. Or do farmers tend to report their expected or desired water use?

Using the same survey information, expanded by a few hundred farms, and a more advanced formulation of water demand determination, Moore, Gollehon, and Carey (1994) generate additional demand elasticities. Overall, computed demand elasticities are strikingly low again, estimated for four distinct regions to be -0.1, -0.06, -0.03, and $+0.03$ (870). General statistical performance for this data set appears to be deficient, implying that confidence intervals about these elasticity estimates may be large.

Thus far, we have only discussed statistical analyses of irrigation's *ground water* demand because energy costs offer a tractable price variable. Farmers with their own access to surface water pay little for pumping energy, so there is little demand estimation that can be done for self-supplied surface water. On the other hand, many irrigators buy water from an irrigation district or similar water authority. Drawing on the success of residential water demand analyses, isn't it possible to use consumption and price data from irrigation districts to estimate agricultural water demand? It is possible, but there are some problems to confront.

The most significant barrier for statistical analysis is dealing with how irrigation water is usually priced by districts. In both past and contemporary settings, acreage charges are an important billing device—often the only billing device (Michelsen et al. 1999). In recent times, district rate structures have begun to embrace metering and volumetric pricing, but progress has been both slow and short. Widespread agricultural reluctance to use water rates as a rationing instrument has meant that volumetric rates have been low, inferring that a small range of demand functions are being revealed. Most districts in the western United States continue to benefit from federally subsidized water, which represents another force limiting the information relayed in irrigation usage data. Metered water information can also be suspect in agricultural settings, as unpressurized flows to individual farms are challenging to meter accurately, and some of the metering technologies are not fully reliable or tamper resistant. The reduced practicality of using statistical analysis to study water demand infers that other methods tend to be utilized.

A rare example of statistical analysis of irrigation demand is provided by Bain, Caves, and Margolis (1966, 175–179). They use 1958 data from thirty-four irrigation districts to estimate water use per irrigated acre as a function of the average water price per acre (thirty-four observations). Interestingly, water price is calculated using all revenue sources, including flat charges such as tax assessments. A log-log form is the only functional form reported. Price elasticity is found to be −0.64, and the authors nicely disclose the 95 percent confidence interval for this estimate, −0.42 to −0.87.

9.16 Summary

Determining water demand is a more inquisitive pursuit than determining water value. Whereas water demand is a functional relation between quantity demanded and price, a marginal value of water is a single point on this function and a total value is an area for a interval under this function. Ultimately, knowledge of the function is more useful than knowing a single value.

The theory and empirics of demand analysis help us to understand the shortcomings of "requirement" thinking. Like demands for all other goods and resources, the demand for water is not a single quantity per person, per household, per $1,000 of output, per ton of product, or per anything. If we are to generate useful advice and action for rising water scarcity, then it is time to move beyond myths. The reality is that rising scarcity does and should alter the quantity demanded. This principle is verified by the methods and results examined here.

Water demand estimation is a serious task requiring serious methods. Most of this chapter has been devoted to explaining and interrelating eight general methods having some ability to disclose water demand. Then, empirical findings of water demand are reviewed for three sectors: residential, commercial/industrial, and agricultural. The empirical findings offer a useful reflection on the methods. Empirical progress for the three sectors is clearly dominated by two approaches, direct statistical regression and mathematical programming. Hence, these methods have the greatest demonstrated relevance for rival uses of water.

Two additional methods also have strongly proven worth. Armed with elasticity or slope information provided by another method, the point expansion method has some special abilities owing to its ease of application and capacity to generate quick advice. Residual imputation is a fundamental method, for it forms the backbone of math programming. The alternative activities of a math program are individual exercises of residual imputation.

Although we only "sampled" the available evidence, the reviewed empirical results offer useful quantitative guidance about the nature of water demand. This information can be directly adopted for water planning scenarios that are appropriately consistent, or it can help design original studies pertaining to new circumstances or deeper inspections.

9.17   Exercises

1. Imagine a river basin with a water supply that is large in relation to water use by any single user group. Enter this water supply as a fixed quantity, $\overline{W}$, on a two-axis (w, $) graph. Within this basin, let's abstractly call the user groups "people factories" and assume that they are all identical. Draw a MNB function for a single factory on the graph, scaling the function appropriately for the setting described thus far.

a. As long as the summed demand of all people factories does not challenge the available basin supply, what point on the single MNB function best describes a factory's "requirement"? Why?

b. Make use of your graph in a discussion that portrays the growth process as a slow, incremental increase in the number of people factories. (Every n years a new factory pops up.) Assume that water use by these factories is strictly rival. Illustrate aggregate natural water demand as a complement to your discussion and include it within your discussion. Is the idea of a requirement misdirected throughout this basin's history?

2. Program the point expansion method into a spreadsheet or other computer program. Set it up so that you may easily enter the three required numbers: elasticity, point quantity, and point price. The program should output four clearly labeled functions or parameters for these four functions: linear demand, inverted linear demand, constant elasticity demand, and inverted constant elasticity demand. Once completed, you should be able to change any of the three input numbers and automatically get all four functions. Use these inputs in the final, saved, and printed edition of your program: $\varepsilon = -0.4$ and $(w, p) = (160, 2.5)$.

3. Redraw figure 9.1 for a three-activity setting with the following parameters: $K = 30$, $\{w_1, w_2, w_3\} = \{2400, 1000, 400\}$, and $\{\pi_1, \pi_2, \pi_3\} = \{200, 100, 50\}$. Precisely label the relevant axes markings. For example, do not simply label p′ on the price axis; put a number there.

4. Use the specifications of the prior problem to compose a precisely stated linear programming problem, like that produced in box 9.1.

5. The availability of an actual data set for box 9.2 allows you to conduct your own regression analysis of residential water demand. Many computer programs are capable of doing ordinary least squares regression—for example, Excel does this. Using the 1,080 observation data set given on the Web site, reestimate demand using the

marginal price (MP) variable instead of average price. What differences occur? (By the way, the use of AP or MP specifications has been highly debated in the water demand literature.)

Appendix 9.A: Joining Point Expansion and Residual Imputation Methods

For a well-defined production activity constituting a substantial portion of an agent's total water use, the *average* water value emerging from the residual imputation (RI) procedure may not approximate the desired *marginal* water value. If the analyst's purpose for conducting RI is to generate a point to which an elasticity will be applied for further analysis, however, then we may combine the RI and point expansion methods to produce a mutually consistent demand function in which the RI-based point does express marginal benefits.

Suppose that the production activity under inspection is the least productive (most marginal) use of water in the firm, and it consumes Δw units of water, as portrayed in figure 9.A.1. w^* is the total amount of water demanded by this agent for all purposes. Δw is the amount of water consumed in the production activity analyzed by

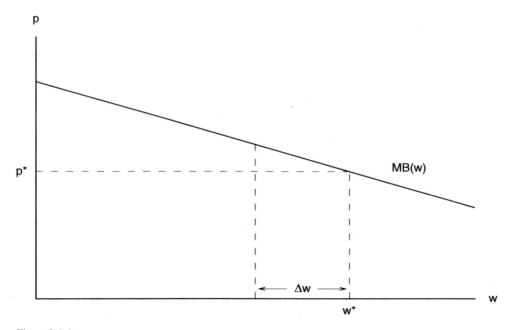

Figure 9.A.1
Point expansion with residual imputation

RI, and it yields a residual value (total, not average) of TV. (It is possible that $\Delta w = w^*$.) TV must be the area under the demand curve from $w^* - \Delta w$ to w^*:

$$TV = \int_{w^* - \Delta w}^{w^*} D^{-1}(w)\, dw. \tag{9.16}$$

The Linear Case

If the presumed demand function is linear, then we can arbitrarily write

$$w = -\frac{1}{b}p + \frac{a}{b}, \tag{9.17}$$

or in equivalent inverse form,

$$MB = -bw + a, \tag{9.18}$$

where a and b are coefficients to be determined. We are also interested in determining the marginal benefits provided by the $w^{*\text{th}}$ unit of water, which is expressed by $MB(w^*)$.

If it is possible to presume a specific elasticity, ε, at the demand point $(w^*, MB(w^*))$, then the limit definition of elasticity (equation (2.13)) may be combined with (9.18) to obtain a relation between a and b. This task is completed by the following sequence of equations.

$$\varepsilon = \frac{dw}{dp} \cdot \frac{p}{w} < 0$$

$$= -\frac{1}{b}\frac{p}{w}$$

$$= -\frac{1}{b}\frac{MB(w^*)}{w^*}$$

$$\varepsilon w^* = -\frac{1}{b}MB(w^*)$$

$$= -\frac{1}{b}(-bw^* + a)$$

$$= w^* - \frac{a}{b}$$

Therefore,

$$a = bw^*(1 - \varepsilon). \tag{9.19}$$

Combining (9.16) and (9.18) where TV is known from RI,

$$TV = \frac{1}{2}\Delta w(-b(w^* - \Delta w) + a - bw^* + a),$$

implying

$$TV = \frac{1}{2}\Delta w(-2bw^* + 2a - b\Delta w). \tag{9.20}$$

Substituting (9.19) into (9.20), the following finding for b is obtained after a little algebra:

$$b = \frac{2TV}{(\Delta w)^2 - 2\varepsilon w^* \Delta w}. \tag{9.21}$$

The resolution of b via (9.21) and then a via (9.19) means that the demand function is known. Also known is $MB(w^*)$ once the demand function (9.18) is obtained by inserting the calculated b and a, and it is interesting to contrast this with the average water value that is resolved by RI alone.

The Constant Elasticity Case

The derivation procedure above can be retraced for a demand function presumed to exhibit constant elasticity ($w = kp^\varepsilon$). The results depend on whether $\varepsilon = -1$ or not. Only the results are stated here:

Box 9.A.1
A Demonstration

A regional group of farming agents irrigate hay as their least valued crop. Hay receives 10 percent of the water these irrigators use in aggregate. The irrigators get fifteen thousand acre-feet annually from their water provider and routinely apply fifteen hundred acre-feet to hay in a normal growing season. Careful application of the residual imputation procedure indicates that the residual value of all this hay is $12,000, or $8 per acre-foot. With a downward-sloping demand for irrigation water, we know that this average value overestimates the marginal value, but by how much?

Analysis

Suppose that the elasticity of water demand across all these farmers and their crops is thought to be -1.0. Using this information in (9.21), (9.19), and (9.18) tells us that the marginal benefit of the last unit of water is $1.33. This is substantially different than $8, having sizable implications for project and policy analysis. Larger elasticities (more negative) bring the marginal value closer to the average value. For example, if $\varepsilon = -2$, then $MB(w^*) = \$2.29$. This value is still not approximated by the average value, attesting to the potential importance of this method or, arguably, indicating an incongruency of using point expansion with linear demand. Average and marginal values are much closer in this case if a constant elasticity demand function is used.

If $\varepsilon = -1$,   then $MB = \dfrac{k}{w}$ and $k = TV \Big/ \ln\left(\dfrac{w^*}{w^* - \Delta w}\right).$ (9.22)

If $\varepsilon \neq -1$,   then $MB = \left(\dfrac{w}{k}\right)^{1/\varepsilon}$ and

$$k = \left(\frac{\varepsilon}{(1+\varepsilon)TV}\right)^{\varepsilon} \cdot \left((w^*)^{(1+\varepsilon)/\varepsilon} - (w^* - \Delta w)^{(1+\varepsilon)/\varepsilon}\right)^{\varepsilon}.$$ (9.23)

Empirical application of either (9.22) or (9.23) should yield marginal benefit estimates that are more in line with average benefits (as opposed to the findings of box 9.A.1). That is, the use of linear demand with a single presumed elasticity is less likely to yield consistent results. The application of these findings to the setting posed within box 9.A.1 is undertaken by a Mathematica file available at the text's Web site.

10 Supply Analysis

How do we obtain marginal cost functions?

In the case of demand, economics focuses on how the continuum of water use translates into marginal benefits (MB) for consumers. Every human agent and perhaps every business agent is a water consumer, so there are many agents of significance. Simplified techniques such as point expansion can expediently address aggregate water demand, but a general demand elasticity must first be determined. Such information can be hard to obtain, and as demonstrated in the previous chapter, economists have mobilized many methods that might be of assistance.

Things are different for water supply. Whereas demand estimation involves a variety of techniques, the methods available for water supply estimation are more limited. To a large extent, this is a consequence of the number of agents on the water supply side (few). As we shall soon see, this feature of supply constrains the available methods and data in important ways.

When investigating water supply economics, we are most concerned about the marginal costs (MC) of transforming natural water into retail water.[1] If attention is merely focused on the physical shortages of water relative to the "demand" for water, as is common in noneconomic discussions and writings, then progress toward real solutions is seriously hampered. The water issues faced by society are not adequately illuminated by emphasizing the physical scarcity of water. The true issues pertain to the economic scarcity of water. Economic scarcity incorporates physical scarcity, but physical scarcity itself is too underspecified for advanced water management.

---

1. For reasons relating to institutional constraints (on water-pricing issues, for example) or approximation (of MC), we might be satisfied with knowledge of average costs instead of marginal costs. Of course, if the functional dependence of total costs on water deliveries can be ascertained, either marginal or average costs can be computed.

The paucity of suppliers also gives rise to the privatization question due to the monopoly status of individual water suppliers. Monopoly managers are endowed with powers that can be abusive to economic efficiency. Unfortunately, that's true of *both* profit-focused and not-for-profit management. As most people are generally aware, uncontrolled private monopolies can keep service as well as output levels below efficient levels in order to reduce costs and increase price. On the other hand, public utilities and districts can be wasteful and favor nonefficiency objectives in their decision making, leading to overly expensive services. An awareness of these issues can be an important matter for water resource professionals.

In this chapter, we shall look at the economic techniques used to estimate retail water's economic supply. We shall also examine key aspects of the privatization debate even though it is not a central concern for supply estimation techniques. Finally, some of the empirical evidence of supply estimation will be considered.

10.1   The Roles of Supply Information

To refine the empirical job to be tackled in estimating MCs, first recall the manners in which the right information can be used to advance water resource decision making. Looking back over the trail thus far and looking forward to the scarcity issues that confront water managers, economically defined supply information is seen to be useful—if not critical—in several areas. The following items summarize the major applications in which supply knowledge is necessary or fruitful.

Allocation and Aggregation   To efficiently apportion limited water across different agents or agent groupings, it is necessary to value common units. Because of retail water's *differential processing* (see section 2.4) for different sectors, adjustments must be made for processing costs before different demands can be added or compared. The simplest adjustment is to emphasize natural water value (MB_{nrtl}). This is accomplished by targeting the marginal net benefits of retail water, which is defined by

$$MB_{ntrl}(w) = MNB(w) = MB(w) - MC(w). \tag{10.1}$$

Once this adjustment is performed, we can either add the resulting demands for natural water (MB_{nrtl}) to obtain the total natural water demand (as in figure 2.10) or equate natural water's marginal benefits to find the optimal allocation of water across different agents or sectors (as in figures 2.11 and 2.12 as well as equation [2.31]). None of this is possible until MC is known for providing water to each agent or group.

Optimal Depletion and Dynamic Scheduling   Once the static concepts of efficiency are correctly extended to dynamic issues, marginal costs maintain relevancy. (Determining optimal depletion rates for ground water is an example issue faced here.) MNBs are again a key concept, so knowledge of MC remains crucial. See figure 3.3 and/or equations (3.14) or (3.15).

Policy Analysis The analysis of policy options for managing scarcity is strongly dependent on our ability to foresee impacts on both benefits and costs. On the water supply side, knowledge of either total costs, marginal costs, or average costs is pivotal. Most forms of policy analysis require attention to supply-side impacts. See, for example, figures 5.2 through 5.8 and the accompanying discussions. If MBs and MCs are combined into the MNB function reiterated in (10.1), then a great deal of empirical policy analysis can be readily performed.

Project Analysis The typical water project acquires or retains water that will be further processed and conveyed before it can be used by consumers. Therefore, valuation of a water project's net benefits and net present value requires cost information, in the same manner required for *supply-shifting policy*. So again, the MNB of retail water is crucial information for analysis.

Water Marketing Water marketing pertains to the exchange of natural water for money. The net gains available from such trades, as well as the incentives motivating agents to trade, are strongly determined by the MNBs experienced by water users. See, for example, figure 7.1 along with equations (7.2), (7.4), (7.5), and (7.10).

Water Pricing A central pricing recommendation for retail water is that the supplier should establish a volumetric price for water. To achieve economic efficiency, such a price should include the marginal cost of processing water as well as the scarcity values of natural water, depletable water, and system capital. Therefore, MC has both a direct and an indirect role in establishing well-priced water. Marginal cost is a direct element of the efficient water price (equations [8.2] through [8.5]), and through its impact on the regional scarcity value of natural or depletable water (the first two items above), it also has an indirect effect.

In virtually all of these applications, supply information in the form of MC functions is utilized alongside demand information in the form of MB functions. As with the demand side, cost functions are envisioned as continuously dependent on water deliveries. When both the MB and MC functions are known, they can either be employed separately yet conjunctively, or be linearly combined into a MNB function that then captures both benefits and costs. As an example of the first alternative, new policies or projects have water supply benefits that can be ascertained using MB while the accompanying water processing costs are measurable using MC. For the second alternative, net benefits are either measured or optimized using the collective function, MNB.

10.2   The Primary Feature of Supply Empiricism: Single Suppliers

Several of these six applications occur at the local level, even though a higher level of authority (e.g., state or federal) may be making the decisions, such as project approval. Whenever the *accounting stance* of decision making is local, there will ordinarily be a single water supplier of interest. In single-supplier cases, there is a single source of data pertaining to the supply costs. Consequently, other ways of accomplishing the water supply "mission" of transforming natural water into retail water are not being attempted, so a wide range of cost experience is not being generated; the absence of competition calls into question whether the supplier is actually operating in ways that minimize costs; and the single data stream emerging from this supplier may not offer robust information for extrapolating future costs.[2] With respect to the latter consequence, the small data set certainly constrains statistical opportunities for studying supply costs. This is in stark contrast to demand studies, where data are sometimes extensive, as with residential demand by numerous households.

For decisions involving larger accounting stances, the matter of single suppliers is still pertinent. Although there may be several-to-many water suppliers of relevance, they do not normally constitute alternatives or choices in any real sense. Each supplier possesses a distinct and normally exclusive service area. Unique features such as topography, water right holdings, surface water impoundments, environmentally sensitive areas, shifting or rocky soils (into which pipe is laid), and management or pricing traditions may perplex any analytic attempts to aggregate cost data for general statistical analysis. Still, such analyses are sometimes performed, and it will be useful to consider some of this literature.

10.3   The Process of Processing Water

To better appreciate processing costs, consider the range of expenditures made by water utilities and districts. Focusing on water services only (and ignoring wastewater collection and processing functions), figure 10.1 separates a water supplier's activities into three areas: administration and compliance, continuing production activities, and new production activities.

Regardless of the presence of demand growth, *administration* by a central body is applied within every water supply system. Whereas day-to-day administration is often conducted by a professional staff, these managers commonly report to elected or appointed board/council members who provide leadership pertaining to "big pic-

---

2. Recall from chapter 2 that economic efficiency in water allocation embeds cost minimization as a necessary element.

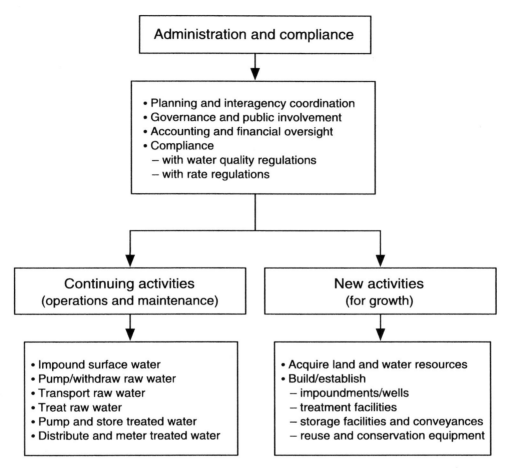

Figure 10.1
Water processing tasks

ture" issues. Studies are regularly conducted regarding management options and consequences. Interagency planning communications are common. Effort is devoted to complying with all rules set forth by higher levels of government. Choices are made by applying a variety of decision criteria and management styles. Interfacing with client groups can be important and difficult, especially with the attention water issues sometimes attract. Whereas some decisions may be made more or less democratically, as with voting by a city council, other decisions will be resolved through more corporate or bureaucratic mechanisms. Overall, these administrative functions can be expensive, and growth in these expenses over time may be weakly related to the total water use.

The day-to-day *continuing activities* of a water supplier pertain to the physical steps of processing water, utilizing *existing* infrastructure. This includes the impounding and pumping of surface water from natural watercourses, pumping ground water to the surface using wells, treating natural water to improve its quality, and the distribution of finished water to final consumers. Whereas treatment may be minimal or nonexistent in some settings, as in purely agricultural supply systems, in other circumstances water treatment may be extensive—perhaps entailing screening, desilting, aeration, cooling, demineralization, chlorination, dechlorination, fluorination, and many other forms of quality augmentation. These continuing activities are distinctive in that their total costs are better related to total water use than are costs for the other two areas. That is particularly true for continuing inputs such as pumping energy and treatment chemicals. Nevertheless, some continuing activity costs will not change in proportion to water use.

Supply system growth is the domain of *new activities*. For the most part, these costs are dominated by new (not replacement) infrastructure, installation work, land for siting the new infrastructure, and additional natural water supplies. In typical circumstances, infrastructure and its installation are the dominant costs. As discussed previously, especially in chapter 8, these costs can be poorly related to water use.

10.4 Conceptualizing Costs

The marginal cost of water supply is the normally needed information, depending on the water management issue at hand. In a few situations, it may be more useful to work with average costs. Either marginal or average costs may be obtained from a disclosure of total costs, so that is a great starting place for empirical work. Whereas elementary economics considers $C(W)$ to be the proper total cost form, accounting- and engineering-based examinations find this to be too simplistic for accuracy. That is not surprising once the full range of costs are considered. There are too many water supply costs that are poorly related to water deliveries.

While there are undoubtedly other possibilities warranted by the exact water issue(s) being confronted at any point in time, recall that a strong enhancement of the elementary economic vision of total costs is captured by

$$C(\Delta N, W, N), \tag{10.2}$$

where

C is the aggregate water supply cost function during an analysis period,
ΔN is the number of new connections during the period,
W is the total water deliveries during the period, and
N is the number of active connections during the period.

For both alternatives, C(W) and C(ΔN, W, N), the standard presumption is that total costs, C, includes all *financial* outlays including (1) operation and maintenance (O&M) costs, and (2) appropriate estimates of capital costs. Economic literature typically refers to these two groupings as variable and fixed costs. Fixed (capital) costs are often amortized across the presumed life span of individual capital items. The tradition is that these two categories (variable and fixed) are mutually exclusive and complete. That is, all financial costs fall in one category, but not both. Because C includes only financial outlays, there are likely to be nonfinancial costs to be separately considered, especially the scarcity value (opportunity cost) of water and capital (MVW, MUC, and MCC). Because our customs continue to exclude nonfinancial costs from the cost function, it is important to be careful about the ways in which cost functions are constructed and utilized.

The functional concept of costs observed by (10.2) was originally forwarded as (8.1). It is an outgrowth of cost allocation studies of water supply performed by accounting specialists. These accountants have determined that substantial portions of water supply costs are better "explained" by system growth and customer numbers than by water deliveries. Such findings are rooted in the capital intensity (i.e., high fixed costs) of water supply systems. Most water storage and conveyance facilities have costs that are functionally dependent on their volumetric displacements or one-dimensional lengths, rather than on the flow of water through these storage and conveyance structures. To a large degree, these displacements and lengths are better related to customer numbers than to water deliveries. For example, each customer tends to add to the capacity demand of the water production system and the spatial coverage of the water distribution system.

Thought of another way, there can be a big difference in water supply costs depending on whether one hundred typical consumers either double their water demand or are added to the system. Whereas both additions represent the same amount of water quantity demanded for all levels of water price, it is the one hundred new customers who add to the distribution infrastructure (as well as added meter reading, billing, and customer service attention).

Within the six categories of application enumerated previously, most water management issues involve growth in both customer numbers and water demand. Hence, the cost conception displayed by (10.2) is more appropriate than C(W). In isolated cases, however, C(W) may be suitable. This is only sound when customer numbers are fixed (as in a nonexpanding irrigation district) *and* no crosscutting matters are being encountered.[3]

---

3. A crosscutting issue would occur if the water management decision under consideration has other implications. For example, more efficient volumetric water pricing in an irrigation district could induce a reduction in irrigated acreage with cost implications depending on the spatial distribution of the remaining

10.5   Basic Methods of Supply Estimation

If C(W) is believed to be an appropriate representation of water processing's total costs and if other conditions are satisfied, then it may be possible to estimate processing costs quite simply.

In *rate-based supply estimation*, either the average or marginal costs of processing water are presumed to be accurately described by observed water rates. So if it is observed that a certain supplier (or an average supplier) is charging $4 per thousand gallons, then it might be presumed that $4 is the marginal or average cost of water processing for *all* levels of water supply. If contact with the supplier(s) suggests that rates are based on average costs, as is disappointingly typical, the observed rates should not be regarded as marginal costs unless the distinction is arguably minor in the instance at hand.

The most surprising attribute of this technique is the resulting horizontal supply curve displayed in figure 10.2. Whereas $4 may be a good estimate of average or even marginal costs for some range of W, it is unlikely to be accurate across all W. Known as the *constant costs assumption*, this method does not produce a believable supply function outside some *unknown* range of W, but it does "get the job done" by allowing analysts to focus on other matters of importance. Economists often apply this method without scrutinizing its accuracy or impact.

A similar method, *revenue-based supply estimation*, looks to suppliers' reported revenue for evidence of average costs. Knowing both the collected revenue for a given period and the quantity of water deliveries, division yields average revenue per unit of water. If the analyst believes rates have been established so as to recover long-run total costs, then the average revenue may approximate the long-run average costs. Instead of dividing revenue by water quantity, the actual total costs may be divided by water quantity to arrive at average costs (*cost-based supply estimation*). The latter is a more direct approach to average costs, but the capital expenditures made by suppliers can be uneven over time due to the lumpiness of supply expansion activities. Focusing on revenue might yield a smoother perspective on average costs, depending on the supplier's accounting practices and rate-making procedures. Many variants of these approaches are conceivable. An important one is to subtract from total revenue or total costs those costs not associated with water production (e.g.,

---

irrigated acreage. If the remaining acreage is compact, then there can be cost reductions due to canal closures, reduced conveyance losses, and lowered canal maintenance. If the remaining acreage is distributed as a patchwork throughout the district's service area, then the cost savings will be much lower. Indeed, if all conveyance facilities continue to be operated, then conveyance losses and maintenance must be shouldered by a shrinking acreage, with obvious implications for the meter/acreage components of the rate structure. In this case, emphasis on a C(W) specification of total costs would be misleading.

$

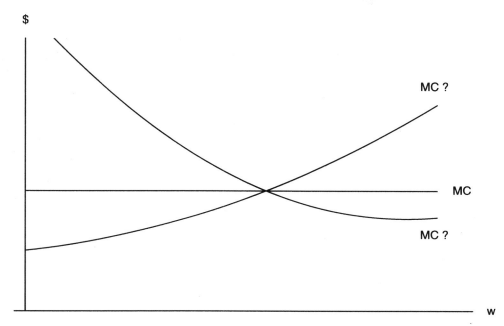

MC ?

MC

MC ?

W

Figure 10.2
Are constant costs realistic?

system expansion to new customers). The constant costs assumption is normally applied with all of these methods.

As a basic approach not assuming a horizontal supply curve, *point expansion* is a
potential means of estimating supply, just as it is for demand. In the case of supply,
all that is needed is a point on the supply curve and a supply elasticity (or slope).
Generally, the point is a (W, p) ordered pair, and it is the same point employed for
the point expansion of demand.[4] Whereas demand elasticity is presumed to be negative, water supply elasticity *may* be positive, inferring that point expansion will produce a positively sloped supply function.[5] Because point expansion is incapable of

4. It can be claimed that supply equals demand at this point. Yet the observed (W, p) point may be a better indication of demand than it is of supply. The water supplier establishes rates before the actual conditions unfold (especially climate), meaning that rates are based on *expected* rather than actual water
deliveries. In addition, whereas the economic ideal of water supply is the marginal costs of delivering
water, typical rate-making policy is not well focused on identifying efficient rates, as observed in chapter 8.

5. The classic presumption of declining average and marginal costs of water supply would imply a negative supply elasticity and a negatively sloped supply curve. The classic presumption may be false in many
contemporary settings, however. For example, "economies of scale" may become exhausted once a water
supply system reaches a certain size. As a second example, the efficiency-based argument of separate prices
for water, connections, and new connections moves many capital costs away from volumetric rates, thereby altering the primary basis for negatively sloped *water* supply functions. Whether supply is positively or

Box 10.1
Pitching Water to Mid Town

You are a sales agent for a new corporate venture. Your company buys/leases natural water resources from right holders, and using long-term contracts, you plan to rent these assets to water-using industries and communities. Due to your firm's specialization, you believe your firm's "brokerage services" are cost-effective alternatives for both small right holders and small buyers. In a forthcoming presentation to the city planners of Mid Town, you want to underscore the cost of your water relative to the (1) costs of other water sources and (2) Mid Town's water use benefits. To perform the computations needed for (2), one informational requirement is the town's marginal cost of processing water. There are other analyses to be prepared, so you want to use something simple, yet respectable, for the marginal processing costs.

Analysis

Mid Town's utility administrators have provided some basic information in response to your earlier inquiries. Consequently, you know Mid Town's current rate structure and its accounting experience with respect to water resource development. In recent years, the town has been increasing its natural water supply about 1.5 percent annually. Only new acquisitions of water are reflected in the water utility's annual budget, and rates are unaffected by the town's accumulated and paid-for water right holdings. Over 80 percent of Mid Town's water deliveries are sold to households for $1,200 per acre-foot. This is the metered price, excluding connection fees and all other charges. If there were no water acquisition costs in the annual budgets, you observe that this rate could be $1,110 per acre-foot. You do not know how Mid Town arrives at its rate structure, but the $1,110 figure is not noticeably different from what you've witnessed elsewhere in the region. Therefore, you are comfortable in your presumption that Mid Town's marginal processing costs are $1,110 per acre-foot. Because your proposal to the city planners will not entail a large increase in their water supply, you are not worried about the "horizontal" feature of presuming constant marginal costs.

generating the elasticity estimate that is needed, other procedures must be employed before point expansion can be conducted. The literature of water resource economics, however, has yet to generate estimates on supply elasticity that can be readily transferred to other study regions.

Statistical regression can be a viable approach for supply estimation, just as it is for demand estimation. Both supply and demand can be simultaneously estimated (as demonstrated by Garcia and Reynaud 2004). As long as suitable data can be assembled, it may be possible to obtain useful estimates of either $C(W)$ or $C(\Delta N, W, N)$. The challenging task is to collect appropriate data. Time-series data for a single water supplier may provide a useful basis for some analysis, but there are important weaknesses in such data. There is little assurance that the supplier is operating with least-cost activities, so the costs may be overestimated. Also, costs

---

negatively sloped then becomes an empirical matter, and it is possible for different water suppliers to encounter differing results on this matter. Moreover, as refined analyses proceed to separate the many activities embedded in retail water supply, we will inevitably find that some activities involve economies of scale while others do not.

are predicated on the installed equipment base that will tend to be fixed within time-series data. Depending on the purpose(s) of analysis, statistical regression using time-series data may be acceptable given the absence of alternatives. Cross-sectional data, involving multiple suppliers, offers a richer look at the possibilities of water supply economics (for a basic example, see Kitchen 1977). Yet the varying physical and client circumstances of different suppliers makes it difficult to apply the generalized results to specific settings.

All of these methods are potentially faulty, depending on the degree to which they attribute all costs to water production and the validity of that presumption for the analysis at hand. For example, using the revenue-based method of supply estimation, one might divide *all* supplier-received revenue by water deliveries, even if much of this revenue resulted from meter charges and other nonwater fees. As a similar example, we might apply statistical regression with only one exogenous variable—the amount of produced or delivered water. While such calculations are supported by the $C(W)$ concept, they may seriously overstate the true average and marginal costs of water deliveries by incorporating expansion costs and consumption-invariant costs (like the costs of meter reading, new water storage and distribution facilities, and even conveyance losses).

Another potential problem is the double counting of surface water values.[6] Our adopted standard is to omit natural water values from cost functions (total, marginal, and average), so that applications of these functions can help to accurately identify natural water value. Then, when we later apply what analysis has discovered about natural water value, as in establishing efficient water prices or determining optimal allocations, we know exactly what to do. If, however, water marketing activities of any type (e.g., leases, sales, options) are present or the accounting practices of suppliers begin to consider natural water value as a financial cost, then adjustments are required. The best approach for estimating cost functions is to omit consistently all natural water values from the costs of processing water. For example, an ably managed district or utility may treat its water right holdings as a valued and costly input, valuing these assets at their current market value as recommended previously. By considering annualized water right values as part of annual operational costs, this practice affects both rates and revenues (while having a positive influence on the economic efficiency of water use). Although this accounting practice is socially advantageous, it can mislead *all* of the techniques noted in the prior section because they are trying to estimate processing costs only. Therefore,

6. It is possible for this same issue to also arise for the marginal user costs of depletable water or the marginal capacity costs of limited infrastructure, but occurrences of these problems have been limited since they are not ordinarily priced into contemporary exchanges or contracts. As practices and economic arrangements mature, however, we can expect these opportunity costs to become financial costs in better-managed jurisdictions.

clear-cut adjustments should be performed on costs, revenues, or rates when applying these methods.

Strengthening Supply-Side Analysis

In spite of $C(W)$'s weak promise as a basis for cost estimation, it still constitutes a fundamental premise in a great deal of economic empiricism. This is an area in which water resource economists can improve analysis by thinking more broadly than $C(W)$ invites. The restrictiveness of $C(W)$ suggests that supply costs are not being investigated with the empirical seriousness they deserve. To be completely fair about this assessment, water resource economists have focused their efforts where they can reap the greatest rewards. The highest social payoff often happens where informational gaps exist, and for the subject of water resource economics these gaps tend to occur in the areas of demand estimation, policy design (including markets and pricing), and policy and project evaluation. Given the recent strides that have been made in these areas, though, perhaps we can begin to assign greater importance to supply-side details. Both cost accounting and engineering subdisciplines have made significant progress that can be usefully applied toward specification of $C(\Delta N, W, N)$.

Cost accountants have a strong history of examining "the books" of water utilities and districts. One purpose of such examinations is to aid the periodic reevaluation of water rate structures. Many water suppliers revisit their rates every year or so, revising rates along the way. As observed and critiqued in chapter 8, water supply managers are strongly oriented toward cost recovery as the justification for water rate changes. Because they wish to link costs and rates, it has been natural to highlight relationships between rising costs and chargeable elements of the rate structure. Equation (10.2) is central in this regard. Each argument of this cost function can be separately monitored for individual clients, and it is easy to attach distinct rates to each argument. Hence, if $C(\Delta N, W, N)$ can be specified for a given water supplier, then a strong basis for rate establishment is achieved. Rate making is not the only reason to specify this form, however, as all supply-side specifications benefit from an accurate estimation of $\partial C / \partial W$. Reliance on $C(W)$ must result in the overestimation of $\partial C / \partial W$.

At the simplest level, $C(\Delta N, W, N)$ might be *additively separable* in its arguments. That is, if the function can be rewritten as summed, independent components without sacrificing accuracy, as in

$$C(\Delta N, W, N) = C_1(\Delta N) + C_2(W) + C_3(N), \tag{10.3}$$

then average-cost pricing for the three fees is easily accomplished.[7] Efficiency is not well served by average-cost pricing, so we are especially interested in the three deriv-

---

7. The diagrammatic representation of the *cost allocation* method contained in figure 8.2 implicitly presumes separability.

Box 10.2
Getting a Cost-Based Estimate of Marginal Costs

Big City has long used an accounting system in which all of the incurred costs are entered into one of four cost classifications: production (water), distribution (water), collection (wastewater), or treatment (wastewater). Production includes surface water impoundment and ground water pumping operations, water quality testing and treatment, and water transmission to elevated storage. Other items, like certain legal costs and a portion of the administration costs, are also assigned to production.

As a result of this accounting system, you possess annual data on production costs and the amount of produced water. One way to use these data is to compute average production costs over the past two years. The result is $1.10 per thousand gallons. Reflecting on (10.3), this value is an empirical estimate of $C_2(W)/W$. You could argue that $1.10 is a good approximation of dC_2/dW, but it is hard to be convincing. As another option, you could use the most recent five years to formulate a five-observation data set. (Don't forget to make inflation adjustments to get to the real values.) Then, simple regression will provide a functional expression of $C_2(W)$. If these statistical results appear sensible, their implications for dC_2/dW can be used.

atives of (10.2) or (10.3) even though these derivatives must be augmented with certain scarcity values before efficient rates can be identified. If the cost function is separable, then these derivatives will be more easily evaluated.

Once the analyst has decided to gather information for the specification of (10.2) or (10.3), what approaches are available? Considering the three procedures noted previously (rate-, revenue-, and cost-based supply estimation), rates and revenues will not be a dependable basis unless they are well-founded. The rate and revenue approaches will be accurate only if rates, and therefore revenues, have been solidly based on costs by the water utility/district. Otherwise, it will be necessary to "build" a cost function for the circumstances at hand. Advanced techniques are not necessary for accomplishing this mission. Care, however, must be exercised. Two avenues for making progress are suggested by accounting and engineering efforts.

Activity-Based Costing

In the *activity-based costing* concept sometimes practiced in the accounting field, actual costs are associated with or "mapped to" specific *cost drivers* (Barfield, Raiborn, and Kinney 1994). The cost drivers are perceived as causal activities. In this sense, then, ΔN, W, and N can be designated as cost drivers. Increases in any of these drivers induce the water supplier to incur added expenditures so as to respond to the increased demand dimension.

The process of activity-based costing is to thoroughly study all expenditures and assign each expenditure to a driver. In this way, cost functions such as $C(\Delta N, W, N)$ or $C_1(\Delta N) + C_2(W) + C_3(N)$ can be resolved by analyzing actual expenses. While this might seem tedious for an extensive water supply system, most modern utilities and districts already classify their costs as they regularly enter actual expenditures into computerized accounting programs. These classification patterns are a large step toward associating each expenditure with a cost driver.

Segmenting Analysis

Whereas the emphasis of accounting can be backward looking—focused on the organization and inspection of incurred expenditures, *cost engineering* is preoccupied with the estimation of costs for upcoming installations. Identifying the prospective costs of new infrastructure is an important matter for engineering design and proposal since it is a rare client that approves new construction without knowing what the costs will be. In general, modern *engineering economics* overlaps heavily with the prescriptive advice of cost-side economics because engineering economics draws its knowledge from accounting and economics (see, for example, Newnan, Lavelle, and Eschenbach 2002). Cost estimation is the major reason that engineering economics exists as a subfield, though, so many of the dimensions of water scarcity economics have yet to be suitably recognized.[8]

Fortunately, the focus of cost engineering has emphasized helpful tools for identifying $C(\Delta N, W, N)$. A strong example is cost engineering's "segmenting" approach to cost estimation. Here, the various aspects of a new endeavor are separated into various segments, costs are estimated for each segment, and then overall costs are obtained as the summed costs of all segments. Within each segment, costs are normally estimated using straightforward procedures, such as hundreds of feet of installed eight-inch pipe times the cost rate per hundred, thousands of person-hours times the cost per thousand, and millions of gallons to be chlorinated times the rate per million. Because segment costs are simplistically computed as quantity times rate, spreadsheet programs are utilized heavily. Hence, segmenting often presumes that costs are linear functions of input quantities. Specialized engineering firms may maintain or subscribe to databases containing unit price estimates for various construction or operational cost components. Such baseline information may also be occasionally published, as was done by Gumerman et al. (1992) for municipal water distribution systems.

Engineering economists become well schooled in applying both amortization-type calculations (like those in chapter 3's appendix 3.A) and escalator indexes designed to reflect the changing nominal (inflation-inclusive) costs of different forms of equipment and installations over time. These procedures can also be combined with the accounting ideal of activity-based costing in order to emphasize the underlying causal factors of costs (Innes, Mitchell, and Yoshikawa 1994). The simplicity and power of segmenting has helped it to become a universal tool. To support the use of

---

8. A secondary reason involves tasks relating to cost control during construction activities (Clark, Lorenzoni, and Jimenez 1997).

this tool, specific cost indexes are available to track changing cost rates. A leading example is the *Engineering News Record*, a weekly publication that is also Web available ($\langle$http://www.enr.com$\rangle$). The *Engineering News Record* tends to be materials focused (lumber, pipe, cement) and watched labor costs pertain more to building construction than water service, but it is still a useful resource.

Blended Methods

Both segmenting and activity-based accounting are consistent with the portrayal of costs provided by (10.3). Yet neither of these approaches enable "quick-and-easy" identification of supply-side parameters. Both necessitate a from-the-ground-up building of the cost function through the itemization of all needed inputs. Ultimately, the task is to attribute these costs in a functional dependence on W and the other drivers. Most cost engineering studies are considered complete when total costs have been estimated. See, for example, Clark et al. (2002) as well as Lauria (2004). For our purposes, however, there is still work to be done in associating these costs with their determining drivers. In the end, these results may be tightly applicable to the specific circumstances for which they were obtained—probably for a single water supplier. The portability of these results to other suppliers will consequently not be well-known.

Statistical or optimization techniques are not as universally helpful in these studies as they are in demand analysis. Here, one must directly confront the nuts and bolts of water pumping, storage, processing, administration, delivery, and building. Available techniques are not especially novel or "academic," so leading literature is not widely available.

It may be possible to combine the various techniques in various ways. In some situations, regression or cost-minimization analyses of one or more components of the overall costs can assist in the identification of C(...). We might use cost minimization to select design parameters (such as pipe sizing and layout) when multiple options exist. We might use spreadsheets and segmenting to develop budgets for water production and treatment facilities of different capacities, and then use the budget-generated data within regression analysis to derive a functional relation for the dependence of these production costs on W.

If spreadsheet programs are to be a central tool, one must be mindful of the linearization inherent to most spreadsheet analysis. If strictly linear relationships, as opposed to piecewise linear ones, are employed for all components, then the resulting cost function will be a linear function of its drivers. This will infer constant-cost supply functions (as in figure 10.2), which are not well accepted given the decreasing and increasing returns to scale (diseconomies and economies of size) that are likely to be actually encountered across different ranges of water supply quantities.

Whenever it exists, increasing returns to scale generates an argument favoring a single supplier for a city *and* its suburbs. Such conditions also commend the merger of irrigation districts. For this reason, some attention has been devoted to estimating water supply costs, just to see if there might be any returns to scale. Different types of analysis has been successfully used to examine this issue, with distinct conclusions for specific aspects of water suppliers' tasks (e.g., water production as opposed to water distribution/conveyance). This work also generates insights for the tasks of water supply estimation. See, for example, Boisvert and Schmit (1997), Kim and Clark (1988), and Clark and Stevie (1981a, 1981b).

Hence, although spreadsheets can serve as a primary vehicle for handling the multitude of input costs encountered in water provision, other methods can serve supporting roles. Recalling figure 10.1 and the many duties involved in water supply, cost analysis can become very extensive. An indication of this fact is contained in the U.S. Bureau of Reclamation analysis of water treatment costs for differing qualities of natural water. A cursory inspection of the spreadsheet available at ⟨http://www.usbr.gov/pmts/water/awtr.html⟩ indicates the depth that may be involved in costing any particular aspect of the water supply mission.[9]

10.6   The Privatization Question

France and the United Kingdom as well as various cities around the world have made strong commitments to infrastructural privatization in recent times. Yet privatization's foothold remains weak in the United States, accounting for less than 15 percent of 1995 water revenues (National Research Council 2002b, 14). Different societies can have different reasons and rationally make different decisions regarding infrastructural privatization. The significance of this topic in contemporary discussions means that water management specialists should obtain greater exposure to it.

In instances of declining average costs for retail water supply, it is inefficient to have multiple water suppliers vying for customers.[10] Natural monopolies such as water suppliers constitute a type of market failure—an instance in which the First Theorem of Welfare Economics does not speak because its assumptions are unmet.

---

9. Although this Bureau of Reclamation–supported analysis emphasizes treatment costs and demonstrates well the role of spreadsheet analysis in water supply estimation, it also indicates the importance being attached to the processing of poor quality waters. One aspect of growing water scarcity is our growing interest in the use of relatively brackish waters. Scarcity motivates an examination of advanced treatment technologies capable of moving salts and other contaminants from otherwise undrinkable water. If we are to harness these sources, then we should understand the technologies and their costs. For this reason, cost analysis of new treatment options such as membrane filtration has been useful (Pickering and Wiesner 1993; Chellam, Serra, and Wiesner 1998).

10. Strictly speaking, declining average costs (or increasing returns to scale) are sufficient grounds for defining a natural monopoly, but they are not necessary (Baumol 1977). A natural monopoly exists when a single producer can provide service more cheaply than two or more producers can. It is quite possible that a natural monopoly might be operating at a level where the average costs are not declining, yet dividing this operating level among two producers would cause higher total costs.

Hence, theoretical support for retail water competition is lost, even though natural water markets are still commendable.

During the past two decades, interest has rapidly increased in the opportunities presented by the privatization of water and wastewater infrastructure. This interest stems, in large part, from favorable public sentiments regarding market institutions. The connection here is a tenuous one, however. Even though economic and political thought often espouses a promarket theology, it should be professionally acknowledged that such opinions yield weak advice in the privatization debate.[11] "'Public versus private' is not the bright line that separates efficient from inefficient management" (Wolff and Palaniappan 2004, 1). "Privatization is not equivalent to competition" (National Research Council 2002b, 5). The truth is that each retail water supplier *can* be well operated under either public or private ownership. In both cases, however, public oversight is advisable lest power corrupt the pursuit of efficiency.

Rather than tolerate the selfish behavior of a profit-minded monopolist, society's polar options are to regulate privately owned suppliers or establish publicly owned suppliers. Both approaches have pitfalls. Fortunately, intermediate selections are also available. Different locales may quite reasonably make different choices among these options. Indeed, the availability of both organizational types adds realism to the threat of dethroning one organizational style in favor of the other, probably motivating more efficient behavior.

The following subsections juxtapose the two polar options, so that the dilemma faced here can be better exposed. Afterward, blends of these two approaches can be entertained.

Public Management

Public water supply organizations are not well respected for their abilities to make economically efficient choices or even cost-minimizing ones. Unlike situations within private corporations, salaries and job security for public water managers are not even partially dependent on the "net benefits" managers enable. No matter how well-intentioned these decision makers may be, if their private rewards are disconnected from economic efficiency, nonefficiency goals can be elevated and economic losses are likely to result. "The fundamental problem with public ownership has been the inability to establish incentives for the relevant agents, chiefly managers and administrators, to act in ways that promote public-interest objectives (which themselves

---

11. This theology becomes scientifically grounded when it corresponds well with the First Theorem of Welfare Economics and its associated principles, which would require accurate attention to axiom assumptions. In less cautious application, promarket idealism becomes detached from the structured developments of economic science. As the disconnect increases, arguments favoring competitive institutions take on an increasing degree of "faith" as opposed to prescriptive accuracy.

have always been vaguely defined). Salaries tend to depend only on rank and are independent of performance" (Spulber and Sabbaghi 1998, 194).

For better and worse, these water supply managers have considerable discretion in the tasks they perform. Skillful decisions can go unrewarded. Poor decisions can go undetected. Public managers are allowed to pass all costs to clients via rates. Given the lack and difficulty of public oversight, public organizations can be wasteful if they are so inclined, or if they do not know any better. Parallel or "control" organizations do not exist, thereby making it hard to gauge performance. Even when there are similar organizations operating in other jurisdictions, their distinctive physical and client circumstances perplex comparisons. Efficiency benchmarks (such as water rates or customer opinion polls) always offer imperfect comparisons. Even when a supplier achieves a favorable benchmark relative to other suppliers, it is not proof of efficiency. Inefficiency may simply be widespread. Client satisfaction is rather moot since customers have almost no basis for knowing what service and rates would result from alternative management styles or decisions. High water rates are not even clear-cut proof of inefficiency, especially in light of chapter 8's observations pertaining to the pricing of scarce water. That is, omitted opportunity costs mean that underpricing is the inefficient norm.

In spite of the difficulty of obtaining worthwhile comparisons, occasional evidence does emerge regarding the efficiency of public water suppliers. For example, in a central California region holding both public and private water suppliers, public suppliers reportedly operate with higher labor costs and more employees per connection (Spulber and Sabbaghi 1998, 194). Later in this chapter, however, we will review some statistical results that are not generally supportive of the hypothesis that costs are higher in publicly owned systems.

Waste can be imposed on public organizations when suppliers' decision making is affected by political influences. City councillors and district board members may have "pet projects" or policies that they wish to advance regardless of the efficiency consequences. Also, prevailing political opinions are that low-priced water encourages desirable business development and growth.[12] Cities are inherently slow to adopt efficient policy modifications (e.g., volumetric pricing, seasonal pricing, marginal-cost pricing, and pricing that incorporates opportunity costs). Aged pricing policies are retained to avoid riling voters or prodevelopment interests (National Research Council 2002b, 42). Labor unions also exercise their political muscle to advance job numbers and wages within public organizations. Existing supervisors and employees are prone to look favorably on larger employee numbers because of their impact on workloads. Indeed, labor interests can be vocal opponents to pri-

---

12. This point also has implications for new and recurring connection charges. The mispricing of any one of the three major charges brings about the mispricing of the others.

vatization. So it turns out that neither administrators nor employees are desirous of privatization.

Public ownership of water supply providers did not dominate in the United States until the 1900s, and the impetus for this domination was the post–World War I introduction of the income tax exemption for municipal bonds (National Research Council 2002b, 28, 30). A national subsidy results because public water suppliers do not have to pay market rates of interest when borrowing construction funds. The implications include lower costs for publicly owned infrastructure—recalling that the water industry is extremely capital intensive—and therefore lower rates for water consumers, unless private operators can counter this advantage with other savings. For example, a wealthy buyer of bonds could easily be in the 35 percent marginal tax bracket for federal taxes and perhaps a 7 percent tax bracket for state taxes. This investor would be indifferent to equally risky corporate bonds paying a 5 percent annual return and municipal bonds paying 2.9 percent. That is a huge advantage in a capital-intensive industry, and it can have sizable implications for water rates. Hence, public suppliers have access to a major subsidy that is not available to private suppliers. It is also often the case that publicly owned property is exempt from property taxes, thus adding to the public subsidy. Differences in exposure to sales taxes can be a factor too.

The taxation rules can be changed to grant private water suppliers access to cheaper capital as well. Indeed, changes of this type are steadily occurring as questions are being raised about the fairness and desirability of the long-standing favoritism. The result may be a reduction in advantage for the public ownership form. Still, not only do these subsidies tilt the field on which public and private operators play they also skew general market conditions. By making water capital (as well as other municipal capital) cheaper, rate-paying water consumers gain. Yet the loss of tax revenue by national and state governments means that taxes must be raised elsewhere. The overall result is a dispersed *loss* in aggregate economic efficiency because the gains do not exceed the losses (National Research Council 2002b, 52; Spulber and Sabbaghi 1998, 196). In addition, water underpricing is aggravated. A more efficient way to level the playing field is to therefore eliminate the public sector's tax advantage.

Privatization

The promise of privatization is mainly cost savings for noninterest construction expenditures and operation costs. Because private companies can generate revenue at multiple water supply locations, they can assemble well-trained, specialized personnel who acquire experience as they work in different settings. By applying this advanced knowledge at many locations, construction planning and execution can be widely bettered. Cost savings also become available from shared administrative staff, purchasing departments, billing departments, facility operators, maintenance technicians, and water-testing laboratories (Raftelis 1993, 98). Specialized private companies learn of innovations and revised regulatory policies more rapidly. The decision-making practices of private companies can be less paralyzed by a desire for widespread consensus, as occurs with public decision making. So privately performed activities can happen more quickly, which is often valuable. When aggregated, these various savings can be sizable.

Competition is undesirable for retail water provision in a single location. Nor is it desirable to give the keys to an unrestricted monopoly franchise. The pursuit of profits by such a franchise will lead to economic inefficiency.[13] Regulation of privately owned suppliers is therefore attractive, and the primary means of regulation are to define expected service levels and control rates. Specifications of service levels can extend to water quality parameters, service reliability, responsiveness to complaints, maintenance expectations, continued investment, and so on.

Rate regulation is a challenging task normally performed by state public utility commissions. If regulation is lax—meaning excessive water rates—the private operator receives inefficiently high profits and consumers lose net benefits. If regulation is too strict, the operator looks for other avenues to earn a profit, perhaps through socially undesirable cost cutting (usually leading to infrastructural deterioration) or, in the extreme, some manner of exiting the franchise. Consumer desire for low rates and supplier desire for high rates creates a tension that must be constantly mediated by regulation. Gaming can emerge, as when the supplier engages in promotional public relations campaigns or lobbying for more favorable rules. Regulation in this environment is not a low-cost enterprise, and costs can be sufficiently high to offset the savings that might be provided by privatization. Although regulation responsibilities largely fall to state agencies—not the local areas that have chosen privatization—the social cost is a real one.

The U.S. model of rate regulation is to determine water rates yielding a fair rate of return on investment, similar to what could be achieved in the general marketplace. This infers a need to (1) value the private supplier's assets, (2) establish a target rate of return (e.g., 5 percent), (3) forecast operation and maintenance costs, and (4) set

---

13. Whereas individual, competing firms understand their lack of impact on market price and therefore choose production levels matching marginal cost to price, a profit-maximizing monopoly knows that its production level influences both its marginal costs and market price. As a consequence, monopoly decision making departs from economic efficiency. A simple, formal model demonstrates this idea. Let the aggregate water demand function, $MB(W)$, be written as $p(W)$ to underscore the dependency of retail water price on the amount of retail water supplied. Using the simplistic supply model, the costs depend only on the amount of retail water: $C(W)$. Monopoly profit is then $p(W) \cdot W - C(W)$. Differentiating with respect to W and letting p' represent the first derivative of $p(W)$, an ungoverned water monopolist chooses W where $p' \cdot W + p - MC = 0$. The only significant circumstance in which this decision is socially efficient occurs when $p' = 0$—that is, when the supplier thinks that price is unaffected by the supplier's production level. Monopolists do not think this.

rates covering both (3) and (1) times (2). Although this procedure is not markedly different from any rate-setting practice, the dependence of profitability on asset value underscores the problems encountered in step (1) and perturbs the operator's incentives.

With respect to incentives, the owner will wish to value assets as highly as possible, inferring that self-valuation is untenable. Also, the owner will favor capital investment as a preferred means to address water supply tasks. Widely known in the economics literature as the Averch-Johnson effect (after Averch and Johnson 1962), rate regulation of this type spurs overinvestment in capital.[14] This tendency can be manifested in several inefficient ways, all of which involve overcapitalization.[15] The term *gold plating* can be an apt description of this problem, in that expensive capital produces more profits than ordinary capital.

Hence, not only might inefficiency arise from errant rate levels (due to the difficulties of achieving accurate regulation) but regulation can skew the input mix away from least-cost supply activities. These problems, combined with the national subsidy of publicly owned capital, challenge the ability of full-fledged privatization to emerge as an economically preferred option.

The Middle Ground

With the dominance of public ownership in the United States (85 percent of revenue), a major transition would be required before privately owned water supply could become significant. For this to occur, private ownership would have to offer more relative advantages than it does currently. Moreover, the transition itself would be costly, posing yet another barrier.

A slippery slope is traversed when transferring public assets to private ventures. If the infrastructural assets are to be sold to the new owner, they must be assessed, and the public must understand that the buyer will have to recoup this payment in forthcoming rates. There is also the thorny matter of what the public sector should do with the one-time windfall. Should other public services be increased, should debt be retired, should each client receive a check, or should the money be invested in case the privatization is unsuccessful and the public sector decides to reacquire its assets? Because the public sector will not divest itself of the water supply system unless it believes the change to be a net improvement, there will be contractual elements to be worked out regarding service expectations, public involvement in future

---

14. Kahn (1988, 2:49–50) respectfully calls this the Averch-Johnson-Wellisz effect in recognition of Wellisz's independent work (1963).

15. To elevate the amount of capital, private operators might make incomplete use of peak-load pricing, maintain excess "standby capacity," not share capacity efficiently with neighboring suppliers, resist the use of "capital-saving technologies," have a "reluctance to lease facilities," prefer "excessively high . . . standards of reliability," and not be forceful bargainers during capital purchases (Kahn 1988, 2:49–53).

Table 10.1
Partial privatization options

Option	Description
Service outsourcing	
External	The private contractor performs a task without operating any public facilities
Internal	The private contractor operates and maintains publicly owned facilities
Facility outsourcing	
Simple contract	The contractor installs capital according to public suppliers' specifications
Design-build	The contractor designs and builds capital to meet a specified need of a public supplier
Design-build-operate (DBO)	After designing and building a facility, the contractor will operate it for a prespecified period
Build-own-transfer (BOT)	Same as DBO except the contractor will own the facility during the life of a contract and transfer ownership to the public supplier at the end of the contract

Source: Some elements of this table are suggested by the National Research Council (2002b, 70).

decisions, penalty/reward consequences, and dispute resolution. Being visionary about desirable contract terms is difficult for local public administrators. After all, they are unlikely to have any experience in such matters. This stage of privatization can also produce corruption and rent seeking, as contending private companies try to secure advantage using campaign contributions and illicit payments to officials (Beecher 2001).

For these reasons, the full privatization of retail water suppliers is not commonly desirable unless public management is faulty and irreparable. But there are useful avenues for blending private sector advantages within the public ownership model. Some of these alternatives are sufficiently attractive that they have become widely applied in many utilities and districts.

Table 10.1 contains a nonexhaustive listing of the major modes of public-private cooperation in retail water supply. While retaining ownership of its existing infrastructure and maintaining its dominant role in management, a publicly owned supplier can "outsource" various components of its mission. It can separately outsource individual tasks (services) and the construction of new facilities. Some of these elements are so commonplace that public managers do not think of them as privatization practices.

In service outsourcing, the public supplier contracts out continuing tasks, such as legal support, meter reading, customer billing, water quality testing, rate analyses, or plant operations. External outsourcing is most common. Here, the private contractor provides the labor, materials, and physical equipment (including office space) necessary to complete the desired task. Internal contracting entails operation of public suppliers' infrastructure by the contractor. A simplistic example is the use of "temps" or temporary office workers. Of greater emphasis in contemporary thinking is the use of contractors for the operation and maintenance of specific water or wastewater plants.

With the high cost of establishing new infrastructure and the attendant difficulties of environmental compliance, many public water suppliers are looking for ways to ease the tasks of building new facilities. Such facilities include new or replacement conveyances, storage reservoirs or tanks, pumping stations, control facilities, and processing units. Table 10.1 includes four alternatives of progressively increasing private involvement. Depending on the extent of involvement, the selected private contractor may build a facility according to publicly specified design parameters; perform design and construction; design, build, and subsequently operate the facility; or design, build, own, and operate the facility. The more complex of these arrangements might even include project financing using private funds, but the subsidized cost advantage of public funds is generally hard to supplant. Interest in making subsequent operations part of these contracts is enhanced by public suppliers' desire to encourage forward-thinking design components impacting operation costs and reliability. Normally, the public authority requests formal proposals and solicits bids before establishing any of these contracts.

These options are potentially underutilized by contemporary water suppliers, but again, public suppliers may lack the motivation to search out efficient opportunities. Moreover, it is difficult for public managers to remain fully knowledgeable about these opportunities and consistently forge advantageous relations with profit-minded firms. Therefore, public-private partnerships should not be regarded as a panacea for inefficiency unless publicly employed managers are vigilant, which takes us full circle to the original issue.

Statistical Analyses of Ownership Effects

Statistical examination of the public versus private issue becomes possible when similar cost data are available from both public and private suppliers. The key is to discover if ownership has a statistically significant effect on total costs, after accounting for other cost-affecting factors. Economists have published various studies of this type, using different variables and data from different locales. Because cost observations must lie on or above the cost function being estimated, advanced econometric techniques are recommended for the estimation technique. That is, it may be inappropriate to fit a curve *through* data when the data must be bounded by the cost function. Unlike investigations seeking $C(W)$ or $C(\Delta N, W, N)$, these studies inject a wider array of exogenous variables, often including a binary (0/1, dummy) variable for ownership. An abridged review of this literature offers some interesting perspectives regarding this policy issue.

Such studies commonly discuss the efficiency of the alternative ownership modes, but readers are counseled that "efficiency" means something different in the public versus private context. A narrower vision is being applied. This research is emphasizing a form of technical efficiency: Is the product being delivered at the least possible cost? Therefore, the efficient allocation of scarce water is not being addressed. It is worth recalling that both aggregate and neutral economic efficiency insist on least cost processing, but then go on to assess allocative efficiency as well. Our dominant criterion, aggregate efficiency, also requires equal marginal net benefits across all rival uses in a watershed.

With the context established, let's consider some of the most recent work.

• Using 1995 data from fifty distinct water supply systems operating in twenty-nine countries, Estache and Rossi (2002) could not find a statistically significant difference attributable to private/public involvement. Because of the variety of private/public blends evidenced in these organizations, the researchers employ three separate dummy variables in this investigation. None turn out to be significant. This means the data do not identify an efficiency advantage for either ownership form.

• Two studies by Bhattacharyya and others (1994, 1995a) investigate 1992 American Water Works Association data from more than two hundred U.S. water suppliers. More than 10 percent of these suppliers are private, indicating both the imbalance of the data and the predominance of public management. Overall, evidence of inefficiency in *both* ownership forms is suggested by the findings. Public operations are found to be "less inefficient" than private ones, but the difference is found to be a small one, applicable primarily to larger systems.

• Looking at rural water utilities in Nevada, Bhattacharyya et al. (1995b) include suppliers that are operated by private owners, counties, municipalities, or water districts. These 1992 data include two private and twenty-four public water suppliers. Although their findings are muted by the small number of private suppliers in the sample, the private suppliers are found to have slightly higher technical efficiencies. District-run suppliers suffer the lowest-average efficiencies, with county-operated systems only slightly better. The efficiency metric for the four ownership types ranges from 86 to 91 percent, so the differences are not great.

• Another regional examination is that of Teeples and Glyer (1987), who do not find significant efficiency differences among 119 southern California suppliers. These 1980 data are better balanced, possessing 36 cities, 31 districts, and 52 private operations.

• Examinations of much earlier American Water Works Association data are provided by two additional studies. Feigenbaum and Teeples (1983) apply their model to 1970 data for 57 private and 262 public suppliers. No statistical difference is uncovered. Bruggink (1982) employs the 1960 version of the American Water Works Association data. This analysis pertains to 9 private and 77 public systems. Here, costs are found to be 24 percent lower for public systems, with this difference showing some statistical significance, depending on which of the two models is viewed.

All told, it is tough to find systematic, contemporary evidence supporting a recommendation for one ownership style over another. So-called efficiency differences (actually cost differences) tend to be small even when they are detectable. Hence, one ownership type may not be universally better than another. Perhaps this is an empowering finding. Regardless of the organizational form established for a water supply system, there are no inherently insurmountable disadvantages. Yet both private and public systems are capable of being inefficient. A recognition of this fact should motivate the constant search for improvement opportunities by management personnel within both types of organizations.

10.7   Summary

The empirical contributions of water resource economics in the supply-side analysis of cost functions have yet to be fully developed. Although economics provides strong conceptual insights here, these ideas are not often matched by empirical depth. The richness and intensity that might emerge from more detailed supply empiricism are still awaited. Opportunities abound. The methods that do exist are more often exercised by accountants and cost engineers. Even here, though, little effort has been devoted to the estimation of $C(W)$ or $C(\Delta N, W, N)$, with the sole exception of accounting work in support of rate analysis (as considered in chapter 8).

In concert with the constant costs assumption and the $C(W)$ form, supply costs can be easily estimated using rate-, revenue-, or cost-based supply estimation. Disappointing, however, are the consequently horizontal supply curves. Such simplistic visions may not provide accurate assistance in water planning unless project/policy-induced movements turn out to be small. Point expansion is a valid approach to supply estimation, but supporting information concerning supply elasticity or slope is scarce. Helpful avenues are provided by segmenting analyses, statistical regression, cost minimization, and spreadsheet programs. Often, these methods can be combined in various ways to build cost functions by inventorying and assessing all inputs. To properly perform supply estimation, it is always necessary to finally relate these input costs to the cost drivers that motivate them (such as ΔN, W, and N).

Because of its relationship to costs, it has been natural to raise the privatization question here. The natural monopoly status of water suppliers requires us to face a fundamental organizational issue: Should any particular supplier be privately or publicly owned? A consideration of the theoretical evidence does not point down either road. Both management approaches have propensities to underperform, in the sense of operating too expensively. Empirical studies of the relative performance of these ownership types have had mixed findings, but the most common finding is a statistical indifference to the two types. Today, various combinations of private and public responsibilities are being tried in an effort to harness each one's comparative advantages. Perhaps an awareness of these issues and opportunities can galvanize efforts for increasing cost effectiveness within individual organizations.

10.8 Exercises

1. A town has recently built its first desalinization plant, allowing the town to make use of the immense quantity of saline ground water in its region. The town also takes advantage of a limited supply of high-quality surface water flowing nearby. Suppose that the marginal processing costs of each of these sources are constant, and that the overall marginal costs are given as follows:

$$MC(w) = \begin{cases} k_1 & \text{if} \quad w \leq W' \\ k_2 & \text{if} \quad w > W', \end{cases}$$

where W' is the amount of available surface water and k_2 is much higher than k_1. Assuming that we are only concerned with variable (i.e., operation and maintenance) costs and the town can build as much desalinization capacity as it wants, determine functions for both total variable costs (TVC) and average variable costs (AVC). (Plant construction costs have no relevance because the town properly uses new connection charges to pay for them.) Illustrate both $MC(w)$ and $AVC(w)$ on the same graph.

2. Extend the point expansion program constructed for exercise 2 of the prior chapter. Add one additional input, supply elasticity, and set up the program to generate four additional output functions (the various supply functions).

11 Modeling with Demand and Supply

How are demand and supply linked in empirical analysis?

Combining economic expressions of water demand and supply can be a simple task. It can be complex too. The degree of difficulty depends on a model's level of abstraction. Less abstraction (greater realism) requires more details and, inevitably, more analytic effort. Fortunately, many matters of interest can be illuminated with simple models.

Models of water demand and supply were introduced in chapter 2, and we have been applying minimalist models ever since. The most basic water demand and supply models (DSMs) begin with the natural water demands of two or more agents and a single, physically fixed water availability. Natural water demands have been defined as the MNBs of retail water, so they are given by MB – MC (retail water demand minus retail water supply). The intersection of summed MNBs with a vertical line depicting water availability reveals much about the optimal allocation of water between the agents and the worth of natural water (figure 2.10). It also tells us the efficient price of retail water. Or the three-axis model (figure 2.11) can be utilized to reveal exactly the same things using exactly the same information. Although they are simple constructs, such models generate useful advice as well as improved intuition in support of more complex modeling.

To better grasp the practice of water demand and supply modeling, one can study actual models. That's the emphasis of this chapter. Following a brief review of modeling's place and some of its features, we will consider previously published DSMs. Two models will be examined in some depth. Other models will be overviewed. Due to the foundation established within earlier chapters, it is practical to perform this review quickly.

11.1 Moving from Theory to Empiricism

The models developed in chapters 2–5 are obviously theoretical in nature. It is a short step, however, to convert them into empirical models, as many examples here begin to demonstrate. Empirical application is accomplished by specifying real-world MB and MC functions, and then performing the theoretically directed calculations.

When the differing approaches of theoretical and empirical policy analysis were compared early in chapter 5, it was observed that theoretical analysis is a powerful ally for policy study (and that all water scarcity matters are ultimately policy problems). As long as the analyst understands water resource economics well and utilizes its principles accurately, a lot can be achieved without resorting to empiricism. That is a wonderful possibility because empiricism is neither cheap nor quick.

Still, well-grounded theoretical arguments do have their limits. Theory tends to tell us the direction of needed change without telling us the magnitude. For example, theory might indicate that a water rate should be increased because opportunity costs have been ignored or that instream flows are too low because market transactions underappreciate nonrival goods. But this theory does not isolate the best water rate or the optimal level of instream flow. Knowing magnitudes is not always necessary to establish better policy, but sometimes it is helpful. Sometimes it is paramount. Moreover, theory may tell us that a change will improve efficiency, but it will not generally tell us if the increase in social net benefits (or net present value) is large or small. Even when theory has the sharpness to discern water policies with the ability to increase social welfare, it will not quantify the distribution of these policies' gains and losses across affected parties. If we want to know more before revising institutions, then it may be necessary to resort to empiricism. While the basic models of the earlier discussion appear helpful, they also seem coarse, in the sense that real-world issues are populated by many people with many options operating in unique physical settings.

To use empirical models to even greater advantage, more must be put into them. Of course, more cannot be gleaned from a model than is put in. Every assumption is a potential abstraction from reality, increasing the distance between model results and real-world consequences. In the end, models only offer glimpses of actual policy performance. For this reason, empirical modeling is not to be regarded as the ultimate tool of the economic arsenal, even though it can be helpful.

11.2 Features of More Advanced Models

There are two broad areas in which DSMs can be progressively enhanced. Either the economic or physical features can be improved. As economic tools are being developed here, it is appropriate to emphasize that side, but some of the physical prospects are interesting too. Indeed, many of the needed economic details are compelled by physical considerations.

Popular ideas for improving DSMs are distinguished within figure 11.1. On one side, there are the physical features of a given problem setting to consider. On the

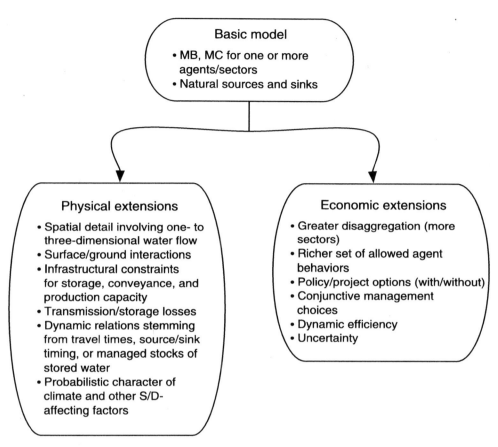

Figure 11.1
Demand and supply modeling options

other side, there are the economic details. When incorporated in modeling, each of these additions yields more accurate results—at least that is the hope. Yet each new element adds to the expense and time of model construction. Were it not for the added complexities, all of these enhancements would be desirable. So model builders face a host of similar trade-offs for each component of figure 11.1. What things should be included to generate the best possible planning advice? What things should be skirted to achieve focus and practicality?

The *physical aspects* of improved DSMs include several realities. If the study area is composed of a number of agents linked by flowing water, it is often desirable to move beyond a lumped parameter model. Modeling one-dimensional or networked flow may be adequate for a surface watercourse; more dimensions might be useful for ground water. Hydrologic interactions between surface and ground water may be important to model. If infrastructural capacities represent potentially binding problems, as they often do, these constraints are strong candidates for modeling. Water losses incurred in storage or transmission always seem to be worth modeling because it is easy (see this chapter's appendix for more specifics about these adjustments).

More advanced models may be advisable for settings with dynamic or stochastic elements. In water scarcity situations, dynamic modeling often emerges from storage issues, where either reservoirs or aquifers can be managed. Means for addressing stochastic matters are usually applied to probabilistic climate, which may impact both water supply and water demand.

The *economic aspects* of more advanced DSMs include items that operate in concert with the physical aspects and those that are independent. An ever-present opportunity for refinement is the level of agent aggregation. Since it is a rare model that attends to individual businesses, farms, and households, greater disaggregation is usually possible. The number of agent groupings (sectors) can range from a few to thousands, so analysts face an important decision here. The power of a DSM to say something about the distribution of scarcity's impacts is tightly determined by a model's level of agent aggregation. For this reason, model builders often find it practical to increase a model's disaggregation over successive editions of a model while commencing with something manageable.

Most DSMs are math programming models, and they embed demand-side activities for water use. Unless individual water-use activities are explicitly price responsive in a DSM, demand is being discontinuously modeled through the range of activities selectable by modeled agents (exactly as developed in chapter 9). In this case, results will be strongly affected by the choices embedded in these activities. So a crucial matter is the realism and range of the included activities. Are the activities sufficiently refined to avoid an overly "lumpy" conception of demand (recalling figure 9.3, which shows horizontal segments for a demand function)? The economic perspective is that a DSM must incorporate economic visions of demand and supply. Do activities include novel, yet realistic possibilities for achieving reduced water use as scarcity rises? It is good to remember that the future will involve different choices than those witnessed now, so it may be worthwhile to incorporate a richer set of behavioral options.

When the analyst is examining a given policy or project strategy for redressing scarcity, an important consideration is whether to compose "with" and "without" versions of the model. By comparing two successive "runs" of the model—one with and one without the strategy—information about the effects of the strategy can be obtained. The change in overall net benefits or net present value can be especially illuminating. It is not always necessary to employ the with/without approach to assess a proposal, but it is a direct approach.

The remaining economic extensions of figure 11.1 require parallel attention on the physical side of a DSM. If the conjunctive use of ground and surface water is to be an economically explored alternative, then the appropriate hydrologic details must be available. Whenever dynamic efficiency is the chosen optimization objective, there must be dynamic elements within the physical model. Whenever probabilistic occurrences are important features on the physical side, as is often the case due to climate, it will be necessary to select an economic approach to uncertainty. When the purpose and focus of modeling rests on policy analysis—that is, public strategies for managing scarcity—risk is pooled across many agents. This may lessen the significance of attending to risk aversion, but there can be settings in which risk considerations are important in modeling agent behavior.

With all of these alternatives, there is a wealth of decisions to be made by model designers. Regrettably, there is no set method for choosing what to include and what to omit in a model. Model building is a blend of art and science. For this reason, a good development practice is to investigate previously constructed DSMs. In the remaining sections of this chapter, we do just that.

11.3 A First Model

With its lack of obscuring details, a low-complexity DSM helps us envision modeling's major elements and promise. One such model for which a computer program is also available is a five-sector model of the Lower Rio Grande Valley in Texas. This region has an active water market, as noted in chapter 7.

Major simplifying assumptions within this particular model are constant-elasticity, point-expansion demand functions, constant-cost supply functions, and conveyance losses that are linear functions of water use (Characklis, Griffin, and Bedient 1999). To study optimal allocation in this region and the "worth" of water rights under different water flow scenarios, the area's water users are partitioned into five groups: small municipalities, large municipalities, irrigators of field crops (e.g., cotton, corn), vegetable irrigators, and citrus irrigators. The analysis can be easily replicated using the available program, so let's use this model while undertaking a couple of departures from the original specifications—just because the programming code makes it easy to do.

Although optimization is used by this mathematical programming model, the conditions are simple enough to be investigated with a spreadsheet. For each sector, an annual price-quantity pair and an elasticity are used to parameterize a demand function, $q_i = A_i P_i^{\varepsilon_i}$ (where $i = 1, 2, \ldots 5$). q_i indicates retail water consumed in sector i, P_i is water value, and A_i and ε_i are demand parameters. Q_i is diversions from the river for sector i. Because it is important to use common units, all parameters should

Table 11.1
First model parameters

| Sectoral activity | Demand point | | A | ε | L |
	Q (1000 af)	p ($/1000 af)			
muni–sm	40.0	440000	2046.70	−0.32	0.2
muni–lg	100.0	400000	5583.44	−0.32	0.1
ag–field	547.5	20000	448947.00	−0.70	0.2
ag–veget	371.9	24000	16811.30	−0.40	0.2
ag–citrus	227.5	22000	9932.09	−0.40	0.2

be expressed in terms of natural/raw river water. (The simple details of this normalization procedure are in this chapter's appendix). Due to transmission losses given by a constant ratio, L_i, it is presumed that $q_i = (1 - L_i) \cdot Q_i$. With each sector's water-related supply costs given linearly by $C_i q_i$, summed net benefits across all five sectors are

$$\sum_{i=1}^{5} \left[A_i^{-1/\varepsilon} \frac{\varepsilon_i}{\varepsilon_i + 1} ((1 - L_i)Q_i)^{(\varepsilon_i + 1)/\varepsilon_i} - C_i(1 - L_i)Q_i \right]. \tag{11.1}$$

Because this sum must be maximized subject to available water, the Lagrangian method is applicable. Less finesse can be employed by entering each sector's MNB function in a spreadsheet column, however, computing each for various Q_i amounts and looking for $(Q_1, Q_2, Q_3, Q_4, Q_5)$ combinations yielding equal MNBs, as required by economic efficiency. (Spreadsheet options are explored by two exercises at the end of this chapter.)

Table 11.1 contains all the parameters used in this edition of the model.[1] Table 11.2 holds the key optimization results where (11.1) is successively maximized for alternative water availabilities ranging from 800,000 to 1.3 million acre-feet. For each level of total water, marginal net benefits and the efficient allocations are recorded. The marginal net benefits identify the marginal value of natural water. This column's only negative entry merely tells us that all sectors are oversatiated (MC > MB) when 1.3 million acre-feet is optimally divided. This occurs because the five quantities of

---

1. An interesting feature of the original model is the use of a "choke price" for field crop demand. Because there are dryland growing options for field crops and irrigation's profitability is modest for field crops, a positive quantity demanded for all price levels may seem extreme. Yet all constant elasticity demand functions have this property. Rather than assume demand is asymptotic to the price axis, field crop demand is simply truncated in the original study once water's marginal value rises to a choke price, presumed to occur where profitability is near zero. The only noteworthy departures from the original model are that the price components of the expansion points have been changed for the municipal sectors and we will set aside the single choke price for greater simplicity.

Table 11.2
First model results

Supply (1000 af)	MNB $/af	Q_1 – sm	Q_2 – lg	Q_3 – fld	Q_4 – veg	Q_5 – cit
		-----------------------------------1000 af-----------------------------				
800	31.09	38.9	97.4	257.1	253.0	153.5
900	19.85	39.3	98.3	311.2	280.0	171.1
1000	12.24	39.6	98.9	367.9	305.3	188.3
1100	6.85	39.8	99.4	426.7	329.1	205.0
1200	2.88	39.9	99.7	487.5	351.7	221.1
1300	−0.11	40.0	100.0	550.2	372.8	237.0

the demand expansion points (table 11.1) add up to 1.286 million acre-feet, and that is the maximum amount of natural water demanded by these sectors (unless processing costs decline or the sectors grow larger).

Also observe that rising water scarcity is best absorbed by the irrigation sectors. As water availability falls, the optimal municipal allocations change by a few percentage points while agriculture curtails water use greatly, especially for field crops.

11.4 What Has Been Gained, Really?

Contemplating this model's results so as to better perceive all modeling efforts, what has been achieved here? That is, in what ways might the water planning mission have been advanced? Careful reflection, guided by the developments discussed previously, yields important answers to this question.

1. Two scenarios, one without some policy/project and one with it, have *not* been examined (as endorsed in chapters 5 and 6). So a particular scarcity-fighting strategy is not being directly assessed. Instead, this model is being used to gain insight about optimal allocation under differing supply conditions. It can be said that such models yield knowledge about worthwhile directions for future management as compared to the existing system.

2. The water quantities in the last five columns of table 11.2 are interesting. Yet their importance is easily overextended. Rarely would there be a policy scenario in which the optimal water quantities could become regulations or the basis of rights. That is, it is unrealistic to think that each Q_i would be established by fiat. Also, because each sector is composed of many water-using agents, it should be realized that optimal partitioning *within* each sector has been assumed by this model. Such efficiency achievements might easily be an unresolved policy issue.

3. The reported marginal net benefits are of greater policy significance than the water quantities. These values directly measure scarcity. Also, knowing these values could help to set efficient retail water prices by providing estimates of natural water value.

4. Studies such as this are often accompanied by an inference that the results confirm or simulate marketplace efficiency. Strictly speaking, this is a weak suggestion in all studies to date, even when the envisioned market is an idealized one.[2] Too much is omitted to associate results with potential market results. The behaviors of individual agents (true market agents) are not represented, and the frictional transaction costs of market activity are neglected too. Agents' transaction costs would include the costs of finding desirable trades, getting legal and professional assistance, and obtaining governmental approval of each exchange. These can be large omissions in that transaction costs can be high relative to seller-buyer discrepancies in natural water values. Indeed, these costs are especially hard to model. Because they tend to be non-linear and lumpy, they cannot be modeled as if they were "transportation costs." The Rio Grande case involves low transaction costs, as noted in an earlier chapter, but it is still unrealistic to think that table 11.2 results would emerge from an actual market.

5. In spite of the model's weak relationship to prospective market results, it does provide a useful depiction of *efficient* water allocation and valuation. In formal terms, the determined optimum is the aggregately efficient allocation, and it is one of the infinitely numbered, neutrally efficient allocations. Therefore, it is more prudent to describe model results as "efficient" rather than "market." Reflecting on the optimization objective of the empirical model makes this point very clear. The objective function embodies aggregate efficiency, not a market equilibrium. The two are equivalent if the First Theorem applies, but that is a separate matter, and it is a matter not illuminated by a DSM.

6. Low-complexity models such as this have few parameters. A normal consequence is that model results will be sensitive to individual parameter levels. If there happens to be low confidence in the selected parameter levels, low confidence should also be presumed for the precision of results. We should be careful not to overstate the accuracy achieved here. Sensitivity analysis might be used to see how key results change in response to parameter changes.

---

2. Remembering that the First Theorem of Welfare Economics establishes the economic efficiency of idealized markets (absent market failures), there is not good cause to associate DSM results with market results. An efficiency-seeking demand and supply model does not show that water marketing achieves efficiency. What model results do show is the characteristics of efficient water allocations: how water should be used, its value, and the net benefits it enables. That's a sufficiently nice achievement. Whether or not water markets can get us there is a fully separate matter.

7. Such models often have a low predictive ability, so it is advisable to interpret results in a relativistic manner, rather than an absolute one. Hence, instead of being confident about the individual entries in table 11.2, it is safer to rely on the magnitudes they convey. In this vein, example "findings" would be that net benefits increased by 14 percent, the marginal value of water increased $10 from baseline conditions, or the optimal use of water dropped twice as much for sector A as for sector C.

These are good points to keep in mind as one considers the findings of any DSM. With this background in place, now is a good time to consider the range of models contributed by many researchers.

11.5 A Brief Survey of Studies

Models such as the one above can be extended in many ways, as noted earlier. Let's characterize the range of available empirical work—doing so creates a foundation that can be built on when constructing a new model. Different approaches have pros and cons that are useful to consider. Prior research also helps to jump-start new studies with the structure they establish and insights they yield.

Several modern DSMs are listed in table 11.3. This is not a complete tabulation of the available work, but it is a broad selection, indicative of model types. These publications also cite the work of other DSM builders. Table 11.3 identifies some of the properties of these models. Prior to discussing each of these models in turn, note two important commonalities.

All of these studies represent *mathematical programming models*. Each optimizes an objective function by choosing various activity levels in the presence of multiple constraints. Economic demands may be explicitly entered, as in the "first model" above, or demands may be implicit to the activity choices available within the model. DSMs are almost always of the math programming variety. The other known possibilities, simultaneous equation systems and computable general equilibrium models, are rarely exercised in water settings owing to the secondary data customarily required for these models. Normally for these two methods, weakly available water use data for individual sectors render a water-focused model too aggregate to generate helpful information. For a water-focused example of a computable general equilibrium model, see Goodman (2000).

All of these models share the property that *transaction costs are omitted*. There are no published examples of DSMs with endogenous transaction costs. Thus, a preferred interpretation of model results is that they depict economic efficiency under various modeling scenarios.

Table 11.3
Contemporary water demand and supply models

	Single basin?	Ground or surface water	Value-based demands[1]	Objective function	Dynamic elements?	Stochastic elements?	Base language
Booker and Young (1994)	yes	sw	A, H, T, U	NB	no	no	GAMS
Willis and Whittlesey (1998)	yes	both	A	NB	no	yes	?
McCarl et al. (1999)	yes	gw	A, I, M	NB	no	yes	GAMS
Tisdell (2001)	yes	sw	A	NB[2]	no	no	?
Newlin et al. (2002)	no	both	A, C, G, H, I, R	NB	no	no	HEC-PRM
Sunding et al. (2002)	no	both	A	NB	no	no	three models
Azaiez (2002)	yes	both	A	ETDC[3]	yes	yes	LINGO

Notes:
1. A = agricultural irrigation, C = commercial, G = government, H = hydropower, I = industrial, M = municipal (C/R blend), R = residential, T = thermal energy, U = urban (C/I/R blend).
2. Tisdell also examines another objective minimizing the "sum of squared differences between the actual and natural flow regime" in the river of interest.
3. Minimizing "expected total discounted costs" is equivalent to maximizing expected NPV.

• Booker and Young (1994) construct a multistate DSM for the Colorado River basin. Interesting features of this model are its spatial extensiveness and attention to water use feedbacks concerning water salinity. Basinwide net benefits are maximized for four scarcity-sensitive demand sectors located at different places along the river. The modeling pertains to a surface water resource and is neither dynamic nor stochastic. The application of focus is to inspect differences in results depending on allowed intrastate or interstate reallocations of water. GAMS is the base computer language, as is the case with many of the DSMs that have been published (⟨http://www.gams.com⟩).

• Willis and Whittlesey (1998) report an irrigation-only DSM for the Walla Walla River basin of Oregon and Washington. The emphasis is placed on the agricultural implications of a probabilistically met instream flow requirement that is relevant to fish migration and reproduction. With and without scenarios are explored for various project and policy options. Other related DSM articles by these authors are available within this same journal issue.

• McCarl et al. (1999) provide a ground water study of a Texas aquifer. Like most DSMs, the regional net benefits are maximized across multiple sectors. As this particular ground water body is primarily a flow resource, much like surface water, the model is functionally static although it attends to variable climate. The primary application is to compute and contrast costs for different policy approaches to spring-flow protection.

• Tisdell (2001) presents an irrigation-only DSM for an Australian river basin. The model is static and deterministic. The emphasis is on the streamflow implications of alternative allocation policies. As in most other models, the net benefits are maximized, but there is also a model run that minimizes the sum of squared differences between the natural and extractive monthly use patterns.

• Newlin et al. (2002) develop a several-sector, spatially intense model of water allocation in southern California. Other editions and applications of this model are also available (Jenkins, Lund, and Howitt 2003; Pulido-Velazquez, Jenkins, and Lund 2004; Jenkins et al. 2004). The model's "minimize costs" objective function formulation is equivalent to maximizing net benefits because the costs modeled here include lost benefits. Both surface and ground water allocation are addressed. The model accounts for conjunctive use opportunities, and determines water use and storage decisions as if future conditions could be perfectly forecast. By performing model runs with/without both reallocation and conjunctive use, the value of different policies are investigated. Also emergent is the marginal value of additional water supplies and infrastructure, which might be pursued using new projects.

• Sunding et al. (2002) assemble three agriculturally focused models of California's Central Valley. Each of these models is separately applied to analyze the economic consequences of greater reservations of water for environmental flows. The issue of focus is how the agricultural opportunity costs depend on intra-agricultural water reallocation. The three models differ in their detail and assumptive bases, yet the results are reported to be consistent.

• Azaiez (2002) describes an agriculturally oriented model involving irrigation in Tunisia. The emphasis is on the dynamic scheduling of surface water use where ground water use and artificial recharge are possibilities. The model incorporates both dynamic and stochastic dimensions. Expected discounted costs, including opportunity costs, are minimized in the guiding theory, but the short-term application (three years) causes the author to select a discount rate of 0 percent. Minimizing discounted costs is equivalent to maximizing net present value. Due to absent data, some model specifications are hypothetical, rendering the model more abstract than the others reviewed here.

Several of these studies include some attention to minimum streamflow thresholds, without portraying these water uses as economic demands. The modeled thresholds are requirement constraints, often derived from endangered species protections. This fact underscores the current importance of streamflow reservations in policy deliberations, and it points to an inadequate knowledge base for representing instream flow as an economic, scarcity-sensitive demand. This is not so much a modeling failure as it is an acceptable expedience to the difficulty of valuing nonmarket demands. Until nonmarket valuation techniques become more widely applied to instream water demands (as in Johnson and Adams 1988; Ward and Lynch 1996), requirement thresholds serve as a useful stopgap measure in modeling.

As another point of interest, all of the studies tabulated here are published in different journals. A central literature "home" for this corpus of work does not exist, adding to the challenge of staying in touch with evolving advancements.

Reading these studies, one finds very little attention being devoted to water-processing costs. Demand details tend to be better discussed, thereby indicating the relative importance of these topics in the minds of researchers. The same observation applies to the "first model" discussed previously: demand parameters are modeled with greater complexity and detail than water-processing costs. To recognize how greater accuracy can be obtained for supply-side economics, let's briefly explore one final DSM.

11.6 A Second Model

The depth of the Simsboro aquifer makes it expensive to access ground water in a Texas county. Wells tapping this aquifer are over two thousand feet deep. While the expense of such wells deters all individual water users, two cities and one university operate separate water systems and pump from the aquifer extensively. Annual pumping has grown to exceed natural recharge, and induced saline water intrusion is progressively rendering the most southern wells useless as they become intersected by the "bad water line." New wells are drilled northward, but at considerable expense. Merrill (1997) offers an economic investigation of this issue, with a couple of unique features:

· To obtain a long-run look, Merrill's dynamic efficiency model uses a twenty-period planning horizon. Each period is five years. Hence, ground water use is optimally scheduled for one hundred years.

· Water-processing and wastewater treatment costs are modeled using a linear version of the $C(\Delta N, W, N)$ cost function. Cost factors are capacity expansion (internally driven by population growth), water consumption, and infrastructural operations independent of water use.

· Water consumption benefits are expressed on a per capita basis, so as to underscore policy's effect on the average consumer.

· Although the results of these scenarios will not be reviewed here, Merrill also examines two nonefficiency model runs that limit pumping to natural recharge and require a nondeclining water table.

Structural Overview

An overview of the model is quickly gained from its optimization problem, quoted here with some of the constraints remaining implicit:

$$
\begin{aligned}
\operatorname*{Max}_{PEQ_{it}, NQ_{it}, BWells_{it}} \sum_{t=1}^{20} \delta_t &\left\{ \sum_{i=1}^{3} \left[\left(Z + \Phi_i^{-1/\varepsilon} \cdot \frac{\varepsilon}{1+\varepsilon} \cdot W_{it}^{(1+\varepsilon)/\varepsilon} \right) \cdot \Omega_{it} \right. \right. \\
&- \theta_{PE} \cdot r_i \cdot PEQ_{it} \cdot Lift_{it} \cdot PEwells_i \\
&- \theta_{new} \cdot r_i \cdot NQ_{it} \cdot Lift_{it} \cdot Newwells_{it} - SEC_i \cdot BWells_{it} \\
&- MW_i(PEwells_i + Newwells_{it}) - \{WPC_i + (1 - \varsigma_i) \cdot WDC_i \\
&\left. \left. + \varsigma_i \cdot (WWC_i + WWT_i)\} \cdot Q_{it} - (WDE_i + WWCE_i) \cdot \Omega_{it} \right] \right\}
\end{aligned} \tag{11.2}
$$

subject to

$$
A \cdot S \cdot \frac{dh_{it}}{dt} = 3.0689 \cdot \left(R - \sum_{i=1}^{3} Q_{it} \right), \tag{11.3}
$$

and

$$Q_{it} < \rho \cdot Wcap_{it}. \tag{11.4}$$

Detailed variable descriptions are contained in table 11.4, but an accurate sense of this model is readily communicated by three points:

· The three groups of decision variables are water pumping from existing wells (PEQ), pumping from new wells (NQ), and the number of new wells to "build" (BWells). The last of these decisions is integer valued. All decision variables are dimensioned by the number of periods, twenty, and the number of agents, three. Hence, there are nine optimizing decisions to be computed for each period.

· The first line of the objective function (11.2) is familiar in form; it includes the present value of total benefits using constant elasticity demand functions. The baseline, real discount rate used for this model is 3 percent. The next four lines of the objective function are the present values of various linear costs: pumping lift costs from existing wells; pumping lift costs from new wells; costs of building new wells and the associated infrastructure; well repair and maintenance costs; postpumping, water-dependent production, distribution, and wastewater costs; and population-driven distribution and wastewater collection expansion costs.

· The constraint given by (11.3) relates the aquifer's height, and therefore pumping lift, to natural recharge and total pumping. This style of constraint was previously used in the Gisser and Sánchez (1980) model visited in section 7.11. Constraint (11.4) enforces the requirement that pumping cannot exceed the installed capacity.

Key Results

Ground water depletion is doubly harmful in this setting—there's the normal marginal user cost attributable to depletion and the lost productive capacity of salinity-influenced wells. As wells are expensive to establish, it is important to ration their capacity as well as the productive capacity of all infrastructure. Two opportunity costs are therefore relevant: the marginal user cost and the marginal capacity cost. Because there are multiple agents involved, these costs are the source of an externality problem too. If these three agents are self-serving yet thoughtful about the future effects of current decision making, they will still overpump because they will ignore future impacts on each other.

By maximizing net present value across all three agents, the dynamic efficiency model accounts for all opportunity costs and externality relationships. Of the model's many results, one of the most telling is the schedule of opportunity costs shown in figure 11.2 for the three agents labeled as A, B, and C. These opportunity costs are equal to MUC + MCC. When compared to the optimal water prices shown in figure

Table 11.4
Second model terms

Term	Unit	Meaning
Decision variables		
PEQ_{it}	MG/5Y	Pumpage per previously existing well (continuous)
NQ_{it}	MG/5Y	Pumpage per newly built well (continuous)
$BWells_{it}$	well/5Y	New well-building activity in a five-year period (integer)
State and accounting variables		
$Newwells_{it}$	well/5Y	Total number of new wells built by agent
Q_{it}	MG/5Y–capita	Total pumping per agent in time t
W_{it}	MG/5Y	Per capita (or per student) consumption per agent at time t
$WCap_{it}$	MG/5Y	Production capacity of agent at time t
h_{it}	feet	Hydraulic head in the agent's well field at time t
$Lift_{it}$	feet	Total lift in the agent's well field at time t
Model parameters		
δ_t	%	Social discount term at time t
Z	—	Very large number
Φ_i	\$-MG/5Y–capita	Parameter describing demand of agent
ε	—	Elasticity of demand of water
Ω_{it}	—	Population of agent at time t
r_i	\$/KWH	Kilowatt-hour charge on electricity for agent
θ_{PE}	hours	Parameter used to fit previously existing well pump costs
θ_{new}	hours	Parameter used to fit newly built well pumping costs
$PEwells_i$	—	Number of previously existing wells by agent
ξ	MG/5Y	Supply capacity of newly built wells
SEC_i	\$/well	Supply capacity expansion cost of agent
MW_i	\$/well	Cost to maintain existing wells by agent
WPC_i	\$/MG	Cost to run the water production system of agent
ς_i	%	System losses of agent
WDC_i	\$/MG	Water distribution system costs of agent
ζ_i	%	Wastewater to water production treatment ratio of agent
WWC_i	\$/MG	Wastewater collection system costs of agent
WWT_i	\$/MG	Wastewater treatment system costs of agent
WDE_i	\$/capita	Water distribution system expansion costs of agent
$WWCE_i$	\$/capita	Wastewater collection system expansion costs of agent
A	acres	Areal extent of Simsboro formation
S	—	Storativity of Simsboro formation
R	MG/5Y	Natural recharge to Simsboro formation
ρ	%	Peak demand capacity ratio
Alt_i	feet	Altitude of agent's well field
$h_{i,0}$	feet	Initial level of hydraulic head in the agent's well field

Source: Merrill (1997, 74).

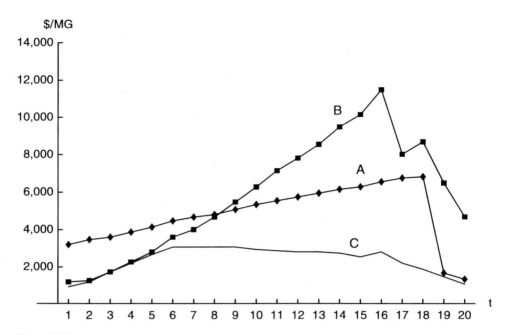

Figure 11.2
Opportunity cost schedules (Merrill 1997)

11.3, it is apparent that regularly uncharged opportunity costs compose a sizable and growing portion of the optimal retail water prices.

Especially pertinent is period 1 optimal policy since the model can be re-solved in advance of period 2 policy choices. If period 1 opportunity costs are $1,000 per million gallons, as they minimally are for all agents, rates should be raised $1 per thousand gallons. Such a healthy increase should invite strong public reaction. Current policy, however, does not include opportunity costs in water rates, so current policy will sacrifice some net present value as compared to optimal policy. The current generation of water users are losers under optimal policy, but future generations' gains (even when discounted) more than offset these losses. Moreover, decision makers might be advised that if this ground water resource were privately owned, resource owners would require compensation and their market behavior would acknowledge the rising value of this natural resource. As we have observed previously, current pricing policy assigns no value to scarce water when water marketing is absent; rates are entirely attributable to the value of nonwater resources used in processing.

The contribution of this DSM is mainly to quantify what theory has already relayed. Theory tells us what is awry in depletion situations and what policy revisions

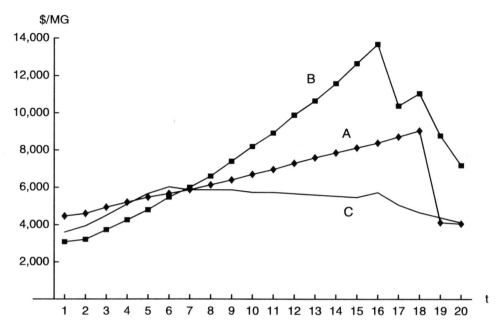

Figure 11.3
Water price schedules (Merrill 1997)

are desirable. Yet measurement of the crucial opportunity costs is not practical without a DSM such as this one.

11.7 Summary

It is a major challenge to produce a credible model of water demand and supply. Demand- and supply-side details must be well accounted for, and the internal linkages must be appropriately designed. Because the typical model is of the math programming variety, an objective function must be selected. This function contains demand and supply factors, both of which embed major economic precepts. Due to the earlier groundwork provided by prior chapters, it has not been necessary to delve into fundamentals, but the overall intensity of these tasks should be evident.

Several published works have been reviewed here so as to highlight distinctive elements and provide a point of access for future model builders. Two actual demand and supply models have been specified in greater depth. The first of these models offers a simple platform for inquiring about the legitimate contributions of such models. It is important for model builders to carefully consider their intended contributions, for such thinking can affect both model design and the application of results.

By appraising modeling's potential accurately, we can model more sharply when it is needed and avoid modeling when the rewards are slight. Except to satisfy intellectual curiosities, there is no need to model unless new insights can be generated. When empiricism has no advantages over theory, theory can be the preferred tool.

Modeling water demand and supply may be worthwhile for many reasons. The reasons generally pertain to the quantification of variables having policy relevance, the measurement of changes in social net benefits, and the measurement of impacts on different agent groups.

11.8   Exercises

1. Expand the retail water demand point (eight million, \$1.50) using an elasticity of -0.3. Suppose that the relationship between retail water deliveries and natural water pumping is given by $W_{rtl} = 0.8W_{ntrl} - 500000$. What is the demand for retail water expressed in units of natural water? (Note: your answer is not the demand for natural water because processing costs are not included.) If you mistakenly used average conveyance losses to perform this conversion, what would your answer be?

2. For each of the five sectors within the first model of chapter 11, enter the marginal net benefits formula in the evenly numbered columns of a spreadsheet. Use the first twenty rows after your heading row(s). Put water quantities in the odd-numbered columns. Hence, each pair of columns will pertain to a single sector. Using different quantity ranges for each sector, enter quantities that are evenly spaced. After setting this up correctly and computing twenty MNBs for each sector, pinpoint five quantities (one for each sector) yielding proximate MNBs. Add these five quantities and discuss whether your results correspond with table 11.2.

3. For each of the five sectors within the first model of chapter 11, enter the inverted marginal net benefits formula in the second through sixth columns of a spreadsheet. Make these entries functionally dependent on values in column 1. Use the first twenty rows after your heading row(s). Let entries in the seventh column be sums across columns 2–6. Place evenly spaced, ascending values for MNBs in the first column. Discuss whether your results correspond with table 11.2. (Clearly, this approach is more direct than that of the previous question, but it is only available when MNB functions are simple enough to be inverted.)

Appendix 11.A: Converting Functions for Water Type

Demand or supply functions can conceivably use either natural or retail water as their quantity measures. When performing multisectoral analyses as well as other types of analysis, it is often desirable to convert all functions to units of natural water. The economic conversion accounting for processing costs was discussed in chapter 2, but there may also be a physical conversion to perform because of conveyance losses. Suppose that a function $f_c(c)$ has been obtained for either marginal benefits, marginal costs, or marginal net benefits, and this function depends on the amount of retail water consumed (c). If this function must be accurately rewritten as a function of the natural water diverted (d), then we must know something about conveyance losses. A great deal of conveyance losses may be independent of the transported water quantity, especially in pressurized systems. As is usual in economic analysis, *marginal* conveyance loss is the key concept for incorporating conveyance losses in economic modeling. Due to nonlinearities and fixed conveyance losses, average conveyance loss may be a poor approximation of marginal loss.

Let L be the marginal loss ratio $(0 < L < 1)$, so that $\partial c / \partial d = 1 - L$. Let $K = 1 - L$. This information permits the resolution of a function $f_d(d)$ that accurately replaces $f_c(c)$. The pivotal element to observe is that both functions must produce equivalent total values. Hence,

$$\int_0^{KD} f_c(c)\, dc = \int_0^D f_d(d)\, dd. \tag{11.5}$$

If f_c is a linear form with known intercept and slope parameters, then f_d is also linear and (11.5) can be used to determine the parameters of f_d. Merely substitute linear expressions into (11.5), evaluate the integrals, and compare the results:

$$\int_0^{KD} (a_c + b_c c)\, dc = \int_0^D (a_d + b_d d)\, dd$$

$$\left[a_c c + \tfrac{1}{2} b_c c^2\right]_0^{KD} = \left[a_d d + \tfrac{1}{2} b_d d^2\right]_0^D$$

$$a_c KD + \tfrac{1}{2} b_c K^2 D^2 = a_d D + \tfrac{1}{2} b_d D^2.$$

So, $a_d = K a_c$ and $b_d = K^2 b_c$.

A second procedure generating the same result is to set $K \cdot f_c(c)$ equal to $f_d(d)$ where $c = Kd$:

$$K \cdot f_c(Kd) = f_d(d)$$

$$K \cdot (a_c + b_c Kd) = a_d + b_d d$$

$$K a_c + K^2 b_c d = a_d + b_d d.$$

If the marginal value function (MB, MC, or MNB) is a constant elasticity functional form, then the elasticity will be preserved on conversion because it is unitless. Still, the remaining parameter requires conversion to account for conveyance losses. First, we have that $c = a_c p^\varepsilon$ is invertible to

$$f_c(c) = \left(\frac{c}{a_c}\right)^{1/\varepsilon}.$$

Applying the second procedure,

$$K \cdot \left(\frac{Kd}{a_c}\right)^{1/\varepsilon} = \left(\frac{d}{a_d}\right)^{1/\varepsilon}$$

$$K^\varepsilon \cdot \frac{Kd}{a_c} = \frac{d}{a_d}$$

$$\frac{K^{\varepsilon+1}}{a_c} = \frac{1}{a_d}$$

$$a_d = \frac{a_c}{K^{\varepsilon+1}}.$$

12 The Water Challenge

What is truly different about water? (And what can be done about it?)

Humanity and the earth's other life-forms evolved in the presence of abundant water. So it is completely natural and expected that most species make heavy use of water. Water is a stable compound, a fluid, and the most important solvent. These properties make it incredibly useful. Our biological systems circulate the "goods" and "bads" using water as the carrier. The food we eat is the product of similarly operating biologies. Interestingly, production and economic systems also make strong use of water to move goods and bads via flow. In light of these and other facts, it is undoubtedly true that water's total value to humans is an enormously large figure.

All things considered, perhaps the most significant feature of water is its flow character. It is certainly the most economically perplexing attribute. Following the "consumption" of water in any common use, those same units of water again become available. Yet the renewed availability might not be immediate, might not be in the same place, and might not have the same qualities. It depends. That's pretty unique when compared to other goods (e.g., timber, fish, gasoline, oranges, televisions), most of which tend to be highly consumed by a single user. Water's flowing passage through production and consumption activities is to society's advantage since it extends water availability momentously. On the other hand, this flowing character requires special treatment—in terms of our theories, institutions, and modeling.

Humanity's footprint on the earth now tests our sizable water endowments. Even more ominously, the "future forces" outlined in chapter 1 promise to raise water scarcity everywhere, albeit unevenly. Because they are acting in unison, the forces of continued population growth, economic growth, environmental demands, pollution, ground water depletion, global warming, infrastructural decay, reservoir sedimentation, and energy scarcity will weigh heavily on scarcity's scale.

If water planners and managers are to rise to this challenge, having new tools, policies, projects, and ways of thinking will be extremely helpful.

12.1   Economically Inspired Principles

In this final chapter, the most distinguished contributions of economics toward these challenges will be reassembled. The purposes are to collect the important insights and aid awareness of their crosscutting messages. In some ways the following points serve as a review—to foster visualization of the "forest" where we have been preoccupied with the trees. In other places, extensions of prior material are warranted too.

The order of these ideas is not intended as a ranking. Nor should the listing be regarded as definitive. For the purpose of expediency, technical details are not repeated.

Marginalism

Even though the value of water to humankind is high, economics maintains that total values lack practical significance. The decisions a society faces exact *changes* in the total value, and it is only the changes that matter in rational decision making. The *net* benefits or *net* present value attributable to new policies and projects is a decisive factor, computable as a change between the before and after consequences. Due to efficiency's optimization goals, economics instructs us to focus on water's *marginal* values, especially the marginal benefits and marginal costs of retail water. Their difference, marginal net benefits, represents the actual demand for natural water.

Go with the Flow

Because a water consumer only enjoys a transitional benefit from any given unit of water and because the same unit may move on to provide other benefits to other users, there are matters of reuse, nonrivalness, and jointness to address. These challenges affect both the methodologies of economic analysis and the design of good institutions—that is, policies. Marginal net benefits are differently calculated and differently aggregated depending on use and flows. The efficiency of different institutions is heavily influenced by the flow-affected details. Policies that work well for ordinary goods can be inept for particular water-based situations. Yet in some water scenarios these policies work well. Disentangling good policies from poor ones can be a tough task requiring specialized knowledge and careful treatment.

Not Needed, Not Required

In deference to our biological dependence on water, economic methods and economically commended policies reject the idea that humans or human activities have water needs that might be relevant to planning, at least in developed countries. The water-planning decisions we face do not affect the amount of water allocated to our needs.

True "needs" get serviced in both before and after regimes, so there are no corresponding changes attributable to new policies or projects. Demand is scarcity dependent, so the quantity of water demanded rises as water's scarcity and value decline. As a consequence, emphasizing needs is too superficial to aid management.

The Efficiency Objectives

Economic objectives applicable to water problems are the same ones employed to analyze nonwater issues. Under the general rubric of "allocative efficiency," there are both static and dynamic versions of economic efficiency as well as aggregate and neutral versions. The choice of static (maximize NBs) or dynamic (maximize NPV) is dictated by the physical and economic conditions. If both current and future net benefits are affected by a prospective decision, a dynamic treatment is preferred. The choice between aggregate and neutral efficiency is prescribed by the chosen ethical stance regarding how people are to be weighed relative to one another. The aggregate objective is normally applicable, but distributional considerations can emerge to recommend neutral efficiency. Neutral efficiency is less resolute. Because of the differing circumstances encountered across the full range of water issues, all of these efficiency variants have found application within this text. Regardless of which is employed, however, all commensurable effects are considered and included. Other conceivable objectives such as increasing water conservation or keeping water cheap turn out to be redundant or deficient.

Pay Attention to Opportunity Costs

Achieving efficient water use is fundamentally about recognizing water's opportunity costs. The main worry here is for omitted natural water values, but infrastructure's opportunity costs are often neglected too. The paid accounting costs of transforming natural water into retail water are regularly acknowledged in decision making about water. Yet three opportunity costs are consistently forgotten or understated. They are the marginal value of water for surface water (MVW), the marginal user cost of ground water depletion (MUC), and the marginal capacity costs of constrained infrastructure (MCC). Improved policies either have the ability to signal these opportunity costs to users or are quantitatively established in light of these changing values.

Appreciate Program Packages

There is no single, social solution to water scarcity. In most settings, multipronged approaches will advance efficiency better. The choice set includes selections from both supply-enhancing and demand-managing classifications. Some of these options are structurally oriented "projects," but several highly useful policies involve no construction at all, just better management. For each scarcity setting, planners should search for the institutional and structural elements of the best program package, being fully aware that this package will evolve along with rising scarcity. Taking one step at a time by focusing on the merits of a single policy/project is often advisable, but at each step analysts and decision makers should understand the action's context within the larger, evolving package of strategies. All available strategies are implicitly competing with one another for membership in the most efficient package. Rising scarcity means that some strategies age poorly while others become indispensable.

Refine Institutions

Mounting water scarcity is caused by a changing world, so planners should strive to keep pace through institutional change and well-timed projects. Institutions (formal and informal rules) cease to be economically justified once they no longer support efficient outcomes. There is a menu of available property forms applicable to natural water. Feasible legal doctrines for surface water and ground water may emerge from private, common, or state property forms. Laws can take on a myriad of differing elements. They can be uniquely blended to develop new rules. The choice of laws impinges greatly on the efficiency of water allocation. Economic theory can be usefully applied to critique available laws, even without empiricism.

Be Critical of Missed Opportunities

Political correctness asks us to tolerate institutions as we find them. Informed observers are supposed to understand that certain things change slowly. From an economically trained perspective, examining the full body of water laws and other water-related rules, it is easy to become disappointed. Laws conflict with one another and often raise transaction costs to the point of cannibalizing the net benefits that society was supposed to receive from its water. Inefficient rules are applied long after their economic expiration dates. The conjunctive management of hydrologically linked surface and ground waters is frustrated by contradictory legal doctrines that damage incentives. Ground water depletion is loosely addressed, if at all, in that well users cannot reap gains from conservation, so why should they bother? On top of this, rent seeking—the development and exercise of political power to establish privately favorable institutions—abounds, erecting a major obstacle to the achievement of improved water management. It is universally understood that rent seeking acts on rule choice within a democratic society. Of possibly greater importance in water management, rent seeking bears heavily on both rule operations and interpretations as pressure is applied on/within administering agencies. Economic studies have not been effective in countering these forces. We get so accustomed to witnessing failures that we become desensitized and sanguine about the sacrificed net benefits. More vigilance would be helpful. Economics has key abilities that can make a big difference.

Conduct Policy/Project Analysis

Whenever theoretical analysis is insufficient and the stakes are high, it is appropriate to empirically analyze proposed policies and projects. The analytic goals are to assess efficiency and improve policy/project design in the interest of efficiency. Policy and project analysis are similar tasks employing closely related techniques. For both, the benefit and cost measures are obtainable as areas under MB and MC curves.

Enable Markets, but Be Realistic

Water marketing refers to a group of instruments (e.g., sales, leases, options, ranching) involving the exchange of natural water rights by their owners. Such markets have the power to help manage scarcity, especially under fortuitous conditions, but this instrument's ability to achieve widespread efficiency faces constraints. The flow character of water is at the root of certain market failures, so private property must be blended with public oversight of exchanges. All things considered, the First Theorem of Welfare Economics loses some prescriptive power here as compared to other resources and goods. Because the management of market failures moves us to adopt institutional blends and market restraints, water marketing is not normally a panacea even when it is an important element of the policy arsenal.

Improve Pricing

Better water pricing is a potentially powerful scarcity tool. It remains seriously underemployed in nearly all jurisdictions. Efficient water rates incorporate three essential components, two of which offer important scarcity-signaling services and may regularly include one or more of the three opportunity cost categories (MVW, MUC, and MCC). Doing a better job of pricing is not a simple enterprise, but it can be highly rewarding for society. Here lie great opportunities for advancing efficiency.

Overrated Secondary Economic Effects

Water issues attract a lot of publicity, which is unfortunate when coupled with errant opinions. Public discussion assigns an unsubstantiated "specialness" to water resources—maintaining, among other things, that cheap retail water creates social benefits through economically linked commerce and job creation. New water projects are favorably regarded by many people. As a result, efficient policy changes are commonly rejected by decision makers and more expensive measures are substituted. We should work to improve understanding that all resources have value and all contribute to the production/employment process. Under most conditions, it is not sensible to regard secondary effects as policy/project benefits or costs because they are merely relocated, not new. In the same vein, prohibiting water export so as to protect areas of origin detracts from water's total benefits, even when some members in the area of origin gain. It should be recognized, however, that the neutral and aggregate versions of economic efficiency offer contrasting perspectives on the area-of-origin issue. Although these differences might invite acceptance of either argument (protect areas of origin or don't), analysts facing this issue should become well educated about these economic doctrines.

Empirical Practices

Considerable methodology has been established for demand estimation and demand-supply modeling. New efforts should derive insight and confidence from these bodies of work. Methodologies used for supply estimation have yet to establish an equal footing, thus meriting additional care in original efforts. Although numerous methods of demand analysis are available, applied work is dominated by point expansion, residual imputation, math programming, and statistical regression. Contingent valuation has strong potential for isolating nonmarket demands, but little water *demand* estimation work is yet available from this method.

Privatization

Promarket sentiments are often overextended into favoritism for the private ownership or management of water supply facilities. This is conceptually unfounded. Water suppliers are classified as natural monopolies. It is always challenging to decide whether to operate a natural monopoly as a rate-regulated privateer or a non-profit public agency. Both have tendencies to operate inefficiently. Considered collectively, empirical studies have not spoken conclusively about a favored ownership or management form. Hybrid operations are now the norm in many places, so it has become inaccurate to think of this as an either-or choice.

12.2 Making a Difference

The mounting problems of water scarcity ask that we sharpen our wits. This is the task to which this book is devoted. As testified by the foundation of expanding literature on which this book is built, this text is neither a first nor final step.

Once sharpened, we must then apply our wits. It was observed much earlier that the rise and fall of societies is affected by their institutional choices, and that we lack automatic mechanisms to identify and correct poor institutions. Policy design is then a deliberate, yet difficult process. Every time we do a bad job of policy choice, a social burden is added.

Water resource economics performs strong service by pinpointing many opportunities for bettering water management. It finds that numerous policies impacting water scarcity should be improved or replaced. It finds that new projects are not the solutions they once were. By consciously applying the tools of water resource economics, it is possible to visualize better choices, especially relating to water policies and projects. Visualizing this change is an important step, yet not the last. Once better strategies to scarcity are recognized, change should be pursued. In doing so, one will inevitably hear challenges from people who are content with the status quo. Many people do not see the current system as broken (or do not want to admit it for strategic reasons). Many people do not want to risk policy changes that might weaken their individual welfare. Education and investigation emerge as key tools in either case. Better education yields the knowledge to understand. Investigation yields particularized information for individual situations. Both types of messages should be passed on to those decision makers who can best use them. Decision makers cannot be expected to perform well without understanding the key ideas. For these reasons, water resource economics is worth knowing *well*, so that it may be passed to others.

Glossary

accounting stance   The accounting jurisdiction defining the boundary for what counts; usually local, state/provincial, or national; only impacts within this jurisdiction matter for decision making.

aggregate economic efficiency   The efficiency goal of finding the allocation that maximizes summed net benefits; sometimes called *potential* Pareto optimality in the formal literature.

allocative efficiency   The best allocation of resources, across all available production and consumption activities as well as all available agents (present and future); there are alternative versions of allocative efficiency that have been formalized (neutral, aggregate, static, and dynamic).

alternative cost procedure   The challenging practice of measuring an action's benefits as the costs thought to be avoided as a result of the action.

annualized net benefits   The recurring, constant stream of net benefits that would yield the same net present value as a proposed change.

anthropocentric   A humanly focused perspective where the only relevant things are things that matter to humans, and all things that matter to humans are relevant.

area of origin   The region containing the original, pretrade place of use in a water right transfer.

area of receipt   The region hosting the new, post-trade place of use in a water right transfer.

banking   A water marketing device in which a public intermediary procures water rights from sellers and subsequently transfers the water to other users.

benefit-cost ratio   The discounted sum of benefits for a proposed change divided by the discounted sum of costs for the proposed change.

Coase Theorem   The principle addressing whether the achievement of allocative efficiency via the First Theorem of Welfare Economics is affected by who is granted newly created private property.

commensurable   An effect on agents that can be economically valued.

common property resource   A resource owned by a common (a group of people enjoying similar rights) and managed according to the adopted social institutions of the common.

connection charge   The one-time element of water rates that occurs when service is first initiated for a given location.

constant costs assumption   The assumption that the average or marginal water cost function of a water supplier is strictly constant.

consumer surplus   The net gains received by one or more consumers as a result of their consumption of some quantity of a good.

consumptive use The amount of water withdrawn or pumped by a user and not returned to the watercourse; this concept is affected by the accounting stance since all water tends to return somewhere.

contingent valuation A method of nonmarket valuation involving the direct questioning of agents, usually applied to elicit values, but conceivably applicable for estimating demand functions.

cost allocation A division of cost responsibilities for a project or the process of resolving such a division.

cost-based supply estimation A method of estimating marginal or average cost functions using mainly the actual costs and the cost classifications reported by a water supplier.

cost-benefit analysis The economically focused examination of individual project proposals to resolve whether each might yield enough benefits to merit undertaking its costs.

cost drivers The independent, demand-based variables that determine the total costs of operating a water supply system.

demand function The relationship between the price and the quantity of water an agent wants to buy; in economic theory, the demand function is indicated by the marginal benefit function for either rational consumers or profit-motivated businesses.

demand management A scarcity strategy that operates by lowering the water demand or reallocating limited water to more valued uses.

discount rate Equivalent to the **time value of money**: "a balancing interest rate originating from peoples' preference for things now over things future." As with the rate of time preference, there are both private and social versions of the discount rate, and it is normally argued that the private discount rate is higher than the social discount rate.

dry-year option Also called an option; a water marketing agreement whereby a water right owner consents to temporarily surrender water to the buyer whenever prespecified future conditions occur.

dynamic Time sensitive.

dynamic efficiency The efficiency goal of finding the temporally defined allocation that maximizes net present value.

dynamic improvement A policy/project or a reallocation yielding more net present value.

economic efficiency Equivalent to allocative efficiency when expressed generally; equivalent to aggregate economic efficiency when interpreted specifically (as a matter of standardization in this text).

elasticity A measure of function responsiveness, defined as the percentage change in a dependent variable that will occur for a 1 percent change in an independent variable; most often used to describe the response of a demand function to the good's price.

equivalent single price A normalized index for expressing the relative costs of some scarcity strategies, computable as the present value of all net costs divided by the present value of added water; mainly useful for comparing alternative water marketing proposals as well as other supply-shifting policies.

externality A type of market failure where there is an interdependence among economic agents for which a market or corrective policy is not in place.

First Theorem of Welfare Economics A formal theorem stating that if certain assumptions are met, the resource allocations resulting from a system of competitive markets will achieve neutral economic efficiency.

ground water ranching The exchange of land mainly to convey attached ground water use rights.

hedonic pricing A method of nonmarket valuation that statistically infers values from market transactions of broader goods, especially land; not a promising method for identifying water demand functions, though useful for generating a single water value.

incommensurable   An effect on agents that can be quantitatively described in physical terms, but cannot be economically valued.

indifference curve   A mapping (usually continuous) of ordered pairs that all generate the same outcome for an agent; hence, the agent is indifferent between all points of a single indifference curve.

inflation   A general reduction in the buying power of money, measured as the rate of cost increase for a well-specified basket of goods.

institutions   Formal and informal rules.

intangible   An effect on agents that can neither be quantitatively described nor economically valued.

internal rate of return   The rate of discount that would generate a zero-value net present value for a proposed change.

marginal capacity cost   The contribution to net benefits of added infrastructure capable of providing another unit of water; nonzero only when the infrastructural capacity is economically constraining.

marginal costs   The function displaying how costs change in response to changes in the quantity supplied; the first derivative of the total cost function.

marginal user cost   The present value of an extra unit of a depletable good in the future; normally applicable to natural ground water.

marginal utility   The function displaying how satisfaction changes in response to changes in consumption; the first derivative of the utility function.

marginal value of water   The value of an extra unit of natural water; normally applicable to surface water, but also relevant for renewable units of ground water.

market failure   A condition in which an assumption of the First Theorem of Welfare Economics is unmet, resulting in the suspect efficiency of a system of competitive markets.

mathematical programming   A method of determining demand functions or optimal allocations by expressing agents' or society's objectives as well as options in an optimization form solvable by computer.

meter charge   The element of water rates that recurs every billing period and is independent of metered water quantity.

natural monopoly   A type of market failure in which supply competition for a good/resource is not efficient because of the large costs that must be replicated by each supplier; hence, the most cost-effective production is by a single supplier—the natural monopoly.

natural water   Water as found in a natural state and location, either on the earth's surface or underground.

net present value   The discounted sum of net benefits for a proposed change.

neutral economic efficiency   The efficiency goal of finding all allocations that cannot be modified without harming at least one agent; also called Pareto optimality.

nominal price   An actually observed price; a price that is unadjusted for its inflationary content.

nonexclusive   A property of a good/resource occurring when it is technically impossible or too expensive for society to exclude agents from using the good/resource.

nonrival   When the use of specific units of a good/resource by an agent does not diminish the availability of those same units for use by another agent at the same time.

open access resource   A resource having no rules pertaining to its use or exploitation (a rare situation in today's world).

opportunity costs The value of the next most valuable option sacrificed once a resource commitment is made; in a well-operating economic system, all opportunity costs are well represented by accounting costs.

option Also called a dry-year option; a water marketing agreement whereby a water right owner consents to temporarily surrender water to the buyer whenever prespecified future conditions occur.

overdiscounting A type of market failure occurring when *social* dynamic efficiency cannot be achieved by agents because they are applying *private* rates of time preference in their decision making.

point expansion A method of extrapolating a function from knowledge of a point on the function *and* slope or elasticity at that point; normally used for demand function estimation, but also amenable to supply function estimation.

private property resource A partitioned resource entitling owners to exclusive use and having a rule allowing individual owners to transfer their ownership to others.

private rate of time preference A time value of money that is strictly derived from the preferences of one or more current people.

privatization Ownership, or perhaps only management, of water supply infrastructure by private agents.

producer surplus The net gains received by one or more producers of a good when they produce a good for sale.

production function The technical relationship between the amounts of inputs used and the amount of output generated in a given production process.

public good A type of market failure in which the use of the good/resource in question possesses two technical conditions: nonrivalness and nonexclusivity; note that this definition is not contingent on any ownership characteristics.

rate-based supply estimation A method of estimating marginal or average cost functions using mainly the rates charged by a water supplier.

real prices Prices that are analytically adjusted to remove their inflationary components; such prices express only scarcity values and not the changing buying power of money.

residual imputation A method of resolving an ordered price-quantity pair that may constitute a demand point; also used as a foundation method within the math programming approach to demand estimation.

retail water Water that has been stored, transported, and/or processed so that it is more directly usable by agents.

revenue-based supply estimation A method of estimating marginal or average cost functions using mainly the revenues reported by a water supplier.

secondary economic effects The accumulated impacts of a policy or project on the agents that are economically linked, perhaps remotely or distantly, to directly affected agents.

separable costs-remaining benefits A particular procedure for apportioning repayment responsibilities; a method of cost allocation.

social rate of time preference A time value of money reshaped by social preferences for things now relative to things in the future; rooted in the preferences of people (and therefore the private rate of time preference), but arguably lowered by greater concern for future people.

state property resource A resource owned by a level of government and for which the government establishes rules that agents must follow if they are to use the resource.

static Time insensitive.

supply function   The relationship between the price and the quantity of water a provider is willing to supply; in economic theory, the supply function is equivalent to the marginal cost function for profit-motivated suppliers operating in a competitive environment; in water settings, marginal costs may omit certain opportunity costs and do not always capture the suppliers' goals.

supply enhancement   A scarcity strategy that operates by expanding the water supply.

time value of money   Basically, a balancing interest rate originating from peoples' preference for things now over things future.

transaction costs   Information costs; applicable to both market transactions and nonmarket policies.

travel cost method   A method of nonmarket valuation that statistically infers values from the travel costs that people willingly incur to visit recreational sites; not an especially promising method for identifying water demand functions, though useful for generating a single water value.

utility   The psychological satisfaction a person receives from the consumption of any good.

utility function   The relation between the amount(s) of good(s) consumed and the consequent amount of utility received by the consumer.

water marketing   The transfer of natural water rights by their owners.

References

Ahmad, Mahmood. 2000. Water Pricing and Markets in the Near East: Policy Issues and Options. *Water Policy* 2 (July): 229–242.

American Water Works Association. 1984. *Before the Well Runs Dry*. Denver, CO: American Water Works Association.

American Water Works Association. 1991. *Water Rates*. 4th ed. Denver, CO: American Water Works Association.

American Water Works Association. 2000. *Principles of Water Rates, Fees, and Charges*. 5th ed. Denver, CO: American Water Works Association.

Amir, I., and F. M. Fisher. 1999. Analyzing Agricultural Demand for Water with an Optimizing Model. *Agricultural Systems* 61: 45–56.

Anderson, Terry L. 1983a. *Water Crisis: Ending the Policy Drought*. Baltimore: Johns Hopkins University Press.

Anderson, Terry L., ed. 1983b. *Water Rights: Scarce Resource Allocation, Bureaucracy, and the Environment*. Cambridge, MA: Ballinger Publishing Company.

Anderson, Terry L., Oscar R. Burt, and David T. Fractor. 1983. Privatizing Groundwater Basins: A Model and Its Application. In *Water Rights: Scarce Resource Allocation, Bureaucracy, and the Environment*, ed. Terry L. Anderson, 223–248. Cambridge, MA: Ballinger Publishing Co.

Anderson, Terry L., and Ronald N. Johnson. 1986. The Problem of Instream Flows. *Economic Inquiry* 24 (October): 535–545.

Anderson, Terry L., and Clay J. Landry. 2001. Exporting Water to the World. *Water Resources Update* 118 (January): 60–67.

Angeletos, George-Marios, David Laibson, Andrea Repetto, Jeremy Tobacman, and Stephen Weinberg. 2001. The Hyperbolic Consumption Model: Calibration, Simulation, and Empirical Evaluation. *Journal of Economic Perspectives* 15 (Summer): 47–68.

Archibald, Sandra O., and Mary E. Renwick. 1998. Expected Transaction Costs and Incentives for Water Market Development. In *Markets for Water: Potential and Performance*, ed. K. William Easter, Mark W. Rosegrant, and Ariel Dinar, 95–117. Boston: Kluwer Academic Publishers.

Au, Tung. 1988. Profit Measures and Methods of Economic Analysis for Capital Project Selection. *Journal of Management in Engineering* 4 (July): 217–228.

Averch, Harvey, and Leland L. Johnson. 1962. Behavior of the Firm under Regulatory Constraint. *American Economic Review* 52 (December): 1052–1069.

Azaiez, M. N. 2002. A Model for Conjunctive Use of Ground and Surface Water with Opportunity Costs. *European Journal of Operational Research* 143 (December 16): 611–624.

Bain, Joe S., Richard E. Caves, and Julius Margolis. 1966. *Northern California's Water Industry*. Baltimore: Johns Hopkins Press.

Balleau, W. P. 1988. Water Appropriation and Transfer in a General Hydrogeologic System. *Natural Resources Journal* 28 (Spring): 269–291.

Barakat and Chamberlin, Inc. 1994. *The Value of Water Supply Reliability: Results of a Contingent Valuation Survey of Residential Customers.* Sacramento: California Urban Water Agencies.

Barfield, Jesse T., Cecily A. Raiborn, and Michael R. Kinney. 1994. *Cost Accounting: Traditions and Innovations.* 2nd ed. St. Paul, MN: West Publishing Co.

Bator, Francis M. 1958. The Anatomy of Market Failure. *Quarterly Journal of Economics* (August): 351–379.

Baumann, Duane D., John J. Boland, and John H. Sims. 1984. Water Conservation: The Struggle over Definition. *Water Resources Research* 20 (April): 428–434.

Baumol, William J. 1977. On the Proper Cost Tests for Natural Monopoly in a Multiproduct Industry. *American Economic Review* 67 (December): 809–822.

Baumol, William J., and Wallace E. Oates. 1988. *The Theory of Environmental Policy.* 2nd ed. Cambridge: Cambridge University Press.

Beecher, Janice A. 2001. The Ethics of Water Privatization. In *Navigating Rough Waters: Ethical Issues in the Water Industry,* ed. Cheryl K. Davis and Robert E. McGinn, 245–261. Denver, CO: American Water Works Association.

Beecher, Janice A., Patrick C. Mann, and James R. Landers. 1991. *Cost Allocation and Rate Design for Water Utilities.* Columbus, OH: National Regulatory Research Institute.

Bennett, Lynne Lewis, and Charles W. Howe. 1998. The Interstate River Compact: Incentives for Noncompliance. *Water Resources Research* 34 (March): 485–495.

Bennett, Lynne Lewis, Charles W. Howe, and James Shope. 2000. The Interstate River Compact as a Water Allocation Mechanism: Efficiency Aspects. *American Journal of Agricultural Economics* 82 (November): 1006–1015.

Bernardo, Daniel J., Norman K. Whittlesey, Keith E. Saxton, and Day L. Bassett. 1987. An Irrigation Model for Management of Limited Water Supplies. *Western Journal of Agricultural Economics* 12 (December): 149–157.

Bernardo, Daniel J., Norman K. Whittlesey, Keith E. Saxton, and Day L. Bassett. 1988. Valuing Irrigation Water: A Simulation/Mathematical Programming Approach. *Water Resources Bulletin* 24 (February): 149–157.

Bhattacharyya, Arunava, Thomas R. Harris, Rangesan Narayanan, and Kambiz Raffiee. 1995a. Specification and Estimation of the Effect of Ownership on the Economic Efficiency of the Water Utilities. *Regional Science and Urban Economics* 25: 759–784.

Bhattacharyya, Arunava, Thomas R. Harris, Rangesan Narayanan, and Kambiz Raffiee. 1995b. Technical Efficiency of Rural Water Utilities. *Journal of Agricultural and Resource Economics* 20 (December): 373–391.

Bhattacharyya, Arunava, Elliott Parker, and Kambiz Raffiee. 1994. An Examination of the Effect of Ownership on the Relative Efficiency of Public and Private Water Utilities. *Land Economics* 70 (May): 197–209.

Blumenschein, Karen, Magnus Johannesson, Krista K. Yokoyama, and Patricia R. Freeman. 2001. Hypothetical versus Real Willingness to Pay in the Health Care Sector: Results from a Field Experiment. *Journal of Health Economics* 20: 441–457.

Boisvert, Richard N., and Todd M. Schmit. 1997. Tradeoff between Economies of Size in Treatment and Diseconomies of Distribution for Rural Water Systems. *Agricultural and Resource Economics Review* (October): 237–346.

Boland, John J. 1993. Pricing Urban Water: Principles and Compromises. *Water Resources Update:* 7–10.

Boland, John J., and Dale Whittington. 1998. *The Political Economy of Increasing Block Tariffs in Developing Countries.* ⟨http://www.eepsea.org⟩.

Booker, James F., and Robert A. Young. 1994. Modeling Intrastate and Interstate Markets for Colorado River Water Resources. *Journal of Environmental Economics and Management* 26 (January): 66–87.

Brealey, Richard A., and Stewart C. Myers. 2003. *Capital Investment and Valuation*. New York: McGraw-Hill.

Bromley, Daniel W. 1989. *Economic Interests and Institutions: The Conceptual Foundations of Public Policy*. New York: Basil Blackwell Inc.

Bromley, Daniel W. 1991. Testing for Common versus Private Property: Comment. *Journal of Environmental Economics and Management* 21 (July): 92–96.

Brown, Donald J., Walter P. Heller, and Ross M. Starr. 1992. Two-Part Marginal Cost Pricing Equilibria: Existence and Efficiency. *Journal of Economic Theory* 57: 52–72.

Brown, Gardner, Jr., and M. Bruce Johnson. 1969. Public Utility Pricing and Output under Risk. *American Economic Review* 59 (March): 119–128.

Brown, Thomas C., Icek Ajzen, and Daniel Hrubes. 2003. Further Tests of Entreaties to Avoid Hypothetical Bias in Referendum Contingent Valuation. *Journal of Environmental Economics and Management* 46 (September): 353–361.

Bruggink, Thomas H. 1982. Public versus Regulated Private Enterprise in the Municipal Water Industry: A Comparison of Operating Costs. *Quarterly Review of Economics and Business* 22 (Spring): 110–125.

Burness, H. Stuart, and Thomas C. Brill. 2001. The Role for Policy in Common Pool Groundwater Use. *Resource and Energy Economics* 23 (January): 19–40.

Burt, Oscar R. 1964. The Economics of Conjunctive Use of Ground and Surface Water. *Hilgardia* 36: 31–111.

Burt, Oscar R. 1967. Temporal Allocation of Groundwater. *Water Resources Research* 3: 45–56.

Cameron, Trudy Ann. 1992. Combining Contingent Valuation and Travel Cost Data for the Valuation of Nonmarket Goods. *Land Economics* 68 (August): 302–317.

Chang, Chan, and Ronald C. Griffin. 1992. Water Marketing as a Reallocative Institution in Texas. *Water Resources Research* 28 (March): 879–890.

Characklis, Gregory W., Ronald C. Griffin, and Philip B. Bedient. 1999. Improving the Ability of a Water Market to Efficiently Manage Drought. *Water Resources Research* 35 (March): 823–831.

Chellam, Shankararaman, Christophe Serra, and Mark E. Wiesner. 1998. Estimating Costs for Integrated Membrane Systems. *Journal of the Amerian Water Works Association* 90 (November): 96–104.

Chiang, Alpha C. 1984. *Fundamental Methods of Mathematical Economics*. 3rd ed. New York: McGraw-Hill Book Company.

Chiang, Alpha C. 1992. *Elements of Dynamic Optimization*. New York: McGraw-Hill, Inc.

Ciriacy-Wantrup, S. V. 1956. Concepts Used as Economic Criteria for a System of Water Rights. *Land Economics* 32 (November): 295–312.

Ciriacy-Wantrup, S. V., and Richard C. Bishop. 1975. "Common Property" as a Concept in Natural Resources Policy. *Natural Resources Journal* 15 (October): 713–727.

Clark, Forrest D., A. B. Lorenzoni, and Michael Jimenez. 1997. *Applied Cost Engineering*. New York: Marcel Dekker, Inc.

Clark, Robert M., Mano Sivaganesan, Ari Selvajumar, and Virendra Sethi. 2002. Cost Model for Water Supply Distribution Systems. *Journal of Water Resources Planning and Management* 128 (September/October): 312–321.

Clark, Robert M., and Richard G. Stevie. 1981a. Analytical Cost Model for Urban Water Supply. *Journal of the Water Resources Planning and Management Division, American Society of Civil Engineers* 107 (October): 437–452.

Clark, Robert M., and Richard G. Stevie. 1981b. A Water Supply Cost Model Incorporating Spatial Variables. *Land Economics* 57 (February): 18–32.

Clyde, Steven E. 1989. Adapting to the Changing Demand for Water Use through Continued Refinement of the Prior Appropriation Doctrine: An Alternative to Wholesale Reallocation. *Natural Resources Journal* 29 (Spring): 435–455.

Coase, Ronald H. 1960. The Problem of Social Cost. *Journal of Law and Economics* 3: 1–44.

Colby, Bonnie G. 1988. Economic Impacts of Water Law: State Law and Water Market Development in the Southwest. *Natural Resources Journal* 28 (Fall): 721–749.

Colby, Bonnie G. 1990a. Enhancing Instream Flow Benefits in an Era of Water Marketing. *Water Resources Research* 26 (June): 1113–1120.

Colby, Bonnie G. 1990b. Transactions Costs and Efficiency in Western Water Allocation. *American Journal of Agricultural Economics* 72 (December): 1184–1192.

Colby, Bonnie G. 1995. Regulation, Imperfect Markets, and Transaction Costs: The Elusive Quest for Efficiency in Water Allocation. In *The Handbook of Environmental Economics*, ed. Daniel W. Bromley, 475–502. Cambridge, UK: Blackwell Publishers Ltd.

Conrad, Jon M., and Colin W. Clark. 1987. *Natural Resource Economics*. Cambridge: Cambridge University Press.

Cooke, Stephen C. 1991. The Role of Value Added in Benefit/Cost Analysis. *Annuals of Regional Science* 25 (July): 145–149.

Coppock, Ray, Brian E. Gray, and Edward McBean. 1994. California Water Transfers: The System and the 1991 Drought Water Bank. In *Sharing Scarcity: Gainers and Losers in Water Marketing*, ed. Harold O. Carter, Henry J. Vaux, and Ann F. Scheuring, 21–40. Davis: University of California Agricultural Issues Center.

Cox, William E. 1982. Water Law Primer. *Journal of Water Resources Planning and Management* 108 (March): 107–122.

Cropper, Maureen, and David Laibson. 1999. The Implications of Hyperbolic Discounting for Project Evaluation. In *Discounting and Intergenerational Equity*, ed. Paul R. Portney and John P. Weyant, 163–172. Washington, DC: Resources for the Future.

Crouter, Jan P. 1987. Hedonic Estimation Applied to a Water Rights Market. *Land Economics* 63 (August): 259–271.

Cummings, Ronald G., and Laura O. Taylor. 1999. Unbiased Value Estimates for Environmental Goods: A Cheap Talk Design for the Contingent Valuation Methods. *American Economic Review* 89 (June): 649–665.

Dahlman, Carl J. 1979. The Problem of Externality. *Journal of Law and Economics* 22 (April): 141–161.

Dalhuisen, Jasper M., Raymond J. G. M. Florax, Henri L. F. de Groot, and Peter Nijkamp. 2003. Price and Income Elasticities of Residential Water Demand: A Meta Analysis. *Land Economics* 79 (May): 292–308.

Dandy, Graeme C., Edward A. McBean, and Bruce G. Hutchinson. 1985. Pricing and Expansion of a Water Supply System. *Journal of Water Resources Planning and Management* 111 (January): 24–42.

Darwin, Roy. 1999. The Impact of Global Warming on Agriculture: A Ricardian Analysis: Comment. *American Economic Review* 89 (September): 1049–1052.

Dasgupta, Partha S., and Geoffrey M. Heal. 1979. *Economic Theory and Exhaustible Resources*. New York: Cambridge University Press.

Davis, Robert K., and Steve H. Hanke. 1971. *Planning and Management of Water Resources in Metropolitan Environments*. Final report to the Office of Water Resources Research, Natural Resources Policy Center, George Washington University, U.S. Department of the Interior, Washington, DC.

Deason, Jonathan P., Theodore M. Schad, and George William Sherk. 2001. Water Policy in the United States: A Perspective. *Water Policy* 3: 175–192.

Debreu, Gerard. 1959. *Theory of Value: An Axiomatic Analysis of Economic Equilibrium*. New Haven, CT: Yale University Press.

DeOreo, William Butler, James Patrick Heaney, and Peter W. Mayer. 1996. Flow Trace Analysis to Assess Water Use. *Journal of the American Water Works Association* 88 (January): 79–80.

De Rooy, Jacob. 1974. Price Responsiveness of the Industrial Demand for Water. *Water Resources Research* 10 (June): 403–406.

Diamond, Peter A., and Jerry A. Hausman. 1994. Contingent Valuation: Is Some Number Better Than No Number? *Journal of Economic Perspectives* 8 (Fall): 45–64.

Dixon, Lloyd S., Nancy Y. Moore, and Susan W. Schechter. 1993. *California's 1991 Drought Water Bank: Economic Impacts in the Selling Regions.* Santa Monica: Rand.

Domenico, Patrick A. 1972. *Concepts and Models in Groundwater Hydrology.* New York: McGraw-Hill Book Company.

Domenico, Patrick A., D. V. Anderson, and C. M. Case. 1968. Optimal Ground-Water Mining. *Water Resources Research* 4 (April): 247–255.

Dubin, Jeffrey A. 1985. *Consumer Durable Choice and the Demand for Electricity.* New York: Elsevier Science Publishing.

Duffield, John W., Christopher J. Neher, and Thomas C. Brown. 1992. Recreation Benefits of Instream Flow: Application to Montana's Big Hole and Bitterroot Rivers. *Water Resources Research* 28: 2169–2181.

Dunning, Harrison C. 1993. Instream Flows and the Public Trust. In *Instream Flow Protection in the West,* ed. Lawrence J. MacDonnell and Teresa A. Rice, 4-1/30. Rev. ed. Boulder: Natural Resources Law Center, University of Colorado School of Law.

Dupuit, Jules. 1969. On the Measurement of the Utility of Public Works. In *Readings in Welfare Economics,* ed. Kenneth J. Arrow and Tibor Scitovsky, 255–283. Homewood, IL: Richard D. Irwin, Inc.

Dziegielewski, Ben. 2000. Efficient and Inefficient Uses of Water in North American Households. In *Tenth International Water Resources Association World Water Congress.* Melbourne, Australia.

Easter, K. William, Mark W. Rosegrant, and Ariel Dinar. 1998. *Markets for Water: Potential and Performance.* Boston: Kluwer Academic Publishers.

El-Ashry, Mohamed T., and Diana C. Gibbons. 1986. *Troubled Waters: New Policies for Managing Water in the American West.* Washington, DC: World Resources Institute.

Emel, Jacque L. 1987. Groundwater Rights: Definition and Transfer. *Natural Resources Journal* 27 (Summer): 653–673.

Ernst & Young. 1992. *1992 National Water and Wastewater Rate Survey.*

Espey, M., J. Espey, and W. D. Shaw. 1997. Price Elasticity of Residential Demand for Water: A Meta-Analysis. *Water Resources Research* 33 (June): 1369–1374.

Estache, Antonio, and Martin A. Rossi. 2002. How Different Is the Efficiency of Public and Private Water Companies in Asia? *World Bank Review* 16: 139–148.

Feigenbaum, Susan, and Ronald Teeples. 1983. Public versus Private Water Delivery: A Hedonic Cost Approach. *Review of Economics and Statistics* 65 (November): 672–678.

Feldman, Stephen L., John Breese, and Robert Obeiter. 1981. The Search for Equity and Efficiency in the Pricing of a Public Service: Urban Water. *Economic Geography* 57 (January): 78–93.

Flyvbjerg, Bent, Mette Skamris Holm, and Soren Buhl. 2002. Underestimating Costs in Public Works Projects. *Journal of the American Planning Association* 68 (Summer): 279–295.

Freeman, A. Myrick, III. 1993. *The Measurement of Environmental and Resource Values.* Washington, DC: Resources for the Future.

Garcia, Serge, and Arnaud Reynaud. 2004. Estimating the Benefits of Efficient Water Pricing in France. *Resource and Energy Economics* 26 (March): 1–25.

Gardner, B. Delworth. 2003. Weakening Water Rights and Efficient Transfers. *Water Resources Development* 19 (March): 7–19.

Gardner, Richard L., and Robert A. Young. 1984. Effects of Electricity Rates and Rate Structures on Pump Irrigation: An Eastern Colorado Case Study. *Land Economics* 60 (November): 352–359.

Getches, David H. 1990. *Water Law in a Nutshell.* 2nd ed. St. Paul, MN: West Publishing Co.

Gillilan, David M., and Thomas C. Brown. 1997. *Instream Flow Protection.* Washington, DC: Island Press.

Gisser, Micha. 1983. Groundwater: Focusing on the Real Issue. *Journal of Political Economy* 91 (December): 1001–1027.

Gisser, Micha, and David A. Sánchez. 1980. Competition versus Optimal Control in Groundwater Pumping. *Water Resources Research* 16 (August): 638–642.

Gittinger, J. Price. 1982. *Economic Analysis of Agricultural Projects.* 2nd ed. Baltimore: Johns Hopkins University Press.

Gleick, Peter H. 2001. Making Every Drop Count. *Scientific American* (February): 41–45.

Goldfarb, William. 1984. *Water Law.* Boston: Butterworth Publishers.

Goldstein, James. 1986. Full-Cost Water Pricing. *Journal of the American Water Works Association* 78 (February): 52–61.

Gonzalez, Amable Sanchez. 1989. Ground Water Externalities. In *Groundwater Economics*, ed. E. Custodio and A. Gurgui, 361–371. New York: Elsevier.

Goodman, D. Jay. 2000. More Reservoirs or Transfers? A Computable General Equilibrium Analysis of Projected Water Shortages in the Arkansas River Basin. *Journal of Agricultural and Resource Economics* 25 (December): 698–713.

Gould, George A. 1988. Water Rights Transfers and Third-Party Effects. *Land and Water Law Review* 23 (Spring): 1–41.

Gray, S. Lee, and Robert A. Young. 1984. Valuation of Water on Wildlands. In *Valuation of Wildland Resource Benefits*, ed. George L. Peterson and Alan Randall, 157–191. Boulder, CO: Westview Press.

Griffin, Adrian H., William E. Martin, and James C. Wade. 1981. Urban Residential Demand for Water in the United States: Comment. *Land Economics* 57 (May): 252–256.

Griffin, Ronald C. 1991. The Welfare Analytics of Transaction Costs, Externalities, and Institutional Choice. *American Journal of Agricultural Economics* 73 (August): 601–614.

Griffin, Ronald C. 1995. On the Meaning of Economic Efficiency in Policy Analysis. *Land Economics* 71 (February): 1–15.

Griffin, Ronald C. 1998. The Fundamental Principles of Cost-Benefit Analysis. *Water Resources Research* 34 (August): 2063–2071.

Griffin, Ronald C. 2001. Effective Water Pricing. *Journal of the American Water Resources Association* 37 (October): 1335–1347.

Griffin, Ronald C., and Chan Chang. 1990. Pretest Analyses of Water Demand in Thirty Communities. *Water Resources Research* 26: 2251–2255.

Griffin, Ronald C., and Chan Chang. 1991. Seasonality in Community Water Demand. *Western Journal of Agricultural Economics* 16 (December): 207–217.

Griffin, Ronald C., and Gregory W. Characklis. 2002. Issues and Trends in Texas Water Marketing. *Water Resources Update* 121 (January): 29–33.

Griffin, Ronald C., and Manzoor E. Chowdhury. 1993. Evaluating a Locally Financed Reservoir: The Case of Applewhite. *Journal of Water Resource Planning and Management* 119 (November/December): 628–644.

Griffin, Ronald C., and Shih-Hsun Hsu. 1993. The Potential for Water Market Efficiency When Instream Flows Have Value. *American Journal of Agricultural Economics* 75 (May): 292–303.

Griffin, Ronald C., and James W. Mjelde. 2000. Valuing Water Supply Reliability. *American Journal of Agricultural Economics* 82 (May): 414–426.

Griffin, Ronald C., John M. Montgomery, and M. Edward Rister. 1987. Criteria for Selecting Functional Form in Production Function Analysis. *Western Journal of Agricultural Economics* 12 (December): 216–227.

Gumerman, Robert C., Bruce E. Burris, Debra E. Burris, and Richard G. Ellers. 1992. *Standardized Costs for Water Distribution Systems.* Environmental Protection Agency Risk Reduction Engineering Laboratory. EPA/600/SR-92/009 (available only from National Technical Information Service).

Halvorsen, Robert, and Michael G. Ruby. 1981. *Benefit-Cost Analysis of Air-Pollution Control.* Lexington, MA: Lexington Books.

Hamilton, Joel R., Norman K. Whittlesey, M. Henry Robison, and John Ellis. 1991. Economic Impacts, Value Added, and Benefits in Regional Project Analysis. *American Journal of Agricultural Economics* 73 (May): 334–344.

Hamilton, Joel R., Norman K. Whittlesey, M. Henry Robison, and John Ellis. 1993. Economic Impacts, Value Added, and Benefits in Regional Project Analysis: Reply. *American Journal of Agricultural Economics* 75 (August): 763.

Hanak, Ellen. 2003. *Who Should Be Allowed to Sell Water in California? Third-Party Issues and the Water Market.* San Francisco: Public Policy Institute of California.

Hanemann, W. Michael. 1994. Valuing the Environment through Contingent Valuation. *Journal of Economic Perspectives* 8 (Fall): 19–43.

Hanke, Steve H. 1978. A Method for Integrating Engineering and Economic Planning. *Journal of the American Water Works Association* 71 (September): 487–491.

Hanke, Steve H. 1981. Water Metering and Conservation. *Engineering and Management* (October): 57–59.

Hanke, Steve H. 1982. On Turvey's Benefit-Cost "Short-Cut": A Study of Water Meters. *Land Economics* 58 (February): 144–146.

Hanley, Nick, and Clive L. Spash. 1993. *Cost-Benefit Analysis and the Environment.* Brookfield, VT: Edward Algar Publishing Company.

Hardin, Garrett. 1968. The Tragedy of the Commons. *Science* 162: 1243–1248.

Harrison, Glenn W., and James C. Lesley. 1996. Must Contingent Valuation Surveys Cost So Much? *Journal of Environmental Economics and Management* 31 (July): 79–95.

Hartman, L. M., and R. L. Anderson. 1962. Estimating the Value of Irrigation Water from Farm Sales in Northeastern Colorado. *Journal of Farm Economics* 44: 207–213.

Hartman, L. M., and Don Seastone. 1970. *Water Transfers: Economic Efficiency and Alternative Institutions.* Baltimore: Johns Hopkins University Press.

Heaney, James P., William DeOreo, Peter Mayer, Paul Lander, Jeff Harpring, Laurel Stadjuhar, Beorn Courtney, and Lynn Buhlig. 1998. Nature of Residential Water Use and Effectiveness of Conservation Programs. *Colorado Water* 15 (October): 5–10.

Hearne, Robert R. 1998. Institutional and Organizational Arrangements for Water Markets in Chile. In *Markets for Water: Potential and Performance*, ed. K. William Easter, Mark W. Rosegrant, and Ariel Dinar, 141–157. Boston: Kluwer Academic Publishers.

Herrington, P. 1987. *Pricing of Water Services.* Paris: Organisation for Economic Co-operation and Development.

Hexem, Roger W., and Earl O. Heady. 1978. *Water Production Functions for Irrigated Agriculture.* Ames: Iowa State University Press.

Holland, Stephen P., and Michael R. Moore. 2003. Cadillac Desert Revisited: Property Rights, Public Policy, and Water-Resource Depletion. *Journal of Environmental Economics and Management* 46 (July): 131–155.

Hotelling, Harold. 1931. The Economics of Exhaustible Resources. *Journal of Political Economy* 39 (April): 137–175.

Howe, Charles W. 1979. *Natural Resource Economics.* New York: John Wiley and Sons.

Howe, Charles W. 1993. Water Pricing: An Overview. *Water Resources Update*: 3–6.

Howe, Charles W., Dennis R. Schurmeier, and William D. Shaw Jr. 1986a. Innovations in Water Management: Lessons from the Colorado-Big Thompson Project Conservancy District. In *Scarce Water and Institutional Change*, ed. Kenneth D. Frederick, 171–200. Washington, DC: Resources for the Future, Inc.

Howe, Charles W., Dennis R. Schurmeier, and W. Douglas Shaw Jr. 1986b. Innovative Approaches to Water Allocation: The Potential for Water Markets. *Water Resources Research* 22 (April): 439–445.

Howe, Charles W., and Mark Griffin Smith. 1993. Incorporating Public Preferences in Planning Urban Water Supply Reliability. *Water Resources Research* 29 (October): 3363–3369.

Howe, Charles W., and Mark Griffin Smith. 1994. The Value of Water Supply Reliability in Urban Water Systems. *Journal of Environmental Economics and Management* 26 (January): 19–30.

Howitt, Richard E. 1994a. Effects of Water Marketing on the Farm Economy. In *Sharing Scarcity: Gainers and Losers in Water Marketing*, ed. Harold O. Carter, Henry J. Vaux, and Ann F. Scheuring, 97–132. Davis: University of California Agricultural Issues Center.

Howitt, Richard E. 1994b. Empirical Analysis of Water Market Institutions: The 1991 California Water Market. *Resource and Energy Economics* 16: 357–371.

Howitt, Richard E. 2002. Drought, Strife, and Institutional Change. *Western Economics Forum* 1 (Fall): 11–14.

Howitt, Richard E., William D. Watson, and Richard M. Adams. 1980. A Reevaluation of Price Elasticities for Irrigation Water. *Water Resources Research* 16 (August): 623–628.

Hughes, David W., and David W. Holland. 1993. Economic Impacts, Value Added, and Benefits in Regional Project Analysis: Comment. *American Journal of Agricultural Economics* 75 (August): 759–762.

Innes, John, Falconer Mitchell, and Takeo Yoshikawa. 1994. *Activity Costing for Engineers.* New York: John Wiley and Sons Inc.

Intriligator, Michael D. 1971. *Mathematical Optimization and Economic Theory.* Englewood Cliffs, NJ: Prentice Hall.

James, L. Douglas, and Robert R. Lee. 1971. *Economics of Water Resources Planning.* New York: McGraw-Hill Book Company.

Jenkins, Marion W., Jay R. Lund, and Richard E. Howitt. 2003. Using Economic Loss Functions to Value Urban Water Scarcity in California. *Journal of the American Water Works Association* 95 (February): 58–70.

Jenkins, Marion W., Jay R. Lund, Richard E. Howitt, Andrew J. Draper, Siwi M. Msangi, Stacy K. Tanaka, Randall S. Ritzema, and Guilherme F. Marques. 2004. Optimization of California's Water Supply System: Results and Insights. *Journal of Water Resource Planning and Management* 130 (July/August): 271–280.

Johns, Gerald. 2003. Where Is California Taking Water Transfers? *Journal of Water Resources Planning and Management* 129 (January/February): 1–3.

Johnson, Neal S., and Richard M. Adams. 1988. Benefits of Increased Streamflow: The Case of the John Day River Steelhead Fishery. *Water Resources Research* 24 (November): 1839–1846.

Johnson, Ronald N., Micha Gisser, and Michael Werner. 1981. The Definition of a Surface Water Right and Transferability. *Journal of Law and Economics* 24 (October): 273–288.

Jones, C. Vaughan, John J. Boland, James E. Crews, C. Frederick DeKay, and John R. Morris. 1984. *Municipal Water Demand: Statistical and Management Issues.* Boulder, CO: Westview Press.

Jones, Douglas N., and Patrick C. Mann. 2001. The Fairness Criterion in Public Utility Regulation: Does Fairness Still Matter? *Journal of Economic Issues* 35 (March): 153–172.

Just, Richard E., Darrell L. Hueth, and Andrew Schmitz. 2004. *The Welfare Economics of Public Policy.* Northampton, MA: Edward Elgar Publishing, Inc.

Kahn, Alfred E. 1988. *The Economics of Regulation: Principles and Institutions.* Two vols. Cambridge: MIT Press.

Kamien, Morton I., and Nancy L. Schwartz. 1991. *Dynamic Optimization: The Calculus of Variations and Optimal Control in Economics and Management.* 2nd ed. New York: North Holland.

Kanazawa, Mark T. 1998. Efficiency in Western Water Law: The Development of the California Doctrine. *Journal of Legal Studies* 27 (January): 159–185.

Kaplow, Louis, and Steven Shavell. 1996. Property Rules versus Liability Rules: An Economic Analysis. *Harvard Law Review* 109: 713–790.

Kelso, Maurice M., William E. Martin, and Lawrence E. Mack. 1973. *Water Supplies and Economic Growth in an Arid Environment: An Arizona Case Study.* Tucson: University of Arizona Press.

Kennedy, John O. S. 1988. Principles of Dynamic Optimization in Resource Management. *Agricultural Economics* 2: 57–72.

Kennedy, Peter. 2003. *A Guide to Econometrics.* 5th ed. Cambridge: MIT Press.

Kim, H. Youn, and Robert M. Clark. 1988. Economies of Scale and Scope in Water Supply. *Regional Science and Urban Economics* 18 (November): 479–502.

Kindler, J., and C. S. Russell, ed. 1984. *Modeling Water Demands.* London: Academic Press.

Kitchen, Harry M. 1977. A Statistical Estimation of an Operating Cost Function for Municipal Water Provision. *Urban Analysis* 4: 119–133.

Kloezen, Wim H. 1998. Water Markets between Mexican Water User Associations. *Water Policy* 1 (August): 437–455.

Koss, Patricia, and M. Sami Khawaja. 2001. The Value of Water Supply Reliability in California: A Contingent Valuation Study. *Water Policy* 3: 165–174.

Koundouri, Phoebe. 2004. Current Issues in the Economics of Groundwater Resource Management. *Journal of Economic Surveys* 18 (December): 703–740.

Krautkraemer, Jeffrey A. 1998. Nonrenewable Resource Scarcity. *Journal of Economic Literature* 36 (December): 2065–2107.

Krulce, Darrell L., James A. Roumasset, and Tom Wilson. 1997. Optimal Management of a Renewable and Replaceable Resource: The Case of Coastal Groundwater. *American Journal of Agricultural Economics* 79 (November): 1218–1228.

Kulshreshtha, S. N., and J. A. Gillies. 1993. Economic Evaluation of Aesthetic Amenities: A Case Study of River View. *Water Resources Bulletin* 29 (March/April): 257–266.

Kulshreshtha, Suren N., and Devi D. Tewari. 1991. Value of Water in Irrigated Crop Production Using Derived Demand Functions: A Case Study of South Saskatchewan River Irrigation District. *Water Resources Bulletin* 27 (April): 227–236.

Landry, Clay. 1998. Market Transfers of Water for Environmental Protection in the Western United States. *Water Policy* 1 (October): 457–469.

Lansford, Notie H., Jr., and Lonnie L. Jones. 1995. Recreational and Aesthetic Value of Water Using Hedonic Price Analysis. *Journal of Agricultural and Resource Economics* 20 (December): 341–355.

Lauria, Donald T. 2002. Behavioural Studies of the Domestic Demand for Water Services in Africa: A Response by Donald T. Lauria. *Water Policy* 4: 89–91.

Lauria, Donald T. 2004. Discussion of "Cost Models for Water Supply Distribution Systems" by R. M. Clark et al. *Journal of Water Resources Planning and Management* 140 (July/August): 353–355.

Leonard, Daniel, and Ngo Van Long. 1992. *Optimal Control Theory and Static Optimization in Economics.* Cambridge: Cambridge University Press.

Lippai, Istvan, and James P. Heaney. 2000. Efficient and Equitable Impact Fees for Urban Water Systems. *Journal of Water Resources Planning and Management* 126 (March/April): 75–84.

List, John A., and Jason F. Shogren. 2002. Calibration of Willingness to Accept. *Journal of Environmental Economics and Management* 43 (March): 219–233.

Livingston, M. L. 1995. Designing Water Institutions: Market Failures and Institutional Response. *Water Resources Management* 9 (August): 203–220.

Loomis, John B. 2003. Estimating the Benefits of Maintaining Adequate Lake Levels to Homeowners Using the Hedonic Property Method. *Water Resources Research* 39 (September): 1259–1264.

Loomis, John B., Thomas Brown, Beatrice Lucero, and George Peterson. 1996. Improving Validity Experiments of Contingent Valuation Methods: Results of Efforts to Reduce the Disparity of Hypothetical and Actual Willingness to Pay. *Land Economics* 72 (November): 450–461.

Loomis, John B., Katherine Quattlebaum, Thomas C. Brown, and Susan J. Alexander. 2003. Expanding Institutional Arrangements for Acquiring Water for Environmental Purposes: Transactions Evidence for the Western United States. *Water Resources Development* 19 (March): 21–28.

Lund, Jay R. 1992. Benefit-Cost Ratios: Failures and Alternatives. *Journal of Water Resources Planning and Management* 118 (January/February): 94–100.

Lund, Jay R. 1995. Derived Estimation of Willingness to Pay to Avoid Probabilistic Shortage. *Water Resources Research* 31 (May): 1367–1372.

Maass, Arthur, and Raymond Anderson. 1978. *And the Desert Shall Rejoice: Conflict, Growth, and Justice in Arid Environments.* Cambridge: MIT Press.

Mann, Dean. 1982. Institutional Framework for Agricultural Water Conservation and Reallocation in the West: A Policy Analysis. In *Water and Agriculture in the Western U.S.: Conservation, Reallocation, and Markets*, ed. Gary D. Weatherford, 9–52. Boulder, CO: Westview Press.

Martin, William E., Helen M. Ingram, Nancy K. Laney, and Adrian H. Griffin. 1984. *Saving Water in a Desert City*. Washington, DC: Resources for the Future.

Mas-Colell, Andreu, Michael D. Whinston, and Jerry R. Green. 1995. *Microeconomic Theory*. New York: Oxford University Press.

McCarl, Bruce A., Carl R. Dillon, Keith O. Keplinger, and R. Lynn Williams. 1999. Limiting Pumping from the Edwards Aquifer: An Economic Investigation of Proposals, Water Markets, and Spring Flow Guarantees. *Water Resources Research* 35 (April): 1257–1268.

McKenzie, George W. 1983. *Measuring Economic Welfare*. Cambridge: Cambridge University Press.

McPhail, Alexander A. 1994. Why Don't Households Connect to the Piped Water System: Observations from Tunis, Tunisia. *Land Economics* 70 (May): 189–196.

Mendelsohn, Robert, and Ariel Dinar. 2003. Climate, Water, and Agriculture. *Land Economics* 79 (August): 328–341.

Mendelsohn, Robert, and William Nordhaus. 1999. The Impact of Global Warming on Agriculture: A Ricardian Analysis: Reply. *American Economic Review* 89 (September): 1053–1055.

Merrett, Stephen. 2002. Behavioural Studies of the Domestic Demand for Water Services in Africa. *Water Policy* 4: 69–81.

Merrill, Kathryn Ann. 1997. Economic Analysis of the Dynamically Efficient and Sustainable Use of a Rechargeable Aquifer. PhD diss., Texas A&M University.

Mettner, Jeanne. 1997. Water Pricing Should Reflect Its Variety of Uses. *U.S. Water News* 14 (May): 7.

Michelsen, Ari M. 1994. Administrative, Institutional, and Structural Characteristics of an Active Water Market. *Water Resources Bulletin* 30 (December): 971–982.

Michelsen, Ari M., R. G. Taylor, Ray G. Huffaker, and J. Thomas McGuckin. 1999. Emerging Agricultural Water Conservation Price Incentives. *Journal of Agricultural and Resource Economics* 24 (July): 222–238.

Michelsen, Ari M., and Robert A. Young. 1993. Optioning Agricultural Water Rights for Urban Water Supplies during Drought. *American Journal of Agricultural Economics* 75 (November): 1010–1020.

Miller, Jon R., and Daniel A. Underwood. 1983. Distributional Issues in Western Municipal and Industrial Water Supply. *Water Resources Bulletin* 19 (August): 631–640.

Miller, Kathleen A. 1987. The Right to Use versus the Right to Sell: Spillover Effects and Constraints on the Water Rights of Irrigation Organization Members. *Water Resources Research* 23 (December): 2166–2173.

Milliman, J. W. 1959. Water Law and Private Decision-Making: A Critique. *Journal of Law and Economics* 2 (October): 41–63.

Mills, Edwin S. 1993. The Misuse of Regional Economic Models. *Cato Journal* 13 (Spring/Summer): 29–39.

Mishan, E. J. 1976. *Cost-Benefit Analysis*. New York: Praeger Publishers.

Mitchell, Robert Cameron, and Richard T. Carson. 1989. *Using Surveys to Value Public Goods: The Contingent Valuation Method*. Washington, DC: Resources for the Future.

Moeltner, Klaus, and Shawn Stoddard. 2004. A Panel Data Analysis of Commercial Customers' Water Price Responsiveness under Block Rates. *Water Resources Research* 40 (January), W01401, doi: 10.1029/2003WR002192.

Moncur, James E. T., and Yu-Si Fok. 1993. Water Pricing and Cost Data: Getting the Right Numbers. *Water Resources Update* 92 (Summer): 35–37.

Moncur, James E. T., and Richard L. Pollock. 1988. Scarcity Rents for Water: A Valuation and Pricing Model. *Land Economics* 64 (February): 62–72.

Moncur, James E. T., and Richard L. Pollock. 1996. Accounting-Induced Distortion in Public Enterprise Pricing. *Water Resources Research* 32 (November): 3355–3360.

Moore, Michael R., Noel R. Gollehon, and Marc B. Carey. 1994. Multicrop Production Decisions in Western Irrigated Agriculture: The Role of Water Price. *American Journal of Agricultural Economics* 76 (November): 859–874.

Mulholland, Catherine. 2000. *William Mulholland and the Rise of Los Angeles.* Berkeley: University of California Press.

Myles, Gareth D. 1995. *Public Economics.* Cambridge: Cambridge University Press.

National Research Council. 1992. *Water Transfers in the West: Efficiency, Equity, and the Environment.* Washington, DC: National Academy Press.

National Research Council. 2002a. *The Missouri River Ecosystem: Exploring the Prospects for Recovery.* Washington, DC: National Academy Press. ⟨http://www.nap.edu⟩.

National Research Council. 2002b. *Privatization of Water Services in the United States.* Washington, DC: National Academy Press.

Neuman, Janet C. 1998. Beneficial Use, Waste, and Forfeiture: The Inefficient Search for Efficiency in Western Water Use. *Environmental Law* 28 (Fall): 919–996.

Newlin, Brad D., Marion W. Jenkins, Jay R. Lund, and Richard E. Howitt. 2002. Southern California Water Markets: Potential and Limitations. *Journal of Water Resources Planning and Management* 128 (January/February): 21–32.

Newnan, Donald D., Jerome P. Lavelle, and Ted G. Eschenbach. 2002. *Engineering Economic Analysis.* 8th ed. New York: Oxford University Press.

Ng, Yew-Kwang, and Mendel Weisser. 1974. Optimal Pricing with a Budget Constraint—The Case of the Two-Part Tariff. *Review of Economic Studies* 41 (July): 337–345.

Nieswiadomy, Michael L. 1985. The Demand for Irrigation Water in the High Plains of Texas. *American Journal of Agricultural Economics* 67 (August): 619–626.

Nieswiadomy, Michael L. 1988. Input Substitution and Irrigation. *Western Journal of Agricultural Economics* 13 (July): 63–70.

North, Douglass C. 1991. Institutions. *Journal of Economic Perspectives* 5 (Winter): 97–112.

Oamek, George Edward. 1990. *Economic and Environmental Impacts of Interstate Water Transfers in the Colorado River Basin.* Ames: Center for Agricultural and Rural Development, Iowa State University.

Ogg, Clayton W., and Noel R. Gollehon. 1989. Western Irrigation Response to Pumping Costs: A Water Demand Analysis Using Climatic Regions. *Water Resources Research* 25 (May): 767–773.

Olson, Mancur. 1982. *The Rise and Decline of Nations.* New Haven, CT: Yale University Press.

Organisation for Economic Co-operation and Development. 1999. *The Price of Water: Trends in OECD Countries.* Paris: Organisation for Economic Co-operation and Development.

Organisation for Economic Co-operation and Development. 2003. *Improving Water Management: Recent OECD Experience.* Paris: Organisation for Economic Co-operation and Development.

Ortolano, Leonard, and Katherine Kao Cushing. 2002. Grand Coulee Dam Seventy Years Later: What Can We Learn? *Water Resources Development* 18: 373–390.

Ostrom, Elinor. 1990. *Governing the Commons: The Evolution of Institutions for Collective Action.* New York: Cambridge University Press.

Pattanayak, Subhrendu K., Jui-Chen Yang, Dale Whittington, and K. C. Bal Kumar. 2005. Coping with Unreliable Public Water Supplies: Averting Expenditures by Households in Kathmandu, Nepal. *Water Resources Research* 41.

Pickering, Karen D., and Mark E. Wiesner. 1993. Cost Model for Low-Pressure Membrane Filtration. *Journal of Environmental Engineering* 119 (September/October): 772–797.

Pindyck, Robert S., and Daniel L. Rubinfeld. 1991. *Econometric Models and Economic Forecasts.* 3rd ed. New York: McGraw-Hill, Inc.

Portney, Paul R. 1994. The Contingent Valuation Debate: Why Economists Should Care. *Journal of Economic Perspectives* 8 (Fall): 3–17.

Portney, Paul R., and John P. Weyant, eds. 1999. *Discounting and Intergenerational Equity.* Washington, DC: Resources for the Future.

Prest, A. R., and R. Turvey. 1965. Cost-Benefit Analysis: A Survey. *Economic Journal* 75 (December): 683–735.

Provencher, Bill. 1993. A Private Property Rights Regime to Replenish a Groundwater Aquifer. *Land Economics* 69 (November): 325–340.

Pulido-Velazquez, Manuel, Marion W. Jenkins, and Jay R. Lund. 2004. Economic Values for Conjunctive Use and Water Banking in Southern California. *Water Resources Research* 40 (March), W03401, doi: 10.1029/2003WR002626.

Raftelis, George A. 1993. *Comprehensive Guide to Water and Wastewater Finance and Pricing.* 2nd ed. Boca Raton, FL: Lewis Publishers.

Raje, D. V., P. S. Dhobe, and A. W. Deshpande. 2002. Consumer's Willingness to Pay More for Municipal Supplied Water: A Case Study. *Ecological Economics* 42 (September): 391–400.

Randall, Alan. 1981. *Resource Economics.* Columbus, OH: Grid Publishing, Inc.

Rees, Judith Anne. 1969. *Industrial Demand for Water: A Study of South East England.* London: Lowe and Brydone Ltd.

Reisner, Marc. 1986. *Cadillac Desert.* New York: Penguin Books.

Renzetti, Steven. 1992a. Estimating the Structure of Industrial Water Demands: The Case of Canadian Manufacturing. *Land Economics* 68 (November): 396–404.

Renzetti, Steven. 1992b. Evaluating the Welfare Effects of Reforming Municipal Water Prices. *Journal of Environmental Economics and Management* 22: 147–163.

Renzetti, Steven, ed. 2002a. *The Economics of Industrial Water Use.* Northampton, MA: Edward Elgar Publishing, Inc.

Renzetti, Steven. 2002b. *The Economics of Water Demands.* Boston: Kluwer Academic Publishers.

Rogers, Peter. 2002. Water Is an Economic Good: How to Use Prices to Promote Equity, Efficiency, and Sustainability. *Water Policy* 4:1–17.

Rollins, Kimberly, Jim Frehs, Don Tate, and Oswald Zachariah. 1997. Resource Valuation and Public Policy: Consumers' Willingness to Pay for Improving Water Servicing Infrastructure. *Canadian Water Resources Journal* 22: 185–195.

Rosenblum, Eric, and Michael Stanley-Jones. 2001. Present Value, Future Value: Intergenerational Ethics for Water Engineers. In *Navigating Rough Waters: Ethical Issues in the Water Industry,* ed. Cheryl K. Davis and Robert E. McGinn, 197–211. Denver, CO: American Water Works Association.

Rothbard, Murray N. n.d. *Biography of A. R. J. Turgot.* 〈http://www.mises.org/turgot.asp〉.

Russell, R. Robert, and Maurice Wilkinson. 1979. *Microeconomics: A Synthesis of Modern and Neoclassical Theory.* New York: John Wiley and Sons.

Samuels, Warren J. 1972. Welfare Economics, Power, and Property. In *Perspectives of Property,* ed. Gene Wunderlich and W. L. Gibson Jr., 61–148. University Park: Institute for Research on Land and Water Resources, Pennsylvania State University.

Sassone, Peter G., and William A. Schaffer. 1978. *Cost-Benefit Analysis.* New York: Academic Press.

Scheierling, Susanne M., John B. Loomis, and Robert A. Young. 2005. Irrigation Water Demand: A Meta-Analysis of Price Elasticities. *Water Resources Research,* in review.

Schmid, A. Allan. 1972. Analytical Institutional Economics: Challenging Problems in the Economics of Resources for a New Environment. *American Journal of Agricultural Economics* 54 (December): 893–901.

Schmid, A. Allan. 1989. *Benefit-Cost Analysis.* Boulder, CO: Westview Press.

Schmidt, Ronald H. 1992. Diamonds and Water: A Paradox Revisited. *Federal Reserve Bank of San Francisco Weekly Letter,* December 4, 1–3.

Schumpeter, Joseph. 1954. *History of Economic Analysis.* New York: Oxford University Press.

Scott, Anthony, and Georgina Coustalin. 1995. The Evolution of Water Rights. *Natural Resources Journal* 35 (Fall): 821–979.

Shupe, Steven J., and Lawrence J. MacDonnell. 1993. Recognizing the Value of In-Place Uses of Water in the West: An Introduction to the Laws, Strategies, and Issues. In *Instream Flow Protection in the West,* ed.

Lawrence J. MacDonnell and Teresa A. Rice, 1–122. Rev. ed. Boulder: Natural Resources Law Center, University of Colorado School of Law.

Simon, Benjamin M. 1998. Federal Acquisition of Water through Voluntary Transactions for Environmental Purposes. *Contemporary Economic Policy* 16 (October): 422–432.

Smith, Adam. 1776. *An Inquiry into the Nature and Causes of the Wealth of Nations.* Two vols. Dublin: Printed for Messrs. Whitestone and others.

Smith, Rodney T. 1989. Water Transfers, Irrigation Districts, and the Compensation Problem. *Journal of Policy Analysis and Management* 8: 446–465.

Smith, Vernon L. 1977. Water Deeds: A Proposed Solution to the Water Valuation Problem. *Arizona Review* 26 (January): 7–10.

Smith, Zachary A. 1989. *Groundwater in the West.* San Diego, CA: Academic Press.

Spulber, Nicolas, and Asghar Sabbaghi. 1998. *Economics of Water Resources: From Regulation to Privatization.* 2nd ed. Boston: Kluwer Academic Publishers.

Steiner, Peter O. 1965. The Role of Alternative Cost in Project Design and Selection. *Quarterly Journal of Economics* 79 (August): 417–430.

Stoevener, Herbert H., and Roger G. Kraynick. 1979. On Augmenting Community Economic Performance by New or Continuing Irrigation Developments. *American Journal of Agricultural Economics* 61 (December): 1115–1123.

Stokey, Nancy L., and Robert E. Lucas Jr. 1989. *Recursive Methods in Economic Dynamics.* Cambridge: Harvard University Press.

Sturgess, Gary L. 1997. Transborder Water Trading among the Australian States. In *Water Marketing— The Next Generation,* ed. Terry L. Anderson and Peter J. Hill, 127–145. Lanham, MD: Rowman and Littlefield Publishers, Inc.

Sunding, David, David Zilberman, Richard Howitt, Ariel Dinar, and Neal MacDougall. 2002. Measuring the Costs of Reallocating Water from Agriculture: A Multi-Model Approach. *Natural Resource Modeling* 15 (Summer): 201–225.

Swallow, Stephen K., and Carlos M. Marin. 1988. Long Run Price Inflexibility and Efficiency Loss for Municipal Water Supply. *Journal of Environmental Economics and Management* 15 (June): 233–247.

Tarlock, A. Dan. 1991. *Law of Water Rights and Resources.* No. 3 release ed. New York: Clark Boardman Company, Ltd.

Taylor, Donald C. 1989. Designing Electricity Rate Structures for Irrigation. *Land Economics* 65 (November): 394–409.

Teeples, Ronald, and David Glyer. 1987. Cost of Water Delivery Systems: Specification and Ownership Effects. *Review of Economics and Statistics* 69 (August): 399–408.

Terza, Joseph V., and W. P. Welch. 1982. Estimating Demand under Block Rates: Electricity and Water. *Land Economics* 58 (May): 181–188.

Texas Center for Policy Studies. 2002. *The Dispute over Shared Waters of the Rio Grande/Rio Bravo: A Primer.* ⟨http://www.texascenter.org/borderwater⟩.

Thomas, John F., and Geoffrey J. Syme. 1988. Estimating Residential Price Elasticity of Demand for Water: A Contingent Valuation Approach. *Water Resources Research* 24 (November): 1847–1857.

Tietenberg, Tom. 2003. *Environmental and Natural Resource Economics.* 6th ed. Boston: Addison-Wesley.

Tisdell, J. G. 2001. The Environmental Impact of Water Markets: An Australian Case-Study. *Journal of Environmental Management* 62 (May): 113–120.

Toman, Michael A. 1994. Economics and "Sustainability": Balancing Trade-offs and Imperatives. *Land Economics* 70 (November): 399–413.

Turner, R. Kerry, David Pearce, and Ian Bateman. 1993. *Environmental Economics: An Elementary Introduction.* Baltimore: Johns Hopkins University Press.

Turnovsky, Stephen J. 1969. The Demand for Water: Some Empirical Evidence on Consumers Response to a Commodity Uncertain in Supply. *Water Resources Research* 5 (April): 350–361.

Turvey, Ralph. 1969. Marginal Cost. *Economic Journal* 78 (June): 282–299.

Turvey, Ralph. 1970. Public Utility Pricing and Output under Risk: Comment. *American Economic Review* 60 (June): 485–486.

Turvey, Ralph. 1976. Analyzing the Marginal Cost of Water Supply. *Land Economics* 52 (May): 158–168.

Tyler, Daniel. 1992. *The Last Water Hole in the West.* Boulder: University of Colorado Press.

U.S. Bureau of Reclamation. 2004. Change in Discount Rate for Water Resources Planning. *Federal Register* 69 (December 9): 71425–71426.

U.S. Environmental Protection Agency Office of Water. 2002. *The Clean Water and Drinking Water Infrastructural Gap Analysis.* EPA–816–R–02–020.

U.S. Global Climate Change Research Program. 2000. *Climate Change Impacts on the United States (Overview).* Cambridge: Cambridge University Press.

U.S. Statutes at Large. 1944. *Treaty between the United States of America and Mexico Respecting Utilization of Waters of the Colorado and Tijuana Rivers and of the Rio Grande.* Vol. 59, 1219–1267. Washington, DC: U.S. Government Printing Office.

U.S. Water Resources Council. 1983. *Economic and Environmental Principles and Guidelines for Water and Related Land Resource Implementation Studies.* Washington, DC: U.S. Government Printing Office. ⟨http://www.iwr.usace.army.mil/iwr/products/reports/reports.htm⟩.

van der Leeden, Frits, Fred L. Troise, and David Keith Todd. 1991. *The Water Encyclopedia.* 2nd ed. Chelsea, MI: Lewis Publishers.

Varian, Hal R. 1992. *Microeconomic Analysis.* 3rd ed. New York: W. W. Norton and Company.

Vaux, H. J., Jr., and William O. Pruitt. 1983. Crop-Water Production Functions. *Advances in Irrigation* 2: 61–97.

Wahl, Richard W. 1989. *Markets for Federal Water: Subsidies, Property Rights, and the Bureau of Reclamation.* Washington, DC: Resources for the Future.

Walski, Thomas M. 1984. Estimating O&M Cost When Costs Vary with Flow. *Journal of Water Resources Planning and Management* 110 (July): 355–360.

Walski, Thomas M. 2001. The Wrong Paradigm—Why Water Distribution Optimization Doesn't Work. *Journal of Water Resources Planning and Management* 127 (July/August): 203–205.

Ward, Evan R. 2003. *Border Oasis: Water and the Political Ecology of the Colorado River Delta, 1940–1975.* Tucson: University of Arizona Press.

Ward, Frank A. 1987. Economics of Water Allocation to Instream Uses in a Fully Appropriated River Basin: Evidence from a New Mexico Wild River. *Water Resources Research* 23 (March): 381–392.

Ward, Frank A., and Thomas P. Lynch. 1996. Integrated River Basin Optimization: Modeling Economic and Hydrologic Interdependence. *Water Resources Bulletin* 32 (December): 1127–1138.

Ward, Frank A., and Ari Michelsen. 2002. The Economic Value of Water in Agriculture: Concepts and Policy Applications. *Water Policy* 4: 423–446.

Warford, Jeremy J. 1997. *Marginal Opportunity Cost Pricing for Municipal Water Supply.* ⟨http://www.eepsea.org⟩.

Water Strategist. 1997. "ESP" Valuation of Water Contracts. Vol. 10 (Winter): 1–9.

Wellisz, Stanilaw H. 1963. Regulation of Natural Gas Pipeline Companies: An Economic Analysis. *Journal of Political Economy* 71 (February): 30–43.

Western Water Policy Review Advisory Commission. 1998. *Water in the West: The Challenge for the Next Century.* Springfield, VA: National Technical Information Service.

Whittington, Dale. 2002a. Behavioural Studies of the Domestic Demand for Water Services in Africa: A Reply to Stephen Merrett. *Water Policy* 4: 83–88.

Whittington, Dale. 2002b. Municipal Water Pricing and Tariff Design: A Reform Agenda for Cities in Developing Countries. Issue brief 02-29. Washington, DC: Resources for the Future.

Willis, David B., and Norman K. Whittlesey. 1998. Water Management Policies for Streamflow Augmentation in an Irrigated River Basin. *Journal of Agricultural and Resource Economics* 23 (July): 170–190.

Wilson, Paul N. 1997. Economic Discovery in Federally Supported Irrigation Districts: A Tribute to William E. Martin and Friends. *Journal of Agricultural and Resource Economics* 22 (July): 61–77.

Wirl, Franz. 1997. *The Economics of Conservation Programs*. Boston: Kluwer Academic Publishers.

Wolff, Gary H., and Meena Palaniappan. 2004. Public or Private Water Management? Cutting the Gordian Knot. *Journal of Water Resources Planning and Management* 130 (January/February): 1–3.

World Bank. 2002. *The World Bank Annual Report*. Vol. 2, *Financial Statements and Appendixes*. Washington, DC: World Bank.

World Commission on Dams. 2000. *Dams and Development: A New Framework for Decision-Making*. London: Earthscan Publications Ltd.

Yoe, Charles. 1993. *National Economic Development Procedures Manual: National Economic Development Costs*. Fort Belvoir, VA: Institute for Water Resources, U.S. Army Corps of Engineers. Report 93–R–12.

Yoe, Charles E. 1995. *Draft Planning Manual*. Alexandria, VA: Institute for Water Resources, U.S. Army Corps of Engineers. Report 95–R–15.

Yolles, Peter L. 2001. Update 2000: Progress and Limitations in Developing a Water Market in California. *Water Resources Update* 118 (January): 74–82.

Young, Robert A. 1970. Safe Yield of Aquifers: An Economic Reformulation. *Journal of the Irrigation and Drainage Division* 96 (December): 377–385.

Young, Robert A. 1986. Why Are There So Few Transactions among Water Users? *American Journal of Agricultural Economics* 68 (December): 1143–1151.

Young, Robert A. 1996. *Measuring Economic Benefits for Water Investments and Policies*. Washington, DC: World Bank.

Young, Robert A. 2005. *Determining the Economic Value of Water: Concepts and Methods*. Washington, DC: Resources for the Future.

Young, Robert A., and S. Lee Gray. 1972. *Economic Value of Water: Concepts and Empirical Estimates*. Springfield, VA: National Technical Information Service.

Young, Robert A., and S. Lee Gray. 1985. Input-Output Models, Economic Surplus, and the Evaluation of State or Regional Water Plans. *Water Resources Research* 21 (December): 1819–1823.

Zerbe, Richard O., Jr., and Dwight D. Dively. 1994. *Benefit-Cost Analysis in Theory and Practice*. New York: HarperCollins College Publishers.

Ziegler, Joseph A., and Stephen E. Bell. 1984. Estimating Demand for Intake Water by Self-Supplied Firms. *Water Resources Research* 20 (January): 4–8.

Zimmerman, W. R. 1990. Finite Hydraulic Conductivity Effects on Optimal Groundwater Pumping Rates. *Water Resources Research* 26 (December): 2861–2864.

Index